RELIGION IN VIRGIL

BY

CYRIL BAILEY

OXFORD

AT THE CLARENDON PRESS

1935

OXFORD
UNIVERSITY PRESS
AMEN HOUSE, E.C. 4
London Edinburgh Glasgow
New York Toronto Melbourne
Capetown Bombay Calcutta
Madras Shanghai
HUMPHREY MILFORD
PUBLISHER TO THE
UNIVERSITY

PRINTED IN GREAT BRITAIN

NOTE

I WISH to express my gratitude to the University of California, which gave me leisure during my visit as Sather Professor in 1932 to collect much of the material for this book; to the University of Oxford for my appointment as University Lecturer and to the Jowett Memorial Trustees for my election as Jowett Lecturer, thanks to which I have had the opportunity to write it.

It was my intention that this study should be based on an independent investigation, but I hope that I have given sufficient references in footnotes to guide readers to other discussions of broad questions and individual passages.

C. B.

CONTENTS

INTRODUCTION

MUCH has been written[1] about Virgil's religion, in the endeavour to extract from his poems his own belief as to the government of the world and the relation of men to the gods. Attention has been generally called, and rightly called, to his conception of Iuppiter and his relation to Fate, to the development of the character of 'pius Aeneas', and to the great description of the underworld in the sixth book of the *Aeneid*. Outside these elements it has been usual to regard his treatment of the anthropomorphic deities as a literary retention of the conventional 'epic machinery', and his constant introduction of allusions to Italian cults and sacred places as proofs of his antiquarian interest in the religious traditions of his country. While it would be unreasonable to suggest that such distinctions are not in the main correct, it is not possible to regard them as finally satisfactory. For in the works of so impersonal a poet as Virgil it is not easy to distinguish with certainty between belief and interest, between acceptance and understanding, and to say with confidence, 'Here we have Virgil the historian and antiquarian, there we see Virgil the man of religious convictions.'

It is the purpose of this essay not primarily at any rate to seek for Virgil's own personal religion, but to conduct a rather more detailed examination than has perhaps hitherto been made into the religious ideas and practices which find their place in his poems. There can be little doubt that just as he designed the *Aeneid* to be an epitome of the history and character of the Roman people and of their civilization, as he intended to enshrine in it by way of

---

[1] e.g. Sellar, *Virgil*, pp. 364–74; Warde Fowler, *Religious Experience of the Roman People*, c. xviii; Glover, *Studies in Virgil*, cc. x–xii; Heinze, *Virgils epische Technik*, pp. 288–316; Norden, *Vergilius, Aeneis Buch vi*.

B

imitation and recollection what was best and greatest in Roman literature, so on the religious side he wished it, and to a less degree his other poems, to recall beliefs and practices which at one period or another had been alive and vital at Rome or among the Italian peoples. Yet this was not pure antiquarianism, for it is clear too that part of Virgil's aim was to give expression to the beliefs of his age, and in the *Aeneid* at least to forward that fusion of the Greek and Roman elements in religion, which it was the object of Augustus' reforms to fix and establish. Perhaps, too, to some extent, he wished to reconcile or to put into juxtaposition the conclusions of philosophy and the beliefs of religious tradition. An examination such as is proposed might then, apart from its own intrinsic interest, throw some light on the question which out of all the strange medley of beliefs and practices that had survived to the Augustan age, still had meaning and reality, and possibly, by causing the central ideas of the poems to stand out in their framework, might bring into clearer definition the conceptions which were most real to the poet himself.

If the study of religion in Virgil on these lines is to be of value, it is necessary to have constantly in mind the elements of which this medley of belief and practice in Virgil's time was composed. I have elsewhere[1] endeavoured to trace the many strains of thought and cult which had come to Rome in the course of her long history, and they may be studied in the works[2] of Wissowa, Boissier, and Warde Fowler. In this book, too, I shall prefix to each section a brief account of Virgil's 'data'. But here, as the start, a short résumé of these strains will serve to bind the

[1] *Phases in the Religion of Ancient Rome*, Sather Classical Lectures, Oxford University Press, 1932.

[2] Wissowa, *Religion und Kultus der Römer*, ed. 2; Boissier, *La Religion romaine*; Warde Fowler, *Roman Festivals*, *The Religious Experience of the Roman People*.

investigation together and to show its general plan.
Roughly speaking there are four such strains which can be
traced in Virgil. Firstly, there is the element of magic and
superstition, very primitive in the religions of the world,
and in Rome, as elsewhere, not only persisting in popular
beliefs but embodied even in the ritual of the State-cult.
Secondly, there is the early Animism, the belief in vague
'spirits' of place and function, which was the foundation of
Italian religion and survives, often in disguise, into its most
complicated stages. In the third place stands the Graeco-
Roman anthropomorphism, which, coming to Rome
firstly through Etruria,[1] then through the Greek cities in
southern Italy, and lastly from Greek literature, dominated
the State-religion of the Republic and the writings of the
Roman poets. Lastly, there is the element of philosophy,
which began to be studied at Rome in the second century
B.C., and, as may be seen in the dialogues of Cicero, profoundly affected the religious views of the educated classes.
It must not be supposed that to Virgil and his contemporaries these elements, except the last, were in any way
distinct. Ovid in the *Fasti*, when endeavouring to explain
the rites of the Roman Calendar, will appeal indifferently
to folk-lore or magic, to the old animistic spirit, to Greek
legend, or to philosophical rationalism without any apparent sense of incongruity. It is in fact the painstaking
researches of modern scholars which have separated out
the various elements. Yet one of the interesting results of
the investigation of Virgil's treatment of religious ideas is
to reveal that he had a clearer consciousness than most
of his contemporaries at least of the distinction between

---

[1] It is possible, as F. Altheim (*Griechische Götter im alten Rom*) has recently
endeavoured to show, that the period of Greek influence must be placed
earlier than has usually been supposed. The perusal of his work leaves
me suspicious of his ingenious trains of argument, though with the sense
that his general conclusions may be sound.

Greek and Roman, and shows some care, as may be seen
in his treatment of deities with both Greek and Roman
names, to keep apart the elements in their conception and
worship which originated from the two different sources.
He knew the Graeco-Roman religion as one, yet seems to
have been conscious of its double source. Whole-heartedly
he seconded Augustus' scheme of 'rebuilding the temples'[1]
of Rome, but he knew whose temples they were.

It will be noticed that of one element in the 'medley of
religions' which was in fact very prominent among Virgil's contemporaries no mention has been made, namely,
the Oriental cults, which during the preceding century
had begun to invade Rome, and had won a great place in
the popular mind. This is because Virgil would have none
of them; beyond a contemptuous reference[2] in his picture
of the battle of Actium they are not mentioned. For it was
essential to Augustus' endeavour to reinstate the sober
Graeco-Roman cult that these emotional interlopers
should be rejected. His struggle with Antony and Cleopatra had been a struggle between East and West, and in
religion, no less than in other fields, the victory of the
West must be undisputed. Propertius, in his earlier books,
when he was not in the court circle, could refer to the
rites of Isis, but Ovid in the *Fasti* and Horace will know
nothing of them or any other of the orgiastic gods.
Bacchus and the Magna Mater are exceptions even in
Virgil, but they appear as the traditional figures of the
Graeco-Roman cult and not as the objects of orgiastic
rites in Italy.

It is the function of the critic to disentangle these
strands in Virgil's work and to analyse his use of them.

---

[1] Cf. *Mon. Anc.* xx. iv. 17; Hor. *Od.* iii. vi.   [2] *Aen.* viii. 698.

I
MAGIC, OMEN, AND PROPHECY

THERE is much that lies at the back of religion which may be classed generally as magic. It rests on the belief that man by his words or actions can constrain nature or the powerful spirits, whom he believes to surround him, to his own ends. It is sometimes held that such practices are not really religious, because they do not involve an appeal to 'powers' outside man's self to aid him and give him their strength, but they do undoubtedly make an appeal to a supernatural force and thus contain in them the germs of religion. Yet religion has always regarded magic as something alien, if not hostile, to itself, and any developed religion has been at pains, as were the Roman pontifices, to exclude it. In spite of this it has nearly always survived in popular belief and practice, and not infrequently, as at Rome, elements of magic have become embodied unconsciously in accepted religious rites.

Magic practice is not very often referred to by Virgil, but in two conspicuous passages he describes it with great elaboration. That it had persisted to his time in private use, especially for the love-charm, there is abundant evidence in inscriptions and elsewhere, and Alphesiboeus in *Eclogue* viii sang of what Virgil's contemporaries no doubt still practised. There are references first to simple instances from country life. Menalcas[1] in the third *Eclogue* complains that 'some evil eye is casting a spell over my lambs', a common belief among agricultural peoples. Italian shepherds,[2] as the poet tells us in the *Georgics*, 'hang up soft masks on the lofty pine'; it is true that Virgil says

---

[1] E. iii. 103 nescio quis teneros oculus mihi fascinat agnos.
[2] G. ii. 388 et te, Bacche, vocant per carmina laeta, tibique
oscilla ex alta suspendunt mollia pinu.

that this was done in honour of Bacchus, but the *oscilla* themselves were really nothing but charms to ward off evil spirits. Not infrequently Virgil mentions the professional witches who 'mingle herbs and harmful words'[1] or 'with their brazen knives seek in the moonlight for downy herbs with the milk of black poison'.[2] It is these witches too who for their evil purposes gather the 'hippomanes'[3] from the loins of the mare and snatch the caul from the head of the new-born foal, before the mother can eat it. Such a witch of more than usual power Dido had once visited on the confines of Aethiopia:[5] 'She engages with her spells to free men's minds, when she wishes, or to fasten on others cruel care, to stay the water in the rivers and turn the stars back; she too can raise ghosts at night; you may see the earth groan beneath her feet and ash-trees come down from the mountains.' This is magic of Thessalian quality. We must reckon too as magic the famous golden bough,[6] which gave a safe entry to the lower world to the men who could pluck it from its tree, and the strange rite of cutting a lock from the head of the dying and dedicating it to Dis in order to secure a safe passage to the underworld[7]—a rite which the dying Dido had forgotten to perform for herself and Iuno sent Iris from heaven to do it for her.

[1] G. iii. 283 miscueruntque herbas et non innoxia verba.
[2] A. iv. 513 falcibus et messae ad lunam quaeruntur aënis
    pubentes herbae nigri cum lacte veneni.
[3] G. iii. 280 hic demum, hippomanes vero quod nomine dicunt
    pastores, lentum destillat ab inguine virus,
    hippomanes, quod saepe malae legere novercae.
cf. Theocr. ii. 48.
[4] A. iv. 515 quaeritur et nascentis equi de fronte revulsus
    et matri praereptus amor.
[5] A. iv. 483 ff.
[6] A. vi. 136 ff., 185 ff.; see esp. 140–1
    sed non ante datur telluris operta subire
    auricomos quam qui decerpserit arbore fetus.
See also p. 269.
[7] A. iv. 696 ff. See p. 246.

But the two principal descriptions of magic rites in
Virgil are of course the love-spell[1] in *Eclogue* viii, and
Dido's pretended preparations for casting a similar spell
over Aeneas,[2] when she is really preparing the pyre for her
own death. These are worth examining in some detail,
as they show an intimate knowledge on Virgil's part of
magical practice and belief. The incantation in *Eclogue*
viii represents a woman enacting a love-spell in order to
regain the affection of her unfaithful lover, Daphnis. It is,
of course, modelled on the incantation of Simaitha in the
sacred *Idyll* of Theocritus, but the imitation is not too close
and it contains several features which are very distinctly
Italian. The most notable of these is in the refrain:
whereas in Theocritus it is the ἴυγξ on the magic wheel
which is to work the charm, in Virgil's version the power
resides in the spoken word: 'Bring Daphnis from the city,
my charms, bring Daphnis home, my songs.'[3] This is
typically Italian, for with the Italians the force of the charm
lies most often in the magic formula and Virgil is true to the
Italian idea when he emphasizes the power of *carmina*.[4]
The setting too is Roman: the lustral water is brought,
an altar set up and decorated with ribbons, the sacred
herbs (*verbenae*), here probably the witches' herbs, are
burnt with incense.[5] There is a wax image of Daphnis,[6]
which is to be adorned with triple fillets of three colours
and carried three times round the altar: 'god rejoices in an
uneven number'; three was always sacred or magic. The
three colours are to be tied in three knots, 'the bonds of
Venus';[7] the constraining power of a knot was always

---

[1] E. viii. 63 ff.   [2] A. iv. 494 ff.
[3] E. viii. 68, &c. ducite ab urbe domum, mea carmina, ducite Daphnim.
[4] 69–71.   [5] 64–65.   [6] 73–5.
[7] 77–8: for the power of the knot see Servius, *ad Aen.* iii. 370: 'in ratione
sacrorum par est et animae et corporis causa; nam plerumque quae non
possunt circa animam fieri, fiunt circa corpus, ut solvere vel ligare, quo
possit anima, quod per se non potest, ex cognatione sentire.'

recognized in Rome, as, for instance, in the provision that
the flamen Dialis, who must be ceremonially free, must
never have a knot on his person.

In the next stanza[1] we find that there is not only wax in
the fire, as in Theocritus' poem, but also clay: 'as this clay
hardens and as this wax melts in one and the same fire,
so may Daphnis with love for me.' This is obscure and
Servius' note appears to confuse two explanations, one
that there are two images, the clay image of the woman
herself, which hardens, and the wax image of the lover,
which melts, or that both images are symbolic of the man
over whom a spell is cast that he may harden towards all
others and melt towards his mistress. The latter view
seems the more probable. The sacred meal[2] is added to
the flames and laurel (Δάφνη) burned with pitch to sym-
bolize, as the poet says, the burning of the woman's heart
for Daphnis. This sounds a sophisticated explanation and
probably in the rite it was only a further symbol of the
consumption of the man's image. Certain relics[3] (*exuviae*),
presumably hair, wearing-apparel, &c., which are pledges
(*pignora*) of Daphnis, are to be buried beneath the threshold—always a sacred place; by their intimate association
with him they will be effective in bringing him back.
Finally,[4] there are to be added to the fire magic herbs
given to the celebrant by Moeris, a noted wizard, who had
often with them turned himself into a werewolf, raised
spirits from the tombs, and charmed crops from their
fields; for the last we may compare the regulation in the
Twelve Tables *neve alienam segetem pellexeris*. As the fire
burns down,[5] an attendant is bidden to take ashes and cast

---

[1] 80–81; cf. Theocr. ii. 28.   [2] 82–83; cf. Theocr. ii. 18, 23–6.

[3] 91–3; for the *exuviae* compare the parallel phrase of the 'relics' of Aeneas
in A. iv. 496; cf. also Theocr. ii. 53.

[4] 95–9; for the casting of a spell on crops cf. also Tibull. i. 8. 19 cantus
vicinis fruges traducit ab agris.   [5] 101–2; cf. Theocr. xxiv. 93.

them over her shoulder into the flowing stream without looking back; this precept comes from another poem of Theocritus and is not typically Roman. When all these rites have been duly performed at last comes the promise of success. The ashes blaze up on the altar and the dog barks on the threshold;[1] thus all ends with a characteristic country omen.

This elaborately worked out description shows a deep acquaintance with the magic practices of Italy, for although many details come straight from Theocritus, yet there are others which Virgil has added from his own knowledge and experience. Not less interesting—if only because some of the main points in *Eclogue* viii recur again— is the description at the end of the fourth *Aeneid*.[2] It will be remembered that Dido, wishing to construct a funeral pyre for herself without arousing suspicion, pretends to her sister that, like the woman in the *Eclogue*, she is preparing a charm to recover Aeneas' love,[3] or free herself from it, and refers to the wardress of the temple of the Hesperides, from whom she learnt the art, whose skill has been already noticed (p. 6). Virgil dwells on the details of Dido's preparations with the same interest as in his earlier description. 'In the recesses of her palace beneath the open air she erects the huge pyre with pine logs and billets of holm-oak: she adorns the spot with garlands and crowns it with leaves to suit her funeral', just as the lover crowned the altar. 'On it she places the relics of Aeneas (note the im-

---

[1] 105–7.

[2] A. iv. 492–521: as links of connexion with *Eclogue* viii we may note— E. viii. 66 magicis . . . sacris; A. iv. 493 magicas . . . artis; E. viii. 91 has olim exuvias; A. iv. 496 exuviasque omnes; 507 exuvias; E. viii. 74 terque haec altaria circum | effigiem duco; A. iv. 508 effigiem-que toro locat; E. viii. 82 sparge molam; A. iv. 517 ipsa mola manibusque piis.

[3] A. iv. 478 inveni, germana, viam (gratare sorori)
    quae mihi reddat eum vel eo me solvat amantem.

portance of this love-charm again) and the sword he had
left. She places an image on a couch, well knowing her-
herself what was to come. Around stand altars and the
priestess with streaming hair (loosened in religious rites to
avoid all knots) thunders the names of the three hundred
gods, Erebus and Chaos and the triple Hecate, the three
aspects of the virgin Diana' (see p. 162). The appeal to the
underworld gods in a magic rite would be natural, but it is,
of course, ironically appropriate in view of Dido's coming
suicide. 'She had sprinkled water feigned to come from
the source of Avernus, and downy herbs with the milk of
black poison, cut in the moonlight with a bronze sickle and
the caul torn from the forehead of a colt at birth, the love-
sign snatched from his dam'; the magic power of all these
has already been noted (p. 6). Dido 'herself with the
sacred meal (the Roman offering again) and pure hands
at the altar's side, with one foot loosed from its thongs[1] and
robe girt back, calls on the gods before her death and the
stars that knew her destiny'. Religion is mingled with magic
here in the appeal to the gods, and the invocation of the

---

[1] This feature is of peculiar interest, but not easy to explain. The loosing
of the one foot is intended to free it from magic restraint, but why is the other
left bound? Servius says that the purpose is to loose Dido and bind Aeneas,
and Frazer (*G.B.*[3], part ii, 'Taboo', &c., pp. 310–13) is inclined to adopt
this explanation. It is borne out by A. iv. 478 (quoted in n. 3, p. 9)
and would have a certain parallel in the two images in *Eclogue* viii (see p. 8),
if it is true that there the clay represents the woman and the wax her lover,
but it does not seem convincing. The practice was embedded in both Italian
and Greek folk-lore, for we find it again in the story of Jason, who appeared
with one sandal before his uncle Pelias (Pindar, *Pyth.* iv. 129, Ap. Rhod. i. 7);
in the *Aeneid* itself it is repeated as a feature in the costume of some of the
Italian troops (vii. 689); and in history it is seen in Thucydides' account
(iii. 22. 2) of the outbreak from Plataea, where a rationalizing explanation is
given. The idea of the binding of the enemy is no doubt applicable in all
these cases, but it seems too artificial a symbolism. The notion should rather
be of the partial freeing of the wearer from magic restraint, but it is hard to
see how it could apply. See also an interesting note in Irvine, *Loves of Dido
and Aeneas*, pp. 113–14.

stars suggests the later cosmological ideas of the astrologers and the Stoics, but the main body of thought is pure primitive magic.

These two major incidents testify clearly to Virgil's interest in the details of the magic art, but, if unsupported, they might be taken to be purely conventional. The song of the *Eclogue* is an imitation of Theocritus, and the action of Dido might well be regarded as part of epic tradition— modelled again perhaps on the wizardry of Apollonius' Medea, who is in many respects Dido's prototype. But the casual allusions to magic elsewhere, especially in *Eclogues* and *Georgics*, imply its continued vitality in country life. As for Virgil's own interest, it would probably be true to say that it is mainly that of curiosity and that there is no reason to suppose that he himself had any belief in the efficacy of magic or spell. It is for him a survival of the primitive, which is at once picturesque and indicative of the strange workings of the human mind.

Not far remote from magic is the spirit in which early man is influenced by omens, or accidental indications that his actions are likely to be prosperous or the reverse. In the earlier stage of thought such omens seem to have possessed their own validity and to be just symbols of 'luck'; as such they survive in folk-lore and in popular sayings. Later, when the religious belief in divine beings has been fully established, they are regarded as significant of the will of some divine power, specially sent to proclaim that will. As such they were incorporated at Rome in the elaborate system of augury and auspice, which played so large a part in the State-religion. Omens from the flight and song of birds and from the occurrence of lightning and thunder formed the basis of the system; the Greek practice of extispice, the examination of the entrails of victims to obtain omens, was never officially recognized at Rome, but it became known to the Romans through Etruria and was occasionally practised by Etruscan *haruspices* brought to Rome for the purpose.

Omen and augury are far more frequently represented in Virgil's poems than magic, and appear in several stages with no sense of inconsistency. Of the simplest form of omen, where the accidental occurrence is itself felt to influence men's fate or foretell their future, there are many traces, not always distinguishable from the 'religious' type of omen, but based at least on a more primitive idea. As might be expected, several of the most obvious folk-lore omens occur among the peasant-folk of the *Eclogues*, the dumbness cast upon Moeris by the wolves who saw him before he caught sight of them,[1] the evil prognostication given by the lightning-struck oaks,[2] and the crow that gave warning of trouble as it croaked on the left from the hollow holm-oak.[3] These are all straightforward omens of an unsophisticated superstition, which carry their force in themselves. There are similar instances in the *Aeneid*, where natural occurrences or sights are interpreted as having a warning or encouraging significance. Several of these are connected naturally with the voyage of Aeneas. When, under the mistaken interpretation of an oracle bidding them seek 'the country of their fathers',[4] the Trojans land and prepare to settle in Crete, a pestilence warns them that they are wrong and must journey on. Later on, when they touch the shores of southern Italy, four white horses, 'the first omen', are seen grazing;[5] Anchises inter-

[1] E. ix. 54   lupi Moerim videre priores.
[2] E. i. 16 saepe malum hoc nobis, si mens non laeva fuisset,
      de caelo tactas memini praedicere quercus.
[3] E. ix. 14   nisi me quacumque novas incidere lites
      ante sinistra cava monuisset ab ilice cornix.
Repeated in the probably spurious line E. i. 18.   [4] A. iii. 137 ff.
[5] A. iii. 537 quattuor hic, primum omen, equos in gramine vidi
      tondentis campum late, candore nivali.

prets the omen as foretelling war, and then remembers as an afterthought that horses are also harnessed to chariots and bear reins; they may be an omen of peace. It should, however, be noted that in both these instances the later religious idea is added in an appeal to a deity to confirm the omen, in the first place to Phoebus, in the second to Pallas. To these warning omens must be added two favourable portents, which, if we may set aside the prophecies of their occurrence, have all the marks of the primitive omen, the famous incident of the 'eating of the tables',[1] and the discovery of the white sow and her thirty young on the site of Alba Longa.[2] An extension of this simple idea in an almost metaphorical sense is seen when Aeneas, leading his host to battle, encourages his followers by his mere presence and is described as an 'omen of the fight'.[3] There are other instances in which not only is the interpretation of the occurrence supernatural, but the occurrence itself; this suggests a less simple state of mind, but one not essentially different. Dido in her first despair is encouraged to suicide,[4] when the wine which she pours on the altar is turned into blood, and the bursting of Acestes' arrow into flames[5] at the funeral games of Anchises is hailed as an omen of the future honour of his house. A more peculiar

---

[1] A. vii. 116 heus, etiam mensas consumimus, prophesied by the Harpy in A. iii. 255-7.

[2] A. viii. 81 ff., prophesied by Helenus in A. iii. 388 ff., and by the Tiber god in A. viii. 42 ff.

[3] A. x. 310   primus turmas invasit agrestis
        Aeneas, omen pugnae.

[4] A. iv. 452 ff.

[5] A. v. 522 ff. Notice here the accumulation of the words associated with divination:

    hic oculis subitum obicitur magnoque futurum
    augurio monstrum: docuit post exitus ingens,
    seraque terrifici cecinerunt *omina* vates;

and 533   nam te voluit rex magnus Olympi
        talibus *auspiciis* exsortem ducere honores.

instance is seen in the bloody roots of the cornel tree torn up by Aeneas,[1] which denote the presence of the corpse of the murdered Polydorus; natural and supernatural are here mingled. Finally, there are omens of the fully-developed religious type, deliberately sent by the gods. After Evander has consented to send his son Pallas to help Aeneas in the battle, 'suddenly lightning flashed from the heaven with thunder . . . and the bray of a Tuscan trumpet seemed to echo through the sky';[2] Aeneas bids Evander not to inquire 'what chance these portents bring', for he remembers that his mother Venus had promised to bring him the armour forged by Vulcan; the lightning and thunder were 'Cythera's sign'. In the last book of the *Aeneid*,[3] Iuturna, to encourage Turnus and the Rutulians, sends the omen of an eagle, who swoops and seizes a swan: 'the Rutulians greet the augury with a shout', and later in the book[4] Iuppiter sends one of the Dirae in the form of a bird, bidding her 'meet Iuturna as an omen'. It is not accidental that in these divinely sent occurrences the omen is lightning or a bird, as in the orthodox Italian science of augury.

This sketch of the range of Virgil's conception of omens may be illustrated and amplified by an examination of his use of the main words connected with divination; we find them used, as would be expected, both in a loose general sense and also in closer connexion with the principles of augury and ritual in the State-cult.

Omen itself is, as has been seen in several instances already, a word of very general application ranging from

[1] A. iii. 22 ff.
[2] A. viii. 524 ff.
[3] A. xii. 244 ff.; note 257 tum vero augurium Rutuli clamore salutant.
[4] A. xii. 845 ff.; note 853
    harum unam celerem demisit ab aethere summo
    Iuppiter inque omen Iuturnae occurrere iussit.

the simple folk-lore idea to something approaching the more elaborate conception of 'auspice'. Thus when the nymphs,[1] which were once his ships, appear to Aeneas and, warning him of Ascanius' danger in the camp, push his boats so that they increase their pace, 'he is amazed and bewildered, yet his spirits rise at the omen'; the omen here is just the strange and significant occurrence. So Turnus begs Amata not to weep and 'send him to the fight with such an omen',[2] the evil omen of her tears; and the shepherd during the great pestilence 'sits' (if the text be right) 'praying the gods for better omens';[3] here the 'omens' are almost equivalent to the fortune which they predict. But when the Latins, roused to fury by Amata, 'demand war against the omens',[4] or when Diana laments that Camilla is joining the fight 'with unlucky omen',[5] the idea is approaching that of the *auspicia*, which the Roman general had to take before a battle. In other passages again we find the idea of the professional seer, almost the Roman augur, whose business it is to interpret the omens sent by the gods. So Sinon speaks of Calchas 'thus he sets out the omens';[6] Aeneas addresses Helenus as one who 'knows the meaning of the stars and the tongues of birds and the omens of the flying wing'[7] (astrologer and augur combined), and in a more elaborate phrase Asilas is described as 'interpreter of gods and men, whom the entrails of sheep and the stars of heaven obey and the tongues of birds

[1] A. x. 249   stupet inscius ipse
       Tros Anchisiades: animos tamen omine tollit.
[2] A. xii. 72   ne, quaeso, ne me lacrimis neve omine tanto
       prosequere in duri certamina Martis euntem.
[3] G. iii. 456   aut meliora deos sedet omina poscens; omina *det. quidam*; omnia *MR*, &c.
[4] A. vii. 583   ilicet infandum cuncti contra omina bellum . . . poscunt.
[5] A. xi. 589   tristis ubi infausto committitur omine pugna.
[6] A. ii. 182   ita digerit omina Calchas.
[7] A. iii. 360 · · · · · · · · · · qui sidera sentis
       et volucrum linguas et praepetis omina pennae.

and the fires of the prophetic lightning';[1] here Greek extispice too is added to the accomplishments of the seer. In a few passages, Virgil seems characteristically to stretch the meaning of the word in a way which conventional speech would hardly admit. A borderline instance[2] is the description of Dido's first marriage to Sychaeus, 'to whom her father had given her as a virgin and had yoked her with the first omens'; the expression is no doubt derived from the auspices before the marriage ceremony, just as later[3] it is said that the 'portents of the gods' were against the marriage of Turnus and Lavinia, but the 'omens' here come very near to meaning the rite itself. So when Helenus is urging Aeneas to veil his head in sacrifice 'lest amid the sacred flames and the ceremony of the gods some hostile form should meet your eyes and disturb the omens',[4] the meaning is 'disturb the rite by evil omens'. A severe strain is put upon the word when it is said of Latinus' palace: 'here it was the omen for kings to receive their sceptres and first lift the fasces';[5] *omen* perhaps means 'a custom sanctioned by favourable omens'. Virgil's extensions are, as often, audacious, but it is always possible to trace the connexion of the new usage with the original sense and to see the appropriateness of the innovation.

With *omen* go naturally three other words used to express a strange or ominous occurrence, *monstrum*, *portentum*, and *prodigium*; Virgil is fond of the first, but uses the other two

---

[1] A. x. 175   hominum divumque interpres Asilas,
     cui pecudum fibrae, caeli cui sidera parent
     et linguae volucrum et praesagi fulminis ignes.
[2] A. i. 345 cui pater intactam dederat primisque iugarat
     ominibus.
[3] A. vii. 58 sed variis portenta deum terroribus obstant.
[4] A. iii. 406 ne qua inter sanctos ignis in honore deorum
     hostilis facies occurrat et omina turbet.
[5] A. vii. 173 hic sceptra accipere et primos attollere fascis
     regibus omen erat.

sparingly. Three times he applies to marvellous events the expression *mirabile monstrum*, which, if *monstrum* is really derived from the root of *monere*, we may translate 'a wondrous warning'. It is used of the flame that appeared on the head of Ascanius,[1] of the bloody roots on Polydorus' grave,[2] and of the transformation of Aeneas' ships into nymphs.[3] Similarly, after the visit of Iris to the Trojan matrons to urge them to burn their ships in Sicily, they were 'astounded by the portent';[4] Amata, maddened by Allecto, is 'deep-stirred by the mighty portent';[5] and Andromache, at her first sight of Aeneas and his Trojans, is 'terrified by this great portent'.[6] In all these instances the meaning is straightforward and equivalent to the use of *omen* in its most general sense. When the bursting of Acestes' arrow into flame is described as 'a portent which is to be of great augury',[7] there is a greater solemnity about it and something of the notion of a State auspice, and in other passages the *monstra* are said definitely to be signs sent by the gods. After his adventure at the tomb of Polydorus, Aeneas refers 'the portents of the gods'[8] to the chieftains and Anchises, and when the Palladium in the Greek camp showed its miraculous signs, 'by no doubtful portents did Tritonia give those signs'.[9] The vague ominous occurrence has here become the manifestation of the god's will. Finally, there is a 'faded' sense of the word in which it is used in a concrete way of any strange or outlandish object, though even here a supernatural touch

---

[1] A. ii. 680.   [2] A. iii. 26.   [3] A. ix. 120.

[4] A. v. 659 tum vero attonitae monstris actaeque furore
        conclamant.

[5] A. vii. 376   ingentibus excita monstris.

[6] A. iii. 307   magnis exterrita monstris.

[7] A. v. 523; see p. 13, n. 5.

[8] A. iii. 58 delectos populi ad proceres primumque parentem
        monstra deum refero.

[9] A. ii. 171 nec dubiis ea signa dedit Tritonia monstris.

may often be detected. The Trojans listening to the rumblings of Aetna 'endure all night those *immania monstra*';[1] the unnatural calm of the sea is a *monstrum* to Palinurus;[2] the wooden horse, always suspected of some religious purpose, is a *monstrum infelix*;[3] the Egyptian deities on Cleopatra's ship are 'monstrous gods of every kind'[4] with their uncanny animal heads. Even Polyphemus, 'the vast dreadful monster',[5] has the element of 'taboo' about him and is what the Germans would call *ungeheuer*.

The rarer words *portentum* and *prodigium* follow the same lines. The 'portents of the gods' which opposed Turnus' marriage with Lavinia have already been noticed,[6] and Aeneas' reference to the thunder and trumpet sounds in the sky as 'portents'.[7] The word occurs once again[8] when Diomedes tells Aeneas' envoys that the misfortunes which beset the Greeks returning from Troy have not yet ceased: 'even now portents of terrible aspect beset us', and his companions are changed into birds, a miraculous occurrence telling of the displeasure of heaven. *Prodigium* has a rather wider range. The Harpy prophesies to the Trojans their 'eating of the tables':[9] it is 'a new and unspeakable prodigy', here simply an omen in the wide sense. So it is when Aeneas tells Palinurus that the neighbouring peoples 'driven by prodigies from heaven'[10] will give him burial. But when Iris disguised as Beroe tells the Trojan matrons of

[1] A. iii. 583 noctem illam tecti silvis immania monstra
       perferimus.
[2] A. v. 849   mene huic confidere monstro?
[3] A. ii. 245 et monstrum infelix sacrata sistimus arce.
[4] A. viii. 698 omnigenumque deum monstra.
[5] A. iii. 658 monstrum horrendum, informe, ingens.
[6] A. vii. 58; see p. 16, n. 3.   [7] A. viii. 533; see p. 14.
[8] A. xi. 271 nunc etiam horribili visu portenta sequuntur.
[9] A. iii. 365 sola novum dictuque nefas Harpyia Celaeno
       prodigium canit.
[10] A. vi. 378 nam tua finitimi, longe lateque per urbes
       prodigiis acti caelestibus, ossa piabunt.

her vision of Cassandra who warned her that Sicily was to be their home and adds, 'prodigies so great brook no delay'[1], *prodigium* is equivalent to a prophetic utterance. Finally there is a 'faded' use, exactly like that of *monstrum*, when Hercules is said to have slain 'the Cretan prodigies'.[2]

Augurium and *auspicium*, the two characteristic words of the State science of divination, have, as might be expected, a rather more restricted and technical sense in Virgil. An *augurium* in the strict augural sense might be of two kinds, *oblativum*, a sign voluntarily sent by the gods which required interpretation, or *impetrativum*, a sign asked for by man and sent in answer to his request. Acestes' arrow, so often referred to, is 'a portent which is to be of great augury';[3] it was an unasked sign, but its interpretation is clear. When the nymphs have appeared to Aeneas and hastened the course of his boats down the Tiber, he prays to Cybele 'do thou duly bring near thy augury',[4] a strange phrase which must mean 'fulfil this sign which thou hast given me'. So Latinus in giving his consent to Aeneas' marriage with Lavinia prays 'may the gods prosper our undertaking and their own augury',[5] the augury being here the oracles of Faunus which foretold Lavinia's marriage with a foreigner. A vaguer use of the same idea occurs at the beginning of the fifth *Aeneid*;[6] the Trojans, sailing away from Carthage, see flames rising from the walls, and the remembrance of Dido's love and sorrow and

---

[1] A. v. 638   iam tempus agi res,
          nec tantis mora prodigiis.
[2] A. viii. 294 tu Cresia mactas prodigia.
[3] A. v. 522; see p. 13, n. 5.
[4] A. x. 254   tu rite propinques augurium.
[5] A. vii. 259   di nostra incepta secundent
          auguriumque suum!
[6] A. v. 5   duri magno sed amore dolores
          polluto, notumque furens quid femina possit,
          triste per augurium Teucrorum pectora ducunt.

'the knowledge of what a frenzied woman can do lead the hearts of the Trojans through a sad path of augury'; there is no divine intervention here and the word really means little more than 'conjecture'—another Virgilian extension. These are all cases of the *augurium oblativum*. Even more interesting, because nearer to Roman ideas, are the instances of the *impetrativum*. The second book supplies a fine example:[1] Anchises, in doubt whether to leave the burning Troy, has seen the tongue of flame on Ascanius' head: this is an omen. But he is not yet convinced, and prays to Iuppiter: 'if by our piety we deserve it, give us now thy augury, Father, and confirm these omens.' Iuppiter sends a star falling through the sky; Anchises is reassured, 'this, ye gods, is your augury, Troy is in your power'.[2] There is a perfect contrast between the *oblativum* and the *impetrativum*. Landing in Delos, Aeneas enters Apollo's temple and prays for guidance as to his course: 'give us, Father, thy augury';[3] in answer comes Phoebus' oracle. And when Iuturna sends the eagle as her sign to the Rutulians, 'then indeed the Rutulians greet the augury with a shout, and first of all Tolumnius the augur cries "this it was, this for which I have often asked in my prayers" ';[4] the sign may have been *oblativum* to the Rutulian host, but to the old augur it was the *impetrativum* for which he had prayed. It is interesting to find Virgil, in these examples, keeping so close to the true Roman idea of augury. There remain two instances in which the word is used for the art of augury. Nisus on his expedition with

[1] A. ii. 690   si pietate meremur,
        da deinde augurium, pater, atque haec omina firma.
[2] A. ii. 703 vestrum hoc augurium, vestroque in numine Troia est.
[3] A. iii. 89 da, pater, augurium.
[4] A. xii. 257 tum vero augurium Rutuli clamore salutant
        expediuntque manus, primusque Tolumnius augur
        'hoc erat, hoc, votis' inquit 'quod saepe petivi.'

Euryalus slays Rhamnes, 'a king he was and an augur most
beloved of Turnus, but he could not by his augury keep
off his doom'.[1] Apollo himself had given his beloved Iapyx
'all his arts and gifts, augury and the lyre and the swift
arrows'.[2]   Finally, we have a direct reference to the State
augury of Rome in the description of the figure of Picus
in the hall of Latinus 'holding the *lituus* of Quirinus and
girt in the short trabea',[3] the tunic of purple and yellow,
which Servius tells us was the official garb of the augur.

Auspicia are strictly the omens taken before an undertaking to see whether or no it has the approval of the gods;
in the State-cult it is used specially in reference to the
magistrate entering on his office or the general about to
enter the field; then in a derivative sense it is used of the
'leadership' or 'command' of the general appointed with
favourable auspices. Virgil has examples of the word in
all these senses, though most frequently in the first and
more general sense. Aeneas bidding farewell to Helenus
and Andromache tells them that they have founded a new
Troy 'with better auspices, I hope, and less exposed to
the Greeks' attack',[4] even as Helenus had previously
assured Aeneas that it was 'with greater auspices that he
was making his way across the deep'.[5] Acoetes, once
Evander's squire, 'was then going as comrade to his dear
charge (Pallas) with less happy auspices'.[6] In a curious

---

[1] A. ix. 327 rex idem et regi Turno gratissimus augur,
      sed non augurio potuit depellere pestem.
[2] A. xii. 393 ipse suas artis, sua munera, laetus Apollo
      augurium citharamque dabat celerisque sagittas.
[3] A. vii. 187 ipse Quirinali lituo parvaque sedebat
      succinctus trabea.
[4] A. iii. 498   melioribus, opto,
      auspiciis, et quae fuerit minus obvia Grais.
[5] A. iii. 374   nam te maioribus ire per altum
      auspiciis manifesta fides.
[6] A. xi. 32   sed non felicibus aeque
      tum comes auspiciis caro datus ibat alumno.

passage, where the text is uncertain, Aeneas assures Acestes after his omen that 'the great king of Olympus has willed thee by such auspices to hold peculiar honours';[1] it is as if he were entering on a magistracy. In a slightly developed sense Aeneas tells Dido that he would gladly have rebuilt Troy and lived on there, 'if the fates had suffered me to live my life with my own auspices',[2] that is, with such auspices as I would have chosen. Drances the orator, attacking Turnus, says that it is 'through his ill-omened auspices and unlucky character'[3] that so many evils have overtaken the Latins: *auspicium* here is almost 'leadership', yet there is the idea too that Turnus' character was the omen of his fate. Finally, there are two instances where Virgil has preserved exactly the technical idea of auspices as applied to a ruler; in both the expression is the same *paribus auspiciis*. Latinus remembers Faunus' prophecy that 'a stranger would be called to share his kingdom with equal auspices',[4] and Iuno in her false overtures to Venus proposes that they should share in the rule over the Carthaginians 'with equal auspices'.[5] The idea in both cases is just that of the two consuls who held their imperium 'with equal auspices'; the official meaning of the word could not be better brought out.

In his use then of the words connected with omen and augury Virgil, though he makes here, as elsewhere, his characteristic extensions, is scrupulously true to traditional

[1] A. v. 533   nam te voluit rex magnus Olympi
              talibus auspiciis exsortem ducere honores.
[2] A. iv. 340 me si fata meis paterentur ducere vitam
              auspiciis.
[3] A. xi. 347 cuius ob auspicium infaustum moresque sinistros . . .
              lumina tot cecidisse ducum . . . videmus.
[4] A. vii. 256   paribusque in regna vocari
              auspiciis.
[5] A. iv. 102 communem hunc ergo populum paribusque regamus
              auspiciis.

ideas, the more definite and technical the associations of the words. In this connexion it is interesting to note the sources from which the more formal of his auguries and auspices are drawn.[1] On the most solemn occasions the will of heaven is declared, as in Roman augury, by lightning and thunder. Thus, when Aeneas has made his prayer on landing on Italian soil, 'the almighty father thrice thundered clear from the high heaven, and showed from the sky, shaking it in his own hand, a cloud bright with golden rays of light'.[2] When Ascanius is making his first essay in battle and asks for a blessing, 'the father heard and from a clear region of the sky, thundered on the left',[3] choosing the side of good omen. Venus, bringing the new gift of armour to Aeneas, gave a still more notable sign, 'For all at once lightning flashing from the sky came with thunder and of a sudden all the heaven seemed to fall, and the bray of a Tuscan trumpet bellowed through the high air'.[4] To this lightning augury must be referred also the star which lit upon the head of Ascanius,[5] and possibly the arrow of Acestes which burst into flame.[6] Auguries from the flight of birds are much rarer in Virgil, and it may be noted that the flight of 'twice six swans',[7] scattered by the eagle and returning again, which greet Aeneas on his way to Carthage, are sent by Venus, not Iuppiter, and that the similar omen greeted by the Rutulian augur Tolumnius proved deceptive.[8] Heinze[9] believes that

[1] See Heinze, *Virgils epische Technik*, p. 313.
[2] A. vii. 141 hic Pater omnipotens ter caelo clarus ab alto
             intonuit, radiisque ardentem lucis et auro
             ipse manu quatiens ostendit ab aethere nubem.
[3] A. ix. 630 audiit et caeli Genitor de parte serena
             intonuit laevum.
[4] A. viii. 524 namque improviso vibratus ab aethere fulgor
              cum sonitu venit et ruere omnia visa repente,
              Tyrrhenusque tubae mugire per aethera clangor.
[5] A. ii. 680 ff.   [6] A. v. 522 ff.
[7] A. i. 393 ff.   [8] A. xii. 244 ff.   [9] *V.E.T.*, p. 313.

Virgil here reflects the practice of his times, in which the *praepetis omina pennae* were much more rarely used. Finally, it may be noted that the non-Roman custom of extispice is only referred to once,[1] and then as practised by Dido. Virgil then was following Roman practice closely; omen and augury were still very much alive both in the thoughts of the country folk and in the practice of the State, and so had for him the reality of a vital element in the experience of individual and community.

The future might be foretold not only by omen and augury, but by prophecy and oracle, and though, in its Greek form at least, oracle belongs to a later and more definitely religious stage than the ideas which have hitherto been considered, the connexion with the more primitive notions is so close that it may naturally be treated here.

There is a great difference in this matter between Virgil's inheritance from Italy and that from Greece. The oracle given by the priest or priestess of a god at a definite oracular seat, like Delphi or Delos, is unknown to the Italian mind; there were no such seats in Italy before the time of Greek influence. Prophecy might be given by the spoken word of a specially gifted human being, or by an animistic spirit, such as a nymph or a faun. So Ennius, in a famous line,[2] speaks of 'the verses, which of old the Fauns and seers chanted'. The word *fatum*[3] appears originally to have meant to an Italian the 'spoken word' of the prophet, not the oracular utterance of a god; in this connexion the seer would be described as *fatidicus* and the name of Faunus himself was derived by some Latin scholars from *fari* and

[1] A. iv. 63   pecudumque reclusis
       pectoribus inhians spirantia consulit exta.
[2] Quoted by Varro, *L.L.* vii. 36 versibu' quos olim Fauni vatesque canebant.
[3] See pp. 205–7. For the name *fatuus* applied to Faunus see Servius *ad Aen.* vii. 47.

to him was applied the epithet *fatuus*. Similarly *oraculum*
seems at first to have denoted the utterance of a human seer,
and Seneca explains it as meaning 'the will of the gods,
announced by the mouth of men'.[1] It is perhaps noticeable
that the Romans never spoke of the oracle of Apollo at
Cumae, but always of the oracles of the Sibyl, his human
mouthpiece. Such prophecy might be given by a seer at
any time or place and specimens of early prophecies have
come down to us; by a prophetic nymph it would naturally
be given at the source or spring where she was worshipped
and by Faunus in a sacred grove or field; to him were
attributed mysterious cries of encouragement which are
said to have urged on the Roman troops in battle.[2] The
Italian conception of prophecy thus belongs to an animistic stage of religion; the seer is the important person and
he is thought of as having behind him the inspiration of
a divine spirit.

Greek influence introduced two new conceptions, firstly
that of the dream-vision, in which the future might be
revealed, whether as an independent prophetic scene, or
as the direct utterance of a divine person, foretelling the
future. But what was far more important, it brought the
fully anthropomorphic idea of the organized seat of an
oracle, in which a god delivered his will or his foretelling of
the future through the words of a human priest or priestess,
who was but his instrument, and was known by some
general title, such as Pythia or Sibylla, which tended to
conceal the human personality. The most prominent of
the prophetic gods of Greece was of course Apollo, who
had his seats at Delphi, Delos, and in many other places.
Rome came to know him no doubt through the cities of

---

[1] Sen. *Contr.* 1 praef. quid est enim oraculum? nempe voluntas divum
hominis ore enuntiata.
[2] Cf. Cic. *de Div.* i. 45. 101; *de Nat. Deor.* ii. 2. 6.

Magna Graecia and above all at his home at Cumae, and often in history, besides employing the Sibylline oracles, sent for enlightenment to Delphi and elsewhere.

Virgil's treatment of prophecy is, as will be seen later in many other fields, a skilful combination of Italian and Greek elements. There is not in Virgil an example of the human *vates* of the Italian sort; Helenus, Calchas, and of course the Sibyl are Greek in their conception. But in Carmentis, 'the prophetess of fate, who sang the coming greatness of Aeneas' sons',[1] we have an example of the prophetic nymph, though it is somewhat contaminated by the euhemerism which has turned her into the mother of Evander. A still more interesting reference occurs to Faunus in his prophetic capacity, which for its combination of Italian and Greek elements deserves study at length. Latinus, alarmed by omens in his household, 'approaches the oracle of Faunus, his prophetic father, and consults the groves beneath lofty Albunea, which greatest of all holy woods resounds with sacred springs and breathes forth the foul mephitis'.[2] Here, so Virgil tells us, the Italian peoples used to practise 'incubation'; after an offering of sheep the inquirer would sleep the night in the temple and there 'he sees many a shape flitting round him in wondrous wise, and hears various voices, and enjoys

---

[1] A. viii. 339   Nymphae priscum Carmentis honorem,
                     vatis fatidicae, cecinit quae prima futuros
                     Aeneadas magnos.
Cf. p. 36.

[2] A. vii. 81–106. See esp. 81 ff.
        at rex sollicitus monstris oracula Fauni,
        fatidici genitoris, adit lucosque sub alta
        consulit Albunea, nemorum quae maxima sacro
        fonte sonat saevamque exhalat opaca mephitim;
and 87 ff.
        cum . . . pellibus incubuit stratis somnosque petivit,
        multa modis simulacra videt volitantia miris,
        et varias audit voces, fruiturque deorum
        colloquio, atque imis Acheronta affatur Avernis.

converse with the gods and addresses Acheron in the depths of Avernus'. Latinus followed the custom and heard a voice from the grove bidding him not to hesitate to give his daughter in marriage to Aeneas. Here there is the genuine Italian prophetic Faunus, and the mysterious Albunea, which here appears to be a mountain or a grove (perhaps a tree-clad hill) but in Horace[1] is undoubtedly a spring, may be in origin a prophetic nymph.[2] But the localization of the oracle of Faunus in a particular spot is Greek, even though it retains an Italian open-air form: much more so is the process of 'incubation', as practised in Greek temples, and the idea of prophecy by means of a dream-voice.

This instance then leads naturally to the Greek side of Virgil's accounts of prophecy. The dream-prophecy occurs both in the vision of Hector in the second book of the *Aeneid*,[3] which is Aeneas' first warning to flee from Troy, and in the strange sleep-vision of the Penates in the third book,[4] from which Aeneas first realizes that Italy is his goal; it was a master-stroke of Virgil's genius for conflation to make the essentially Italian deities appear in this Greek manner. Comparatively independent prophecy is made in the fourth book of the *Georgics*[5] by Proteus on the analogy of Homer, and by the harpy Celaeno,[6] who, however, admits in true Greek fashion that her prophecies are derived from Apollo: 'Mark my words, which the Almighty Father foretold to Phoebus, Phoebus Apollo to me, and I the greatest of the Furies set them forth for you.' For,

[1] Hor. *Od.* i. 7. 12 domus Albuneae resonantis.
[2] See Heinze, *Virgils epische Technik*, p. 174, n. 2.
[3] A. ii. 270 ff.   [4] A. iii. 147 ff.   [5] G. iv. 450 ff.
[6] A. iii. 245 ff. See esp. 250 ff.

>accipite ergo animis atque haec mea figite dicta,
>quae Phoebo Pater omnipotens, mihi Phoebus Apollo
>praedixit, vobis Furiarum ego maxima pando.

indeed, in Virgil's mind over the whole realm of prophecy Apollo[1] is supreme and he accepts without reserve the Greek conception of his oracular temples and his delivery of oracles by the mouth of his priest or priestess; even from Troy the Greeks send Eurypylus 'to inquire the oracles of Phoebus'.[2] Virgil knows of his oracular temples at Delos, Claros, and Actium,[3] and elsewhere, but above all at Cumae, where the Sibyl is his priestess. The account of her inspiration[4] is a fascinating study and it must be noted that all through the Sibyl is merely the god's mouthpiece; he dominates her and speaks through her lips. So, too, it is significant that Helenus,[5] though, as one might say, a prophet in his own right, yet leads Aeneas to the temple of Apollo, that he may receive fuller inspiration. Virgil truly represents the Greek theory that the god is all-important and the man but his instrument.

Thus in the matter of prophecy and oracle, though Virgil is true to Italian ideas, he is much more profoundly influenced, as indeed he was bound to be, by the organized Greek oracular practice. And if we ask in reference to all these modes of divination whether Virgil and his contemporaries had a belief in them, it is not possible to give a certain answer. But a significant clue is afforded by the statement of the harpy Celaeno that she derived her prophetic knowledge from Phoebus, and Phoebus from Iuppiter. Iuppiter, as will be seen later, implied to Virgil the divine government of the world, and it is perhaps legitimate to build so far on the harpy's dictum as to suppose that Virgil may have believed that the course of that divine government might be revealed to man.

---

[1] For a fuller account of Apollo see pp. 163–172.
[2] A. ii. 114 suspensi Eurypylum scitatum oracula Phoebi
　　　　mittimus, isque adytis haec tristia dicta reportat.
[3] Delos A. iii. 162; vi. 12; Claros A. iii. 360; Actium A. viii. 704.
[4] A. vi. 77 ff.　　　　　　　　　　　　　　[5] A. iii. 371 ff.

II

THE OLD ITALIAN RELIGION

DEITIES AND CULTS

IF there is any one passion in Virgil's life of which we may
feel certain, it is his devotion to the Italian country-side
and the farmer's life. His boyhood was spent on his father's
farm near Mantua, in the *Eclogues* he gives thanks to
Octavian for its restitution to him, the *Georgics* are his
hymn of praise to Italy and his prayer for the revival of the
simple farm-life, and the *Aeneid*, too, is full of the spirit of
the country. And in this strong feeling for the country
religion plays a large and vital part. If magic was to Virgil
mainly an object of curiosity, there can be no doubt of his
affectionate devotion to the old animistic religion of the
Italians. He loves to recall the spirits of field and woodland
and the many agricultural deities who played their part
in the country festivals, the details of the old cults and their
underlying ideas have an obvious and permanent fasci-
nation for him, and his poems are redolent of the sacred
words of the old religion, *numen, religio, sacer, pius,* and of
their spirit. Here we feel him as something more than an
antiquarian; if it is not possible to say that he believed in
the existence of all and every of these ancient deities, yet
it may fairly be claimed that the sense of higher powers
behind the outward occurrences of life, which is the
essential of an animistic religion, was to Virgil a vivid
reality.

A study in some detail of the attitude of Virgil to the old
religion will reveal not only the extent of his own interest in
it, but its own religious vitality. It is not always possible to
disentangle the old ideas and conceptions from their later
accretions—they were not always distinct in Virgil's mind

—but an attempt will be made here to collect descriptions and ideas in which earlier thought survives amid the developments of later and more sophisticated practice or belief. It will be remembered that Italian animism was rooted in the conception of spirits (*numina*) inhabiting special places; these are recognized in many of the deities of the countryside, the Fauns, the nymphs, Silvanus, and particularly in the more clearly defined deities of the household, Ianus, Vesta, the Penates, the Lar, and the Genius. In this early conception the sex of the spirit is often uncertain (*sive mas, sive femina; sive deus, sive dea*) and the spirits are often known by a collective plural designation. But the Italians had also reached the more advanced conception of spirits whose activity was not limited to any particular spot, but showed itself in some special function, wherever it might be exercised. This idea is seen in its natural development in the series of spirits which watched over the operations of the agricultural year and whose worship was embodied in the ancient festivals of the calendar. The cult of these spirits was embodied in simple operations of offering, prayer, and purification, and the attitude of the worshipper expressed in such words as *religio*, the feeling of awe, and *pietas*, the spirit of devotion. We may trace Virgil's relation to the deities, to worship, and to the underlying words and ideas.

A. *Deities of the Household and Country-side*

Of the spirits of the door and the hearth in the household, Ianus and Vesta, Virgil makes comparatively little mention; he is more interested in them as State-gods, worshipped as their protectors by the Roman people as a whole. But there are times when he recurs to their simple worship in the household. It is, for instance, the Ianus *bifrons* [1] of the household whose image stands with that of 'old Saturn' in the hall of Latinus' palace, and probably by him,[2] rather than the deity of the State, that Latinus takes the treaty-oath, though we may note there the typically Virgilian mingling of nature-cult, Graeco-Roman deities, and the old animistic god. Clearer is his recollection of the household Vesta. When, after the departure of the vision of Anchises in the fifth *Aeneid*,[3] Aeneas performs his act of worship, 'rousing the ashes and the slumbering flames', he venerates 'with the pious gift of corn and the full censer the Lar of Pergamus and the shrine of hoary Vesta'; it is the simple cult of the household which the poet has in his vision.

So, too, the Penates have their own peculiar place in the *Aeneid* as the State-gods whom Aeneas brought from Troy with a view to the establishment of a new city (a strange conception which must be examined later); yet from time to time the simpler thought of the Penates as house-deities seems to emerge. After his night in Evander's house, Aeneas rises early in the true spirit of a Latin paterfamilias, 'approaches the Lar he worshipped yesterday and the little Penates';[4] the picture is the family hearth, on which last night's fire is roused to flame and the household gods worshipped collectively. In view of the conception of the Trojan Penates brought to Italy, it is interesting to notice that Virgil seems to regard the worship of the Penates as natural and universal in all lands. Thus in Troy itself in the centre of Priam's palace beneath the open air was 'a

---

[1] A. vii. 180 Saturnusque senex Ianique bifrontis imago
vestibulo astabant.
[2] A. xii. 197 haec eadem, Aenea, terram, mare, sidera iuro,
Latonaeque genus duplex, Ianumque bifrontem.
[3] A. v. 743 haec memorans cinerem et sopitos suscitat ignis,
Pergameumque Larem et canae penetralia Vestae
farre pio et plena supplex veneratur acerra.
[4] A. viii. 543 hesternumque larem parvosque Penatis
laetus adit.

vast altar and hard by an ancient laurel, bending over the altar and with its shade embracing the Penates'.[1] Dido in her new palace in Carthage has 'fifty handmaids whose care it was in long array to set in order the store and with flames to worship the Penates';[2] we may notice here the scrupulous connexion of the Penates with the store (*penus*), which is their true sphere of activity. So again in an interesting passage in the fifth book, when Aeneas is making preparations for the establishment of the annual worship of his father Anchises as a hero, he bids his comrades 'bring to the feast both the Penates of your fathers and those whom our host Acestes worships'.[3] So, too, when Sychaeus, Dido's first husband, was murdered by his brother, 'the Penates were besmirched with a brother's blood',[4] and Diomedes in enumerating the misfortunes of the Greeks refers to 'the overthrow of the Penates' of Idomeneus.[5] The assumption in all these places is that the Penates must be worshipped in every home in every land. Finally we may notice here that there are passages where the Penates have lost their personality and the word is used in the conventional sense, commoner in the other Augustan poets than in Virgil, of 'home'. Evander begs Aeneas to enter his 'Penates',[6] the Tiber-god assures Aeneas that here on Italian soil is 'his destined home and destined Penates',[7] and in the fourth book of the *Georgics* Virgil tells us that the bees alone among animals 'know a

[1] A. ii. 512 aedibus in mediis nudoque sub aetheris axe
　　　　　ingens ara fuit iuxtaque veterrima laurus,
　　　　　incumbens arae atque umbra complexa Penatis.

[2] A. i. 703 quinquaginta intus famulae, quibus ordine longo
　　　　　cura penum struere et flammis adolere Penatis.

[3] A. v. 62　　　　　　　　　　　adhibete Penatis
　　　　　et patrios epulis et quos colit hospes Acestes.

[4] A. iv. 21　　　　　sparsos fraterna caede Penatis.

[5] A. xi. 264 versosque Penatis Idomenei.

[6] A. viii. 123　　　　nostris succede penatibus hospes.

[7] A. viii. 39 hic tibi certa domus, certi (ne absiste) Penates.

fatherland and fixed Penates'.[1] This phenomenon of the 'faded personality' will meet us frequently in the case of other deities.

The Lar occurs curiously rarely, and it is remarkable that Virgil in accordance with the regular usage of Rome, until on the analogy of the Lares Praestites of the State two Lares were thought of in the household also, never uses the plural. His combination with the Penates in Aeneas' morning worship at Evander's home,[2] and with Vesta in his prayers after the vision of Anchises,[3] have already been noticed; in both these cases the combination represents the sum total of the household gods. Ascanius in his oath to Nisus[4] combines all three, for he swears 'by the great Penates and the Lar of Assaracus and the shrine of hoary Vesta'. All these instances are in the true spirit of the household cult, though a little contaminated by the idea of the importation of the Trojan household gods by Aeneas. The Lar, too, like the Penates, is twice used in the *Georgics* in the 'faded' sense of 'home'. The wandering African herdsman is said to carry with him 'his house and his Lar',[5] and it is reported that bees have been known to 'dig out a hiding-place and keep their Lar beneath the soil'.[6]

The Genius is only mentioned twice and then not as a household god, the spirit of the *paterfamilias*, but as the *genius loci*, the protecting spirit of a place, a derived notion fully in accord with Roman practice. Aeneas, seeing the serpent issue from his father's tomb, doubts 'whether it is

[1] G. iv. 155 et patriam solae et certos novere Penatis.
[2] A. viii. 543; see p. 31, n. 4.   [3] A. v. 743; see p. 31, n. 3.
[4] A. ix. 258   per magnos, Nise, Penatis,
        Assaracique larem et canae penetralia Vestae.
[5] G. iii. 343   omnia secum
        armentarius Afer agit, tectumque laremque.
[6] G. iv. 42 saepe etiam effossis, si vera est fama, latebris
        sub terra fovere larem.

the genius of the spot, or his father's attendant spirit'; [1] the snake was the emblem both of the genius of the living and of the spirit of the dead. Similarly, on the first landing in Latium he prays to 'the genius of the spot and Earth, first of the gods, and the nymphs and the streams which as yet he knows not' [2]—a fine early Italian combination.

Virgil, then, in his treatment of the old household gods is perfectly true to the genuine Italian conceptions, but their character is somewhat obscured, as indeed it was in actual fact at Rome, by their larger development in the State-cult. On the other hand, his full enthusiasm goes out to the deities of the country-side, 'all the gods and goddesses, whose care is to protect the fields', [3] the *di agrestes*, [4] whom to know is to be happy, and in his treatment of them he comes nearest to the true spirit of Italian animism. Not only are the *Georgics* rich with their presence, as might be expected, but in the *Aeneid*, too, Virgil loves to recur to them, re-counting the deities and their cults with a fond care. He [5] seems to know and to recognize a stratum of religion before even the coming of Saturn, to which belong the spirits of fountain and river, the vague groups of Nymphs and Fauns, and the wilder spirit of the woods, Silvanus; they are put together in the opening address in the *Georgics*: [6] 'You, the countrymen's deities ever-present, ye Fauns, yea Fauns and Dryad maidens, come hither together.' There are passages even simpler and more

[1] A. v. 95 incertus geniumne loci famulumne parentis
    esse putet   See p. 293.
[2] A. vii. 136   Geniumque loci primamque deorum
        Tellurem Nymphasque et adhuc ignota precatur
        flumina.
[3] G. i. 21 dique deaeque omnes, studium quibus arva tueri.
[4] G. ii. 493 fortunatus et ille deos qui novit agrestis.
[5] See A. viii. 314 ff., a very interesting passage in which Virgil gives his ideas of Italian 'pre-history' and early religion.
[6] G. i. 10 et vos, agrestum praesentia numina, Fauni,
        ferte simul Faunique pedem Dryadesque puellae.

animistic than this. Aeneas in his oath before the single combat calls on many deities, but the list ends with 'the fountains and streams',[1] and on his first landing in Italy he prays to 'the rivers he as yet knows not'.[2] Among rivers the special sanctity of the Tiber is of course recognized. Aristaeus, received beneath the earth, sees the sources of all rivers, 'where father Tiber breaks forth and the stream of Anio'.[3] Aeneas, asleep on the river-bank, has a vision of 'old Tiber, god of the spot',[4] who foretells the settlement in Italy and the foundation of Alba, and on waking he makes sacrifice and addresses 'the nymphs of Laurentum, from whom the rivers take their being, and thou, O Tiber our father, with thy sacred stream'.[5]

More frequently, as in the opening verses of the *Georgics*, streams and fountains are personified as Nymphs and associated often with the Fauns, the female spirits of the streams with the male spirits of the fields. So in the famous exclamation in the second book of the *Georgics*: 'blessed too is he who knows the gods of the country-side, Pan (*sc.* Faunus) and old Silvanus and the sister nymphs.'[6] So, too, when Silenus in the sixth *Eclogue* begins his song 'you might have seen the Fauns and the wild things dancing in time'.[7]

---

[1] A. xii. 181 fontisque fluviosque voco.   [2] A. vii. 136; see p. 34, n. 2.

[3] G. iv. 368   unde altus primum se erumpit Enipeus,
　　　　　unde pater Tiberinus et unde Aniena fluenta.

[4] A. viii. 31 huic deus ipse loci fluvio Tiberinus amoeno
　　　　　populeas inter senior se attollere frondes
　　　　　visus.

[5] A. viii. 71 Nymphae, Laurentes nymphae, genus amnibus unde est,
　　　　　tuque, o Thybri tuo genitor cum flumine sancto
(imitated from a famous line of Ennius: tuque, pater Tiberine, tuo cum flumine sancto).

[6] G. ii. 493 fortunatus et ille deos qui novit agrestis,
　　　　　Panaque Silvanumque senem Nymphasque sorores.
It may be noted that in the *Culex* the plural *Panes* is twice used for Fauni (94, 115), though never in the certainly authenticated works of Virgil.

[7] E. vi. 27 tum vero in numerum Faunosque ferasque videres
　　　　　ludere.

In the *Aeneid* Evander opens his story of early Italy: 'these woods Fauns and Nymphs once inhabited, natives of the land.'[1]   Sometimes the Fauns and Nymphs are individualized, and, in a spirit more Greek than Italian, there are stories of their intermarriage and their children. Thus Latinus himself is 'the son of Faunus' (possibly rather, 'of a Faun') 'and the Laurentian Nymph Marica',[2] and Tarquitus who fights against the Trojans 'was born to a Faun of the woods by the nymph Dryope'.[3] The sea-nymphs whom Aristaeus finds beneath the sea,[4] those who accompany Aeneas' fleet on leaving Sicily,[5] and those into whom his ships are finally turned,[6] all have Greek names and are quite foreign to genuine Italian ideas. On the other hand, there are nymphs with Italian names, who had their true place in Italian belief. Iuturna, who by a kind of euhemerism, which must be noticed later, is for the most part the semi-divine sister of Turnus, is yet known by Virgil to be 'a goddess who presides over pools and sounding streams',[7] perhaps an older and wider view of the spirit who in historical times was associated with the *lacus Iuturnae* in the Forum. More important is Carmentis, who appears in the poem as the mother of Evander—a curious attempt of sophistication to link Greek legend with Italian religion. She, like many spring and stream spirits in the old religion, has the gift of prophecy: it was her warnings,[8] together with Apollo's prophecies, which drove Evander

---

[1] A. viii. 314 haec nemora indigenae Fauni Nymphaeque tenebant.
[2] A. vii. 47 hunc Fauno et Nympha genitum Laurente Marica
        accipimus.
[3] A. x. 551 silvicolae Fauno Dryope quem Nympha crearat.
[4] G. iv. 336 ff.   [5] A. v. 825 f.   [6] A. x. 219 ff.
[7] A. xii. 138 extemplo Turni sic est adfata sororem
            diva deam, stagnis quae fluminibusque sonoris
            praesidet.
[8] A. viii. 333 me . . . matrisque egere tremenda
            Carmentis Nymphae monita et deus auctor Apollo.

to seek a new home in Italy, and he proudly shows Aeneas the Carmental Gate, 'the ancient memorial to the nymph Carmentis, the prophetess of fate, who first sang the coming greatness of Aeneas' sons'.[1] The Fauns, too, as well as the nymphs, had the gift of prophecy, and Latinus in his first difficulties on the arrival of Aeneas 'approaches the oracle of Faunus, his prophetic father, and consults the groves beneath lofty Albunea, which greatest of all woods resounds with sacred springs and in its dark shade breathes the foul mephitis'.[2] The description of the grove is very characteristic of early animism.

With the Nymphs and the Fauns, the deities of streams and the open country, is closely associated Silvanus, the deity of the woods outside the settlements, who always remained a rather outlandish and slightly hostile personality in Roman thought.[3] To Virgil he is just one of the rustic deities and is coupled with them in the great passage in the second book of the *Georgics*.[4] In the exordium to the first book he is greeted as 'Silvanus, who bearest the tender cypress tree torn from its roots';[5] here he is a real woodland god. So, too, he is one of the mourners for Gallus in the tenth *Eclogue*: 'Silvanus came too, his head decked with rustic ornament, shaking the flowery fennel and the great lilies.'[6] His one independent appearance is in the descrip-

---

[1] A. viii. 339   Nymphae priscum Carmentis honorem,
       vatis fatidicae, cecinit quae prima futuros
       Aeneadas magnos.
[2] A. vii. 81   oracula Fauni,
       fatidici genitoris, adit lucosque sub alta
       consulit Albunea, nemorum quae maxima sacro
       fonte sonat saevamque exhalat opaca mephitim.
For further consideration of this passage see p. 26.
[3] Thus precautions were taken to keep off Silvanus from the new-born child (Aug. *de Civ. Dei*, vi. 9), see p. 41.   [4] G. ii. 493; see p. 35, n. 6.
[5] G. i. 20 et teneram ab radice ferens, Silvane, cupressum.
[6] E. x. 24 venit et agresti capitis Silvanus honore,
       florentis ferulas et grandia lilia quassans.

tion of his grove at Caere, near which the Tuscan host under Tarcho encamped: 'the story runs that the old Pelasgians dedicated to Silvanus, god of fields and flocks, a grove and a festal day, they who long ago were the first to dwell in the regions of Latium.'[1] It may be noticed here that Silvanus is just one of the gods of country life, but he seems to retain his old character in the grove dedicated to him; the attribution of the cult to the Pelasgians is an indication of belief in its very ancient origin.

Besides the deities of country-side and springs and woods, the truest survivors of the old animistic spirits of place, Virgil knew, of course, as well the functional spirits associated with the festivals of the farmer's year. But many of these had become so deeply overladen with the ideas connected with their Greek counterparts that they will best be treated later on. The two old corn-spirits, 'Liber and gracious Ceres',[2] are involved together at the outset of the *Georgics*, but Ceres had assumed much of the character of the Greek Demeter, and Liber had merged his own functions in that of the Greek Bacchus, so that he is appealed to here not as a corn-deity, but as the god of the vine. The vine is no longer in Virgil's day under the care of Iuppiter, as it was in the earliest times, nor even, as in the later Italian period, of Venus, but, as in many places of the second book of the *Georgics*, it is in the charge of Bacchus, or of Liber as his equivalent. So, too, the olive is in the care of Minerva, not as the Italian deity of handicraft, but as the representative of Pallas Athena. In both cases the supplanting is complete.

There are, however, one or two of the agricultural deities, whom Virgil mentions, who were not merged in

[1] A. viii. 600 Silvano fama est veteres sacrasse Pelasgos,
    arvorum pecorisque deo, lucumque diemque,
    qui primi finis aliquando habuere Latinos.

[2] G. i. 7 Liber et alma Ceres.

Greek equivalents, and of these a word may be said here.
In Aeneas' first prayer in Italy, combined with the genius
of the spot, the nymphs, and the rivers, is Tellus, 'Earth,
first of all the gods'.[1] The earth, that bears the crops, is one
of the oldest of Italian deities and has her place with Ceres
in the January festival of the Feriae Sementivae. In a
strange passage, when Aeneas and Dido are driven by a
thunderstorm into the cave, which was the scene of their
wedlock, 'Tellus first and Iuno, harbinger of marriage,
gave the sign'.[2] It might be thought that there was Greek
influence here, but Servius[3] tells us that Tellus presides
over marriage and is called on by the bride at the wedding
auspices; this being so, we have probably here, too, a
genuine Italian custom.

Pales, the ancient deity of the flocks and herds, whose
sex even was uncertain, was still worshipped, as we know
from Ovid, at the Parilia. To her Virgil appeals at the outset of the third book of the *Georgics*,[4] and later in the
book[5] when he starts to give detailed instructions for the
care of the flocks. In the *Culex*,[6] probably an early poem of
Virgil's, Pales appears twice as the principal agricultural
deity. Here, too, may be mentioned Priapus, who though a
Greek god in origin, had been thoroughly acclimatized in
Italy as the protector of gardens. To Virgil he seems to
have become little more than a venerable scarecrow, 'the

[1] A. vii. 136; see p. 34, n. 2.
[2] A. iv. 166   prima et Tellus et pronuba Iuno
                    dant signum.
[3] Servius ad loc.: quidam sane Tellurem praeesse nuptiis tradunt; nam
et in auspiciis nuptiarum vocatur.
[4] G. iii. 1 te quoque, magna Pales, et te memorande canemus
                    pastor ab Amphryso.
[5] G. iii. 294 nunc, veneranda Pales, magno nunc ore sonandum.
[6] Culex, 20 et tu, sancta Pales, ad quam ventura recurrit
                    agrestum bona sors, cui rura serena, tenesque
                    aerios nemorum saltus silvasque virentis.
Ibid. 77 et nemus et fecunda Pales.

guardian of the poor man's garden',[1] 'the sentinel against thieves and birds';[2] it is notable that he is told to be content with 'a bowl of milk and cakes', the simplest form of rustic offering before wine and incense became known in Italy.

This old Italy, the farmers' Italy, with its indigenous gods and its simple modes of worship is to Virgil more than all else 'the land of Saturn',[3] 'Saturn's fields'.[4] Saturnus was in fact one of the oldest of Italian deities, and probably, in spite of philological difficulties and rival modern theories, the spirit who watched over the winter sowing. The only trace of this original character in Virgil occurs in the second book of the *Georgics*, where the pruning-knife of the vine cultivator is described as 'the curved tooth of Saturn'.[5] His development is twofold; with his identification with the Greek Kronos and its consequences it will be more appropriate to deal later (see p. 104), but here may be noticed a curious phenomenon, prominent in Virgil's treatment of several of these old Italian gods, which by a kind of euhemerism transforms them into legendary kings. Saturn thus brought laws and civilization to Latium and established his golden reign, 'the reign of Saturn', as it is called in a famous line of the *Eclogues*.[6] He is in fact an historical figure; it was he who established the citadel on the Capitol, as Ianus founded the Ianiculum;[7] his statue, again

[1] E. vii. 33 sinum lactis et haec te liba, Priape, quotannis
　　　　　exspectare sat est; custos es pauperis horti.
[2] G. iv. 110　　custos furum atque avium cum falce saligna
　　　　　Hellespontiaci servet tutela Priapi.
[3] G. ii. 173 salve, magna parens frugum, Saturnia tellus,
　　　　　magna virum.
[4] A. i. 569 seu vos Hesperiam magnam Saturniaque arva,
　　　　　sive Erycis finis regemque optatis Acesten.
[5] G. ii. 406　　　　curvo Saturni dente relictam
　　　　　persequitur vitem.
[6] E. iv. 6 iam redit et Virgo, redeunt Saturnia regna.
[7] A. viii. 357 hanc Ianus pater, hanc Saturnus condidit arcem;
　　　　　Ianiculum huic, illi fuerat Saturnia nomen.

in association with Ianus, stands in Latinus' hall among his ancestors.[1] This is all the result of Greek rationalism, but behind it lies the shadowy figure of the old Italian deity. A similar euhemerism has transformed two other Italian deities into divine kings, Picus, the grandfather of Latinus, and Pilumnus, the ancestor of the Rutulian Turnus. Now Picus,[2] whether or no he was an Italian woodpecker deity, was certainly one of the old rustic *numina*, but to Virgil he has become definitely and solely the divine king. We have the whole genealogy in the seventh *Aeneid*: Latinus is the son of Faunus and the nymph Marica, 'Picus was the father of Faunus, and he counts thee, Saturn, as his sire; thou art the first founder of the stock'.[3] Thus Picus, too, has his place among the ancestors in Latinus' hall and he is described in the full garb of an augur, 'with the rod of Quirinus, girt in a short cloak (*trabea*), bearing on his left arm the sacred shield, Picus, tamer of horses'.[4] Virgil adds the story of his transformation into a bird by Circe, an assimilation to the Δρυκολάπτης legend of Crete. Pilumnus in the old religion was a more specialized spirit, one of those summoned at the birth of a child to expel evil influences—or, as later ideas defined it, to avert Silvanus. But he, too, in Virgil assumes the character of a divine king, the ancestor of Turnus, to whom Orithyia had given a team of chariot-horses, 'who excelled the snow in whiteness and the winds in speed'.[5] As to his precise relation to

[1] A. vii. 180 Saturnusque senex, Ianique bifrontis imago
           vestibulo astabant.
[2] See W. R. Halliday, *Class. Rev.* xxxvi. 110.
[3] A. vii. 48   Fauno Picus pater, isque parentem
      te, Saturne, refert, tu sanguinis ultimus auctor.
[4] A. vii. 187 ipse Quirinali lituo parvaque sedebat
        succinctus trabea, laevaque ancile gerebat,
        Picus, equum domitor.
[5] A. xii. 82 poscit equos . . .
      Pilumno quos ipsa decus dedit Orithyia,
      qui candore nives anteirent, cursibus auras.

Turnus Virgil seems uncertain. Once Turnus is represented as 'sitting in a holy valley in the grove of Pilumnus,
his parent'[1]—possibly a vague general term; in another
passage[2] Pilumnus is said to be grandfather to Turnus, and
in yet another[3] he is his great-grandfather. Turnus' genea-
logical tree does not seem so clearly worked out as that of
Latinus, but there is no doubt that Pilumnus is a venerated
ancestor and has the same character of divine king as Picus.
Similar in character we must imagine Venilia,[4] the mother
of Turnus, who is described by Servius as a nymph; there
is perhaps something in his suggestion that Virgil chose
Venilia as a counterpart of Aeneas' mother, Venus.

If this euhemerizing tendency was prompted by the
desire to provide the inhabitants of Italy with a divine
ancestry which could match that of the Trojans, it may
fairly be said that Virgil not only knows the old ideas and
associations of these old 'spirit-gods' of primitive Italy, but
has for them a genuine and affectionate regard. Some
instinct seemed to lead him back to the spirit of the animistic religion and to dwell on it with a peculiar love,
which he did not feel so strongly for the more clear-cut
anthropomorphic figures of the State-cult and the Graeco-
Roman pantheon.

B. *Worship*

Almost more than the old deities do the rites and ceremonies of the old religion claim Virgil's interest and devotion. In a poem so filled with the spirit of religion as the
Aeneid, it is not surprising that there should be many
descriptions of religious rites, but it is noticeable that the
vast majority of such descriptions are of old Italian modes
of worship rather than of the more elaborate ceremonies

---

[1] A. ix. 3   luco tum forte parentis
     Pilumni Turnus sacrata valle sedebat.
[2] A. x. 76 cui Pilumnus avus, cui diva Venilia mater.
[3] A. x. 619 Pilumnusque illi quartus pater.   [4] A. x. 76; see n. 2.

of the State-cult. It is usually the simple ceremonies of the household and the fields which he loves to depict, though, as will be seen, his accounts are not free from the contamination of Greek ideas.

Some mention has already been made (pp. 30–33) of the part played in the *Aeneid* by the worship of the household gods, the Penates, Vesta, and the Lar. Here Virgil is scrupulously accurate in his description of the rites and offerings. Two further points may be noticed, firstly the repeated mention of the morning sacrifice to the household gods by the rekindling of yesterday's ashes,[1] which was the first daily duty of the pious Roman, and secondly the making of the offerings by Anchises or Aeneas as *paterfamilias* without any intervention of a priest. This was always the household tradition and the priest is unknown till the development of the State-cult.

We may now consider in some detail Virgil's treatment of the various cult-acts inherent in the old religion. Of the rites of the most common act of worship, the *sacrificium*, there are many accounts, and in them the various stages of the proceedings are carefully recounted. There are to begin with accurate descriptions of the preparation and adornment of the victim; in the *Georgics* Virgil tells us how in the time of the great pestilence the victim would often die in the hands of the ministrants 'as it stood as an offering at the altar amid the worship of the gods, while the woollen fillet with its snowy ribbon was being bound about its head'.[2] So the treacherous Sinon narrates that 'the

---

[1] A. v. 743   cinerem et sopitos suscitat ignis,
        Pergameumque Larem et canae penetralia Vestae
        farre pio et plena supplex veneratur acerra.
Cf. A. viii. 543; see p. 31, n. 4.
[2] G. iii. 486 saepe in honore deum medio stans hostia ad aram,
        lanea dum nivea circumdatur infula vitta,
        inter cunctantis cecidit moribunda ministros.

sacred rites were prepared for me; the salted corn (the *mola salsa*) and the fillet around my temples',[1] and he refers later to 'the fillets of the gods, which I bore as a victim'.[2] Elsewhere the gilded forehead of the victim is referred to, a feature due probably to Homeric precedent.[3]

The slaughter of the victim is many times described[4] and the sacredness of its blood is more than once referred to (see p. 74, n. 13). A particularly interesting description of a sacrifice occurs in the account of Latinus' visit to the grove of Faunus to obtain his oracular advice as to the marriage of Lavinia: 'he sacrificed duly a hundred fleecy sheep and lay resting on their skins and strewed fleeces.'[5] Here, though the offering of sheep is appropriate to the old Italian Faunus, the large number sacrificed is more Greek than Italian (a 'hecatomb'), and the lying on the fleeces for 'incubation' comes from the practices in Greek temples.

The choice of the right victim to be offered to a particular deity—always an important matter in Italian ritual—is often insisted on by Virgil. The bull is offered to the Di Superi, to Iuppiter,[6] and to Neptune;[7] black animals[8] are offered to the gods of the lower world by Aristaeus at the

---

[1] A. ii. 132   mihi sacra parari
      et salsae fruges et circum tempora vittae.
[2] A. ii. 156   vittaeque deum, quas hostia gessi.
[3] A. ix. 627 et statuam ante aras aurata fronte iuvencum | candentem.
Cf. Hom. *Od.* iii. 425.
[4] e.g. A. vi. 38 nunc grege de intacto septem mactare iuvencos
            praestiterit, totidem lectas de more bidentis.
[5] A. vii. 93 centum lanigeras mactabat rite bidentis,
            atque harum effultus tergo stratisque iacebat
            velleribus.   See p. 26.
[6] A. iii. 20   superoque nitentem
        caelicolum regi mactabam in litore taurum.
[7] A. ii. 201 Laocoon, ductus Neptuno sorte sacerdos,
            sollemnis taurum ingentem mactabat ad aras.
[8] G. iv. 545 inferias Orphei Lethaea papavera mittes
            et nigram mactabis ovem.

bidding of Cyrene and by the Sibyl on behalf of Aeneas.[1] The ritual in the latter case is strange; the Sibyl pours wine on to the victims' foreheads and plucking the topmost hairs from between the sheeps' horns she throws them on to the flames 'as a first offering'; here again is Greek influence, this time directly from Homer.[2] A very interesting sacrifice is made by Anchises on Delos,[3] a bull to Neptune, a bull to Apollo, a black sheep to Hiems, a white sheep to the Zephyrs. Apollo is lord of Delos, and the other deities are concerned with the Trojans' voyage, but the difference in the colour of the victims is strange, as Hiems, an unusual personification, is not chthonic. The explanation probably is, as is hinted in Servius' note, that the black offering is made to the power you wish to discourage, the white to the deity for whose help you look; this may indeed be the underlying thought in the offering of black victims to the chthonic deities. With similar care Virgil refers to the pig, which was always the proper offering at the making of a treaty.[4]

The simpler bloodless offerings are also often mentioned in Virgil, the *mola salsa*[5] made of spelt (*far*), incense,[6]

[1] A. vi. 153 duc nigras pecudes.
A. vi. 243 quattuor hic primum nigrantis terga iuvencos
constituit.
[2] Hom. *Od.* iii. 445.
[3] A. iii. 118 sic fatus meritos aris mactavit honores,
taurum Neptuno, taurum tibi, pulcher Apollo,
nigram Hiemi pecudem, Zephyris felicibus albam.
See Servius on 120: bono usus est ordine ut prius averteret mala, sic conciliaret optanda.
[4] A. viii. 641 caesa iungebant foedera porca; A. xii. 170 saetigeri fetum suis.
[5] A. ii. 133 salsae fruges; A. xii. 173 dant fruges manibus salsas; E. viii. 82 sparge molam; A. iv. 517 ipsa mola manibusque piis altaria iuxta; A. v. 745 farre pio et plena supplex veneratur acerra.
[6] A. i. 416   centumque Sabaeo
ture calent arae sertisque recentibus halant.
A. xi. 481 succedunt matres et templum ture vaporant; E. viii. 65 verbenasque adole pinguis et mascula tura.

wine,[1] and the primitive offering of milk.[2] The use of flowers for the decoration of the altar is also frequently referred to.[3]

Not only in the offering, but also in the prayer which accompanies it, Virgil follows tradition, though not so closely. He makes little attempt to represent the stereotyped formulae in which prayers were set, but in his invocations, sometimes to deities carefully chosen as appropriate for the purpose in hand, sometimes in the inclusive spirit of the old religion, to all deities who might be concerned, he is acting in full accordance with established usage. As an example of the former might be cited Aeneas' prayer[4] when he finds the bloody roots on the tomb of Polydorus, addressed to the Nymphs of the country-side, who would be concerned in the growing of the trees and the bushes, and to Mars, as the deity of the Getic country on which he had landed. A more inclusive invocation[5] is made by Aeneas in swearing his oath before the single combat with Turnus, which is interesting because it represents several strata of religious ideas, first the appeal to Sol and Terra, the cosmological worship of the philosophic thought of his day, then to Iuppiter, Iuno and Mars, the gods of the State-religion, then to the old spirits of stream and river and sky and sea. A peculiarly interesting account is given of the Roman custom of veiling the head in prayer 'lest amid the holy flames and at the offering to the gods any

[1] A. v. 98 vinaque fundebat pateris; A. v. 238 vina liquentia fundam; A. v. 776 vina liquentia fundit; G. i. 344 cui tu lacte favos et miti dilue Baccho.

[2] e.g. G. i. 344 (see n. 1); E. vii. 33 sinum lactis.

[3] G. iv. 276 saepe deum nexis ornatae torquibus arae. Cf. A. i. 417; see p. 45, n. 6.

[4] A. iii. 34   Nymphas venerabar agrestis
    Gradivumque patrem, Geticis qui praesidet arvis.

[5] A. xii. 176 esto nunc Sol testis et haec mihi Terra vocanti . . .
    et Pater omnipotens et tu Saturnia coniunx,
    iam melior, iam diva, precor; tuque inclute Mavors . . .
    fontesque fluviosque voco, quaeque aetheris alti
    religio et quae caeruleo sunt numina ponto.

hostile form should be seen and pollute the omens',[1] an account which cannot be far from the meaning of a custom, which Virgil mentions once again in the same book. In a similar spirit of conformity with old custom Helenus 'prays for the peace of the gods',[2] the *pax divum*, which it was the object of all Roman prayer-ritual to maintain, or to restore, if it were broken.

Other religious ceremonies besides the normal ritual of sacrifice and prayer find their place in Virgil. Thus the ceremony of lustration is performed at the end of the rites at the burying of Misenus: 'three times he bore the pure water round his companions, sprinkling them with light dew from the bough of a fruitful olive and purified the men and spake the last words.'[3] On the arrival at Actium an interesting compound ceremony is performed: 'we are purified before Iuppiter and kindle the altars with our vows and celebrate the Actian shores with our Ilian games.'[4] The same juxtaposition of lustration and vow is found in the *Eclogues*: 'these honours shall be ever thine, both when we pay our annual vows to the Nymphs and when we purify the fields';[5] the reference here is clearly to the *lustratio agri*, described by Cato, which is the counterpart on the individual farm of the rustic festival of the *Ambarvalia*.

The word *votum* is of frequent occurrence in Virgil, and in

[1] A. iii. 405 purpureo velare comas adopertus amictu,
ne qua inter sanctos ignis in honore deorum
hostilis facies occurrat et omina turbet.
Cf. A. iii. 545 et capita ante aras Phrygio velamur amictu.
[2] A. iii. 369 hic Helenus caesis primum de more iuvencis
exorat pacem divum.
[3] A. vi. 229 idem ter socios pura circumtulit unda,
spargens rore levi et ramo felicis olivae,
lustravitque viros dixitque novissima verba.
[4] A. iii. 279 lustramurque Iovi votisque incendimus aras,
Actiaque Iliacis celebramus litora ludis.
[5] E. v. 74 haec tibi semper erunt, et cum sollemnia vota
reddemus Nymphis, et cum lustrabimus agros.

many places it is clear that it has its full force, the 'vow' or 'promise' made by a man to a deity that, if the god will do certain things for him, he will make such and such an offering in return. Thus Cloanthus in the boat-race promises the gods of the sea that, if he is victorious in the race, 'I will sacrifice a white bull on the shore, a debtor to my vow, and will cast the entrails into the waves and pour the liquid wine.'[1] This vow is in due form and contains the technical expression *voti reus*; the word *laetus*, too, is a poetical variation on *libens*, which occurs so often in votive inscriptions and which Virgil uses himself elsewhere.[2] So, too, in the stress of battle Ascanius 'prays to Iuppiter with a vow'[3] and promises to bring annual gifts to his temple and set a white steer with gilded forehead before his altars. In many places we find the regular terms connected with the vow carefully employed by Virgil. Aeneas, gazing on the dead Pallas, wonders whether his father is even now 'making vows' for his return (*vota facit*).[4] The man under the obligation of the vow is, as has been seen, *voti reus*, and the god 'condemns him to his vows'.[5] The fulfilment or payment of the vow (*votum solvere*) is similarly recorded: Helenus tells Aeneas that when his ships have touched Italian soil he must 'build altars and pay his vows on the shore' with veiled head;[6] Aeneas, when morning breaks

[1] A. v. 235 di, quibus imperium est pelagi, quorum aequora curro,
　　　　　　vobis laetus ego hoc candentem in litore taurum
　　　　　　constituam ante aras, voti reus, extaque salsos
　　　　　　proiciam in fluctus et vina liquentia fundam.
[2] A. iii. 438 Iunoni cane vota libens.
[3] A. ix. 624　　　ante Iovem supplex per vota precatus: . . .
　　　　　　ipse tibi ad tua templa feram sollemnia dona,
　　　　　　et statuam ante aras aurata fronte iuvencum
　　　　　　candentem.
[4] A. xi. 49 et nunc ille quidem spe multum captus inani
　　　　　　fors et vota facit.
[5] E. v. 80　　　damnabis tu quoque votis.
[6] A. iii. 403 quin ubi transmissae steterint trans aequora classes,
　　　　　　et positis aris iam vota in litore solves.

after the battle, 'paid his vows for victory to the gods';[1] and in the *Georgics* the sailors saved from the perils of the sea will 'pay their vows' to the sea-deities.[2] The verb is sometimes varied: Aeneas swears that wherever he might be, by land or sea, he would 'carry out' (*exsequerer*) 'his annual vow' in his father's honour;[3] Augustus on the shield of Aeneas is represented as 'consecrating three hundred shrines throughout the whole city,[4] his immortal vow to the gods of Italy.' In the latter case *votum* comes near to the concrete meaning of the votive-offering, which it has in the second book of the *Aeneid*, where the Greeks pretend that the Trojan horse is a 'votive-offering for their return'.[5]

A common phrase in Virgil is 'to summon the gods to (or 'with') the vow'. In the strict sense this should mean to summon them to hear a vow, that is, to make the promise to them. So it seems to be used in two passages referring to the future deification of Augustus: in the *Georgics* he is urged even now to 'grow used to being summoned with vows',[6] and in the opening of the *Aeneid* there is the similar prophecy that 'he too shall be summoned with vows'.[7] If these be taken in conjunction with the passage in the *Eclogues* where it is said that Augustus, too, 'will hold men to their vows', there is little doubt that *votum* is used in its full sense. But in this phrase, as in many others, there is often a looser use of *vota*,

[1] A. xi. 4 vota deum primo victor solvebat Eoo.
[2] G. i. 436 votaque servati solvent in litore nautae
        Glauco et Panopeae et Inoo Melicertae.
[3] A. v. 53 annua vota tamen sollemnisque ordine pompas
        exsequerer.
[4] A. viii. 714 at Caesar . . . dis Italis votum immortale sacrabat
        maxima ter centum totam delubra per urbem.
[5] A. ii. 17 votum pro reditu simulant.
[6] G. i. 42 votis iam nunc adsuesce vocari.
[7] A. i. 290 vocabitur hic quoque votis. See E. v. 80, quoted on p. 48, n. 5.

where it means little more than 'prayer'. Of Turnus, after a prayer to Faunus, it is said that he 'summoned the god's help to no idle prayer':[1] there is no suggestion of a vow in the context and *vota* cannot well mean more than prayer; so the maddened Amata 'called the gods to hear her prayer',[2] and the farmer in the *Georgics* is instructed to 'call the rain in his prayers'.[3] In an interesting passage in the fifth *Aeneid*, Eurytion, about to shoot in the contest 'summons his brother (Pandarus, the great archer) to his prayers';[4] this is probably not to be regarded as an instance of prayer to the dead, rather he is praying for his brother's skill, as the farmer prays for the rain.

This looser sense of *votum* was a later but quite common usage and it is of frequent occurrence in Virgil. Thus *vota* is frequently combined with *preces* as little more than a synonym and with no suggestion of a formal vow;[5] it is found again with the verb *optare*, the regular verb of prayer, or with the less formal *petere*.[6] In many other contexts, though not combined with such significant words, its vague and general meaning is clear.[7] Virgil, then, though not disdaining this commoner and more general use, gives

---

[1] A. xii. 780 dixit, opemque dei non cassa in vota vocavit.
[2] A. vii. 471 divosque in vota vocavit.
[3] G. i. 157 votisque vocaveris imbrem.
[4] A. v. 514 fratrem Eurytion in vota vocavit.
[5] A. vi. 51 cessas in vota precesque? A. iii. 261 sed votis precibusque iubent exposcere pacem; A. xi. 157 nulli exaudita deorum | vota precesque meae.
[6] A. iv. 158 spumantemque dari pecora inter inertia votis
              optat aprum.
A. x. 279 quod votis optastis, adest; A. xii. 259 hoc erat, hoc, votis, inquit, quod saepe petivi.
[7] A. iii. 548 perfectis ordine votis. A. iv. 65 quid vota furentem, quid delubra iuvant? A. vii. 597 votisque deos venerabere seris. A. viii. 60 Iunoni fer rite preces, iramque minasque| supplicibus supera votis. ibid. 556 vota metu duplicant matres; A. ix. 24 oneravitque aethera votis; ibid. 310 prosequitur votis. G. i. 47 votis respondet avari agricolae.

abundant evidence of his knowledge of the formal *votum* and of the place it plays in religious life.

The use of the words *daps* and *epulae* in Virgil is of peculiar interest and shows again his careful tenacity of religious tradition. *Daps* was originally a simple offering made by the farmer, particularly to Iuppiter, and is described fully by Cato (*De agr. cult.* 132); the idea is quite primitive and seems to be just that of providing a meal for the unseen spirit. It is, therefore, comparable to the practice in the household of offering a part of the household meal to the deities of the home by throwing it into the fire on the hearth. When Greek influence began to work it seems to have operated in two ways. In the first place the simple offering was elaborated on anthropomorphic lines into a sacred meal offered to the gods, whose presence was indicated by images set at the board. This was first done at the *epulum Iovis*, celebrated on September 13, the day of the foundation of the Capitoline temple; the three deities of the Etruscan triad were represented by *imagines* at the feast. Whether, as Warde Fowler has suggested (*R.F.*, p. 218), this custom was actually introduced by the Etruscans or whether it represents an Etruscanization of an earlier and simpler Roman custom, this is the only form in which it is known in historical times. A still further development under direct Greek influence came in the introduction about the time of the Punic wars of the *lectisternium*, at which the deities were represented by images on couches (*pulvinaria*) partaking of the meal offered them; this rite might be ordered at any time of religious emergency.

Secondly, the Greek idea of a sacrifice, at which the parts of the victim assigned to the gods were burnt on the altar, while the worshippers partook of the rest of the flesh, affected Roman custom. Such a sacred meal came to be known as *dapes* or sometimes *epulae*. The latter, as Servius points out,[1] is in origin a secular word for a banquet, but it, too, acquired in certain contexts a religious sense equivalent to *dapes*.

A parallel development took place in regard to the dead. It was an old Roman custom on the anniversary of a death or during the State festival of the Parentalia to place food at the grave: this custom would seem, at any rate by Virgil's day, to have become associated with the Greek hero-worship at the tomb, and *dapes* is used of an offering to the dead.

This explanation is needed to follow Virgil's use of the words, for he seems to know them all. A clear instance of the old idea is found in the use of *epulae* in the fifth book,[2] where Aeneas orders that the Penates of the Trojans and those of his Sicilian host Acestes should be invited to the meal; this is but an elaboration of the *daps* of the household gods. Similarly, the palace of Latinus is described as the 'seat of the sacred banquets',[3] the offerings of the king's household, and again, on the arrival at the home of Helenus,[4] libations of wine are poured and *dapes* placed on a golden table or altar. But for the most part Virgil seems to have in mind the more Greek idea of the combination of sacrifice with the human meal. Evander, for instance, describes the sacrifice to Hercules at the Ara Maxima as '*has ex more dapes*',[5] a word quite consonant with the old idea, but it is clear from the context (179–83) that there is a human feast as well, and Dido's serving-men have the

[1] *ad Aen.* iii. 224 dapes deorum sunt, epulae hominum.
[2] A. v. 62   adhibete Penatis
      et patrios epulis et quos colit hospes Acestes.
[3] A. vii. 175 hae sacris sedes epulis.
[4] A. iii. 354 aulai medio libabant pocula Bacchi
      impositis auro dapibus paterasque tenebant.
[5] A. viii. 185   non haec sollemnia nobis,
      has ex more dapes . . . vana superstitio . . . imposuit.

task of 'loading the tables with the sacred meal and placing the cups',[1] before which the Tyrians are at once told to take their place. In two passages this double capacity of the feast, at once divine and human, seems to be emphasized by the combination of the words *dapes* and *epulae* (or the verb). Before the intervention of the Harpies, Aeneas and his men on the shore place their couches and 'feast upon the rich sacred meal';[2] in another place Aeneas and his men 'start the meal and place cakes of bread beneath the sacred meat'.[3] The idea of the *lectisternium* seems clear when Aeolus, telling Iuno that he owes her his divine privileges, says, ''tis thou who dost grant me to take my place at the feasts of the gods'.[4]

Finally, there are places where *dapes* seems to be used of an offering at a hero's grave: Andromache, when Aeneas found her, was offering *dapes* at Hector's tomb;[5] the serpent devoured the *dapes* which Aeneas had placed at his father's tomb in Sicily;[6] and *dapes* are among the offerings made at the burial of Misenus.[7]

Some of the individual features of worship which have been noticed may perhaps be better appreciated in combination, if we look at some of the longer and more detailed descriptions of festivals which Virgil has given us. In the first

[1] A. i. 705 centum aliae totidemque pares aetate ministri,
             qui dapibus mensas onerent et pocula ponant.
[2] A. iii. 223   litore curvo
             exstruimusque toros dapibusque epulamur opimis.
[3] A. vii. 109 instituuntque dapes et adorea liba per herbam
             subiciunt epulis.
[4] A. i. 79 tu das epulis accumbere divum.
[5] A. iii. 301 sollemnis cum forte dapes et tristia dona . . . libabat . . .
             Hectoreum ad tumulum.
[6] A. v. 90   ille agmine longo
             tandem inter pateras et levia pocula serpens
             libavitque dapes.
[7] A. vi. 224   congesta cremantur
             turea dona, dapes, fuso crateres olivo.

book of the *Georgics* he describes a festival of Ceres.[1] It is to be celebrated 'at the fall of the end of winter, when spring is already bright', and the new corn is already sprouting. Its date then would seem to correspond with the Cerealia, the State festival of April 19, but its details are much more like that of the rustic festival of the Feriae Sementivae celebrated in January to Ceres and Tellus. As it also contains a feature drawn from the *agri lustratio* or *ambarvalia*, we may perhaps say that Virgil was more concerned to describe a rustic spring festival than any particular act of worship. He bids all the country-folk join in worshipping Ceres, their offering is to be the rustic gift of honeycombs soaked in milk or wine: meanwhile the blood-victim is to be led thrice round the new crops (this is a feature borrowed from the Ambarvalia), followed by all the crowd, summoning Ceres to their houses. None must lay a sickle to the corn till he has bound his head with the sacred oak, joined in the rude dance, and sung the *Carmina* (presumably the prayer-formula rather than hymns or secular songs).

More suggestive perhaps of the ordered worship of the State-cult is Dido's offering in view of her prospective marriage, but it contains so many features of the *sacrificium* that it is worth quoting in full:[2]

'First they approach the shrines and seek peace (the *pax divum*) from altar to altar; they slay sheep chosen in due manner to Ceres the lawgiver (an assimilation to Demeter θεσμοφόρος), and to Phoebus and to father Lyaeus, above all to Iuno, who has the care of the bonds of marriage. Dido herself in all her beauty holding the sacred platter (*patera*) in her right hand, pours it out between the horns of a white cow, or in the presence of the gods

---

[1] G. i. 338–50: note 340 extremae sub casum hiemis, iam vere sereno; 344 cui tu lacte favos et miti dilue Baccho; 345 terque novas circum felix eat hostia fruges.

[2] A. iv. 56–64.

moves before the rich-laden altars, and opens the new day with gifts, and setting bare the hearts of the victims gazes consulting the still breathing entrails.'

It is really a Roman sacrifice with the wholly Greek conclusion of the extispice.

The most elaborate description of worship in the *Aeneid* is that of the offering to Hercules at the Ara Maxima,[1] on which Evander was engaged when Aeneas landed from the river; here Virgil's archaeological accuracy plays a larger part than usual, and he seems to revel not only in the detailed account of the ceremony, but in Evander's explanation of it. Hercules was not, of course, one of the *di indigetes* of the old Latin cult, but one of the earliest of the *di novensides* to be brought to Rome from Tibur and allowed a place inside the *pomoerium* at the 'Great altar' in the Forum Boarium. His cult,[2] as Virgil reminds us, was in the hands of the two families of the Potitii and the Pinarii, whether they were originally immigrants from Tibur or, as is perhaps more likely, Roman patrons of the people of Tibur. The worship at the Ara Maxima preserved its originally Greek character in that the participants did not veil their head but prayed *aperto capite*, but in other respects it followed the general lines of a *sacrificium*. Virgil's account is much interrupted by talk and speeches, but it is possible to put together a fairly consecutive narrative and it has many points of interest. When Aeneas arrived the initial sacrifice was being performed; Evander with Pallas and his young companions and 'the needy senate were offering incense and the warm blood was still smoking on the

---

[1] A. viii. 102–6, 175–83, 280–8.
[2] A. viii. 269   primusque Potitius auctor
                     et domus Herculei custos Pinaria sacri.
Ibid. 281 iamque sacerdotes primusque Potitius ibant.

altars';[1] blood-offering with incense is a frequent combination. When Aeneas had made himself known and been welcomed, they turned to the sacrificial feast; Evander 'bids the feast and the cups they had moved, to be placed again upon the tables';[2] they sit with Aeneas on the ground, 'chosen youths and the priest of the altar bring the roast flesh of the bulls, and pile upon the baskets the gifts of kneaded Ceres (i.e. bread) and serve Bacchus. Aeneas with them and the Trojan youths feast on the chine of whole ox and the entrails of purification.'[3] We may note here the special priest for the special cult, and the connexion of the entrails with purification. Evander then narrates the origin of the festival, which he solemnly describes as 'this annual rite, this feast of tradition, this altar of the great god'.[4] The story of the contest of Hercules and Cacus, to which he refers it all, is, of course, Graeco-Roman legend, but Virgil seems conscious of Cacus as a semi-divine being associated with the Palatine, as he clearly was in the old Roman religion. His story over, Evander bound his head 'with the twi-coloured poplar with its shade loved of Hercules and it hung with its leaves twined in his hair' (Servius notes that in historic times the officiating priest at the Ara Maxima wore a crown not of poplar, but of laurel) 'and the sacred cup filled his hands. Quickly all gladly pour libation on the table and pray to the

[1] A. viii. 104　　　　　　　　Pallas huic filius una,
　　　　　　una omnes iuvenum primi pauperque senatus
　　　　　　tura dabant, tepidusque cruor fumabat ad aras.
[2] A. viii. 175　　　　　　dapes iubet et sublata reponi
　　　　　　pocula.
[3] A. viii. 179　tum lecti iuvenes certatim araeque sacerdos
　　　　　　viscera tosta ferunt taurorum, onerantque canistris
　　　　　　dona laboratae Cereris, Bacchumque ministrant.
　　　　　　vescitur Aeneas simul et Troiana iuventus
　　　　　　perpetui tergo bovis et lustralibus extis.
[4] A. viii. 185　　　　　　　　　haec sollemnia nobis,
　　　　　　has ex more dapes, hanc tanti numinis aram.

gods.'[1] It was now evening but 'the priests headed by Potitius, girt according to custom in skins, came and bore fresh flames';[2] the feast is renewed both for gods and men; the skin cloak is the mark of a very ancient ritual. Virgil then, as the conclusion of the celebration, says that the Salii appeared round the blazing altars, their heads bound with sprays of poplar, in two bands of seniors and juniors and sang of the deeds of Hercules.[3] This statement has caused great difficulty both to ancient and to modern critics, as the Salii are, of course, at Rome associated with Mars. Macrobius (III. xii), who comments on the passage, tries to explain that Hercules and Mars are one, but incidentally adduces evidence that in his worship at Tibur Hercules had Salii. This is confirmed by inscriptions (see Wissowa, *R.K.*[2], p 272, n. 8) and is much more likely to be right: whether they accompanied him at his first coming to Rome or were still in use at Tibur, or Virgil was reproducing some ancient tradition, it is impossible to say, but once again he seems to have preserved a piece of antiquarian lore.[4] The songs he attributes to them are the Greek legends of Heracles combined with the Cacus story. The final completion of the

---

[1] A. viii. 276 dixerat, Herculea bicolor cum populus umbra
           velavitque comas foliisque innexa pependit,
           et sacer implevit dextram scyphus. ocius omnes
           in mensam laeti libant divosque precantur.

[2] A. viii. 281 iamque sacerdotes primusque Potitius ibant
           pellibus in morem cincti, flammasque ferebant.
           instaurant epulas et mensae grata secundae
           dona ferunt cumulantque oneratis lancibus aras.

[3] A. viii. 285 tum Salii ad cantus incensa altaria circum
           populeis adsunt evincti tempora ramis,
           hic iuvenum chorus, ille senum, qui carmine laudes
           Herculeas et facta ferunt.

[4] It should be noted that in Liv. i. 27. 7, Tullus Hostilius vows twelve Salii to the abstract deities Pallor and Pavor; this suggests that the association with Mars was not so exclusive as we are inclined to suppose. See Wissowa, *R.K.*[2], p. 149.

ritual occurs next morning, when Aeneas revives the smouldering ashes on the altar of Hercules and combines his worship with that of the Lar and the Penates.[1]

From this survey of Virgil's accounts of worship several inferences may be drawn. It is clear in the first place that the old rituals of sacrifice, lustration, and vow were still familiar in their ancient form to Virgil's contemporaries, so that their embodiment in his epic would appear natural to them. This is no doubt due to the extreme conservatism of the Roman religious mind, which even after Greek anthropomorphism had transformed conceptions of the gods and elaborate temples had taken the place of the rustic turf-altar, yet preserved the old forms of rite and ceremony intact. In the pious household, indeed, and in many of the country festivals the ancient forms of worship, as we may learn from Ovid's accounts, were observed in all their details. Secondly, Virgil's description of the worship of Hercules at the Ara Maxima proves that the special features of an extraneous cult were still known and practised. Yet it is equally true that the occasional intrusion of distinctively Greek elements in the worship which he describes cannot have appeared incongruous either to Virgil or to his readers. This cannot be accounted for by any similar contamination in the State-cults, but must rather be due to the Greek epic tradition; indeed, it has been seen in several instances that the intrusions may be traced direct to individual passages in Homer. It is a fusion which is largely, if not entirely, poetic.

And if one asks the further question as to Virgil's own attitude to it all, he remains, as usual, impersonal but never remote. Archaeological interest, which was far

[1] A. viii. 542 et primum Herculeis sopitas ignibus aras
                excitat, hesternumque larem parvosque Penatis
                laetus adit.

deeper with him than with Ovid, would no doubt account for a great deal, but it is difficult to resist the impression that he felt that in this old ritual of worship man could somehow get into relation with the supernatural power which was represented for him in the old animistic deities.

III

THE OLD ITALIAN RELIGION

WORDS AND IDEAS

MUCH light may be thrown on Virgil's religious habits of thought by an examination of his use of some of the leading words connected with the old religion and the ideas which they represent. In employing the majority of such words he keeps very close to the ancient conceptions and shows how vital they still were through all the changes which the religion of Rome had undergone.

(i) *'Numen'*.

After the consideration of Virgil's attitude to the old gods and their worship, it is most natural to begin with the word *numen*, which, though it cannot be assigned historical priority over *deus*, yet more nearly represents the idea of the animistic deity, which was the germ of the old religion. There can be little doubt that the word is derived from *nuere*, 'to nod'; it is found in its most literal sense in a line of Lucretius describing the Curetes in their worship of Cybele 'tossing the terrible crests on their heads with a nod'.[1] So in its religious sense it comes to mean the nod of assent with which the deity expresses his will, as Zeus often does in Homer. Hence it appears to branch out into two slightly different but not always easily distinguishable meanings, firstly the 'will' or 'decree' of a deity, and secondly the 'deity' himself, conceived, however, not as an anthropomorphic *deus*, but rather as a vague 'power' or 'spirit' which has control over some sphere or function. It is supremely well illustrated in Ovid's description of the

---

[1] Lucr. ii. 632 terrificas capitum quatientes numine cristas.

grove on the Aventine 'at the sight of which you might say "there is a spirit in it" '.[1]

Virgil is extremely fond of the word; he uses it some sixty times in both senses and extensions of them both. It will be convenient first to take the more concrete sense of a 'spirit' or 'power', a deity conceived in or near to the strictly animistic conception. An instance, very close to the Ovidian use, occurs where Virgil speaks of the Stygian lake 'by whose spirit the gods fear to swear falsely'.[2] In a more concrete sense the fury Allecto, manifestly a 'power', but never a goddess in the anthropomorphic sense, is described as 'that hated spirit'.[3] A perfect example occurs in the introduction to the first book of the *Georgics*,[4] where the Fauns are described with exactly the feeling of the animistic religion as 'the ever-present spirits of the country-folk'. So in a passage of Aeneas' last prayer, already noted as typical of early thought, he cries: 'I call on the fountains and rivers and all the holy powers (*religio*) in high heaven, and all the spirits (*numina*) in the blue sea.'[5] It is characteristic of the old religion that there is no attempt here to specify the deities of the sea; in the true spirit of animism they are collective and vague. In the same way, on first touching Sicily Aeneas and his comrades 'worship the great spirits of the place'.[6] In other passages of prayer we find formulae reminiscent of the *sive mas, sive femina* and other inclusive phrases in the ancient invocations. 'May the gods', says Aeneas to Dido at their first meeting, 'grant

[1] Ovid, *Fast.* iii. 296 quo posses viso dicere 'numen inest'.
[2] A. vi. 323   Stygiamque paludem,
                    di cuius iurare timent et fallere numen.
[3] A. vii. 570   Erinys,
                    invisum numen.
[4] G. i. 10 et vos, agrestum praesentia numina, Fauni.
[5] A. xii. 181 fontisque fluviosque voco, quaeque aetheris alti
                    religio et quae caeruleo sunt numina ponto.
[6] A. iii. 697 numina magna loci veneramur.

thee due reward, if there be any spirits who look upon the pious.'[1] In the fourth book Dido hopes that Aeneas will be punished 'if the pious spirits have any power',[2] and in her last despair she 'prays to any just and mindful spirit who cares for unrequited lovers'.[3] Here and there Virgil somewhat stretches this primary meaning. When Helenus leads Aeneas to the threshold of Phoebus' temple before he makes his prophecy, the hero is described in an almost untranslatable phrase as *multo suspensum numine*, 'thrilled with the awe-inspiring spirit';[4] the sense of the divine presence is strong upon him. So, again, when Ascanius has exclaimed that they are indeed 'eating their tables' in fulfilment of Helenus' prophecy, Aeneas 'seized the first words from his mouth and stayed his speaking, *stupefactus numine*'.[5] Servius explains that *numen* here means 'the prophecy', but it is surely again the sense of a divine intervention in this very unexpected fulfilment which has awed him.

A very interesting passage occurs in the introduction to the fourth book of the *Georgics*;[6] 'the task', says Virgil, 'of writing about the bees concerns tiny things; but not tiny is the glory, if one is suffered by malignant spirits to accomplish it and Apollo hears the prayer'. Here the *numina laeva* are conceived in the true animistic way, but they are combined with the clear-cut anthropomorphic Apollo. This leads to the more important extension which Virgil, no

---

[1] A. i. 603 di tibi, si qua pios respectant numina, ... praemia digna ferant.
[2] A. iv. 382 si quid pia numina possunt.
[3] A. iv. 520   tum, si quod non aequo foedere amantis
              curae numen habet iustumque memorque, precatur.
[4] A. iii. 371   meque ad tua limina, Phoebe,
              ipse manu multo suspensum numine ducit.
[5] A. vii. 118   primamque (vocem) loquentis ab ore
              eripuit pater ac stupefactus numine pressit.
[6] G. iv. 6 in tenui labor; at tenuis non gloria, si quem
              numina laeva sinunt auditque vocatus Apollo.

doubt following popular usage, gives to the word, for in many passages he uses *numen* as little more than an equivalent of *deus* in the normal sense of the later religion. In several instances this is made clear by the combination of *deus* and *numen*, apparently as synonyms with at the most a nuance of distinction between them. Thus Aeneas begs the Sibyl 'grant that the Teucrians may find a home in Latium, and their wandering gods and the harried *numina* of Troy';[1] this is mere amplification, both the *dei* and the *numina* are the Penates which Aeneas brings with him from Troy. Anchises, when the Harpies appear, calls on the 'great spirits'[2], but his words are, 'Ye gods, ward off this threat', and Aeneas asks the exhausted Dares, 'do you not feel the spirits turned against you?'[3] and adds at once: 'Yield to the god.' A peculiarly interesting combination occurs when the poet describes Orpheus' desolation at the loss of Eurydice: 'with what lamentation could he move the Manes, what spirits with his cry?'[4] Here the Manes are the underworld gods and perhaps in the use of *numina* there may be a faint suggestion that they are not quite full gods like the *di superi*. In other places we find *numen* standing alone, but clearly equivalent to *deus*. It cannot, for instance, be doubted that when Ulysses' ill-fated comrade in narrating the story of the Cyclops says, 'we prayed to the great spirits',[5] he is using the phrase just as it was used of Anchises earlier in the book. So when Latinus addresses Aeneas, 'thou to whose years and race the fates are kindly, thou

[1] A. vi. 65 tuque, o sanctissima vates . . . da . . . Latio considere Teucros,
     errantisque deos agitataque numina Troiae.
[2] A. iii. 263 et pater Anchises passis de litore palmis
     numina magna vocat meritosque indicit honores.
[3] A. v. 466 non viris alias conversaque numina sentis?
     cede deo.
[4] G. iv. 505 quo fletu Manis, quae numina voce moveret?
[5] A. iii. 633   nos magna precati
     numina.   See n. 2.

whom the spirits demand',[1] the combination with the fates shows that the gods are meant by *numina*; this will become clearer later on. Thus Pallas cries to his comrades: 'No spirits are against us, we are mortals pressed by a mortal foe',[2] thinking of the descent of anthropomorphic gods into battle. These instances are in the plural: there are equally clear uses of *numen = deus* in the singular. Proteus tells Aristaeus that 'the wrath of some spirit is harrying thee';[3] in his invocation to the Muse Virgil asks, 'what spirit was offended that Aeneas should suffer such toils?'[4] and gives the answer 'Iuno' in the next line. With even clearer reference to a definite god, Evander calls Hercules' Ara Maxima 'the altar of so great a spirit',[5] and Venus, appealing to Vulcan for the making of Aeneas' armour, calls him 'spirit sacred to me'.[6] Similarly, Venus, addressing her son Cupid, says, 'in supplication I appeal to thy spirit'.[7] Here, too, there is a further and characteristic extension: he uses *numina* of the stars, divine in an astrological sense, when the treacherous Sinon raises his hands to the stars and cries: 'You, eternal fires, I call to witness and your inviolable spirit',[8] and this may be his meaning a few lines earlier when he appeals to the Trojans 'by the gods above and the spirits who know the truth'.[9] Once again he applies the word in anticipation to Octavian, so soon to become a god,

[1] A. viii. 511   tu, cuius et annis
       et generi fata indulgent, quem numina poscunt.

[2] A. x. 375   numina nulla premunt, mortali urgemur ab hoste
       mortales.

[3] G. iv. 453   non te nullius exercent numinis irae.

[4] A. i. 8   quo numine laeso.

[5] A. viii. 186   hanc tanti numinis aram.

[6] A. viii. 382   sanctum mihi numen.

[7] A. i. 666   ad te confugio et supplex tua numina posco.

[8] A. ii. 154   vos aeterni ignes, et non violabile vestrum
       testor numen.

[9] A. ii. 141   per superos et conscia numina veri.

'whether thou wilt come as god of the boundless sea and sailors shall adore thy spirit'.[1]

In two of these extensions of the *deus* sense it will be noticed that Virgil speaks of the *numen* 'of a god' and this is indeed his most frequent use of the word. But it requires careful analysis, for it appears to range from instances where the *numen* of a god is little more than a periphrasis for the god himself, through those in which it seems to have the added idea of 'power' or 'majesty' to cases where it is quite definitely attached to the other derivative meaning of *numen*, the 'will' or 'consent' of a god. The first class is comparatively rare, but must be recognized in several instances in which men are said to pray to the *numen* of a god. So in the third book, 'we pray to the holy *numina* of Pallas';[2] 'pray first', says Helenus, 'to the *numen* of great Iuno';[3] and Iuno herself in the beginning of the first book asks despairingly, 'does any one besides pray to the *numen* of Iuno or in supplication will he lay gifts upon my altar?'[4] It is difficult in these cases to say that the periphrasis means much more than Pallas and Iuno, with possibly an added note of majesty or dignity. So, too, in that mysterious passage of the second book, where Virgil has so marvellously given the sense of a divine catastrophe, 'there appear awful figures and the great *numina* of the gods hostile to Troy'.[5] Here *numina* perhaps gives the sense of 'presence'. Iarbas, again, maddened by the rumour of the wedlock of Aeneas and Dido, 'is said to have made many a prayer to

[1] G. i. 29 an deus immensi venias maris ac tua nautae
    numina sola colant.
[2] A. iii. 543   tum numina sancta precamur
    Palladis armisonae.
[3] A. iii. 437 Iunonis magnae primum prece numen adora.
[4] A. i. 48   et quisquam numen Iunonis adorat
    praeterea aut supplex aris imponet honorem?
[5] A. ii. 622 apparent dirae facies inimicaque Troiae
    numina magna deum.

K

Iuppiter before the altars amid the *numina* of the gods';[1] 'presence' seems here as near the meaning as we can get. So in Aeneas' prayer to the Tiber-god, 'only come and confirm thy presence nearer at hand'.[2]

In a second class of examples the meaning of *numen*, combined with the genitive or with the possessive pronoun, seems rather to be that of 'power'. Such are the passages in which persons or places are said to be in the *numen* of a god or gods, 'power' with the consequent idea of protection. Anchises, determined at last to leave Troy, prays to be preserved by the *di patrii* of Troy;[3] 'this is your augury, and Troy is in your power'; and so Aletes prays to the 'gods of our fatherland, in whose power Troy ever lies'.[4] A similar idea of protection occurs in Evander's prayer to the *di superi*: 'if your power, if the fates preserve Pallas unharmed for me'.[5] Akin to this use is the description of the nymphs, 'whom gracious Cybebe had ordered to have power (*numen*) over the sea',[6] though possibly the meaning may rather be 'to be sea-deities'. And, again, two passages where Iuno laments that her 'powers' (*numina*) are waning: 'forsooth, my powers at last lie exhausted',[7] and a little later, 'if my powers are not great enough'.[8] This 'power' sense has certain derivatives, which should be considered

[1] A. iv. 204 dicitur ante aras media inter numina divum
        multa Iovem manibus supplex orasse supinis.
[2] A. viii. 78 adsis o tantum et propius tua numina firmes.
[3] A. ii. 702 di patrii, servate domum, servate nepotem.
        vestrum hoc augurium, vestroque in numine Troia est.
[4] A. ix. 247 di patrii, quorum semper sub numine Troia est.
[5] A. viii. 574   si numina vestra
        incolumem Pallanta mihi, si fata reservant.
[6] A. x. 220   nymphae, quas alma Cybebe
        numen habere maris . . . iusserat.
[7] A. vii. 297   at, credo, mea numina tandem
        fessa iacent.
[8] A. vii. 310   quod si mea numina non sunt
        magna satis.

here, even though there is not in all cases this peculiar possessive genitive or adjective. Firstly, it is used specially for the 'inspiration' of a god to a follower; the Sibyl seemed to grow in stature 'when she was filled with the inspiration of the god now nearer at hand';[1] Aeneas and his comrades in Troy rush to meet the Greeks 'by no inspiration of our own'.[2] This may possibly be the sense when Virgil himself, as he embarks on his description of the lower world, prays that it may be right for him to tell what he has heard, 'and by your inspiration to disclose things hidden in the deep darkness of earth',[3] though here the meaning may not be more than 'by your consent'. Secondly, this definite sense of inspiration passes into a vaguer sense of 'influence'. Amata, maddened by the poison of the fury Allecto, rushes into the woods, 'simulating the influence of Bacchus',[4] and Venus decides to attempt artifice to win Dido's love for Aeneas, 'lest by some influence she be changed'.[5] Lastly, there are instances where *numen* appears to acquire a more concrete sense of 'an exhibition of power': 'it is a great and notable mark of power,' says Iuno sarcastically to Venus, 'if one woman is overcome by the craft of two gods (you and Cupid)'.[6] Specially is this the case where the meaning of 'inspiration' seems to pass into the concrete sense of the 'oracle' delivered under inspiration. It has been noticed that Servius believes this to be the meaning when Aeneas seized on Ascanius' joking word about the

---

[1] A. vi. 49   maiorque videri
      nec mortale sonans, afflata est numine quando
      iam propiore dei.
[2] A. ii. 396 vadimus immixti Danais haud numine nostro.
[3] A. vi. 266 sit mihi fas audita loqui, sit numine vestro
      pandere res alta terra et caligine mersas.
[4] A. vii. 385 quin etiam in silvas simulato numine Bacchi . . . evolat.
[5] A. i. 674   ne quo se numine mutet.
[6] A. iv. 94   magnum et memorabile numen,
      una dolo divum si femina victa duorum est.

'consuming of the tables', *stupefactus numine*.[1] There are less dubious instances where Ulysses in Sinon's story drags forward Calchas and 'demands of him what are these oracles of the gods',[2] or when his comrades check Ascanius, 'eager for the fight, by the words and oracle of Phoebus';[3] on the former passage Servius notes *numina divum pro oraculis posuit*.

It is difficult to say whether these instances of the 'power' sense and its extensions derive from the meaning of *numen* as 'god' or rather that of 'will'. But there are many places where the latter sense is self-evident. Firstly, there are the passages in which events are said to occur 'not without the will of the gods'. Aeneas comforts Creusa with the thought that the sack of Troy is not so occurring;[4] he tells his comrades that it is not 'without the purpose and will of the gods' that they have come back to Anchises' burial-place in Sicily;[5] Palinurus supposes that it is 'not without the will of the gods' that Aeneas proposes to visit the lower world.[6] Similarly, Neptune rebukes the winds for daring to raise a storm 'without my will';[7] Venus offers to Iuppiter that the Trojans shall pay the penalty 'if without thy sanction and against thy will they have come to Italy';[8] Aeneas rushes into battle in Troy inspired 'by the words of Panthus and

[1] A. vii. 118; see p. 62, n. 5.
[2] A. ii. 123   quae sint ea numina divum
              flagitat.
[3] A. ix. 661 ergo avidum pugnae dictis ac numine Phoebi
              Ascanium prohibent.
[4] A. ii. 777   non haec sine numine divum
              eveniunt.
[5] A. v. 56 haud equidem sine mente, reor, sine numine divum.
[6] A. vi. 368   neque enim, credo, sine numine divum
              flumina tanta paras Stygiamque innare paludem.
[7] A. i. 133 iam caelum terramque meo sine numine, venti,
              miscere et tantas audetis tollere moles?
[8] A. x. 31 si sine pace tua atque invito numine Troes
              Italiam petiere.

the will of the gods',[1] and tells Helenus that 'all the gods persuaded me by their will to seek Italy'.[2] In the last two instances the sense of 'will' is approximating closely to that of 'inspiration' or even 'oracle'. So, too, there are other places where it comes near to the meaning of 'power'. In the last book of the *Aeneid* Aeneas says that 'if Victory has granted us successful warfare (as I rather think and may the gods confirm it by their will), I seek no kingdom for myself';[3] just before he has prayed to Mavors who 'rulest all wars beneath thy will';[4] and in a more conventional phrase Mercurius speaks of Iuppiter as 'he who by his will governs sky and earth'.[5]

This review of Virgil's use of the word *numen* shows that he knows well and loves its primitive sense of a vaguely felt divine presence and the power and will associated with it, but that he has adapted it to the circumstances of the Graeco-Roman anthropomorphic religion, and occasionally strains its sense rather beyond normal usage, but always in close derivation from it.

(ii) *'Religio' and 'religiosus'*.

The derivation of the word *religio* is uncertain, but there can be little doubt that its primary sense to a Roman is the feeling of awe or anxiety experienced in a holy place, believed to be the dwelling of a *numen*. This is the sense which Virgil retains exactly in the majority of instances where he uses the word. It is most fully expressed in some fine lines describing Aeneas' visit with Evander to the hill which

---

[1] A. ii. 336 talibus Othryadae dictis et numine divum
    in flammas et in arma feror.
[2] A. iii. 363   cuncti suaserunt numine divi
    Italiam petere.
[3] A. xii. 188 ut potius reor et potius di numine firment.
[4] A. xii. 180 cuncta tuo qui bella, pater, sub numine torques.
[5] A. iv. 269   caelum ac terras qui numine torquet.

was to be the Capitol: 'even then the spot's dread awfulness (*religio*) brought fear to the timid countrymen; already they quaked before wood and rock. "This grove," said Evander, "this hill with its wooded top some god, what god we know not, has for his dwelling." '¹ This is a magnificently sympathetic expression of the feeling of the old religion: the spot is hallowed, it has a *religio* for the people, and this is due to the presence of some deity, though they know not whom. In the same spirit the poet describes the old cypress-tree which stood by the deserted temple of Ceres in Troy as 'preserved for many a year by the awe of generations':² here the *religio* is not looked on as something possessed by the spot, but felt in the minds of the worshippers. So in the sack of Troy corpses are strewed 'through the houses and the awful thresholds of the gods';³ their presence was a violation of *religio*. So, again, the palace of Picus, now inhabited by Latinus, was a vast building 'fearful for its trees and the awe of ancestors';⁴ the famous gates of Ianus are 'twin gates of war, so they call them, made holy by awe and the dread of cruel Mars';⁵ and the grove by the stream of Caere is 'holy throughout its length through the awe of generations'.⁶ There can be no doubt that in all these instances the old sense is exactly

---

¹ A. viii. 349 iam tum religio pavidos terrebat agrestis
    dira loci, iam tum silvam saxumque tremebant.
    'hoc nemus, hunc', inquit 'frondoso vertice collem
    (quis deus incertum est) habitat deus.'
² A. ii. 714   iuxtaque antiqua cupressus
    religione patrum multos servata per annos.
³ A. ii. 364 plurima perque vias sternuntur inertia passim
    corpora perque domos et religiosa deorum
    limina.
⁴ A. vii. 172 horrendum silvis et religione parentum.
⁵ A. vii. 607 sunt geminae belli portae (sic nomine dicunt)
    religione sacrae et saevi formidine Martis.
⁶ A. viii. 597 est ingens gelidum lucus prope Caeritis amnem,
    religione patrum late sacer.

preserved; the 'feeling of awe' of holy places was still alive in Virgil's time and he was himself aware of it.

He also has his extensions of this primitive use. Sometimes, as not infrequently in Latin elsewhere, *religio* has come to mean 'a religious rite'. Helenus tells Aeneas, when he first touches the shores of Italy, to sacrifice with veiled head, 'this custom in sacrifice do thou and thy companions observe, to this rite may thy pious descendants remain true'.[1] Two interesting examples occur in connexion with the wooden horse. Priam asks the prisoner Sinon, 'why did they fashion the vast bulk of this horse? who prompted it? what is their purpose? what sacred rite (*religio*) is it or what engine of war?'[2] and Sinon replies that Calchas ordered it to be made so vast 'lest it should be able to be received within the gates or dragged within the walls and so protect the people under an ancient rite'.[3] This is something of a stretching of the legitimate meaning, for *religio* here has the sense both of a rite and the protection of a god. A still further extension of this notion is found in the invocation of Aeneas, so often quoted already, before the single combat with Turnus, 'I call on the fountains and streams, on all the holy powers (*religio*) in high heaven and on the spirits in the blue sea.'[4] Here *religio* is almost equivalent to *di* and cannot really be distinguished from *numina* which follows, but both suggest that vague undistinguished sense of divine beings, which is characteristic of the ancient religion. With a still further strain, characteristic of Virgil, he uses the word once almost in the sense of

[1] A. iii. 408 hunc socii morem sacrorum, hunc ipse teneto;
    hac casti maneant in religione nepotes.
[2] A. ii. 150 quo molem hanc immanis equi statuere? quis auctor?
    quidve petunt? quae religio? aut quae machina belli?
[3] A. ii. 187 ne recipi portis aut duci in moenia posset,
    neu populum antiqua sub religione tueri.
[4] A. xii. 181 fontisque fluviosque voco, quaeque aetheris alti
    religio et quae caeruleo sunt numina ponto.

'oracles': 'prospering signs of the gods (so we might translate *religio* here) have foretold all my course and all the
gods have urged me by their will (*numine*) to seek Italy.'[1]
Finally, in the first book of the *Georgics* we have the word
in its much more normal sense of a 'religious scruple':
'there are some things which laws both human and divine
suffer to be done on festal days; no scruple of religion forbids the turning of the streams on to the crops.'[2]

We may notice here two interesting uses of the allied but
contrasted word *superstitio*, which seems to mean a rite
going beyond what is needed, a *religio* where no *religio* need
be. It is used exactly in this sense by Evander, who tells
Aeneas that the worship of Hercules was not set as a bur-
den on his people by any 'idle superstition, ignorant of the
ancient gods'.[3] A more difficult use of the word is in
connexion with the oath by the Styx, which is said to be
'the one superstition assigned to the gods above'.[4] Here
superstitio seems to be almost equivalent to *religio*, as
indeed Servius says in his note, unless Virgil meant to
suggest that the gods by their very nature had no need of
religio.

In his less extended use of *religio* Virgil seems to keep
almost closer to the old meaning than he does in his
employment of *numen*; the simple feeling of 'religious awe'
is almost always present to him and his developments of
it are in accordance with usage.

[1] A. iii. 362 namque omnem cursum mihi prospera dixit
religio, et cuncti suaserunt numine divi
Italiam petere.
[2] G. i. 268 quippe etiam festis quaedam exercere diebus
fas et iura sinunt: rivos deducere nulla
religio vetuit.
[3] A. viii. 185 non haec sollemnia nobis . . .
vana superstitio veterumque ignara deorum | imposuit.
[4] A. xii. 816 adiuro Stygii caput implacabile fontis,
una superstitio superis quae reddita divis.

(iii) '*Sacer*', '*sacratus*', '*sanctus*', '*sollemnis*'.

There is a group of words, all of which roughly imply the notion 'holy', but which had in reality precise and distinct meanings: we may consider how far Virgil here followed tradition. *Sacer* is strictly that which is consecrated to a god; *religiosus* is a wide word which may be applied to any thing or place which causes the feeling of 'awe', whether that be due to association with a god or to some other cause. Thus a place struck by lightning is *religiosus*, so is a tomb, for they are both 'taboo'; you must not tread on them, but neither of them is sacred. But, if the *religio* which affects the spot is due to the presence of a god, then the spot is also *sacer*. Thus in two passages already quoted[1] the gates of Ianus and the grove of Caere are said to be *religione sacer* (*sacrae*); the *religio* in both cases is divine. This sense is most clearly seen when things are definitely said to be *sacer* to a deity. Thus the golden bough is 'sacred to Iuno of the lower world';[2] Aeneas in his pursuit of Turnus halted by a wild olive once 'sacred to Faunus'.[3] Persons are described in the same way: among the warriors in the lower world Aeneas meets Polyboetes, 'sacred to Ceres' (Demeter),[4] Lichas, one of his victims in battle is 'sacred to Phoebus',[5] and Chloreus the priest is 'sacred to Cybele',[6] and with an extension of this idea Virgil speaks of 'calves sacred to the altars',[7] that is, destined for sacrifice.

In many instances where this defining dative is wanting,

[1] A. vii. 607, A. viii. 597; see *religio*, p. 70, nn. 5 and 6.
[2] A. vi. 137   ramus
              Iunoni infernae dictus sacer.
[3] A. xii. 766 forte sacer Fauno foliis oleaster amaris
              hic steterat.
[4] A. vi. 484 Cererique sacrum Polyboeten.
[5] A. x. 315 inde Lichan ferit . . . tibi, Phoebe, sacrum.
[6] A. xi. 768 sacer Cybelae Chloreus olimque sacerdos.
[7] G. iii. 160 aris . . . sacros.

the idea is evidently the same. Thus *sacer* is used of places made 'holy' by the presence of a spirit or deity, of groves,[1] of a mountain-top,[2] of rivers,[3] of a fountain,[4] of a shrine,[5] of the doorposts of Latinus' palace and of Neptune's temple,[6] and of the sacred island of Delos.[7] It is not used absolutely of individual persons—that is *sanctus*—but it is used of the 'sacred body' of Camilla,[8] of the 'sacred band' of nymphs who are Diana's attendants,[9] and of the 'face' of the morning star.[10] Among other 'sacred' things it is most frequently applied to trees, which are known as the special abode of a particular spirit or are sacred as a class to some deity. It is thus used of the oak (Iuppiter) and the laurel (Phoebus), of the shade of a holm-oak (Iuppiter), or, generally, of a sacred grove.[11] Another group of objects to which the epithet *sacer* is applied is composed of things connected with the ritual of sacrifice. It is used of the victim, the goat sacrificed to Bacchus,[12] several times of the victim's blood,[13] of the sacrificial water turned to blood when Dido made her offering,[14] of the fire on the altar,[15] of

[1] A. v. 761 lucus late sacer; A. viii. 345 sacri . . . nemus Argileti.

[2] A. x. 230 Idaeae sacro de vertice pinus.

[3] A. vii. 797 sacrumque Numici | litus; G. ii. 147 saepe tuo perfusi flumine sacro; G. iv. 319 sacrum caput . . . amnis.

[4] A. vii. 242 fontis vada sacra Numici.

[5] A. ii. 525 sacra . . . in sede.

[6] A. vii. 183 sacris in postibus; A. v. 360 Neptuni sacro . . . de poste.

[7] A. iii. 73 sacra mari colitur medio gratissima tellus.

[8] A. xi. 591 quicumque sacrum violarit vulnere corpus.

[9] A. xi. 533 unam ex virginibus sociis sacraque caterva.

[10] A. viii. 591 os sacrum.

[11] E. vii. 13 sacra . . . quercu; A. vii. 59 laurus . . . sacra comam; G. iii. 333 sicubi nigrum | ilicibus crebris sacra nemus accubet umbra; G. i. 148 sacrae . . . silvae; G. ii. 21 nemorumque sacrorum.

[12] G. ii. 395 et ductus cornu stabit sacer hircus ad aram.

[13] A. iii. 67 sanguinis et sacri pateras; A. v. 78 sanguine sacro; A. v. 333 sacroque cruore; G. iv. 542 sacrum . . . cruorem.

[14] A. iv. 454 latices nigrescere sacros.

[15] A. vi. 246 ignibus . . . sacris.

the cup from which the libation was poured,[1] and of the sacrificial feast.[2] The consecration of every object connected with sacrifice is of course an essential idea of the old religion. The epithet *sacer* is similarly applied to a series of objects whose connexion with the *religio* of deities is always close. Thus it is used of the images of the gods,[3] of sacred tripods offered as prizes at the games in honour of Anchises,[4] of the gates of a temple and by an extension of the gates leading to the lower world,[5] of articles of the priest's dress, the crown or fillet or tiara.[6] So, too, of locks of human hair consecrated to a deity,[7] of the boughs of sacred trees,[8] and of Aeneas' ships made of the pines from Cybele's holy mountain.[9] Specially notable is its application to abstract substantives, to the 'commands' of the gods[10] and to the 'custom' (*mos*) of throwing open the gates of Ianus in time of war.[11] Two very special instances are the use of *sacer* as applied to the 'fire' of the pestilence,[12] and in a famous passage to the 'thirst for gold';[13] in these two places it has the sense of 'accursed'. A holy thing was always taboo and it was dangerous to touch it; hence what was 'sacred' might also be 'cursed'. What is true of *sacer* is true also of the participle *sacratus*. It may sometimes be

[1] A. viii. 278 et sacer implevit dextram scyphus.

[2] A. vii. 175 hae sacris sedes epulis.

[3] A. ii. 167 sacram effigiem; A. iii. 148 effigies sacrae divum.

[4] A. v. 110 sacri tripodes.

[5] A. vi. 573 sacrae panduntur portae; A. vi. 109 sacra ostia pandas.

[6] A. iii. 81 vittis et sacra redimitus tempora lauro; A. x. 538 infula cui sacra redimibat tempora vitta; A. vii. 247 sceptrumque sacerque tiaras.

[7] A. iv. 702 hunc [crinem] ego Diti sacrum iussa fero. A. vii. 391 sacrum tibi pascere crinem.

[8] A. iv. 485 sacros servabat in arbore ramos.

[9] A. ix. 109 ratibus sacris; A. ix. 116 sacras . . . pinus.

[10] A. vi. 40 nec sacra morantur iussa viri.

[11] A. vii. 601 mos erat Hesperio in Latio, quem protinus urbes
        Albanae coluere sacrum.

[12] G. iii. 566 contactos artus sacer ignis edebat.

[13] A. iii. 57 auri sacra fames.

said to have a participial force, 'consecrated', but often it seems little more than a synonym of *sacer*; it is noticeable that it occurs four times in the second *Aeneid* where *sacer* only appears twice, as though it were at that time in Virgil's mind as an equivalent. It is applied to objects which fall into just the same categories as those which are *sacra*; thus a grove,[1] a valley,[2] the sacred capitol of Troy,[3] temples or resting-places in them,[4] the sheep brought as offerings to the sacrifice,[5] the consecrated 'head' of Helenus the prophet,[6] and with the extension again to an abstract substantive, 'the sacred oath of loyalty',[7] *sacrata iura* being, as Servius interprets it, equivalent to *sacramentum*.

Sanctus is a more difficult word than *sacer* and its relation to it has to be carefully considered. It is, of course, in origin a participle and it therefore often has the meaning of 'consecrated' like *sacratus*. But it also has a derived sense in which, as Servius[8] points out, it is not the same as *sacer* or *religiosus*, but means instead 'holy', 'pure', 'uncorrupt'. For this reason, though it is often used of things, it is also more frequently applied to people than *sacer* and conveys not merely a sense of consecration, but an indication of personal character as well. In its use of things in Virgil it seems to follow very closely the categories of *sacer* and *sacratus* and no doubt varies but little in meaning: a moun-

[1] A. vii. 778 lucisque sacratis.
[2] A. ix. 4 sacrata valle.
[3] A. ii. 245 et monstrum infelix sacrata sistimus arce.
[4] A. ii. 165 sacrato . . . templo; A. ii. 742 sedemque sacratam; A. i. 681 sacrata sede.
[5] A. xii. 213 rite sacratas . . . pecudes.
[6] A. iii. 370   vittasque resolvit
                          sacrati capitis.
[7] A. ii. 157 fas mihi Graiorum sacrata resolvere iura.
[8] Serv. *ad Aen.* xi. 158 *sanctum* non semper sacrum neque religiosum est; ut hic, ubi *sanctissima* incorruptae castitatis significat; cf. *ad A.* xii. 648.

tain-top is *sanctus*,[1] so is a river,[2] so in a metaphorical sense derived from Lucretius are 'springs',[3] and the star or meteor sent to Anchises and Aeneas to urge their departure from Troy.[4] The connexion with sacred ceremonies is seen in its use of the fire of sacrifice,[5] of the fire kindled by the meteor on the head of Ascanius,[6] and of oracles.[7] It is also used with an abstract noun in the phrase *sancta fides*, where the participial sense comes out, 'the promise that is ratified by a holy pledge'.[8] In its application to gods *sanctus* may perhaps be most nearly represented by 'revered'; it has the old sense of 'holy' and something of the new sense of 'pure' in character. Thus we get it in a vague phrase, borrowed from Ennius and typical of the old religion, 'thou, reverend among gods, whosoever thou art',[9] and twice in connexion with *numen*, once of 'the reverend *numina* of Pallas',[10] and once when Venus, wishing to persuade Volcanus to make Aeneas' armour, addresses him coaxingly as '*numen* reverend to me'.[11] When it is used of persons there is again sometimes still the sense of divinity or divine inspiration uppermost, as when Aeneas speaks of Anchises, after his death, as 'my holy parent',[12] or when he addresses the Sibyl as 'most holy prophet';[13] but when

[1] A. xi. 785 sancti custos Soractis Apollo.
[2] A. viii. 72 tuque, o Thybri, tuo genitor cum flumine sancto.
[3] G. ii. 175 sanctos ausus recludere fontis; cf. Lucr. i. 927 iuvat integros accedere fontis.
[4] A. ii. 700 sanctum sidus adorat.
[5] A. iii. 406 sanctos ignis.
[6] A. ii. 686 sanctos restinguere fontibus ignis.
[7] A. viii. 131 sancta oracula divum.
[8] A. vii. 365 quid tua sancta fides? cf. sacrata iura (A. ii. 157), quoted in n. 7, p. 76.
[9] A. iv. 576 sancte deorum, quisquis es.
[10] A. iii. 543   tum numina sancta precamur
          Palladis armisonae.
[11] A. viii. 382 sanctum mihi numen.
[12] A. v. 80 sancte parens. See p. 293.
[13] A. vi. 65 o sanctissima vates.

Evander calls his wife 'most holy',[1] though there is again
the sense of the divinity of the dead, it probably has more
of the idea of character, 'chaste, pure'. So again, when
Turnus at his death claims that he is going to the lower
world as a *sancta anima*,[2] Servius is probably right in interpreting it as *incorrupta* and Warde Fowler adds the illu-
minating note 'he goes to the shades with a conscience
clear of guilt or of *impietas*'. Twice[3] in a characteristically
Roman sense Virgil uses the word of the senate, the fathers
consecrated to the service of the State. But in none of these
derivative senses is the religious implication lost.

Akin to the words just discussed is *sollemnis*. Its original
use is doubtless for a religious rite which recurs every year;
then for any object made sacred by such a rite, *anniversario
sacrificio religiosus*, as Servius[4] describes it; then more loosely
it approximates to a general meaning of 'sacred'. Virgil is
scrupulous in his use and very conscious of the idea of
annual recurrence. He emphasizes this idea when Aeneas
is founding the funeral games for his father: 'were I caught
in the uttermost parts of the earth,' Aeneas says, 'yet I
would perform my annual vows and this solemn pomp in
due order';[5] *sollemnis pompas* is underlined, as it were, by
annua vota. The expression *sollemnis pompas* occurs also in
the *Georgics*[6] of the annual festival of Bacchus. So the
worship of Hercules at the Ara Maxima is described as
'a solemn honour',[7] and Ascanius vows to Iuppiter that he

---

[1] A. xi. 158 o sanctissima coniunx.
[2] A. xii. 648 sancta ad vos anima atque istius nescia culpae.
[3] G. ii. 473 sanctique patres; A. i. 426 sanctumque senatum (in the latter
case of the senate of Carthage).
[4] Serv. *ad. Aen.* ii. 202.
[5] A. v. 53 annua vota tamen sollemnisque ordine pompas
              exsequerer.
[6] G. iii. 22   iam nunc sollemnis ducere pompas
                    ad delubra iuvat.
[7] A. viii. 102 forte die sollemnem illo rex Arcas honorem . . . ferebat.

will bring 'solemn gifts' to his temple,[1] speaking clearly of a recurrent ceremonial. The plural *sollemnia* is used substantivally of such an annual festival: Evander speaks of the Hercules-cult as 'this annual rite',[2] and Aeneas promises the dead Palinurus that the neighbours will 'send their annual offering' to his tomb.[3] In the more extended sense we find it used of the games at Anchises' tomb,[4] established for annual repetition, of the altar of Neptune at Troy, consecrated, as Servius points out, by an annual offering,[5] and of the offering of Andromache at the tomb of Hector.[6] Lastly, in a context where the meaning can hardly be more than 'sacred' or 'solemn', Aeneas promises that, if he wins in the single combat with Turnus, Latinus shall be his father-in-law and share the *sollemne imperium*.[7] In this instance alone does Virgil seem to have deserted the original sense of the word.

In all this group of words Virgil is on the whole scrupulously observant of their old religious sense, and as a rule only departs from it with a natural amplification. The frequency of their occurrence shows his fondness for the ideas which they convey.

(iv) *'Pius', 'pietas', 'piare', 'piaculum'*.

The words *pius* and *pietas* play a large part in the thought of the *Aeneid*—indeed, Warde Fowler[8] says that '*pietas* is Virgil's word for religion'—and with them are associated, though in a less degree and a more technical sense, the verb *piare* and the substantive *piaculum*. The root

---

[1] A. ix. 626 ipse tibi ad tua templa feram sollemnia dona.
[2] A. viii. 185 haec sollemnia.
[3] A. vi. 380 et statuent tumulum et tumulo sollemnia mittent.
[4] A. v. 605 dum variis tumulo referunt sollemnia ludis.
[5] A. ii. 202 sollemnis taurum ingentem mactabat ad aras.
[6] A. iii. 301 sollemnis . . . dapes.
[7] A. xii. 192 socer arma Latinus habeto, | imperium sollemne socer
[8] *R.E.*, p. 412.

idea of *pius* and *pietas* seems to be harmony or conformity with the will of the gods, or, as the established State-religion put it, conformity to the *ius divinum*.[1] On its formal side then it implied the due performance of the rites and ceremonies required by the worship of the gods; any lapse in such performance must be atoned for (*piare*) by the special offering of a *piaculum*, the effect of which was to bring the man back again into a state of *pietas*. But from the outset—and certainly in Virgil's use—it is more than this, for it implies not only right action but also a right relation of man to god; it has a moral and even spiritual implication as well as a formal content. From this seem to spring three conclusions. Firstly, the gods were always thought of by the Romans as being members of the individual household and citizens of the State.[2] The *pietas*, then, which is the expression of man's relation to the gods, extends itself to the other members of these groups: it is part of *pietas* to the gods to be in the right relation and to act aright towards the members of your own family and towards your State; *pietas* on its human side, which nevertheless has always the divine sanction behind it, is paternal and filial affection at home and loyalty or patriotism in public life. Secondly, as the association between religion and morality developed, the idea of the breach of *pietas* broadened from a technical flaw in ritual to include wrong-doing of other kinds, and the 'expiation' required (*piaculum*) developed from a formal offering to a reparation or purification, sometimes in this life, or, as the idea of punishment after death became accepted, in a future world; there was an approximation to the idea of 'sin' and 'atonement'. Lastly, as the divine beings were members of the communities, so the idea grew that they too had

---

[1] See Warde Fowler, *R.E.*, p. 462.
[2] Cic. *de Leg.* i. 7. 23.

their *pietas* to fulfil towards men, and men in trouble might appeal to them for it; in this sense *pietas* comes near to the conception of 'divine pity'.

If this be an approximately true account of the various meanings of *pius* and its cognates, we can find in Virgil ample illustration of its use in all these senses. The most frequent use is in the root sense of man's relation to the gods. It is the special epithet of the prophet, who has of necessity an immediate and direct relation to a god: so it is used (if *piorum* be the right reading as against *priorum*) in connexion with the prophecies which terrified Dido,[1] and of the 'pious prophets, who spoke words worthy of Phoebus',[2] who have their special abode in the fields of the blessed in the lower world. They, indeed, have a double claim to the epithet, for another of its particular usages is for the 'holy' dead, those who have died after a life of *pietas* on earth; thus Anchises, appearing in a vision to Aeneas, tells him that he now dwells among the 'lovely congregations of the pious in Elysium',[3] and Vulcan on the shield of Aeneas in the picture of the lower world gives the 'pious' their separate place, with Cato as their ruler.[4] But its more general use is of 'piety' in this life: Aeneas prays that Dido may be rewarded by 'any gods who have care for the pious'[5] (here the human relationship of Dido to the Trojans may be included); Anchises prays to the gods to 'preserve the pious' from the Harpies;[6] and in the description of the plague in the third book of the *Georgics* comes the

[1] A. iv. 464 vatum praedicta piorum (*or* priorum).
[2] A. vi. 662 quique pii vates et Phoebo digna locuti.
[3] A. v. 734   amoena piorum
    concilia Elysiumque colo.
[4] A. viii. 670 secretosque pios, his dantem iura Catonem.
[5] A. i. 603 di tibi, si qua pios respectant numina, . . . praemia digna ferant.
[6] A. iii. 265   di talem avertite casum
    et placidi servate pios.

exclamation 'may the gods grant a better fate to the pious'.[1] In this sense the substantive *pietas* is also frequent; 'is this', Venus cries to Iuppiter, 'the due reward for piety?'[2] (the piety of her Trojans), and later in the poem complains that 'no piety can assuage the wrath of Iuno'.[3] Panthus in the sack of Troy was not saved by his 'piety' or by the wreath of Apollo[4] (note again the connexion with service of the gods); Anchises prays Iuppiter to send an omen to tell him whether to leave Troy or not, 'if by our piety we deserve it'.[5] A specially interesting example occurs in Arruns' appeal to Apollo of Soracte,[6] where he refers to the rustic rite in which the farmers run through the midst of the burning fire, 'trusting in piety'; here there is the implication of the god's fulfilment of his relation to his worshippers, as well as of their due performance of what they owe him.

There is, I believe, only one instance in Virgil in which it can be definitely said that *pius*, the adjective, expresses human relation between man and man and nothing more; Nisus was 'renowned for his pious affection for the boy' Euryalus.[7] On the other hand, it is a frequent use of the substantive *pietas*. Iulus on hearing of the resolve of Nisus and Euryalus is struck at heart by the thought of his father's 'love' for him,[8] and in the same phrase Aeneas gazing on the dying Lausus is reminded of Anchises' 'love'

[1] G. iii. 513 di meliora piis.

[2] A. i. 253 hic pietatis honos?

[3] A. v. 781 Iunonis gravis ira . . . quam nec longa dies pietas nec mitigat ulla.

[4] A. ii. 429   nec te tua plurima, Panthu,
                labentem pietas nec Apollinis infula texit.

[5] A. ii. 690   si pietate meremur,
                da deinde augurium, pater.

[6] A. xi. 787   medium freti pietate per ignem
                cultores multa premimus vestigia pruna.

[7] A. v. 295 insignis . . . Nisus amore pio pueri.

[8] A. ix. 294 atque animum patriae strinxit pietatis imago.

for himself[1]—in these instances 'love' seems the only equivalent of *pietas*. So Anchises is addressed by Helenus as 'happy in the love of thy son',[2] and greeting Aeneas in the lower world he asks, 'has thy love proved victorious over this hard journey?'[3] Aeneas just before he kills Lausus cries to him, 'thy love for thy father is betraying thee'.[4] A puzzling instance occurs where Euryalus' mother, hearing of her son's death, rushes out and cries to the Rutulians, 'slay me, if ye have any *pietas*'.[5] It is hard to decide here whether she means 'if you have *pietas* in your own families and so can understand a mother's love' or whether she means 'if you have *pietas* for me', almost in the sense of 'pity'. Perhaps it is quite general, 'if you have any natural feelings'.

In many instances *pius* undoubtedly embraces both ideas of piety towards the gods and affection to family or friends or State; it expresses in fact the full conception of the word in Latin. This is supremely the case in the famous and oft-recurring *pius Aeneas*.[6] But the epithet gains force as the poem proceeds, as in fact the 'piety' of Aeneas develops and broadens.[7] He was from the first meticulous in the performance of his duties to the gods in sacrifice and prayer, and showed the due family *pietas* in his relation both to his father and to his son. But gradually, as his destiny unfolds itself to him, he gains a new and far wider

---

[1] A. x. 824 et mentem patriae subiit pietatis imago.
[2] A. iii. 480   o felix nati pietate.
[3] A. vi. 687   tuaque exspectata parenti
                vicit iter durum pietas?
[4] A. x. 812 fallit te incautum pietas tua.
[5] A. ix. 493 figite me, si qua est pietas. A curious and half-humorous use of *pietas* occurs in *Culex* 225, where the ghost of the gnat appearing to the shepherd and reminding him of his 'deed of kindness', exclaims, 'praemia sunt pietatis ubi, pietatis honores?'
[6] A. i. 220, 378, &c.
[7] See Warde Fowler, *R.E.*, pp. 412 ff.

conception of the will of the gods and his own part in its fulfilment, and at the same time his human *pietas* reaches out from his own family and following to loyalty to the great State which it is his function to found. It is this development, as Warde Fowler has so well pointed out, which constitutes the religious 'plot' of the whole *Aeneid*. Other phrases are used of Aeneas; he is 'famed for his piety',[1] and, as compared with Hector, 'greater in piety'.[2] Nor is it only of Aeneas that *pius* and *pietas* are used in this broad sense: the Trojans in general are 'pious' or 'a pious race',[3] and their offspring, the Romans, will surpass men and gods in their piety.[4] Aeneas Silvius, Aeneas' descendant, is to be 'notable alike in piety or arms',[5] and 'piety' is the characteristic of the young Marcellus;[6] the man in the famous simile who quells the tumult is 'noble in piety and good deeds'.[7] In none of these instances is there any reason to limit the application to the divine or to the human side; they are both included in the perfect Roman character, which Virgil is always wishing to attribute to Aeneas.

The gods, too, can show 'piety'. In one instance[8] the idea is based on the analogy of human character, for Apollo is *pius* because for his mother's sake he chains down the floating Delos. But in others we meet the appeal of men to the 'piety' of the gods to show the affection and devotion which they require. Dido hopes 'if the pious

---

[1] A. vi. 403 Troius Aeneas, pietate insignis et armis; A. i. 10 insignem pietate virum.

[2] A. xi. 292 hic pietate prior.

[3] A. i. 526 parce pio generi; A. vii. 21 pii . . . Troes.

[4] A. xii. 839 supra homines, supra ire deos pietate videbis.

[5] A. vi. 769   pariter pietate vel armis
             egregius

[6] A. vi. 878 heu pietas, heu prisca fides.

[7] A. i. 151 pietate gravem ac meritis.

[8] A. iii. 73 tellus . . . quam pius Arquitenens . . . errantem Mycono e celsa Gyaroque revinxit.

powers avail aught, that Aeneas may be punished for his treachery',[1] Aeneas prays to Iuppiter to spare his fleet 'if thy ancient piety looks upon the sufferings of men',[2] and Priam prays for vengeance on Pyrrhus 'if heaven has any piety'.[3] Here the idea clearly is that there is something which the gods owe to men in return for their piety. The dictionaries give 'justice' as the meaning in such passages; it is surely not that, but rather the divine complement, as it were, of human piety, and if there is any modern word which expresses the meaning, it is rather the derivative 'pity'.

Piare and *piaculum* go back to the original idea of making an expiatory offering for a flaw in ritual, but they have widened out into the more general sense of atonement for sins. Sinon expresses the fear that the Greeks will wreak vengeance for his escape on his father and children, 'and will atone for this sin by their death',[4] and tells the Trojans that the Greeks made the Trojan horse as an offering to Pallas for the stolen Palladium, 'that it might atone for that dark crime'.[5] The sins to be atoned here are moral and not merely technical. In a slightly different sense the Sibyl assures the shade of Palinurus that the neighbours will 'purify his bones'[6] from their unburied taint by the gift of a tomb and offerings. *Piacula* occurs twice[7] in the concrete sense of offerings for expiation or purification, those that Dido bids her sister to bring and those that the Sibyl instructs Aeneas to offer to the underworld gods.

[1] A. iv. 382 si quid pia numina possunt.
[2] A. v. 688 si quid pietas antiqua labores | respicit humanos.
[3] A. ii. 536 si qua est caelo pietas.
[4] A. ii. 140 culpam hanc miser rum morte piabunt.
[5] A. ii. 183 hanc pro Palladio moniti, pro numine laeso
        effigiem statuere, nefas quae triste piaret.
[6] A. vi. 378 nam tua finitimi . . . ossa piabunt.
[7] A. iv. 636 pecudes secum et monstrata piacula ducat; A. vi. 153 duc nigras pecudes; ea prima piacula sunto.

There remains the very difficult and much disputed passage in the description of the judgement of Rhadamanthus.[1] It is usually said that *piacula* here is used in the derived sense of 'an act which requires expiation' and that *commissa* means 'committed', as it is used, for instance, with *scelus*: the meaning is then that Rhadamanthus compels each in turn to confess the crimes committed in the upper world which he has postponed till death, that is, atonement for which he has postponed. This is very awkward, and it appears to me to be much more natural to take *piacula* in its normal sense of the act of atonement and *commissa* to mean 'incurred', as *poenam committere* occurs in Cicero:[2] 'the atonements for sins in the upper world which each man has postponed till death', he made no reparation in life and will now be punished for it.

In all these examples of *pius* and its cognates Virgil is following very closely the traditional meanings of the word and its natural extensions. There remain a few rather looser uses of the adjective, which must not be passed over. In several of these it is applied very naturally to parts of a *pius* person, to the hands of Aeneas[3] and the hands of Dido,[4] to the lips of Deiphobus,[5] and to the blood of Turnus;[6] there is really no looseness here, for in each case the action is one in which piety or impiety would be involved. Less close are two cases where the application is to objects used in ritual—not necessarily the ritual of atonement. The one is to the sacred fillet round the head

[1] A. vi. 566 Gnosius haec Rhadamanthus habet durissima regna,
    castigatque auditque dolos subigitque fateri,
    quae quis apud superos furto laetatus inani,
    distulit in seram commissa piacula mortem.
[2] Cic. *Verr.* II. iii. 12. 30 poenam octupli sine ulla dubitatione commissam.
[3] A. iii. 42 parce pias scelerare manus.
[4] A. iv. 517 ipsa mola manibusque piis altaria iuxta.
[5] A. vi. 530 pio si poenas ore reposco.
[6] A. x. 617 nunc pereat Teucrisque pio det sanguine poenas.

of a ministrant,[1] the other to the sacred meal of spelt used in the sacrifice[2]—a usage found also in Horace, and almost amounting to a constant epithet. *Pius* is here not far from *sacer* or *sanctus*.

The examination of Virgil's use of these characteristic words and ideas of the old religion shows that he is scrupulous in his adherence to the old meanings. Where he breaks away from these, it is often, as in the use of *numen* of the anthropomorphic deities or of *piaculum* of a moral 'sin', to adopt an extension sanctioned and well understood in his day; very occasionally there is that little extra strain of meaning which Virgil was apt in the subtlety of his thought to place on any word, which is rather an adjustment to a new context than an indication of a change of thought. But whereas in the case of the old deities it appeared that Virgil showed an affectionate antiquarian interest rather than any personal belief, it may be said that these old words meant more to him; in them he was able to express his sense of a supernatural presence without acknowledging the existence of individual deities. Especially in the idea of *pietas*, the ready obedience to the will of heaven, which was also the bond of the common life in the family and the State, there lies a conception which was fundamental to his outlook on the world, an entirely religious feeling, which Virgil recognized as a central motive in human and particularly in Roman life.

[1] A. iv. 637 tuque ipsa pia tege tempora vitta.
[2] A. v. 745 farre pio et plena supplex veneratur acerra; cf. Hor. *Od.* iii. 23. 20 farre pio et saliente mica.

IV

THE STATE-CULT

THE old religion of the Italian farmers was transformed in two ways, by the establishment of the State-cult of Rome, and by the introduction, first through Etruria and then by direct contact, of Greek anthropomorphic ideas and methods of worship. The two influences worked together and led to a more conventional and remote form of religion in which the individual had a far smaller part to play. The State-cult took over the gods of the household and the fields and established their official worship as gods of the State; for most of them temples were built in accordance with Greek custom and special priests appointed to maintain their worship; the agricultural festivals were adapted and performed with as near an approach to rural conditions as could be effected in or near the city. Greek influence, working very early through Etruria, led to the erection of temples, and the making of statues representing the gods in anthropomorphic form; it also brought about the identification of many of the old Italian deities with Greek gods of more or less similar functions, and the consequent attachment to the Italian deities of the relationships and legends of their Greek counterparts. It was natural that this Greek conception of divinity should play a great part in the works of the Roman poets, which were so largely based on Greek models and found in Greek myth and legend so ample a material. Virgil was of course affected by both these influences; indeed, though it has been seen that he had a genuine understanding of the old Italian religion and a deep affection for its manifestations, his normal conception of a deity is that of an anthropomorphic State-god. And, just as in the life of the Romans the existence of the State-cult tended to make religion less real to the individual, except in his own household worship, so Virgil's treatment of the Graeco-Roman gods is more conventional and less sympathetic than that of the genuine Italian deities and their cult; there is less of the devoted antiquarianism which distinguishes his attitude to the older religion, and, with the exception of the three great deities of the *Aeneid*, Iuppiter, Iuno, and Venus, who symbolized much of Virgil's ultimate belief in the government of the world, the Graeco-Roman gods are pale figures, introduced as occasion demands, in the traditional Greek contexts. Yet his treatment of them is always of interest as an indication of the thought of his time.

In this chapter we must consider the effects of the State-religion, which, as reflected in Virgil's poems, are seen in the main in the position of the household gods in the State, and in certain developments in cult, chiefly in matters of military ceremonial. We may take first, in some detail, Virgil's treatment of the sacred gods of the household.

(i) *The State Deities*

1. *Ianus*, who in Virgil, as elsewhere, has little recorded of his cult in the household, becomes a figure of great importance in the State as the deity of the famous Ianus Geminus, the double gateway, which, in accordance with what the Augustans believed to be an immemorial tradition, had its gates opened in time of war and closed in peace. The tradition had come into prominence through Octavian's boast[1] that in his day the gates had been closed for the third time in the history of the city. Virgil[2] has a fine description of the opening of the gates.

---

[1] See Liv. i. 19. 3.
[2] A. vii. 607 sunt geminae belli portae (sic nomine dicunt)
religione sacrae et saevi formidine Martis;

'Twin gateways of war there are (so they call them by name) hallowed by divine awe and the dread of savage Mars; a hundred brazen bolts and the lasting bars of brass close the gates, and Ianus the guardian ever sits upon the threshold. These gates, when the fathers have given a firm vote for war, the consul himself, adorned with the robe of Quirinus and the Gabine cincture, unlocks the groaning threshold, and himself summons battles; then all the warrior youths follow his lead, and brazen trumpets cry a braying assent.'

Almost equally impressive is the position which Ianus holds in Latinus' oath before the single combat: 'the same oath, I swear, Aeneas, by earth and sea and stars, and the twin offspring of Latona, and Ianus of the double face, and the power of the gods below and the precincts of cruel Dis.'[1] It is not easy to say here whether this is the Ianus of the household or the Ianus of the State, but his presence in the invocation is a reminder of the ancient habit that all prayers to a plurality of gods should begin with Ianus, as they end with Vesta. As one of the oldest of Italian deities Ianus is twice coupled with Saturnus. In the hall of Latinus' palace stood 'the old Saturn and the likeness of Ianus of the double face';[2] and Evander, when he shows Aeneas the site of the future Rome, points out the Ianicu-

> centum aerei claudunt vectes aeternaque ferri
> robora, nec custos absistit limine Ianus:
> has, ubi certa sedet patribus sententia pugnae,
> ipse Quirinali trabea cinctuque Gabino
> insignis reserat stridentia limina consul,
> ipse vocat pugnas; sequitur tum cetera pubes,
> aereaque adsensu conspirant cornua rauco.

Another reference to the 'Gates of War', though without mention of Ianus, is found in A. i. 293–6.

[1] A. xii. 197 haec eadem, Aenea, terram, mare, sidera, iuro,
Latonaeque genus duplex* Ianumque bifrontem,
vimque deum infernam et duri sacraria Ditis.

     * *sc.* Phoebus and Diana; does he here mean 'sun and moon'?

[2] A. vii. 180 Saturnusque senex Ianique bifrontis imago
vestibulo adstabant.

lum and the Capitol with the words: 'the one citadel Ianus founded, the other Saturn.'[1] In these instances Ianus seems to have suffered the same euhemeristic process which transformed Saturn into a divine king of Italy (see p. 40), but his high position among Italian deities is made clear, and the one characteristic ceremony at his oldest seat, the gate of Ianus Geminus, has its appropriate place in the poem.

2. The *Di Penates publici populi Romani*[2] were prominent in the State-cult, and it was by them and by Iuppiter that the magistrates took their oath on entering office. They were no doubt developed from the household Penates and in two points show a clear analogy. In the first place they were closely allied with Vesta: we do not hear of an independent temple of the Di Penates till 167 B.C., but they were supposed to have their abode in the temple of Vesta, where it was said that very ancient and sacred symbols of the Penates were preserved. Secondly, they always maintained their character of an undefined deity-group without special names; when a Roman asked who the Penates Publici were he doubtless thought of them as a group of the 'high gods' in whose care was the welfare of the State (e.g. Iuppiter, Iuno, and Minerva, the deities of the Capitol), and it was no doubt in this connexion that they were spoken of as the *di magni*. Later legend on this ground identified them with the 'great gods' of Samothrace, and after the growth of the Aeneas story, it was said that he brought the Penates of Troy with him to Italy.

To the State Penates, as such, there are two references in Virgil. In the second book of the *Georgics*, when he is contrasting with the quiet life of the countryman the fevered

---

[1] A. viii. 357 hanc Ianus pater, hanc Saturnus condidit arcem,
         Ianiculum huic, illi fuerat Saturnia nomen.
[2] See Wissowa, *R.K.*², p. 164.

existence of the town, he speaks of the traitor who 'seeks to bring ruin on the city and its sorrowing Penates';[1] the conspirator who, like Catiline, attacks his own State, assaults also its high gods. More definite is the picture of Augustus at the battle of Actium 'leading the Italians to battle, with the fathers and the people, the Penates and the great gods';[2] the *di magni* here are in effect a synonym for the Penates and the conception is exactly that of the *Penates publici populi Romani*.

But in the vast majority of instances Virgil is, as is natural, occupied with the story of the bringing of the Penates of Troy to Italy by Aeneas. He tells in the first place of the Penates in Troy before its capture. In a passage already quoted[3] he describes their altar in Priam's palace overshadowed by an ancient laurel-tree, and Achaemenides, the survivor of Ulysses' men in the home of the Cyclops confesses, in a phrase strongly reminiscent of that quoted from the *Georgics*, 'that he had attacked in war the Penates of Ilium'.[4] In the second Book there is the story of their removal by Anchises and Aeneas: Hector first warns Aeneas in a vision: 'Her sacred symbols and her Penates Troy entrusts to thee; take them as comrades of thy destiny and seek a city for them';[5] as they start to leave, Aeneas bids his father, who, as long as he lives, is the true *paterfamilias*, to 'take in his hand the sacred symbols and the Penates of our fathers',[6] and later, when he returns to seek for the lost Creusa, he 'commends Ascanius and his father Anchises and the Trojan Penates to his comrades

---

[1] G. ii. 505 hic petit excidiis urbem miserosque Penatis.
[2] A. viii. 678 hinc Augustus agens Italos in proelia Caesar
            cum patribus populoque Penatibus et magnis dis.
[3] A. ii. 512; see p. 32, n. 1.
[4] A. iii. 603 bello Iliacos fateor petiisse Penatis.
[5] A. ii. 293 sacra suosque tibi commendat Troia Penatis;
            hos cape fatorum comites, his moenia quaere.
[6] A. ii. 717 tu, genitor, cape sacra manu patriosque Penatis.

and hides them in a winding valley'.[1] So Iris-Beroe later appeals to 'our fatherland and the Penates wrested in vain from the enemy's hand'.[2] Throughout the voyage the Penates are Aeneas' constant care. 'As an exile I am borne to the deep sea', Aeneas says in describing its start, 'with my comrades and my son, with the Penates and the great gods'[3]—once again this solemn combination. As he is journeying on the ocean at night he has the vision of the 'sacred images of the gods and the Phrygian Penates',[4] who cheer him in a fit of despondency and promise that, as they have followed him, 'so we will raise to the stars your descendants that are to be and grant empire to your city'; this is perhaps the most explicit identification of the Penates of Troy with those of Rome. As the Trojans are approaching Italy from Sicily, Iuno in her appeal to Aeolus to raise a storm, tells him that 'a race hostile to me is traversing the Tuscan sea, carrying to Italy Ilium and its conquered Penates';[5] and Aeneas, revealing himself to Dido, exclaims, 'I am pious Aeneas, who bear with me in my fleet the Penates wrested from the enemy's hands.'[6] Even after the final landing in Italy the household gods are still Aeneas' first thought. When the 'eating of the tables' has assured him that the goal is reached, his first

[1] A. ii. 747 Ascanium Anchisenque patrem Teucrosque Penatis
    commendo sociis et curva valle recondo.
[2] A. v. 632 o patria et rapti nequiquam ex hoste Penates.
[3] A. iii. 11   feror exsul in altum
    cum sociis natoque Penatibus et magnis dis.
[4] A. iii. 148 effigies sacrae divum Phrygiique Penates,
       quos mecum ab Troia mediisque ex ignibus urbis
       extuleram, visi ante oculos adstare iacentis
       in somnis. . . .
    158 idem venturos tollemus in astra nepotes
       imperiumque urbi dabimus.
[5] A. i. 67 gens inimica mihi Tyrrhenum navigat aequor
    Ilium in Italiam portans victosque Penatis.
[6] A. i. 378 sum pius Aeneas, raptos qui ex hoste Penatis
    classe veho mecum.

words are a greeting to 'the land due to me by fate' and to 'the faithful Penates of Troy';[1] again the link is established. Later, envoys are sent to Diomedes 'to seek his aid and to tell him that Aeneas has reached Italy in his fleet and is bringing the conquered Penates'.[2] If it was no small part of Virgil's task to connect Rome and Troy, the essential point in that connexion was to establish the religious continuity of the two cities through the imported Penates.

When it is remembered that the Penates are most undoubtedly genuine Italian spirits of the household, the story and the emphasis Virgil lays on it seem strange. It arose in Rome, no doubt, as part of the Aeneas legend, but it is perhaps worth while considering certain beliefs and practices which made the introduction of such a story possible without the violation of accepted religious ideas. In the first place, it may be recalled that it was essential to the Roman conception of religious life that a man migrating to another city should take his *sacra* with him: Aeneas was doing what any Roman changing his home would do. Secondly, as has been already noticed (p. 31), Virgil seems almost at pains to emphasize the idea that every household in every land should have its own Penates. To the passages previously quoted two may be added which illustrate the idea of national Penates other than those of Rome. Ilioneus assures Dido that the Trojans 'have not come to ravage with the sword the Penates of Africa',[3] and in a more striking phrase Aeneas tells how the land of Lycurgus in Thrace had an 'ancient bond of friendship

---

[1] A. vii. 120 continuo 'salve fatis mihi debita tellus,
     vosque' ait 'o fidi Troiae salvete Penates'.
[2] A. viii. 10 qui petat auxilium et Latio consistere Teucros,
     advectum Aenean classi victosque Penatis
     inferre . . . edoceat.
[3] A. i. 527 non nos aut ferro Libycos populare Penatis
     venimus.

with Troy and allied Penates';[1] the human alliance was cemented by that of the gods of the two peoples. This is a new step to the identification of the Penates of two cities or to their migration from one to the other. Finally—and this brings the story near home—it was generally believed in Republican times that the Penates of Rome came from Lavinium and Alba,[2] the cities from which old Roman legend believed that Rome had been founded. When the later legend had attributed the foundation of these cities to Aeneas and his descendants, the extension of the Roman story was not a large one. Thus, however strange the idea of the origin of the Penates of Rome in Troy may seem to us, it would not, probably, have appeared so odd or unorthodox to a Roman. Virgil at least betrays no hesitation as to its veracity. And in his narration of this State-legend there are touches now and then of the affection which surrounded the Penates of the household-cult.

3. *Vesta*, who has already (p. 31) been mentioned as the household deity of the hearth, had in the State-cult her famous temple at the end of the Forum, where the sacred fire of the State was tended by the vestal virgins, and all through the history of Roman religion she remained free from Greek contamination and was never even represented by a sensuous image. She is closely associated with the Penates and has a very special position in the State-cult, which Virgil acknowledges. In the peroration of the first book of the *Georgics* she is named with Romulus alone among all the *di indigetes*,[3] and this combination of Vesta

[1] A. iii. 15 hospitium antiquum Troiae sociique Penates.
[2] Varro, *L.L.* v. 144 oppidum, quod primum conditum in Latio stirpis Romanae, Lavinium; nam ibi di Penates nostri; Plut. *Coriol.* 29 Λαουίνιον ... ὅπου καὶ θεῶν ἱερὰ ᾿Ρωμαίοις πατρῴων ἀπέκειτο, καὶ τοῦ γένους ἦσαν αὐτοῖς ἀρχαὶ διὰ τὸ πρώτην πόλιν ἐκείνην κτίσαι τὸν Αἰνείαν; and for a general discussion of the legend see Dion. Hal. i. 67.
[3] G. i. 498 di patrii, Indigetes, et Romule Vestaque mater.

and Quirinus occurs again on another equally solemn occasion, when Iuppiter promises Venus that 'hoary Honour and Vesta, Quirinus with his brother Remus shall give the laws'.[1] It is a singular combination and it is not easy to find the reason for it. Legend, of course, supplied a link in that Rhea Silvia, Romulus' mother, was a Vestal virgin, but possibly Virgil, in combining a deified hero with one of the great gods, wished to suggest Augustus.

The more usual coupling, even in State contexts, is with the other household gods, the Lar and the Penates. Thus Aeneas at the tomb of Anchises venerates 'the Lar of Pergamum and the shrine of hoary Vesta';[2] though it is the household worship which Virgil is describing, the characteristic epithet of the Lar shows that he has the Trojano-Roman State-gods in view. With a fuller combination, Ascanius swears to Nisus and Euryalus 'by the great Penates and the Lar of Assaracus and the shrine of hoary Venus';[3] here are all the household deities. Both these passages imply a Vesta-cult in Troy, and this is explicit, when Aeneas, during the sack, finds Helen sitting in sanctuary on the threshold of Vesta's temple.[4]

Vesta's divinity, too, like that of the Penates, had its 'faded' aspect and her name is occasionally used as a synonym for 'fire' or 'the hearth'. In the fourth book of the *Georgics*, Cyrene, Aristaeus' mother, pouring libation to Oceanus, 'thrice bathes blazing Vesta with liquid nectar',[5]

---

[1] A. i. 292 cana Fides et Vesta, Remo cum fratre Quirinus
       iura dabunt.
[2] A. v. 744 Pergameumque Larem et canae penetralia Vestae
       farre pio et plena supplex veneratur acerra.
[3] A. ix. 258   per magnos, Nise, Penatis
       Assaracique larem et canae penetralia Vestae | obtestor.
[4] A. ii. 567   limina Vestae
       servantem et tacitam secreta in sede latentem
       Tyndarida aspicio.
[5] G. iv. 384 ter liquido ardentem perfundit nectare Vestam.

and Anchises, urging flight from Troy, 'bears out in his hands from the inmost shrine the fillets and mighty Vesta and the eternal fire';[1] here Vesta is the hearth (*focus*) containing the fire.

4. The *Lar*, who is mentioned with the other household gods in domestic worship, and has his 'faded' use in the sense of 'home' (see p. 33), is definitely attached to Troy in the two passages quoted above,[2] and so takes his place with the State-gods. This again corresponds to Roman usage which recognized the Lares Praestites of the State, two gods, identified in Graeco-Roman days with the Dioscuri and represented with their appearance and attributes.

5. Here may be mentioned certain abstract deities, known in the State-cult and referred to by Virgil. The theory usually held about their origin is that they were offshoots of State-gods through their cult-titles. Thus *Fides*,[3] 'Faith' or 'Honour', whom Virgil couples with Vesta as a lawgiver, is supposed to be an offshoot of Iuppiter, in his capacity of Deus Fidius. Similarly, *Victoria* is regarded as an offshoot of Mars Victor; she is twice mentioned by Virgil; 'Victory', cries Turnus, 'has not so fled in hate from my hands that I would refuse to dare anything for so great a hope',[4] and Aeneas promises an equal share in the kingdom to the Latins 'if Victory shall have granted to us success in the fight'.[5] *Pax*, a deity specially dear to Augustus, appears even in the *Georgics*[6] as the lover of the olive, whose branch was the symbol of peace. There are many other personifications in Virgil, such as Furor,

[1] A. ii. 296 sic ait et manibus vittas Vestamque potentem
        aeternumque adytis effert penetralibus ignem.
[2] A. v. 744; A. ix. 258; see p. 96, nn. 2 and 3.
[3] A. i. 292; see p. 96, n. 1.
[4] A. xi. 436 non adeo has exosa manus Victoria fugit
        ut tanta quicquam pro spe temptare recusem.
[5] A. xii. 187 sin nostrum adnuerit nobis Victoria Martem.
[6] G. ii. 425 hoc pinguem et placitam Paci nutritor olivam.

Discordia, &c., belonging to war, natural powers such as Hiems and the Tempestates, or Greek deities like Somnus (ὕπνος) and Fama (φήμη), but they are poetical and had no place in the State-cult.

(ii) *Worship in the State-cult*

The worship of the State-cult at Rome did not differ in essentials from the old Italian worship of the fields, and apart from the explicit descriptions of the Cerealia[1] and the worship of Hercules at the Ara Maxima,[2] Virgil does not make special reference to religious ceremonials of the State. His usual descriptions of worship in the *Aeneid* are of what might be called the 'epic rites', based on the practices of the old Italian ritual, sometimes elaborated and magnified and sometimes, as has been noticed, contaminated with features drawn from Greek ritual. Nor does he make much use of the official priesthoods of the State-cult; there is never a mention of a *flamen* or a *pontifex*, though *augur* is used of the Italian king Rhamnes,[3] slain by Nisus, of the Latin seer Tolumnius,[4] and in an extended sense of Apollo.[5] Even the most general term for 'priest', *sacerdos*, occurs comparatively rarely. Laocoon is the chosen priest of Neptune,[6] and the 'holy priests'[7] have their place in Elysium. Rhea Silvia, the Vestal virgin, is described as 'the priestess queen',[8] a priestess aids Dido in the preparation of her pyre,[9] and the Sibyl is the priestess of Phoebus and Trivia.[10]

---

[1] G. i. 338–50; see p. 54.   [2] A. viii. 102–6, 175–83, 280–8; see p. 55.
[3] A. ix. 327 rex idem et regi Turno gratissimus augur.
[4] A. xii. 258 Tolumnius augur.   [5] A. iv. 376 augur Apollo.
[6] A. ii. 201 Laocoon, ductus Neptuno sorte sacerdos.
[7] A. vi. 661 quique sacerdotes casti, dum vita manebat.
[8] A. i. 273 regina sacerdos.
[9] A. iv. 509   crinis effusa sacerdos
                    ter centum tonat ore deos.
[10] A. vi. 35 Phoebi Triviaeque sacerdos; cf. above, n. 6.

But there are, especially in the second half of the *Aeneid*, certain references to military religious ceremonials in connexion with the making of treaties, the triumph, and the dedication of trophies, which belong essentially to the State-cult, and these must not be passed over.

The religious ceremony of the making of a treaty is described at length in the twelfth book of the *Aeneid*,[1] where an agreement is made for the single combat of Aeneas and Turnus. In many details Virgil follows closely the proceedings of the fetials and the pater patratus,[2] but allows himself some licence. The ground is first prepared for the combat and 'in the midst they placed the hearths and altars of turf for their common gods, while others brought water and fire, clad in the sacred garment (*limus*) with their temples bound with vervain'.[3] This very carefully follows tradition; the *focus* is the portable hearth for the sacred fire, the altars, like all early altars in Italy, are made of piled turf (*caespes*), and are erected to the gods known to both peoples; the water is for purification and the fire for the sacrifice, and the officiating priests are clad, like the fetials, in the sacred *limus* and wear wreaths of vervain, the sacred herbs (*sagmina*) always plucked in historical times from the Capitol.[4] The kings advance on either side, Latinus and Turnus riding from the city, Aeneas and Ascanius walking from the camp. Then 'the priest in robes unstained brought the offspring of a bristly pig and an unshorn sheep, and led the animals to the blazing altars. The others turning their eyes to the rising sun sprinkle

[1] A. xii. 116 ff.
[2] See Liv. i. 24. 4–9.
[3] A. xii. 118 in medioque focos et dis communibus aras
    gramineas. alii fontemque ignemque ferebant,
    velati limo et verbena tempora vincti. Cf. A. viii. 639–641.
[4] Liv. i. 24. 4 iubente rege, 'sagmina' inquit, 'te, rex, posco'. rex ait:
'pura tollito.' fetialis ex arce graminis herbam puram attulit.

salted meal with their hands and touch the topmost temples of the beasts with their swords and pour libation on the altar from the sacred platters.'[1] Here there is some divergence from tradition; the pig was the regular animal sacrificed in the making of a treaty, but the custom was for the fetial to strike it with a stone, saying, 'So may Iuppiter strike us, if we break our promise.' Virgil includes the pig, but wishes to suggest a sacrifice as well as the treaty rites, and so adds the sheep and the *mola salsa* and the procedure of a *sacrificium*. Servius notes that the use of a sheep in a treaty ceremony was *Graeco more*. Aeneas and Latinus then take their oaths, touching the altars and swearing each most solemnly by many gods, then the consecrated victims are slain over the flames: 'they tear the entrails from them while yet they live and pile the altars with the loaded dishes.'[2] Strictly the ceremony of treaty-making did not involve a sacrifice or a feast; Virgil has added these to give a deeper solemnity to the whole procedure.

The ceremony of hanging the spoils of a conquered foe on a tree and dedicating them to a god, as the *spolia opima* were dedicated on the oak of Iuppiter Feretrius on the Capitol, is described at length at the beginning of the eleventh Book after Aeneas' victory over Mezentius. 'At early dawn Aeneas as victor paid his vows to the gods. On a mound he set up a huge oak, lopping its boughs all round, and hung on it the shining armour, the spoils of the chief

[1] A. xii. 169   puraque in veste sacerdos
saetigeri fetum suis intonsamque bidentem
attulit admovitque pecus flagrantibus aris.
illi ad surgentem conversi lumina solem
dant fruges manibus salsas et tempora ferro
summa notant pecudum, paterisque altaria libant.

[2] A. xii. 213   tum rite sacratas
in flammam iugulant pecudes et viscera vivis
eripiunt, cumulantque oneratis lancibus aras.

Mezentius, a trophy in thine honour, great lord of war.'[1] The procedure is fully correct, but we may notice that the dedication is to Mars and not, as was usual at Rome, to Iuppiter. So Serestus carries back armour won by Aeneas as a trophy to Gradivus;[2] Mezentius, the atheist, whose god is his weapon and his right arm, vows to dress his dead son, Lausus, in Aeneas' armour and dedicate him as a trophy;[3] to honour the dead Pallas, the Trojans 'bring great trophies of those whom Aeneas' arm gave over to death'.[4] There are other passages in the *Aeneid*[5] where the idea is employed in a rather looser sense, and it is applied in the *Georgics*[6] to the triumphs of Augustus in East and West. The triumph of the victorious general is given its full value as a religious ceremony in the passage in the second book of the *Georgics* where Virgil is speaking of the animals raised on the Italian farms: 'the white flocks, Clitumnus, and the bull, greatest of victims, often washed in thy sacred stream, have led Roman triumphs to the temples of the gods';[7] the victims for the sacrifice on the Capitol pass in the triumphal procession. Again, on the shield of Aeneas, the epitome of Roman history—

[1] A. xi. 4 vota deum primo victor solvebat Eoo.
                 ingentem quercum decisis undique ramis
                 constituit tumulo fulgentiaque induit arma,
                 Mezenti ducis exuvias, tibi, magne, tropaeum,
                 Bellipotens.
[2] A. x. 541   arma Serestus
                 lecta refert umeris tibi, rex Gradive, tropaeum.
[3] A. x. 774   voveo praedonis corpore raptis
                 indutum spoliis ipsum te, Lause, tropaeum
                 Aeneae.
[4] A. xi. 172 magna tropaea ferunt quos dat tua dextera leto.
[5] A. xi. 224, 385, 790.
[6] G. iii. 32   duo rapta manu diverso ex hoste tropaea
                 bisque triumphatas utroque ab litore gentis.
[7] G. ii. 146 hinc albi, Clitumne, greges et maxima taurus
                 victima, saepe tuo perfusi flumine sacro,
                 Romanos ad templa deum duxere triumphos.

'Caesar, entering the walls of Rome in triple triumph, was consecrating his immortal vow to the gods of Italy, three hundred great altars throughout the whole city; the streets rang with joyful sports and applause; in all the temples was the chorus of matrons and altars in all; before the altars slaughtered heifers strewed the ground. Caesar himself sitting on the snow-white threshold of gleaming Phoebus, reviews the presents of the peoples and fits them on the proud doorposts; in long array the conquered races passed, how varied in their tongues, their garments and their arms!'[1]

This is a compound picture, for Virgil wished to work in Augustus' dedications and the great temple of Apollo on the Palatine, but it has the true features of the triumph. Again, there are other vaguer allusions to the triumph both in *Georgics* and *Aeneid*.[2] As in the ceremonies of peace so in those of war Virgil shows his love of religious rites and his wish to give religious sanction to the sequence of events.

[1] A. viii. 714–23.
[2] G. i. 504, A. iv. 37, vi. 814, viii. 626, xi. 54.

V

THE GRAECO-ROMAN GODS

I. GODS WITH ROMAN NAMES

THE great majority of the divine beings who appear in Virgil are either Greek gods taken into the Roman religion or adopted by the poets as part of the divine framework, or else gods who had still retained their Roman names but by their assimilation to Greek counterparts had acquired an anthropomorphic personality and often in the process had largely changed their character. It might seem a tedious operation to consider the treatment of all these deities individually in Virgil, but the results are not unimportant. For it is possible by this means to get a clearer idea as to the proportion of Greek and Roman elements in the conception of each god held in Virgil's day. It will be seen that in some the original Italian idea was still vital and was often distinguished from the Greek accretion, in others the two elements are fused almost equally, in others the Greek conception has so far prevailed that there is little trace left of the genuine Roman idea. With yet another class the 'faded' use of the god's name as a concrete or abstract substantive has become so common that there is little of deity left. We can also learn something of Virgil's own mind, for it will be seen that he is often scrupulous in distinguishing the Greek and Italian elements and in observing local and other associations. We can even see something of the development of his interests, for it is noticeable that his allusions to Greek legend and mythology are proportionately far more frequent in *Eclogues* and *Georgics* than in the *Aeneid*. While he was more markedly under the influence of Greek literature, Greek religious associations bulked larger in his mind; when his great Roman theme had possessed him, they to a great extent faded into the background.

For purposes of treatment it will be convenient to consider first the gods known only by their Roman names, secondly those who have both Roman and Greek names, thirdly those which have only Greek names. The true significance of the three great Virgilian deities, Iuppiter, Iuno, and Venus, who alone are actors in the story, will only emerge when they are considered later in connexion with Virgil's conception of Fate and the ultimate government of the world.

The larger number of the gods mentioned by Virgil—as indeed of the gods of the Roman pantheon—were known only by their Roman names, but this did not prevent their Italian character from being modified and sometimes overlaid by that of their Greek counterparts. We may begin by considering two of the deities already noticed as prominent in Virgil's picture of the old Italy, Saturnus and Ceres.

1. *Saturnus* was undoubtedly, whatever be the derivation of the word, an Italian agricultural deity, and the date of his festival, the famous Saturnalia in December, suggests that he was connected with the winter sowing. As has been seen (p. 40), this original character is represented by only one phrase in Virgil,[1] and he has been transformed by a process of euhemerism into the ancient Italian king, whose reign was a golden age, who took part in the foundation of Rome and with Ianus seems specially to represent the majesty of ancient Rome and Italy. Greek learning had identified Saturnus with Kronos, the father of Zeus (Iuppiter), Hera, and Poseidon. It is with these associations that Saturnus appears, particularly in the *Aeneid*. Iuppiter is described as *Saturnius pater*[2] because

---

[1] G. ii. 406 curvo Saturni dente relictam | persequitur vitem.   [2] A. iv. 372.

Zeus was the son of Kronos, Neptunus (Poseidon) is 'Saturn's son, the tamer of the sea',[1] and Iuno (Hera), more than either of these, is again and again 'Saturn's daughter'.[2] This constantly repeated association may be intended to emphasize Iuno's partisanship with the old Italy before the coming of the Trojans, but in all probability it is purely Greek and is to be compared with the constantly recurring Κρονίων or Κρονίδης as an alternative for Zeus in Homer. Saturnus is thus the father of the deities who determine the course of events in the *Aeneid*, but himself takes no part in the action. The *Georgics* give further Greek associations in the references to the strange legend of the appearance of Kronos in the form of a horse when he was courting Rhea,[3] and to the 'star of Saturn',[4] an idea closely derived from Greek astronomical notions.

Nor is the notion of Saturnus' golden reign in Italy unconnected with the Greek Kronos, for he, too, was associated in Greek thought with the 'golden age', and it is worth noticing that in the sixth *Eclogue* 'the reign of Saturnus'[5] is placed in close conjunction with the purely Greek legends of Deucalion and Pyrrha and the sufferings of Prometheus. The two ideas are in fact linked together by Virgil in Evander's account of early Italy; for he describes how Saturnus (Kronos) fled from Olympus, driven out by his son Iuppiter (Zeus) and settled in Italy

---

[1] A. v. 799 Saturnius . . . domitor maris.

[2] A. vii. 572 Saturnia . . . regina; A. xii. 807 dea . . . Saturnia; A. xii. 830 Saturni . . . proles; A. vii. 428 omnipotens Saturnia; A. iii. 380, v. 606, ix. 745, 802, x. 760, xii. 156 Saturnia Iuno; A. i. 23, iv. 92, vii. 428, 622, x. 659 Saturnia as a proper name.

[3] G. iii. 92 talis et ipse iubam cervice effundit equina
     coniugis adventu pernix Saturnus.

[4] G. i. 335 hoc metuens caeli mensis et sidera serva,
     frigida Saturni sese quo stella receptet.

[5] E. vi. 41 hinc lapides Pyrrhae iactos, Saturnia regna,
     Caucasiasque refert volucris furtumque Promethei.

to establish his reign of peace there.[1] This is a typical instance of the kind of legend which grew up in order to smooth over the awkward join between Greek and Italian elements in the new combined conception of a deity. Saturnus, as Virgil shows him to us, is 'double-faced', but the Greek element has prevailed, as it did both in the later Roman conception of him and in his cult. In his temple in the Forum he was worshipped *graeco ritu*,[2] his cult-statue was modelled on the Greek conception of Kronos, and the Saturnalia lost almost all its Italian elements and became unrecognizable as an agricultural celebration.

2. Of *Ceres* and her worship something has already been said (pp. 38, 54) in speaking of the old religion of the country-side, but Virgil's usage may be analysed more closely. The name, Ceres, appears to be connected with the root seen in *creare* and probably in the old Italian noun *cerus* found in the hymn of the Salii. She was thus a goddess of fertility and in particular of the fertility of the crops, and was worshipped in the fields, often in connexion with Liber, another Italian corn-deity, or with Tellus, the earth. In the period of Greek influence she was thus identified with the Greek Demeter, the great earth-goddess, who also had special associations with the crops. In this connexion she formed one of a triad, Ceres, Libera, and Liber, representing the Greek chthonic triad, Demeter, Kore, and Iacchus.

In her old Roman character she is coupled with Liber in the invocation at the outset of the *Georgics*,[3] and later on in the book[4] the performance of the old festival of the Cerealia is fully and beautifully described, though, as has been seen

---

[1] A. viii. 319 primus ab aetherio venit Saturnus Olympo,
        arma Iovis fugiens et regnis exsul ademptis.
[2] Wissowa, *R.K.*[2], p. 205.
[3] G. i. 7 Liber et alma Ceres.   [4] G. i. 338 ff.

(p. 54), the description contains elements belonging to other rustic festivals. In a passage in the *Eclogues*[1] referring to annual offerings to Ceres she is probably still in her Italian shape, for Bacchus with whom she is coupled is here really the Italian Liber, but when Virgil says in the *Georgics* that the farmer who duly hoes and harrows his ground, 'helps the fields, nor does fair-haired Ceres look down in vain on him from high Olympus',[2] it is difficult to know quite what was his thought. No Italian goddess could look down from Olympus, nor even did the Greek Demeter, for her abode was beneath the earth; he is probably using a conventional idea without thinking of its application in the particular case.

In a larger number of instances Ceres appears definitely as Demeter. She is said to have been 'the first to teach mortals to turn the earth with the iron plough';[3] Aeneas and Dido sacrifice to 'Ceres the lawgiver',[4] an obvious translation of Demeter's cult-title Θεσμοφόρος. Virgil seems too to know of a special cult of Demeter in Troy, for the hero Polyboetes is 'sacred to Ceres',[5] and it is at 'the mound and ancient shrine of deserted Ceres'[6] just outside the town that Aeneas and his friends agree to meet for their flight, and on the way there that Creusa is lost.[7] It is

---

[1] E. v. 79 ut Baccho Cererique, tibi sic vota quotannis
    agricolae facient.
[2] G. i. 95   neque illum
    flava Ceres alto nequiquam spectat Olympo.
[3] G. i. 147 prima Ceres ferro mortalis vertere terram
    instituit.
[4] A. iv. 57   mactant lectas de more bidentis
    legiferae Cereri.
[5] A. vi. 484 Cererique sacrum Polyboeten.
[6] A. ii. 713 est urbe egressis tumulus templumque vetustum
    desertae Cereris.
[7] A. ii. 741 nec prius amissam respexi animumve reflexi
    quam tumulum antiquae Cereris sedemque sacratam
    venimus.

probably, too, to the chthonic Demeter that the 'poppy of Ceres',[1] the flower of forgetfulness, is dedicated.

But Ceres, like other deities, had lost her full godhead and had become a mere synonym for 'corn'. It is interesting that she stood for three different stages in the history of the corn. Most often Ceres is the standing corn in the fields. Thus 'the ruddy Ceres is cut in midsummer';[2] of the different kinds of soil 'the heavier is best for Ceres, the thinner for Lyaeus';[3] there is no rest for the farmer all the year round, for there are either the fruits to be gathered, or the young of the flock to be tended, or 'the sheaf of the stalks of Ceres' to be cut.[4] In one passage Ceres is the corn threshed and stored for use; after the shipwreck in the first Book of the *Aeneid,* 'weary from their adventure they set out the corn (Ceres) damaged by the waves and Ceres' implements',[5] which are presumably the cooking utensils. Finally, as the last stage in the process, Ceres is the bread or cakes made of the corn. So in the first evening in Dido's halls, 'the attendants bring water in their hands and serve Ceres in baskets',[6] and after Evander's welcome to Aeneas and his companions, 'chosen youths pile in baskets the gifts of Ceres wrought for eating and serve Bacchus'.[7] But the most notable instance of the use of Ceres as a synonym for bread occurs in the account of the fulfilment of the strange prophesy of the Harpy that the Trojans shall 'eat their

---

[1] G. i. 212 Cereale papaver.
[2] G. i. 297 at rubicunda Ceres medio succiditur aestu.
[3] G. ii. 229 densa magis Cereri, rarissima quaeque Lyaeo.
[4] G. ii. 516 nec requies, quin aut pomis exuberet annus,
    aut fetu pecorum aut Cerealis mergite culmi.
[5] A. i. 177 tum Cererem corruptam undis Cerealiaque arma
    expediunt fessi rerum.
[6] A. i. 701 dant manibus famuli lymphas Cereremque canistris
    expediunt.
[7] A. viii. 180   onerantque canistris
    dona laboratae Cereris Bacchumque ministrant.

tables'.[1] As they lay at their meal 'they pile the plate of bread [lit. 'the substratum of Ceres'] with country apples', and then 'the lack of food drove them to turn their teeth upon the scanty bread (Ceres)'. It is possible that Virgil uses the periphrases here to give a greater air of quaintness and mystery to the occurrence.

Virgil's treatment of Ceres shows again his full consciousness of the old Roman rites, the legends of the identified Demeter, and a singularly prolific ingenuity in the use of the name as a synonym.

From these two rustic gods we may proceed to consider some of the other great deities of the Graeco-Roman State-cult.

3. The treatment of *Mars* in Virgil is peculiarly interesting as indicative of current modes of thought in his day. Mars, in the early Roman religion, was a deity of agriculture and Cato preserves in full the farmer's prayer to him at the lustration of the fields.[2] Of this aspect of Mars there is no trace in Virgil and it is clear that it had become quite obsolete. But he was also from early times the god of war, perhaps in origin the guardian of the young warriors as the deity of all growing things. In this capacity he was known throughout the Roman historical period and it was emphasized by his natural identification with the Greek war-god Ares. But the interesting point about Virgil's usage is that even this conception of Mars seems to have faded into the background, and in far the greater part of his occurrences in Virgil Mars is not consciously felt as a god at all but only as a faded personification of war or even as its synonym.

---

[1] A. vii. 111 et Cereale solum pomis agrestibus augent.
consumptis hic forte aliis, ut vertere morsus
exiguam in Cererem penuria adegit edendi.
[2] *de Agri. cult.* 141.

Virgil, of course, knows and recognizes the old Italian war-god, and true to his usual antiquarian instinct he frequently uses the old by-form Mavors and twice the Italian cult-title Gradivus;[1] once Mars is called by the traditional epithet Bellipotens. There are, moreover, passages in which the worship of Mars is referred to as one of the recognized Roman cults. In Aeneas' great prayer in the last book of the *Aeneid*, among the other gods of Italy he prays to 'thee, Mars, father renowned, who dost guide all wars at thy will'.[2] Twice, too, there is reference to the old custom of offering the spoils of war to Mars; Aeneas places the arms of Mezentius on an oak-stump, 'a trophy to thee, great Lord of war',[3] and Serestus 'bears back from the battle the chosen spoils, a trophy to thee, king Gradivus'.[4] In the same spirit Rome is spoken of as 'Mars' city'.[5]

As a Roman god Mars is associated with the story of the birth of Romulus and Remus, the twin sons of Mars and Ilia, and their suckling by the wolf. In Iuppiter's prophecy to Venus in the first book he tells how Aeneas' descendants will reign three hundred years at Alba, 'until the princess priestess shall conceive of Mars and bear her twin off-spring. Then joying in the tawny guardianship of his wolf-nurse Romulus shall receive rule over the race and found the walls of Mavors' town and call them Romans

[1] Mavors A. vi. 872, viii. 630, 700, x. 755, xi. 389, xii. 179, 332; Gradivus iii. 35, x. 542; Bellipotens xi. 8.
[2] A. xii. 179　　　　　　　　　　　　　　tuque, inclite Mavors,
　　　　cuncta tuo qui bella, pater, sub numine torques.
[3] A. xi. 7 Mezenti ducis exuvias, tibi, magne, tropaeum, | Bellipotens.
[4] A. x. 541 arma Serestus | lecta refert umeris tibi, rex Gradive, tropaeum.
[5] A. vi. 872 quantos ille virum magnam Mavortis ad urbem
　　　　campus aget gemitus.
It would be possible here to take *Mavortis* with *campus*, referring to the campus Martius, but the order is in favour of taking it with *urbem*: possibly it goes with both.

from his own name.'[1] So on the great shield Volcanus 'had
wrought the mother-wolf lying in the green cave of Mavors
and the twin boys playing as they hung about her dugs'.[2]

But equally often the personal Mars is really the Greek
Ares and has attached to him the attributes and legends
of the Greek god. So in the *Georgics* Virgil speaks of 'the
yoked pair of Mars and the chariot of great Achilles, of
which the Greek poets sung',[3] and in the cave of Vulcan
the Cyclops were 'hastening to make a chariot and flying
wheels for Mars, wherewith he rouses men and cities';[4] his
Greek character here is certified because they were also
making an aegis for Pallas. Even less mistakable is the
song which the nymph Clymene sings beneath the sea of
the 'fruitless vigilance of Vulcan and the cunning of Mars
and his sweet treachery';[5] this is nothing but Demodocus'
song in the *Odyssey* of the story of Hephaestus and Ares.
This Greek Ares was particularly associated with Thrace,
and so Virgil quite rightly makes Aeneas, when he lands
in Thrace in the course of his wanderings, worship 'the
nymphs of the country-side and father Gradivus, who is
lord over the fields of the Getae'.[6] For all his typically

---

[1] A. i. 273   donec regina sacerdos
        Marte gravis geminam partu dabit Ilia prolem.
        inde lupae fulvo nutricis tegmine laetus
        Romulus excipiet gentem et Mavortia condet
        moenia Romanosque suo de nomine dicet.
[2] A. viii. 630 fecerat et viridi fetam Mavortis in antro
        procubuisse lupam, geminos huic ubera circum
        ludere pendentis pueros.
[3] G. iii. 90   quorum Grai meminere poetae,
        Martis equi biiuges et magni currus Achilli.
[4] A. viii. 433 parte alia Marti currumque rotasque volucris
        instabant, quibus ille viros, quibus excitat urbes.
[5] G. iv. 345 inter quas curam Clymene narrabat inanem
        Volcani, Martisque dolos et dulcia furta.
Cf. *Od.* viii. 266 ff.
[6] A. iii. 34   nymphas venerabar agrestis
        Gradivumque patrem, Geticis qui praesidet arvis.
Cf. A. iii. 13 terra procul vastis colitur Mavortia campis.

Italian name here, he is the local tribal god, whom Aeneas addresses with the local nymphs: for Thrace, as he has just described it, is 'the Mavortian land with its desert plains' So in a later simile we have once again the Mars of Thrace: 'Even as when bloodstained Mars, awakened by the streams of cold Hebrus, clangs on his shield and rousing war gives rein to his maddened horses.'[1] These references to the Thracian Ares are an interesting proof of the accuracy of Virgil's knowledge of Greek as well as of Roman cults and mythology.

But far more frequent in Virgil than these recollections of the personal divinity Mars or Ares are instances in which Mars has but a 'faded' personality and is little more than a personification of the spirit of war and even a convenient synonym for 'war' itself. There are places in which we can see this transition almost in operation. When Virgil tells us that 'Mars had power to ruin the uncouth race of Lapithae',[2] our first inclination is to suppose a legend of Ares. But Ares had no such connexion in story with the Lapithae, and when we remember their downfall, it is clear that Mars is here only the spirit of war which drove them to fight the Centaurs. Or, to take a Roman instance, when Virgil starts to describe the opening of the gates in time of war, he says: 'twin gates of war there are—for so they call them—consecrated by religious awe and the fear of savage Mars';[3] Mars is not a deity here, for the gates were sacred to Ianus, not to Mars; once again he is but the spirit of war.

---

[1] A. xii. 331 qualis apud gelidi cum flumina concitus Hebri
sanguineus Mavors clipeo increpat atque furentis
bella movens immittit equos.
[2] A. vii. 304   Mars perdere gentem
immanem Lapithum valuit.
[3] A. vii. 607 sunt geminae belli portae (sic nomine dicunt).
religione sacrae et saevi formidine Martis.

It is natural that in this sense we should meet Mars most often in the accounts of fighting, yet even there the degree of personality or personification is sometimes doubtful. When, in the course of battle, 'Mars mighty in arms added spirit and strength to the Latins and laid his keen goads to their breasts',[1] is it the god Mars or the spirit of battle? It is hard to say how Virgil thought of it, but more probably in the second sense. When 'wavering Mars wanders amid the hosts',[2] the epithet seems to decide the question, for a deity can hardly be *dubius*. It is again in this personified sense that the Trojans in the last fight in Troy 'see Mars unconquered and the Danaans rushing to their palaces',[3] and that the maddened Latin people 'weary Mars with their cries',[4] that is, they cry repeatedly for war. Once more, in the prophetic picture of the battle of Actium on Aeneas' shield, 'Mavors rages amid the struggle';[5] here we might take it to be the god himself but that he is set among personifications, the 'Curses' and 'Discord'. So, again, Evander reproaches his dead son: 'not these, Pallas, were the promises thou gavest thy father, with caution to trust thyself to raging Mars';[6] there was no committing himself to the care of a 'raging' divinity, Mars is just 'battle'. So Drances, taunting Turnus, says, 'if you have in you any of your father's Mars [i.e. his warlike spirit], look Aeneas in the face, who calls you',[7] and Turnus in reply

[1] A. ix. 717 hic Mars armipotens animum virisque Latinis
    addidit et stimulos acris sub pectore vertit.
[2] G. ii. 283 dubius mediis Mars errat in armis.
[3] A. ii. 440 sic Martem indomitum Danaosque ad tecta ruentis
    cernimus.
[4] A. vii. 582 undique collecti coeunt Martemque fatigant; cf. A. ix. 766
Martemque cientis.   [5] A. viii. 700 saevit medio in certamine Mavors.
[6] A. xi. 152 non haec, o Palla, dederas promissa parenti,
    cautius ut saevo velles te credere Marti.
[7] A. xi. 373   etiam tu, si qua tibi vis,
    si patrii quid Martis habes, illum aspice contra,
    qui vocat.

Q

asks, 'will your Mars be ever in your windy tongue and flying feet?'[1] The same sense may be recognized in more stereotyped phrases, such as 'the fierce fight of Mars'[2] and 'the contest of panting Mars'.[3] Conspicuous among these are the recurring expressions, *aequo, secundo,* and *adverso Marte*;[4] there can hardly be there any sense of the favour or opposition of a deity, it is the 'even', 'prosperous', or 'adverse' running of the fight. Closely allied to these uses are the expressions 'blind Mars'[5] and 'impious Mars',[6] who breaks the natural relations between man and man.

There are numerous instances in Virgil in which the meaning has long passed beyond even this faded personification, and Mars has become little more than a convenient poetical synonym for *bellum* or *pugna*: a few illustrations will bring this out. Misenus was better than any other man at 'rousing men with his trumpet and kindling Mars with his tune';[7] Mars cannot here be the god, for the verb *accendere* is impossible, and hardly even the 'spirit of fight'—it is just that the trumpeter stirred men to battle. When Turnus cries to the Rutulians, 'what you have prayed for is granted, to break through by your valour; Mars himself is in your hands',[8] he means no more than that 'the fortune of the battle rests with you'. Aeneas, taking the oath before the single combat, says, 'if Victory

---

[1] A. xi. 389   an tibi Mavors
        ventosa in lingua pedibusque fugacibus istis
        semper erit?

[2] A. xii. 124 aspera Martis | pugna.

[3] A. xii. 790 certamina Martis anheli.

[4] aequo Marte A. vii. 540; secundo Marte A. x. 21, xi. 899, xii. 497; adverso Marte A. xii. 1.

[5] A. ix. 518 caeco contendere Marte; A. ii. 335 caeco Marte resistunt.

[6] G. i. 511 saevit toto Mars impius orbe.

[7] A. vi. 164   quo non praestantior alter
        aere ciere viros Martemque accendere cantu.

[8] A. x. 279 quod votis optastis adest, perfringere dextra.
        in manibus Mars ipse, viri.

shall have granted us our Mars',[1] 'our success', that is, 'in battle'; and here we have the strange phenomenon of the personification of the abstract Victory with the real god Mars faded to a common noun. 'The mad love of cruel Mars keeps me under arms', says Gallus in the tenth *Eclogue*;[2] and Venus in similar words tells Iuno that she will rouse the Italians to war and 'kindle their hearts with the love of mad Mars';[3] 'Mars' in either case is just 'fighting'. An even more obviously concrete use of the word occurs at the outset of the description of the battle of Actium: 'you might have seen all Leucate alive with Mars drawn up for battle';[4] here Mars is just 'the fleet'; while the Ianus ceremony is similarly said to be used 'as soon as they move Mars to battle',[5] that is, dispatch the armies from Rome. It is this half-personified, half-concrete sense of Mars which is by far the most frequent in Virgil, and it is significant of the degradation into which even the greatest of the State-deities might fall.[6] Once again Virgil appears to be sensitive to the history of Mars and his Greek equivalent Ares, and yet to accept to the full the current poetical use of the ideas associated with him.

Closely linked with Mars is *Bellona*, in origin probably,

---

[1] A. xii. 187 sin nostrum adnuerit nobis Victoria Martem.
[2] E. x. 44 nunc insanus amor duri me Martis in armis
     tela inter media atque adversos detinet hostis.
[3] A. vii. 550 accendamque animos insani Martis amore.
[4] A. viii. 676   totumque instructo Marte videres
     fervere Leucaten.
[5] A. vii. 603 cum prima movent in proelia Martem.
[6] Other examples are:
A. viii. 495 regem ad supplicium praesenti Marte reposcunt, 'under threat of war';
A. x. 237 tela inter media atque ardentis Marte Latinos;
A. xi. 110 pacem me exanimis et Martis sorte peremptis | oratis?
A. xii. 108 Aeneas acuit Martem et se suscitat ira.
A. xii. 409   it tristis ad aethera clamor
     bellantum iuvenum et duro sub Marte cadentum.
A. xii. 712 invadunt Martem clipeis atque aere sonoro.

like Victoria (see p. 115), an offshoot of Mars, who in the later history of Roman religion became identified with Mâ, a mother-god like Cybele, brought home by the soldiery from Asia Minor. Of this identification there is no trace in Virgil, but in her Roman capacity she has suffered the same fate as Mars himself. In the same description of Actium on Aeneas' shield in which Mars appears as the 'spirit of war', surrounded by the Dirae and Discordia, he is followed by 'Bellona with her bloody scourge'.[1] Here possibly she is the 'spirit of battle', but when Iuno prophesies to Lavinia 'the blood of Trojans and Rutulians shall be thy dowry and Bellona waits to guide thee to the couch',[2] Bellona is little more than 'war', though given an ironical personification by the application of the cult-title *pronuba*, which was Iuno's own.

To the circle of Mars belongs also *Quirinus*, who was probably the chief deity of the Quirinal settlement before it united with that on the Palatine to form Rome, and may therefore have been of Sabine origin; in the earliest days of Rome Iuppiter, Mars, and Quirinus formed an unofficial 'triad' of chief gods. Later he was identified with the deified Romulus, and it is in this capacity only that he is known to Virgil. He appears first in the prophecy of Iuppiter in the first *Aeneid*: 'Quirinus with his brother Remus shall give the laws',[3] and again when Anchises prophecies that Marcellus 'will for the third time hang up the captured arms [the *spolia opima*] to father Quirinus';[4] here there may be a trace of his identification with Mars. In the same sense the epithet *Quirinalis* is applied to the

---

[1] A. viii. 703 quam cum sanguineo sequitur Bellona flagello.
[2] A. vii. 318 sanguine Troiano et Rutulo dotabere, virgo,
    et Bellona manet te pronuba.
[3] A. i. 292 cana Fides et Vesta, Remo cum fratre Quirinus
    iura dabunt.
[4] A. vi. 859 tertiaque arma patri suspendet capta Quirino.

augur's *lituus*[1] and to the consul's *trabea*;[2] they date from Romulus, the augur king. In a slightly wider sense in the phrase 'the arms of victorious Quirinus',[3] the deified hero stands in effect for Rome itself. With these mentions of Quirinus we may couple the invocation at the end of the first book of the *Georgics* to the 'gods of our fathers and our land, Romulus and mother Vesta';[4] it is Quirinus, the deified Romulus, whom Virgil has here in mind.

4. The gods who have hitherto been under consideration show a mingling of Greek and Roman characteristics. As a typical example of a deity whose Italian conception has been completely swamped by identification with a Greek god we may take *Mercurius*. In the old Roman State-cult he was a deity associated with commerce (*merces*).[5] It was no doubt through this association that he was identified with the Greek Hermes, who had a similar connexion, but in Virgil all traces of this original character are gone and Mercurius is simply Hermes, the messenger of the gods. He inherits Hermes' relationships;[6] he was born on Mount Cyllene, the son of Maia, daughter of Atlas, and Evander, the Arcadian, traces his descent to him. So, too, his appearances in the story are Greek. Iuppiter sends him near the beginning of the poem to

[1] A. vii. 187 ipse Quirinali lituo parvaque sedebat
            succinctus trabea.

[2] A. vii. 612 ipse Quirinali trabea cinctuque Gabino
            insignis reserat stridentia limina consul.

[3] G. iii. 27 victorisque arma Quirini.

[4] G. i. 498 di patrii, indigetes, et Romule Vestaque mater.

[5] F. Altheim, *Griechische Götter im alten Rom*, pp. 39 ff., regards him as an Etruscan phallic deity, but his proofs do not seem to me convincing.

[6] A. viii. 138 vobis Mercurius pater est, quem candida Maia
            Cyllenae gelido conceptum vertice fudit;
            at Maiam, auditis si quicquam credimus, Atlas,
            idem Atlas generat caeli qui sidera tollit.

Cf. A. i. 297 Maia genitum demittit ab alto; A. iv. 252 paribus nitens Cyllenius alis | constitit; A. iv. 258 materno veniens ab avo Cyllenia proles; A. iv. 276 tali Cyllenius ore locutus.

prepare the minds of Dido and the Carthaginians to receive Aeneas and his men;[1] later, when Aeneas shows signs of thinking of Carthage as his permanent home, Iuppiter sends him again to warn the hero to depart, and the journey of 'Cyllenius' is described with all the fullness of a Homeric itinerary of Hermes;[2] lastly, when Aeneas, now resolved to go, is yet delaying to sleep instead of hastening away by night, the vision of Mercurius appears to him in a dream.[3] These actions are all those of the Greek Hermes, with whom Mercurius is so completely identified that when he is starting to fulfil Iuppiter's mission he seizes the rod with which 'he summons souls from Orcus, and sends others to gloomy Tartarus below, gives and takes away sleep and unseals men's eyes in death';[4] he is not only the messenger of the gods, but also has Hermes' most characteristic Greek function of Ψυχοπομπός, though it is probable that the idea of opening men's eyes in death is only Roman and implies a Roman notion of the functions of the 'guide of souls'.

5. *Neptunus* is a rather more important figure in Virgil than Mercurius, but he, too, is entirely Greek in conception. In the genuine Roman cult he was a minor and rather obscure figure, who was apparently connected with water. His identification with Poseidon brought him into prominence as the god of the sea, and it is in this capacity that he is met with in Virgil. In the first book of the *Aeneid* he quells the storm which Aeolus has raised at Iuno's request and orders the winds back to Aeolus' cave.[5] After

---

[1] A. i. 297 ff.   [2] A. iv. 222–78.   [3] A. iv. 556–70.
[4] A. iv. 242 tum virgam capit: hac animas ille evocat Orco
              pallentis, alias sub Tartara tristia mittit,
              dat somnos adimitque, et lumina morte resignat.
The whole description is based closely on Hom. *Od.* v. 43 ff. and *Il.* xxiv. 339 ff. For *lumina morte resignat* see Conington's note.
[5] A. i. 124–56.

the funeral games in Sicily Venus appeals to him to grant Aeneas a safe voyage to Italy and he gives his promise,[1] and later he guides the Trojans safely past the rocks of Caria.[2] The helmsman, Palinurus, appeals to him as the heroes sail from Carthage to Sicily in fear of a storm;[3] Mnestheus in the boat-race resigns himself in the belief that victory will rest with the crew he favours.[4] He appears in a more restricted and local sense as 'the Aegean Neptune',[5] the home of Proteus is similarly said to be situated in 'the Carpathian gulf of Neptune',[6] and Proteus' seals are described as 'Neptune's monster flock'.[7] Like Mercurius he assumes his Greek parentage and is described as 'Saturn's son',[8] because Poseidon was the son of Kronos.

He has his share in the regular worship of the gods, and before leaving for Crete Anchises sacrifices a bull to Neptune as he does to Apollo.[9] So Iris, inciting the Trojan women to burn the ships, exclaims, 'Here are four altars for Neptune; the god himself provides torches and courage to use them.'[10] The worship of Neptunus-Poseidon is specially associated with Troy,[11] for he, as Turnus reminds his comrades, built the walls of Troy which yet sank into

---

[1] A. v. 779–826 (cf. 863).

[2] A. vii. 21–4.

[3] A. v. 13 heu quianam tanti cinxerunt aethera nimbi?
    quidve, pater Neptune, paras?

[4] A. v. 195 superent quibus hoc, Neptune, dedisti.

[5] A. iii. 74 Nereidum matri et Neptuno Aegaeo.

[6] G. iv. 387 est in Carpathio Neptuni gurgite vates
    caeruleus Proteus.

[7] G. iv. 394 quippe ita Neptuno visum est, immania cuius
    armenta et turpis pascit sub gurgite phocas.

[8] A. v. 799 tum Saturnius haec domitor maris edidit alti.

[9] A. iii. 118 sic fatus meritos aris mactavit honores,
    taurum Neptuno, taurum tibi, pulcher Apollo.

[10] A. v. 639   en quattuor arae
    Neptuno: deus ipse faces animumque ministrat.

[11] A. ix. 144   at non viderunt moenia Troiae
    Neptuni fabricata manu considere in ignis?

the flames; the ill-fated Laocoon was his special priest,[1] and one of the prizes at the funeral games was a shield torn (on the most probable interpretation of the line) by the Greeks from the door-post of Neptune's temple in Troy.[2] But the sea-god was also worshipped at Rome and on Aeneas' shield is represented with Venus and Minerva as protecting Augustus' fleet at the battle of Actium against the 'barking Anubis' and the other outlandish deities of Egypt.[3]

Other functions of the Greek Poseidon are exercised by Neptune. He is, as ΠοσειΔῶν σεισίχθων, lord of the earthquake; as such he shakes the walls of Troy to their foundations with his trident after the Greek irruption,[4] and makes a rift in the soil to bring forth his favourite animal, the horse.[5] It is probably also as ΠοσειΔῶν ἵππιος that he is thought of as the ancestor of Messapus, 'tamer of horses'.[6] Finally, in the 'faded' sense in which so many of the Graeco-Roman gods appear, Neptunus is used as a mere synonym for 'water'; the bees 'spread their wings to the summer sun, if by chance as they dally the wind has sprinkled them or bathed them headlong in Neptune';[7] the

---

[1] A. ii. 201 Laocoon, ductus Neptuni sorte sacerdos.
[2] A. v. 359 et clipeum efferri iussit, Didymaonis artem,
        Neptuni sacro Danais de poste refixum.
(If this translation is right, we must suppose it was given to Aeneas by Helenus; it may mean 'torn from the Greeks': see Conington's note.)
[3] A. viii. 698 omnigenumque deum monstra et latrator Anubis
        contra Neptunum et Venerem contraque Minervam
        tela tenent.
[4] A. ii. 610 Neptunus muros magnoque emota tridenti
        fundamenta quatit totamque a sedibus urbem
        eruit.
[5] G. i. 12   tuque o, cui prima frementem
    fudit equum magno tellus percussa tridenti, | Neptune.
[6] A. vii. 691 At Messapus, equum domitor, Neptunia proles.
[7] G. iv. 27 pontibus ut crebris possint consistere et alas
        pandere ad aestivum solem, si forte morantis
        sparserit aut praeceps Neptuno immerserit Eurus.

water here is more probably that of river or pond than sea, so that possibly Neptunus comes nearer here to his true Roman character.

Allied to Neptunus is *Portunus*, probably a deity of harbours (*portus*) rather than gates (*porta*) and so clearly thought of in his one casual mention in the *Aeneid*, where he gives Cloanthus' ship the push that brings him the victory.[1]

6. Like Neptunus, *Volcanus*, an old Italian deity of fire, keeps his character most nearly when his name is used by transference for 'fire' itself. This use is frequent in Virgil. The farmer's wife in winter time 'boils down the liquid of sweet musk with Vulcan';[2] in the burning of Troy, 'the great house of Deiphobus falls in ruins as Vulcan gains the mastery';[3] Lavinia, when the altar-fire catches her hair, 'scatters Vulcan throughout the house';[4] when Turnus arms his comrades with torches to fire the Trojan fleet 'the smoky torch gives out a pitchy light and Vulcan lifts the mingling ashes to the stars';[5] and in the simile of the shepherd firing the wood to make a clearing, 'the bristling line of Vulcan stretches through the wide plain'.[6] Here we are closer than in most of the concrete usages to the true Roman conception: for, as Vesta is the spirit in the hearth-flame, so Volcanus is in animistic thought the spirit of flame in general; and in most of the instances a semi-animistic sense survives.

The epithet *Ignipotens*, 'master of fire',[7] which is Vol-

---

[1] A. v. 241 et pater ipse manu magna Portunus euntem | impulit.
[2] G. i. 295 dulcis musti Volcano decoquit umorem.
[3] A. ii. 310   iam Deiphobi dedit ampla ruinam
        Volcano superante domus.
[4] A. vii. 77 totis Volcanum spargere tectis.
[5] A. ix. 75   piceum fert fumida lumen
        taeda et commixtam Volcanus ad astra favillam.
[6] A. x. 407   extenditur una
        horrida per latos acies Volcania campos.
[7] Ignipotens A. viii. 414, 628, 710, x. 243.

R

canus' most common cult-title, is perhaps applicable to the
Roman god, but it has an anthropomorphic ring, which
suggests Greek influence, and the cult-title Lemnius[1] is
directly derived from the Greek Hephaestus, for Lemnos
was his special abode in Greek mythology. The identification is complete when the nymph Clymene attaches to
Volcanus the story of the deception of Hephaestus by Ares
and Aphrodite,[2] which is the theme of the song of Demodocus at the palace of Alcinous. And it is as Hephaestus,
the smith, and not the fire-god, that Volcanus makes his
one great appearance in the story of the *Aeneid*, when at
Venus' request he fashions the arms of Aeneas.[3] He makes
for the caves of the Cyclopes, 'the home of Vulcan, the land
known by Vulcan's name',[4] bids them lay aside the work
on which they were engaged for other gods, and fashions
the magnificent vision of the future greatness of Rome. In
reference to this great gift Turnus later on boasts that he
needs not the arms of Vulcan,[5] and vows that he will go
against Aeneas 'though he play the great Achilles and girds
on to meet me arms fashioned by the hand of Vulcan'.[6]
On two strange occasions Volcanus has an anthropomorphic relation to Italian legend. He is said to be 'the
father of the monstrous Cacus, for belching Vulcan's dark
fires from his mouth he moved on his huge bulk';[7] this

[1] Lemnius A. viii. 454.
[2] G. iv. 345 inter quas curam Clymene narrabat inanem
Volcani, Martisque dolos et dulcia furta.
Cf. *Od.* viii. 266 ff.
[3] A. viii. 370 ff., 626 ff.
[4] A. viii. 422 Volcani domus et Volcania nomine tellus.
[5] A. ix. 148 non armis mihi Volcani, non mille carinis
est opus.
[6] A. xi. 438 ibo animis contra, vel magnum praestet Achillem
factaque Volcani manibus paria induat arma
ille licet.
[7] A. viii. 198 huic monstro Volcanus erat pater; illius atros
ore vomens ignis magna se mole ferebat.

cannot be a genuine Italian myth, but must be a fanciful Greek notion applied to the fire-breathing creature. Still more strangely the Italian hero Caeculus, fighting on the side of Turnus, is said to be 'sprung of the stock of Vulcan';[1] here Virgil must have been thinking of the Greek habit of tracing the descent of a hero back to a god and employed Vulcan, anthropomorphized in the Greek manner, for the purpose. Once more we have the Latin elements, the Greek elements, and the fusion of the two.

7. Among the minor deities with Roman names a passing mention is made of *Feronia*,[2] always a mysterious personage, but here a goddess of childbirth, who had given the Praenestine king Erulus three lives.

8. Among the gods with Roman names—for it is fully Latinized—may be reckoned *Hercules*. There can really be no doubt that he was in fact the Greek Heracles, brought to Italy by the cities of Magna Graecia and then penetrating into Italian towns and finding a special home in Tibur. Thence he was brought to Rome and established at the Ara Maxima in the Forum Boarium, his cult being in the special charge of the families of the Potitii and Pinarii. Virgil has no doubt of his identity with the Greek hero; he speaks of him as Alcides,[3] as Amphitryoniades,[4]

---

[1] A. x. 543 instaurant acies Volcani stirpe creatus
            Caeculus et veniens Marsorum montibus Umbro.
[2] A. viii. 563 et regem hac Erulum dextra sub Tartara misi,
            nascenti cui tris animas Feronia mater,
            horrendum dictu, dederat.
[3] E. vii. 61 populus Alcidae gratissima.
A. v. 414 his magnum Alciden contra stetit.
A. viii. 203 Alcides aderat taurosque hac victor agebat
            ingentis.
A. viii. 362   haec . . . limina victor
            Alcides subiit.
A. x. 461 te precor, Alcide.
[4] A. viii. 103 Amphitryoniadae magno.

and as 'the man of Tiryns'[1] (not altogether unprompted perhaps by the inadmissibility of the nominative *Hercules* in the hexameter), and he knows well the story of the killing of Geryon and the theft of his cattle.[2] He also knows a legend of the visit of Hercules to Sicily and the powers he showed there in boxing against the local hero, Eryx,[3] and a story of his founding of Tarentum,[4] which, unless it refers to the refounding of the city by the Lacedaemonian Phalanthus, a descendant of Heracles, is otherwise unknown. To Heracles Virgil also attributes his sacred tree, the poplar.[5]

The most important and most interesting occurrence of Hercules in Virgil is, of course, the long episode in the eighth *Aeneid*,[6] where Aeneas arriving at the settlement of Evander on the future site of Rome, finds the king and his followers engaged in the worship of Hercules at the Ara Maxima in the Forum Boarium. The ritual of this worship has already been examined (c. ii, p. 55), and there can be little doubt that it was introduced in its Greek form (*aperto capite*) from the cult of Hercules at Tibur. Here we are concerned with the strange myth of Cacus and Hercules, which Evander narrates as the origin of the cult. It is clearly not Greek but Italian and local, indeed it is not known in Roman literature before Virgil and it is

---

[1] A. vii. 661   postquam Laurentia victor
       Geryone exstincto Tirynthius attigit arva.
A. viii. 228 ecce furens animis aderat Tirynthius.

[2] A. viii. 202 tergemini nece Geryonae spoliisque superbus; cf. vii. 661, above, n. 1.

[3] A. v. 410 quid, si quis caestus ipsius et Herculis arma
       vidisset tristemque hoc ipso in litore pugnam?

[4] A. iii. 551 hinc sinus Herculei (si vera est fama) Tarenti | cernitur.

[5] E. vii. 61; see p. 123, n. 3; G. ii. 66 Herculeaeque arbos umbrosa coronae.
A. viii. 276   Herculea bicolor cum populus umbra
       velavitque comas foliisque innexa pependit.

[6] A. viii. 102–304; see Wissowa, *R.K.*[2], pp. 282–3.

impossible to say whether as a story it went far back into the past. But whatever its antiquity—or modernity—we are able here to trace more clearly than usual the growth of an aetiological legend and to piece its elements together. There is a cult of Hercules at an altar in the 'Cattle-market'; there is an association on the Palatine with a mysterious divine being Cacus—apparently one of an old divinity pair Cacus and Caca—attested by the presence of the Scalae Caci.[1] There is also the *motif* of cattle-stealing, frequent in Greek legend, such as that of Hermes and Apollo, and ready to hand in the story of Hercules himself and Geryon. Putting all these elements together it is not difficult to see how the story arose, and it is not necessary to go back, as some commentators have done, to an original Indo-Germanic myth, though that may be the *motif* behind all these kindred legends. Hercules has here then developed an independent Italian or rather Roman association of his own, no doubt after the Greek influence had popularized legends of divine or heroic beings.

There are two offshoots of this story of Cacus and Hercules, which may even be due to Virgil himself. In the first Hercules is represented as the contemporary of Evander and actually paying a visit to him in his little palace on the site of Rome;[2] to this Evander's son Pallas later appeals, when praying to Hercules for aid in the battle.[3] The second is the appearance in the ranks of battle of Hercules' son 'Aventinus', born to him by 'the priestess Rhea, a woman united to a god, after that the man of Tiryns, victor over the slain Geryon, had reached the Laurentian fields and washed his Spanish cattle in the Tuscan

---

[1] For the Scalae Caci see Diod. iv. 21. 2; Plut. *Rom.* 20.

[2] A. viii. 362   haec, inquit, limina victor
        Alcides subiit, haec illum regia cepit.

[3] A. x. 460 per patris hospitium et mensas, quas advena adisti,
        te precor, Alcide, coeptis ingentibus adsis.

stream';[1] he appears duly clad in his father's lion's skin. The name Aventinus is clearly borrowed from the Aventine hill and 'the priestess Rhea' seems to be a counterpart of the mother of Romulus and Remus.

These stories of Hercules are of special interest as showing the way in which definitely Italian legends could spring up after the habit of mythology had been learnt from the Greeks.

There remain the gods of the underworld, Orcus, Dis, and Proserpina, who will be better discussed in a general consideration of the attitude of Virgil to the dead, and the three deities, who are prominent throughout the story and play a continuously active part, Iuppiter, Iuno, and Venus. Their share in the story and their relation to Virgil's conception of Fate we must consider later, but it will be well here to examine their general treatment on the lines adopted in dealing with the other deities.

9. *Venus* in the old Italian religion was a deity of gardens and fruit-trees; she was introduced to Rome from Ardea and superseded Iuppiter as the presiding deity of the festival of the Vinalia. Of this original character there is no trace in Virgil, unless it be in the attribution of the myrtle as the favourite tree of Venus,[2] though this has probably a Greek source; the myrtle is said to have

---

[1] A. vii. 656 ff.; esp. 659:
    collis Aventini silva quem Rhea sacerdos
    furtivum partu sub luminis edidit oras,
    mixta deo mulier, postquam Laurentia victor
    Geryone exstincto Tirynthius attigit arva,
    Tyrrhenoque boves in flumine lavit Hiberas;
and ibid. 667   tegimen torquens immane leonis,
    terribili impexum saeta cum dentibus albis
    indutus capiti, sic regia tecta subibat,
    horridus Herculeoque umeros innexus amictu.
[2] E. vii. 61 populus Alcidae gratissima, vitis Iaccho,
    formosae myrtus Veneri, sua laurea Phoebo.
G. ii. 64 solido Paphiae de robore myrtus.

sheltered Aphrodite when she first rose from the sea. In Roman thought Venus was completely absorbed in her identification with the Greek Aphrodite, the goddess of love. In Virgil she is accordingly associated with the many Greek sites of her cult and is called by the appropriate local cult-titles. Cythera is hers and her most frequent synonym is Cytherea;[1] Amathus[2] and Paphus[3] are hers and Idalium;[4] she is Dionaea[5] and special mention is made of her famous cult on Mount Eryx in Sicily,[6] the foundation of which is attributed to Aeneas. On the mythological side she is the wife of Vulcan,[7] as Aphrodite was of Hephaestus, and so prevails upon him to make the new divine armour for Aeneas, and Diomedes refers without any sense of incongruity to his wounding of Venus in battle before Troy.[8] She has inherited the Homeric traditions of Aphrodite as well as the Greek cults. Lucifer, too, the morning-star, is, as in Greek astronomy, the star of Venus.[9]

It is, too, from Greek mythology that Venus comes back

---

[1] A. i. 680 hunc ego sopitum somno super alta Cythera
        aut super Idalium sacrata sede recondam.
A. x. 51 est Amathus, est celsa mihi Paphus atque Cythera
        Idaliaeque domus.
Ibid. 86 est Paphus Idaliumque tibi, sunt alta Cythera.
Cytherea A. i. 257, 657, iv. 128, v. 800, viii. 523, 615.

[2] Amathus A. x. 51; see above, n. 1.

[3] Paphus G. ii. 64; see p. 126, n. 2; A. i. 415 ipsa Paphum sublimis abit; A. x. 51, 86; see above, n. 1.

[4] Idalium A. i. 681, x. 51, 87; see above, n. 1.
A. v. 759 tum vicina astris Erycino in vertice sedes
        fundatur Veneri Idaliae.

[5] A. iii. 19 sacra Dionaeae matri divisque ferebam; cf. E. ix. 47.

[6] Eryx A. v. 759; see above, n. 4.

[7] A. viii. 370 at Venus . . .
        Volcanum adloquitur, thalamoque haec coniugis aureo
        incipit et dictis divinum aspirat amorem.

[8] A. xi. 276   cum ferro caelestia corpora demens
        appetii et Veneris violavi vulnere dextram.

[9] A. viii. 589 qualis ubi Oceani perfusus Lucifer unda,
        quem Venus ante alios astrorum diligit ignis.
Cf. A. ii. 801, where it is Lucifer who guides Aeneas from the ruins of Troy.

into the story of Rome as the wife of Anchises and the mother of Aeneas. She thus becomes throughout the poem the deity favouring the Trojans and therefore opposed to Iuno (Hera), the natural protectress of the Greeks. The ultimate meaning of this antagonism may be left for future discussion, but here may be noticed Venus' special care for her grandson Ascanius or Iulus.[1] This has an historic significance in that the house of the Iulii claimed descent from Iulus and had a special cult of Venus, and so the comet which appeared at Caesar's death is described by Virgil as 'the star of Dionaean Caesar'.[2] So in another definitely historical context Venus appears on the shield of Aeneas as one of the gods protecting Octavian's fleet against the outlandish deities of Egypt.[3] Venus was not in the historical religion of Rome a special protectress of the city, but she became so through her connexion with the Iulian house, as Apollo did through his association with Augustus.

Like many other of the gods Venus, too, has a 'faded personality' in Virgil and is frequently used, especially in the *Eclogues* and *Georgics*, as a personification or synonym of 'love' and its passions. Thus, to take a few instances, the lover working the charm in the eighth *Eclogue* bids her attendant weave 'the chains of Venus'[4]—a half-way usage; the herds of cattle 'seek Venus on certain days';[5] the old horse is 'cold to Venus';[6] and in the fourth book of

[1] A. x. 132 ipse inter medios, Veneris iustissima cura,
　　　　　Dardanius . . . puer.
Cf. A. i. 691 ff.
[2] E. ix. 47 ecce Dionaei processit Caesaris astrum.
[3] A. viii. 698 omnigenumque deum monstra et latrator Anubis
　　　　　contra Neptunum et Venerem contraque Minervam
　　　　　tela tenent.
[4] E. viii. 78 necte, Amarylli, modo et 'Veneris' dic 'vincula necto.'
[5] G. ii. 329 et Venerem certis repetunt armenta diebus.
[6] G. iii. 97 frigidus in Venerem senior.

the *Aeneid* Anna asks the widowed Dido, 'wilt thou never know sweet children or the joys of Venus?'[1] A peculiarly concrete use is found in the third *Eclogue*, where Damoetas says, 'I have gained the gifts for my Venus', meaning 'for my loved one'.[2]

Closely associated with Venus is her son Amor or Cupido, who is similarly the Greek boy-god Ἔρως. He plays a large part in the first book of the *Aeneid*,[3] when Venus sends him to Carthage to take the place of the young Ascanius, whom she spirits away, and to inflame the heart of Dido with passion for Aeneas, and he appears again in a 'faded' form in the indignant question of Iuno, 'was it with my guidance that the Trojan adulterer stormed Sparta, did I supply weapons or foster war by Cupid?'[4] The usage here is just parallel to the 'faded' meaning of Venus.

10. *Iuno* was one of the oldest of Italian goddesses, whose cult was spread all over the peninsula; indeed, she seems at first to have been more prominent in some other towns than Rome and only to have taken her full place of honour there when she was in the period of Etruscan influence established with Iuppiter and Minerva in the great temple on the Capitol. She was pre-eminently Iuno regina, but primarily a goddess of women and particularly of married women, her festival, the Matronalia, was celebrated by the matrons. She was a protectress in childbirth, Lucina, and of marriage, and was thought in her capacity as *pronuba* to lead the bride to her new home. There are far more traces in Virgil of this original character of Iuno than there are

---

[1] A. iv. 33 nec dulcis natos Veneris nec praemia noris; cf. also G. iii. 64, 137, 210, 267, iv. 199; A. vi. 26, xi. 736.

[2] E. iii. 68 parta meae Veneri sunt munera.

[3] A. i. 657 ff.

[4] A. x. 92 me duce Dardanius Spartam expugnavit adulter,
     aut ego tela dedi fovive Cupidine bella?

of the Italian Venus. There are hints of her cult at Gabii,[1] at Ardea,[2] and on the Alban Mount,[3] and in the description of the great cattle plague in the third book of the *Georgics* the lack of heifers for sacrifice to Iuno is specially noticed.[4] She appears in the *Aeneid* as *regina* or *regia*.[5] As Lucina she occurs in the fourth *Eclogue*, where she is implored to favour the birth of the child to be born,[6] and in the 'faded' sense, as a personification of childbirth, twice in the *Georgics*.[7] As *pronuba*[8] she plays a large part in the wedlock of Aeneas and Dido, and her function has been already hinted at in their first joint sacrifice to the gods.[9] In Italian mythology she is throughout the *Aeneid* the wife of Iuppiter[10] and the daughter of Saturn;[11] in both these attributions of relationship there is no doubt Greek influence.

In the Graeco-Roman period Iuno was naturally enough identified with Hera, the sister and wife of Zeus, and it is this identification which gives her her chief prominence in Virgil. Hera's cult at Argos,[12] the main seat

[1] A. vii. 682 arva Gabinae | Iunonis.
[2] Ardea A. vii. 411–20.
[3] Alban mount A. xii. 134 ff.
[4] G. iii. 531 tempore non alio dicunt regionibus illis
        quaesitas ad sacra boves Iunonis.
[5] A. i. 9 regina deum; A. vii. 572 Saturnia . . . regina; A. x. 62 regia Iuno.
[6] E. iv. 8 tu modo nascenti puero . . . casta fave Lucina.
[7] G. iii. 60 aetas Lucinam iustosque pati hymenaeos
        desinit ante decem.
G. iv. 340 (of a nymph) altera tum primos Lucinae experta labores.
[8] A. iv. 166   prima et Tellus et pronuba Iuno
        dant signum.
[9] A. iv. 57 mactant lectas de more bidentis | . . . Iunoni ante omnis, cui vincla iugalia curae.
[10] A. i. 46 Iovisque | et soror et coniunx; A. iv. 91 cara Iovis coniunx; A. vii. 287 saeva Iovis coniunx; A. vii. 308 magna Iovis coniunx; A. xii. 830 es germana Iovis.
[11] For Saturnia Iuno see p. 105, n. 2.
[12] A. iii. 547 Iunoni Argivae iussos adolemus honores.

of her worship in Hellas, is a
according to the bidding of Helenu
honours enjoined on them to Argive
the seventh book, 'the cruel wife of Iov
from Inachian Argos';[1] Virgil knows, too, of
island of Samos, and speaks of Carthage as 'the
Iuno is said to have cherished more than all lai.
ferring it even to Samos'.[2] Iuno has definitely the ch
ter of Hera in association with the legend of Io: 'with the
pest [the gadfly] in days gone by Iuno wreaked her
terrible wrath, when she devised a plague for the heifer-
daughter of Inachus';[3] and again in connexion with the
story of Heracles, who 'endured a thousand toils under
King Eurystheus by the fate of persecuting Iuno'.[4] Virgil
records a cult of Iuno in Troy,[5] but consistently with his
general view of her attitude makes her lead the Greeks in
the sack of the city.[6] It is, of course, because she is the
traditional protectress of the Greeks that she becomes
throughout the poem the enemy of the Trojans and the
bitter opponent of the foundation of Rome.[7] The more
philosophical meaning of this main feature of the poem
must be discussed later, but here it may be noticed that out
of this hatred of the Trojans arises the special position
which Iuno holds in the *Aeneid* of the patron-goddess of the

[1] A. vii. 286 ecce autem Inachiis sese referebat ab Argis.
[2] A. i. 15 quam Iuno fertur terris magis omnibus unam
    posthabita coluisse Samo.
[3] G. iii. 152 hoc quondam monstro horribilis exercuit iras
    Inachiae Iuno pestem meditata iuvencae.
[4] A. viii. 291   ut duros mille labores
    rege sub Eurystheo fatis Iunonis iniquae
    pertulerit.
[5] A. ii. 761 porticibus vacuis Iunonis asylo.
[6] A. ii. 612   hic Iuno Scaeas saevissima portas
    prima tenet sociumque furens a navibus agmen
    ferro accincta vocat.
[7] A. i. 12–16.

ed emphatically at
out several times in
d Dido engaged in
spot which the god-
ido's prayer at the
ic place at the end.[3]
ill be necessary to
a Iuno of the lower
as sacred,[4] and it is
Dido appeals in her
ate and the Dirae,[5]
usion to the idea of

hen preserves a more equal balance than usual between the Italian and Greek sides of her character, but in the main body of the *Aeneid* all is swallowed up in the mythological conception of the goddess as the bitter enemy of Aeneas and his men. It may be noted that there is no 'faded' meaning for Iuno.

11. *Iuppiter* always held a unique position among the deities of Italy; his name suggests that he was in fact identical with Zeus, and probably he was a common inheritance of both races from the Indo-Germanic stock of which they came. He is primarily a 'sky-god', not in any metaphysical sense, but as controller of the phenomena of the sky, the clouds and rain, the lightning and the thunder-

[1] A. i. 446 hic templum Iunoni ingens Sidonia Dido
   condebat.
[2] A. i. 441 lucus in urbe fuit media laetissimus umbrae,
   quo primum iactati undis et turbine Poeni
   effodere loco signum, quod regia Iuno
   monstrarat, caput acris equi.
[3] A. i. 734 adsit laetitiae Bacchus dator et bona Iuno.
[4] A. vi. 136   latet arbore opaca
   aureus et foliis et lento vimine ramus,
   Iunoni infernae dictus sacer.
[5] A. iv. 608 tuque harum interpres curarum et conscia Iuno.

bolt. He has also his position in the woods, and the oak is specially his tree. Gradually he emerges into a position of supremacy, partly as chief among the other gods, partly as the divine head of the Roman State. This is acknowledged in his position at Rome as the first of the early 'triad', Iuppiter, Mars, and Quirinus, and later of the more official triad, Iuppiter, Iuno, and Minerva, consecrated in the great Capitoline temple.

Of all this Italian character of Iuppiter there are abundant traces in Virgil. He is still clearly a sky-god and has control of the phenomena of weather. He is spoken of as 'the lofty king of the sky,'[1] and in the *Georgics* we are told that 'the Father himself ordained the times of heat and rain and the winds that bring the cold, what are the warnings of the moon in her monthly course, in what sign the winds fall'.[2] He 'covers the sky with shadow when black night takes the colour from things'.[3] He sends the rain when 'the almighty Father Sky descends with fertile showers into the bosom of his fruitful consort [the earth]'[4] and gathers the rainstorm when 'Iuppiter shivering with the winds hurls a watery tempest and bursts the hollow clouds in the heaven'.[5] In this sense he becomes almost a 'faded' synonym for rain; 'Iuppiter is to be dreaded for the ripening grapes',[6] 'Iuppiter will fall in abundance with life-giving showers',[7] 'Iuppiter wet with the south winds

[1] A. xii. 140 rex aetheris altus.
[2] G. i. 352 aestusque pluviasque et agentis frigora ventos
        ipse pater statuit quid menstrua luna moneret,
        quo signo caderent Austri.
[3] A. vi. 271   ubi caelum condidit umbra
        Iuppiter et rebus nox abstulit atra colorem.
[4] G. ii. 325 tum pater omnipotens fecundis imbribus Aether
        coniugis in gremium laetae descendit.
[5] A. ix. 670   cum Iuppiter horridus austris
        torquet aquosam hiemem et caelo cava nubila rumpit.
[6] G. ii. 419 iam maturis metuendus Iuppiter uvis.
[7] E. vii. 60 Iuppiter et laeto descendet plurimus imbri.

thickens the soil that just now was thin'.[1] But his most frequent association as a sky-god is with the thunderbolt and lightning, the association which gave him the cult-titles of Iuppiter Fulgur and Iuppiter Summanus (god of the lightning by night). 'The Father himself in the thick night of clouds wields the lightnings in his flashing hand';[2] Dido prays that 'the omnipotent Father might hurl me with his lightning to the shades';[3] Iuno complains that Pallas had usurped her father's rights and 'hurled Iove's whirling fire from the clouds'[4] to overthrow the Greek fleet, even as the mortal Salmoneus had dared to 'mimic the fires of Iuppiter and the sounds of Olympus'[5] and was hurled by Iuppiter's thunderbolt to the lower realms, where Aeneas saw him paying the penalty for his crime. A passage of considerable mythological interest describes Vulcan and his Cyclopes engaged on fashioning a thunder-bolt 'such as the many which from all across the sky the Father hurls upon the earth'.[6] On earth Iuppiter, like many other of the Italian deities, has an association with the woods; the Cyclopes standing on the cliff are like 'a wood of Iuppiter or a grove of Diana',[7] and Iaera had brought up the two sons of Alcanor 'in a grove of Iuppiter'.[8] But his special care is the oak, 'which, queen of the forest, puts

[1] G. i. 418   Iuppiter uvidus austris
    denset erant quae rara modo.

[2] G. i. 328 ipse Pater media nimborum in nocte corusca
    fulmina molitur dextra.

[3] A. iv. 25 vel pater omnipotens abigat me fulmine ad umbras.

[4] A. i. 42 ipsa Iovis rapidum iaculata e nubibus ignem
    disiecitque rates evertitque aequora ventis.

[5] A. vi. 585 vidi et crudelis dantem Salmonea poenas,
        dum flammam Iovis et sonitus imitatur Olympi, &c., to
    594.

[6] A. viii. 427 fulmen . . . toto genitor quae plurima caelo
      deicit in terras, &c., to 432.

[7] A. iii. 681 silva alta Iovis lucusve Dianae.

[8] A. ix. 673 quos Iovis eduxit luco silvestris Iaera.

forth her leaves for Iuppiter',[1] and the shepherd in the noonday heat seeks a valley where 'the great oak of Iuppiter with its hoary trunk stretches its huge boughs'.[2]

Virgil is sparing of the use of local cult-titles with Iuppiter, but he knows him as 'lord of Anxur',[3] and Evander brings out his association with the Capitoline hill, a spot of very hallowed associations, where 'the Arcadians believe that they have seen Iuppiter, when often he was shaking his black aegis in his hand and summoning the clouds'.[4] But the two titles which he most frequently applies to Iuppiter are *pater* and *rex*, both significant of the position he held in Roman religious thought. They are of course combined in the great phrase which Virgil thrice uses of him, 'Father of gods and king of men',[5] but this title does not imply that he was not also 'king of gods and father of men'. *Pater*, as Warde Fowler has shown,[6] was not intended in the old religion to imply any physical relationship, but was only a term of devotion and an acknowledgement of a god's care for men. It could not be directly applied to Iuppiter, for it was already a part of his very name. But it is very often used by Virgil as an equivalent for Iuppiter,[7] often in conjunction with the epithet *omnipotens*.[8] The synonym *genitor* one would expect to find in a more concrete sense of 'father', and so it is used in the expressions *genitor deum* and the queer *genitor caeli*, where

[1] G. ii. 15 nemorumque Iovi quae maxima frondet | aesculus.
[2] G. iii. 332 sicubi magna Iovis antiquo robore quercus
   ingentis tendat ramos.
[3] A. vii. 799 quis Iuppiter Anxurus arvis | praesidet.
[4] A. viii. 352   Arcades ipsum
   credunt se vidisse Iovem, cum saepe nigrantem
   aegida concuteret dextra nimbosque cieret.
[5] divum pater atque hominum rex, A. i. 65, ii. 648, x. 2.
[6] *Religious Experience*, pp. 155 ff.
[7] pater alone A. ii. 617, v. 690, vi. 780, vii. 558, &c.
[8] pater omnipotens A. i. 60, iii. 251, vii. 141, 770, &c.

caeli stands for *caelicolum*, 'father of the beings in heaven'.[1] But it is often used by itself, apparently as a mere equivalent of *pater*, and like *pater* is combined with the epithet *omnipotens*. The further synonym *sator*[2] has naturally a definitely physical sense and is used twice in the full phrase, 'begetter of men and gods'. *Rex*,[3] or its equivalent *regnator*, has similarly a more concrete sense than *pater*. Iuppiter is sometimes 'king of the gods', sometimes 'king of the dwellers in heaven', but more often 'king of Olympus', a phrase which could, of course, only have originated after the period of Greek influence. But he is also in Virgil *rex* alone, as he would have been in religious terminology, particularly in what is perhaps the most impressive religious phrase in all the *Aeneid*, 'king Iuppiter is the same for all; the fates will find a way'. Besides these titles deriving from the genuine Italian period, Iuppiter, when the Romans had learnt mythology, becomes 'the son of Saturn',[4] just as Iuno was 'the daughter of Saturn', and figures as her brother and husband. As a god of the lower world he is also Stygius[5] and is spoken of by Charon as 'king';[6] but the Iuppiter of the lower world is probably Dis.

Prayer to Iuppiter is, of course, common throughout the *Aeneid* and there are passages where his worship is more fully mentioned. Aeneas urges his comrades to 'pour libation from the platters to Iuppiter;[7] Ascanius vows to him

[1] genitor deum A. vii. 306; caeli A. ix. 630; genitor alone A. viii. 427, xi. 727, xii. 200, 843; genitor omnipotens A. x. 668.

[2] hominum sator atque deorum A. i. 254, xi. 725.

[3] rex deum A. iii. 375, xii. 851; regnator deum A. iv. 268; rex caelicolum A. iii. 21; rex Olympi A. v. 533, x. 621; regnator Olympi A. ii. 779, vii. 558; rex alone A. xii. 849, x. 112 rex Iuppiter omnibus idem, | fata viam invenient.

[4] A. iv. 371   iam iam nec maxima Iuno
              nec Saturnius haec oculis Pater aspicit aequis.
Cf. references given for Iuno on p. 105, n. 2.

[5] A. iv. 638 sacra Iovi Stygio, quae rite incepta paravi,
              perficere est animus.

[6] A. vi. 396 ipsius a solio regis.   [7] A. vii. 133 nunc pateras libate Iovi.

'to bring to thy temple the annual gifts and place before thy altars a white steer with gilded forehead',[1] the white steer being the correct offering to Iuppiter. Particularly interesting are two passages, in one of which we find Iuppiter associated with the ritual of purification,[2] and in the other, a scene on the shield of Aeneas, with the rites of treaty-making,[3] which are succinctly but accurately described: 'thereafter the same kings laying aside their mutual strife were standing armed before the altar of Iove, holding the sacred platters, and by the slaying of a sow were making their treaty.'

There is then abundant evidence that the ancient Italian conception of Iuppiter with its old associations was still surviving and held a large place in Virgil's mind.

The identification of this Italian Iuppiter with the Greek Zeus, since there was real identity, made less difference than most of the Graeco-Roman assimilations, for the Greek Zeus, too, was a sky-god and controlled the weather and its phenomena just as did the Italian Iuppiter: he, too, was 'father' and 'king'. Nevertheless, there are certain attributions made by Virgil to Iuppiter which in reality belong solely to the Greek Zeus. Among these may be placed certain local associations and most notably with Crete, where Zeus was nurtured on Mount Ida by the Curetes: 'In the midst of the Ocean', says Anchises, 'lies Crete the island of great Iuppiter, where is Mount Ida and the cradle of our race',[4] and when it is shown that Crete was not to be

[1] A. ix. 626 ipse tibi ad tua templa feram sollemnia dona
et statuam ante aras aurata fronte iuvencum
candentem.
[2] A. iii. 279 lustramurque Iovi votisque incendimus aras.
[3] A. viii. 639 post idem inter se posito certamine reges
armati Iovis ante aram paterasque tenentes
stabant et caesa iungebant foedera porca.
[4] A. iii. 104 Creta Iovis magni medio iacet insula ponto,
mons Idaeus ubi et gentis cunabula nostri.

the goal of the Trojans' wanderings, the Penates, seen in a vision, say to Aeneas: 'Iuppiter denies the fields of Dicte to thee',[1] denies them, that is, not only by his supreme authority, but also because they are his fields. So, again, in his solemn prayer at the first landing in Italy Aeneas invokes 'Iuppiter of Ida and the Phrygian Mother in due order'.[2] Another famous connexion of Zeus' is mentioned in the third book of the *Georgics*, that with the race-course of Olympia: 'if it is rather thy desire to breed for war and its fierce squadrons, or to glide on wheels past the streams of Alpheus at Pisa and in the grove of Iuppiter to drive thy flying car.'[3] A more remote identification is that with the Libyan Ammon,[4] whom the Greeks, when they discovered his shrine in Africa, had identified with their own Zeus; it is said that Iarbas, the Numidian suitor of Dido, who is himself described as 'the son of Ammon', 'raised a hundred vast temples to Iuppiter in his wide domain, placed in them a hundred altars and consecrated the undying fire, to keep eternal watch for the gods; the floor was rich with the blood of sacrifice and the threshold abloom with gay flower wreaths'. Here is, so to speak, an assimilation twice removed. A local connexion of special importance is that with Troy: Dardanus, the founder of the Trojan race, was said to have been the son of Zeus, born in Italy and migrated to Troy; thus Aeneas, in coming to Italy, was only seeking the country of his Zeus-born race. On this con-

[1] A. iii. 171   Dictaea negat tibi Iuppiter arva.
[2] A. vii. 139 Idaeumque Iovem Phrygiamque ex ordine matrem
                     invocat.
[3] G. iii. 179 sin ad bella magis studium turmasque ferocis,
                     aut Alphea rotis praelabi flumina Pisae
                     et Iovis in luco currus agitare volantis.
[4] A. iv. 198 hic Hammone satus rapta Garamantide nympha
                     templa Iovi centum latis immania regnis,
                     centum aras posuit vigilemque sacraverat ignem,
                     excubias divum aeternas; pecudumque cruore
                     pingue solum et variis florentia limina sertis.

nexion, clearly valuable for the story, Virgil insists often.
The messengers to Latinus claim that 'from Iove is the
origin of our race, the Dardan people boast Iove as their
grandsire, our king himself, Trojan Aeneas, is of the high
race of Iove'.[1] Hence Aeneas' twice-repeated boast that
he is 'of the race of highest Iove'.[2] The idea is expressed
already in the picture of the temple at the opening of the
third book of the *Georgics*: 'there shall stand in it the offspring of Assaracus and the names of the race sprung from
Iove';[3] and it may even lie behind the mysterious title of
the unborn child in the fourth *Eclogue*: 'great offshoot
of Iuppiter.'[4] Iuppiter takes over, too, not only the local
associations, but some of the legends of Zeus. Virgil seems
to have a particular fondness for the story of the defeat of
the giants who rose against the new Olympian régime,
possibly because it suggested a parallel to the rising of the
uncouth easterns against Octavian. In the lower world
are 'the vast bodies of the twin sons of Aloeus, who essayed
to reach the great heavens with their hands and to thrust
Iuppiter from his realm on high';[5] the punishment of the
giants is referred to again in the description of the island
Inarime, 'that hard bed, laid by the orders of Iuppiter on
Typhoeus',[6] and the battle recurs in the description of the
monster Aegaeon, 'who, they say, had a hundred arms

---

[1] A. vii. 219 ab Iove principium generis, Iove Dardana pubes
    gaudet avo, rex ipse Iovis de gente suprema:
    Troius Aeneas tua nos ad limina misit.
Cf. Hom. *Il.* xx. 215 Δάρδανον αὖ πρῶτον τέκετο νεφεληγερέτα Ζεύς.
[2] A. i. 380 et genus ab Iove summo; A. vi. 123 et mi genus ab Iove summo.
[3] G. iii. 35 Assaraci proles demissaeque ab Iove gentis
    nomina.
[4] E. iv. 49 magnum Iovis incrementum.
[5] A. vi. 582 hic et Aloidas geminos immania vidi
    corpora, qui manibus magnum rescindere caelum
    adgressi superisque Iovem detrudere regnis.
[6] A. ix. 715   durumque cubile
    Inarime Iovis imperiis imposta Typhoeo.

and a hundred hands, and fire blazed from fifty mouths
and fifty chests, when against the thunderbolts of Iuppiter
he raised a din with fifty shields and drew fifty swords'.[1]
The story of Salmoneus has already been noticed,[2] and
Iuno, in speaking to Iuturna, makes reference to the in-
numerable legends of Zeus' amours with mortal maidens,
oddly transferring them to an Italian setting: 'thou knowest, nymph, how I have preferred thee to all those nymphs
of Latium who have climbed the thankless couch of great-
souled Iove.'[3] From Zeus, too, is derived the attribution
to Iuppiter of the eagle as his favourite bird. The Trojans
in their first wanderings near Carthage see the twelve
swans, 'whom Iove's bird swooping from the heavenly
region was but now driving along the open sky';[4] on the
cloak which Aeneas gives as a prize for the boat-race is
woven the picture of Ganymede, 'whom the swift squire of
Iuppiter seized aloft from Ida in his crooked claws';[5] the
same description is employed later in a simile,[6] and in a
portent in the twelfth book we have the 'tawny bird of
Iuppiter' driving the shore-birds in rout.[7] Like Zeus, too,
Iuppiter takes his supreme oath by the Styx: 'he spake and
nodded assent to his words by the streams of his Stygian

---

[1] A. x. 565 Aegaeon qualis, centum cui bracchia dicunt
        centenasque manus, quinquaginta oribus ignem
        pectoribusque arsisse, Iovis cum fulmina contra
        tot paribus streperet clipeis, tot stringeret ensis.
[2] A. vi. 585–94; see p. 134, n. 5.
[3] A. xii. 143 scis ut te cunctis unam, quaecumque Latinae
        magnanimi Iovis ingratum ascendere cubile,
        praetulerim.
[4] A. i. 394 aetheria quos lapsa plaga Iovis ales aperto
        turbabat caelo.
[5] A. v. 254   quem praepes ab Ida
        sublimem pedibus rapuit Iovis armiger uncis.
[6] A. ix. 563 qualis ubi aut leporem aut candenti corpore cycnum
        sustulit alta petens pedibus Iovis armiger uncis.
[7] A. xii. 247 namque volans rubra fulvus Iovis ales in aethra
        litoreas agitabat avis.

brother, by the banks boiling with pitch and the black whirlpool and with his nod made all Olympus tremble.'[1] In a different region of legend, derived rather from Hesiod than from Homer, we find the idea of the iron age of Iuppiter contrasted with the golden age of Saturn (Kronos), bringing toil and trouble to men, where before nature had bountifully supplied their wants.[2]

Common to the conception of Zeus and Iuppiter alike was the idea of his supremacy over all the other gods, leading in a more reflective age to an almost monotheistic conception, in which Zeus was equated with fate, and after the prevalence of the Stoic philosophy to the notion of Zeus as the 'world-god'. This idea must be considered more fully in a later chapter, but its foundations may be noticed here. To it in its early stages belongs the frequently recurring title 'almighty' or 'omnipotent', almost a constant epithet in Virgil.[3] The epithet is not in fact confined to Iuppiter, and is applied also to Apollo and Iuno, to Olympus as the seat of Iuppiter, and in a significant manner also to Fortuna, but much more frequently to Iuppiter and in a less conventional sense.[4] What exactly the epithet meant to Virgil, it is not easy to say, but its application to Fortuna as well as to Iuppiter seems to suggest the ultimate divine power in the guidance of the events of the world which will be seen to be Virgil's highest theological conception. Iuppiter's supremacy over the other gods is again emphasized in the title, 'thou highest

---

[1] A. ix. 104 dixerat idque ratum Stygii per flumina fratris,
        per pice torrentis atraque voragine ripas
        adnuit, et totum nutu tremefecit Olympum.
Repeated in A. x. 113–15.

[2] G. i. 125 ante Iovem nulli subigebant arva coloni, &c.

[3] *omnipotens* as applied to Iuppiter G. ii. 325, A. i. 60, ii. 689, iii. 251, iv. 206, v. 687, vii. 141, 770, x. 100, &c.

[4] To Apollo A. xi. 790; to Iuno A. vii. 428; to Olympus A. x. 1, xii. 791; to Fortuna A. viii. 334.

ruler over the gods',[1] applied to him in prayer by Evander.
More interesting are certain passages in which we find an
expression of Iuppiter's relation to fate. This subject must
be discussed more fully later, but we may notice three
significant passages here. When, in the ninth book, Cybele
appeals to Iuppiter to save Aeneas' ships from destruction,
he replies: 'Mother, to what end dost thou summon the
fates? or what seekest thou in thy words [or 'for thy ships']?
can ships made by mortal hand have the rights of im-
mortals, and Aeneas in certainty traverse uncertain dan-
gers? to what god is such power granted?'[2] Here fate seems
to be set supreme above all gods, but the passage need not
in fact imply more than that it is above the will of Cybele;
for fate itself may be the will of god. In the moment before
the final meeting of Aeneas and Turnus, 'Iuppiter himself
holds up two scales with tongue set level and places therein
the divergent fates of the two, to see which his own toil
condemns and beneath whose weight death will sink'.[3]
The passage is imitated from Homer and again seems to
represent Iuppiter as waiting for the ultimate judgement
of fate; yet it is he who holds the scales. And in perhaps the
most majestic of all the utterances of the *Aeneid* Iuppiter
says of himself: 'King Iuppiter is the same for all, the fates
will find a way.'[4] He is perfect fairness and the fates, one
cannot but feel here, are his will. This comes very near to
the Stoic idea of πρόνοια, the divine guidance of the world

---

[1] A. viii. 572 divum tu maxime rector | Iuppiter.
[2] A. ix. 94 o genetrix, quo fata vocas? aut quid petis istis?
       mortaline manu factae immortale carinae
       fas habeant? certusque incerta pericula lustret
       Aeneas? cui tanta deo permissa potestas?
[3] A. xii. 725 Iuppiter ipse duas aequato examine lances
       sustinet et fata imponit diversa duorum,
       quem damnet labor et quo vergat pondere letum.
Cf. Hom. *Il.* xxii. 209.
[4] A. x. 112   rex Iuppiter omnibus idem:
       fata viam invenient.

by a destiny which is the expression of the immanent world-god. Lastly, the idea of the world-god itself is not often explicit in Virgil, but we may see it perhaps in the famous saying of the *Eclogues*: 'all things are full of Iuppiter.'[1] The phrase no doubt goes right back to Thales, but in the Stoic philosophy it had assumed a fuller and a richer content.

The picture of Iuppiter in Virgil is thus one of peculiar interest. It grows from the old Indo-European sky-god, through the early notions of Italy and the mythology of Greece, to a fine conception of a supreme and almost monotheistic deity who guides the destiny of men with righteousness towards a righteous end.

[1] E. iii. 60 Iovis omnia plena.

VI

THE GRAECO-ROMAN GODS

(II) GODS WITH ROMAN AND GREEK NAMES

MANY of the identified deities were known by the poets both by their Roman and their Greek names, and of these we have several in Virgil. The interest in the analysis here lies largely in observing how far essentially Italian functions are reserved for the Roman name and Greek for the Greek name, and how far there was a complete fusion. It will be seen that the combinations differ in individual cases. We may again begin with two of the deities already noticed among the gods of the Italian country-side.

1. *Faunus-Pan.* It has been seen (pp. 35 ff.) how the Fauni, as an unindividualized group of spirits, were recognized in the purest spirit of the old Italian religion among the deities of the country-side, how a single deity, Faunus, was evolved from the group, was given oracular powers, and under the influence of euhemerism became an ancient king of Italy and the father of Latinus. There is little to be added of Faunus himself in his appearances in Virgil, except that he is appealed to by Turnus in his hour of need as one of the Italian deities[1] whose worship he had never neglected. This passage is, however, of particular interest, because it is connected with a characteristic open-air worship of Faunus at an ancient wild olive tree,[2] which the Trojans had torn up to clear the ground with the result that Aeneas' spear, which he had planted there, could not be removed; the violation of the *religio* of the sacred spot

---

[1] A. xii. 777 'Faune, precor, miserere' inquit, 'tuque optima ferrum
　　　Terra tene, colui vestros si semper honorès.'
[2] A. xii. 766–76.

had its immediate effect. There is an additional point of interest in that Virgil tells us that the wild olive was 'a stock long venerated by seamen, on which saved from the waves they were wont to fasten their gifts to the god of Laurentum and hang up the garments they had vowed'.[1] The dedication of their clothes by shipwrecked sailors is, of course, a constant *motif*, but it is not elsewhere known in connexion with Faunus, who is by nature a land deity.

In the period of Greek influence Faunus was assimilated to the Greek Pan in a closer union than usual. They were not merely identified by a similarity of function—for Pan, like Faunus, was a rustic deity with the care, if not of all the flocks, yet at any rate of the goats—but a supposed similarity in their festivals led to the belief that they were actually the same. The festival of the Λύκαια at which Pan was worshipped in his home in Arcadia was taken, largely owing to the name, to be identical with the Lupercalia of the Palatine, with which, at any rate in historical times, Faunus was associated. Hence arose the legend that Evander brought with him the worship of Pan from Arcadia and established it at the Lupercal on the Palatine.[2] To this legend Virgil alludes when Evander is showing Aeneas the sacred sites: 'next he shows the vast grove, which fierce Romulus made the Asylum and the Lupercal beneath its cool grot, named after the Arcadian manner of the Lycaean Pan.'[3] The Greek Pan was conceived as a half-beast, with goat's feet and a horned head: these characteristics are attributed to

[1] A. xii. 766 forte sacer Fauno foliis oleaster amaris
　　　　　hic steterat, nautis olim venerabile lignum,
　　　　　servati ex undis ubi figere dona solebant
　　　　　Laurenti divo et votas suspendere vestis.
[2] Plut. *Rom.* 21; Ov. *Fast.* ii. 271–82.
[3] A. viii. 342 hinc lucum ingentem, quem Romulus acer asylum
　　　　　rettulit, et gelida monstrat sub rupe Lupercal
　　　　　Parrhasio dictum Panos de more Lycaei.

him by Ovid,[1] but never by Virgil. On the other hand he has many of his Greek attributes. He is 'god of Arcadia'[2] and 'lord of Tegea';[3] it was he who, according to a strange Greek story, deceived the moon into wedlock.[4] Above all, Pan was the inventor of the musical reeds, the 'Pan-pipes': 'Pan first taught how to join many pipes with wax',[5] 'Pan first suffered not the reeds to lie idle',[6] Pan, who, if Virgil could only have strength to sing as he would, 'would confess defeat even with Arcadia to judge'.[7] These are all characteristics of the Greek Pan and Virgil never attributes them to Faunus. On the other hand, Pan becomes not only the god of goats, but like Faunus the 'guardian of the sheep':[8] 'Pan cares for the sheep and the sheeps' masters.'[9] And so we find Pan, now fully identified with Faunus, in company with the nymphs and shepherds. It is Pan, not Faunus, who in the famous line of the *Georgics* is placed with 'old Silvanus and the sister nymphs' among the *di agrestes*,[10] and when Daphnis rises to heaven, 'keen joy seizes on the woods and all the fields and Pan and the shepherds and the Dryad nymphs'.[11] These are contexts in which we should certainly have expected to find Faunus.

Virgil then assimilates Pan and Faunus, but assimilates

[1] Ov. *Fast.* ii. 268, iii. 312, v. 99, &c.
[2] E. x. 26, G. iii. 392 Pan deus Arcadiae.
[3] G. i. 18 o Tegeaee.
[4] G. iii. 392 Pan deus Arcadiae captam te, Luna, fefellit
   in nemora alta vocans.
[5] E. ii. 32 Pan primum calamos cera coniungere pluris
   instituit.
[6] E. viii. 24 Panaque, qui primus calamos non passus inertis.
[7] E. iv. 58 Pan etiam, Arcadia mecum si iudice certet,
   Pan etiam Arcadia dicat se iudice victum.
[8] G. i. 17 Pan, ovium custos.
[9] E. ii. 33 Pan curat ovis oviumque magistros.
[10] G. ii. 494 Panaque Silvanumque senem nymphasque sorores.
[11] E. v. 58 ergo alacris silvas et cetera rura voluptas
   Panaque pastoresque tenet Dryadasque puellas.

with discrimination. He knows the legends and characteristics which belong to the Greek god and will not assign them to Faunus; nor will he let Pan take the place of the euhemerized Faunus of Italy. But where the ground is really common, in the case of the flocks, he can speak of Pan and Faunus indifferently.

2. *Liber-Bacchus*. The treatment of this assimilated pair of deities by Virgil forms a marked contrast to that of Faunus-Pan, and no doubt reflects the usage of his age. Liber was in the Italian religion a corn-spirit, who with Libera formed a deity-pair concerned with the growth of the crops; of this ancient conception there is, as has been seen (p. 38), no trace in Virgil. After the Greek influence had come, Liber was identified with the Greek Bacchus in his capacity of god of the vine and of wine; he was also associated in a new triad, Liber, Libera, and Ceres, regarded as the equivalent of the Eleusinian triad, Iacchus, Kore, and Demeter. So completely was he merged in Bacchus that we shall find him in Virgil used as a mere synonym even in legendary passages referring to the Greek Dionysus. But in compensation, as it were, there is a modification in the conception of Bacchus. Sometimes he is the genuine Greek Dionysus, worshipped by the Bacchanals in their wild mountain orgies and at the soberer dramatic festivals at Athens and invested with all the Greek legends. But in his agricultural capacity as god of the vine, he takes on a more distinctly Roman character, which is seen specially in the *Georgics*. It will therefore be most convenient to begin with an analysis of Virgil's treatment of Bacchus.

Bacchus is found as the Greek Dionysus of the Bacchanals when Dido in her frenzy is compared to 'a Thyiad roused by the start of the sacred rites, when hearing the cry of "Bacchus" they spur on the triennial orgies and

Cithaeron at night re-echoes with their cries'.[1] In the
same character he appears in the famous passage of the
seventh book of the *Aeneid*, where Queen Amata, spurred
on by the fury Allecto, 'feigning the inspiration of Bacchus'
rushes into the woods to hide her daughter Lavinia and
save her from marrying Aeneas, 'crying Evoe, Bacchus,
proclaiming that thou alone art worthy of the maid, for in
thine honour does she take up the pliant thyrsus, thee doth
she honour in the dance, and for thee cherish her consecrated locks'.[2] The matrons, roused by the queen and
'mazed by Bacchus, leap through the distant groves in
their inspired bands';[3] this is a transference of the wild
Thracian cult to Italian soil.

So in the fourth book of the *Georgics* Virgil tells how 'the
matrons of the Cicones amid the rites of the gods and the
orgies of Bacchus by night tore asunder the body of Orpheus and scattered his limbs over the wide fields',[4] and
Daphnis in the fifth *Eclogue* is said to have 'taught men to
lead the inspired bands of Bacchus and to weave the pliant
spears with twining leaves';[5] an allusion has been suspected
here to the reintroduction of the cult of Dionysus by Iulius
Caesar. There are hints, too, of the legend of Dionysus

[1] A. iv. 301   qualis commotis excita sacris
                Thyias, ubi audito stimulant trieterica Baccho
                orgia nocturnusque vocat clamore Cithaeron.
[2] A. vii. 385 quin etiam in silvas simulato numine Bacchi . . .
                evolat et natam frondosis montibus abdit . . .
                euhoe Bacche fremens, solum te virgine dignum
                vociferans: etenim mollis tibi sumere thyrsos,
                te lustrare choro, sacrum tibi pascere crinem.
Cf. A. vii. 405 reginam Allecto stimulis agit undique Bacchi.
[3] A. vii. 580   attonitae Baccho nemora avia matres
                insultant thiasis.
[4] G. iv. 520   spretae Ciconum quo munere matres
                inter sacra deum nocturnique orgia Bacchi
                discerptum latos iuvenem sparsere per agros.
[5] E. v. 30   Daphnis thiasos inducere Bacchi
                et foliis lentas intexere mollibus hastas.

in the reference to 'Bacchus' spotted lynxes',[1] and in the charge that 'Bacchus too has given cause for censure, 'twas he who laid low the maddened Centaurs in death',[2] though in the last instance it is perhaps not so much a legend of the god, as an accusation against his product, wine. The Athenian cult of Dionysus and its dramatic performances are the theme of a fine passage in the second book of the *Georgics*,[3] and there is a suggestion of an equivalent performance in Italy[4] which seems to be a kind of combination of the Fescennine ribaldry and the practice of hanging *oscilla* as charms in the fields against evil influences on the crops; essentially Italian practices are here gratuitously identified with a rather remote Greek equivalent. As it were in extenuation of this very unusual assimilation of rites the poet goes on to urge the countrymen to a kind of Graeco-Roman Bacchus ritual: 'therefore with due rites we will pay Bacchus his honour in the hymns of our own country, we will bear platters and cakes (*lances et liba*), and led by the horn the sacred goat shall stand at the altar, and we will roast his fat entrails on spits of hazel.'[5] The whole passage is full of interest, for this blending and identification of Greek and Roman rites is rarer than the blending of the persons of the gods. A further reference to this Graeco-Italian cult is found when Tarchon upbraids the Etruscans:

[1] G. iii. 264 lynces Bacchi variae.

[2] G. ii. 455 Bacchus et ad culpam causas dedit; ille furentis
    Centauros leto domuit.

[3] G. ii. 380–4.

[4] G. ii. 385–9 nec non Ausonii, Troia gens missa, coloni
    versibus incomptis ludunt risuque soluto,
    oraque corticibus sumunt horrenda cavatis,
    et te, Bacche, vocant per carmina laeta, tibique
    oscilla ex alta suspendunt mollia pinu.

[5] G. ii. 393–6 ergo rite suum Baccho dicemus honorem
    carminibus patriis lancesque et liba feremus,
    et ductus cornu stabit sacer hircus ad aram,
    pinguiaque in veribus torrebimus exta colurnis.

'Ye are not slow ... when Bacchus' curved pipe summons you to the dance.'[1]

The narrower conception of Bacchus as the protector of the vine and the producer of wine is prominent in the dedicatory opening of the second book of the *Georgics*:[2] 'Now, Bacchus, of thee will I sing ... hither, father Lenaeus, (here all things are full of thy gifts, for thee the field teems heavy with the tendrils of autumn, the vat foams full to the brim); come hither, father Lenaeus, strip off thy buskins and with me dye thy naked limbs in the fresh must.' The whole book is full of this conception of Bacchus, which, though it is here clothed with Greek cult-titles and expressed with Greek metrical forms and licences, is really Italian in idea: Bacchus is the functional spirit with a limited sphere. Echoes appear in another book of the *Georgics*, in the phrase 'the Massic gifts of Bacchus',[3] and when at Dido's banquet, 'Bacchus, giver of happiness',[4] is summoned to the feast. Incidentally may be noticed the recurrence of the cult-title Lenaeus,[5] and the use of another of Dionysus' epithets, Lyaeus.[6]

Closely linked with this conception of Bacchus as god of wine comes the 'faded' use of his name, so characteristic of the Augustan age when real belief had died away, as a mere synonym for 'wine'. Such phrases as 'mingle the honeycomb with milk and mellow Bacchus', 'the vines

---

[1] A. xi. 737 ubi curva choros indixit tibia Bacchi.

[2] G. ii. 2 nunc te, Bacche, canam ...
　　　huc, pater o Lenaee (tuis hic omnia plena
　　　muneribus, tibi pampineo gravidus autumno
　　　floret ager, spumat plenis vindemia labris)
　　　huc, pater o Lenaee, veni, nudataque musto
　　　tinge novo mecum dereptis crura coturnis.

[3] G. iii. 526 Massica Bacchi | munera.

[4] A. i. 734 adsit laetitiae Bacchus dator.

[5] G. ii. 529 te libans, Lenaee, vocat.

[6] A. iv. 57 　　　　　　　mactant lectas de more bidentis
　　　legiferae Cereri Phoeboque patrique Lyaeo.

flowing with much Bacchus', 'take cups of Maeonian Bacchus', 'enlivening the banquet with much Bacchus', or in a typical combination, 'they load on the baskets the gifts of well-wrought Ceres, and minister Bacchus',[1] and many other similar passages speak for themselves of a purely literary convention, where all religious sense has been lost. It has not perhaps been sufficiently noticed that Bacchus in this deflated and concrete sense is also used for the vine. This is, of course, especially the case in the second book of the *Georgics*: "tis joy to sow Ismarus with Bacchus', 'Bacchus loves the open hills, the cypresses the cold of the north wind', 'the one soil favours corn-crops, the other Bacchus', 'a barren soil will not preserve his stock for Bacchus, nor their names for the fruit-trees', 'Bacchus is as quick to grow in close-packed rich soil';[2] the substitution is everywhere obvious and it is to be noticed how often it is emphasized by the juxtaposition of a common noun for 'plant' or 'tree'. Outside the second book of the *Georgics* we find the same usage: the old bee-keeper's plot 'had no crop fertile for the steers nor suited for the flocks nor fit for Bacchus',[3] and among Turnus' allies were 'those who with their harrows turn Massica fertile in Bacchus'.[4]

The Roman name Liber is used as a mere synonym for

[1] G. i. 344 lacte favos et miti dilue Baccho; G. ii. 190 multoque fluentis . . . Baccho vitis; G. iv. 380 cape Maeonii carchesia Bacchi; E. v. 69 multo in primis hilarans convivia Baccho; A. viii. 180 onerantque canistris | dona laboratae Cereris, Bacchumque ministrant; cf. E. vi. 15, G. ii. 143, iv. 102, 279, A. i. 215, iii. 354, v. 77.

[2] G. ii. 37 iuvat Ismara Baccho | conserere.
　　Ibid. 112 apertos
　　　　Bacchus amat collis, Aquilonem et frigora taxi.
　　Ibid. 228 altera frumentis quoniam favet, altera Baccho.
　　Ibid. 240 Baccho genus aut pomis sua nomina servat.
　　Ibid. 275 in denso non segnior ubere Bacchus.

[3] G. iv. 128 nec fertilis illa iuvencis
　　　nec pecori opportuna seges nec commoda Baccho.

[4] A. vii. 725 vertunt felicia Baccho
　　　Massica qui rastris.

Bacchus in all senses. He appears as the Thracian Dionysus when Anchises tells Aeneas that the nations shall
tremble before Augustus more than before 'Liber, who in
triumph guides his yoked car with reins of tendrils, driving
his tiger from the lofty height of Nysa'.[1] As the god of the
vine he is coupled with 'life-giving Ceres' in the invocation
to the *Georgics*,[2] and when in the *Eclogues* it is said that
'Liber grudges the hills the tendrils' shade',[3] he is the vine
rather than the god.

In the Greek mysteries it was Iacchus rather than Bacchus who was associated with Demeter and Kore, and so
Virgil rightly speaks of 'the mystic winnowing fan of
Iacchus';[4] but elsewhere Iacchus, too, is a mere equivalent
of Bacchus: 'the poplar is dear to Alcides, the vine to
Iacchus',[5] and Silenus has 'his veins puffed, as ever, with
yesterday's Iacchus',[6] the conventional equivalent of wine
once more.

In his treatment of Liber-Bacchus, then, it may be said
that Virgil is fully conscious of all his Greek character and
attributes, but inclines to give a true Latin turn to him as
protector of the vine, and emphasizes this by the 'faded'
concrete uses of his name.

3. *Pallas-Minerva*. The interest here again lies in the
extent of Virgil's assimilation and discrimination. Minerva
was an old Italian goddess of handicraft, especially perhaps
of women's work, who attained to a high position in Etruria
and the neighbouring country; she came to Rome from
the town of Falerii, was the patroness of the craft-guilds,

---

[1] A. vi. 804 nec qui pampineis victor iuga flectit habenis
        Liber, agens celso Nysae de vertice tigris.
[2] G. i. 7 Liber et alma Ceres.
[3] E. vii. 58 Liber pampineas invidit collibus umbras.
[4] G. i. 166 mystica vannus Iacchi.
[5] E. vii. 61 populus Alcidae gratissima, vitis Iaccho.
[6] E. vi. 15 inflatum hesterno venas, ut semper, Iaccho.

and had her place in the great Etruscan temple on the Capitol with Iuppiter and Iuno. Probably through the connexion with crafts, the Greek Pallas, who had similar associations, was identified with Minerva. Pallas Athena was of course in Greek legend the daughter of Zeus. She was a protector of cities (πολιοῦχος) and in particular of Athens; in this capacity she had a shrine in Troy from which Diomede and Ulysses stole her image, the Palladium, and thus incurred her wrath. But in general throughout the Trojan war she was the champion of the Greeks. Her character in Greece was pre-eminently that of a war-goddess, but she had also the love of craftsmen and at Athens was the protectress of the olive, her favourite plant.

Virgil shows his faithfulness to history in that, though he uses Minerva as the equivalent of Pallas—he never speaks of Athena—in almost all her functions, it is Minerva alone who appears as the patron of women's crafts and never Pallas; he is faithful to Minerva's true Italian character.

Let us look then first at Pallas with Minerva as her equivalent. When the Trojans first approach Italy they see on the heights a 'temple of Minerva',[1] and landing they made a prayer to 'the holy deity of Pallas of the rattling arms'.[2] The temple on the heights suggests Pallas πολιοῦχος, in which capacity she appears in the *Eclogues*, 'let Pallas dwell in the citadels she has founded'.[3] So as the patron of Troy she has her temple there: the two sea-snakes on their way to take vengeance on Laocoon make for 'the citadel of fierce Tritonis',[4] and in the sculptures in Dido's new palace the Trojan matrons are seen bearing the peplus to Pallas' temple, just as the Athenian matrons bore it to the

---

[1] A. iii. 531 templumque apparet in arce Minervae.
[2] A. iii. 543 tum numina sancta precamur | Palladis armisonae.
[3] E. ii. 61 Pallas quas condidit arces | ipsa colat.
[4] A. ii. 226 saevaeque petunt Tritonidis arcem.

Parthenon.[1] This temple in Troy is connected with two important incidents in the poem, in which individual Greeks offended against Pallas. The first was the theft of the Palladium during the siege, which is described in the second *Aeneid*, by 'impious Tydides and Ulysses, plotter of crimes';[2] it is alluded to later in the poem by Turnus, who says that he will never have recourse to 'deeds of darkness and the cowardly theft of the Palladium'.[3] The second was the carrying off, during the sack, of Cassandra from 'the temple and shrine of Minerva',[4] where she had taken refuge. This crime was, as Iuno tells us, the deed of Ajax and was the cause of the Greeks' shipwreck on their way home.[5] It is alluded to in a very different context when Anchises in the lower world prophesies that L. Aemilius Paulus will avenge 'the grandsires of Troy and the polluted temple of Minerva'.[6] Yet in spite of these offences Pallas is in the main the champion of the Greeks in the war. It is she who prompts them to construct the wooden horse, built 'by the inspiring art of Pallas'[7] (there may be

---

[1] A. i. 479 interea ad templum non aequae Palladis ibant
　　　　crinibus Iliades passis peplumque ferebant.
The ceremony of the peplus clearly made a great impression on Virgil's mind, for he attributes it also to the city of Latinus:
A. xi. 477 nec non ad templum summasque ad Palladis arces
　　　　　subvehitur magna matrum regina caterva
　　　　　dona ferens.

[2] A. ii. 163 ff.

[3] A. ix. 150　　　　　　　　tenebras et inertia furta
　　　　　　Palladii.

[4] A. ii. 403 ecce trahebatur passis Priameia virgo
　　　　　crinibus a templo Cassandra adytisque Minervae.

[5] A. i. 39　　　　　　　　　Pallasne exurere classem
　　　　　Argivum atque ipsos potuit summergere ponto
　　　　　unius ob noxam et furias Aiacis Oilei?
Cf. A. xi. 259　　　　　　　　　scit triste Minervae
　　　　　　sidus et Euboicae cautes ultorque Caphereus.

[6] A. vi. 840 ultus avos Troiae templa et temerata Minervae.

[7] A. ii. 15 instar montis equum divina Palladis arte
　　　　aedificant.

an allusion here to her patronage of handicraft) and regarded as 'a gift to the maiden Minerva'.[1] And at the end
when the Greeks have taken Troy, 'Tritonian Pallas is
seen seated on the top of the citadel'.[2]

Pallas appears in her general character as goddess of war
both in the prayer already quoted to 'Pallas of the rattling
arms',[3] in the appeal of the Latin matrons to 'Maiden
Tritonia, queen of arms, arbiter of war',[4] and in the description of the Cyclopes, who, when Volcanus came to
them, were working at 'the dread aegis, the arms of wrath-
ful Pallas'.[5] In her capacity as protectress of Athens, Pallas
had particular care of the olive, and this side of her
character naturally finds its place in the *Georgics*: 'stubborn
lands and churlish hills are rich in the woods of Pallas'
long-lived olive';[6] in this capacity, too, 'Minerva, inven-
tress of the olive' is a synonym.[7] In the *Aeneid* also the
envoys of Aeneas to Latinus are 'all veiled in the branches
of Pallas',[8] they had, that is, wreaths of olive, the symbol of
peace. Once, too, Pallas is met with in an association she
rarely has with prophecy, for it was she 'who taught the
aged Nautes and made him famous in many an art'.[9]

In all these contexts Pallas-Minerva is really the Greek
goddess introduced with her attributes, her sympathies,
and her history. But there are places, too, where Minerva,
never Pallas, is the genuine Italian goddess, who has her

[1] A. ii. 31 innuptae donum exitiale Minervae; 189 dona Minervae.
[2] A. ii. 615 iam summas arces Tritonia, respice, Pallas
        insedit.
[3] A. iii. 543; see p. 153, n. 2.
[4] A. xi. 483 armipotens, praeses belli, Tritonia virgo.
[5] A. viii. 435 aegidaque horriferam, turbatae Palladis arma.
[6] G. ii. 179 difficiles primum terrae collesque maligni . . .
        Palladia gaudent silva vivacis olivae.
[7] G. i. 18 oleaeque Minerva | inventrix.
[8] A. vii. 154 ramis velatos Palladis omnis.
[9] A. v. 704   senior Nautes, unum Tritonia Pallas
        quem docuit multaque insignem reddidit arte.

seat in the Capitoline temple and is the deity of handicraft.
On the shield of Aeneas the outlandish gods of Egypt fight
at Actium against 'Neptune and Venus and against
Minerva'.[1] The reason for this list is obscure. Neptune is
presumably the sea-god who favoured Augustus in this
sea-battle, Venus is the protectress of the Julian house
and, as she is all through the poem, of the Roman 'sons of
Aeneas'. Minerva is probably there as the representative
of the Capitoline triad; Iuppiter cannot be here mentioned as he is the ultimate arbiter, and Iuno because in
the *Aeneid* she is the opponent of the Roman race. Minerva
appears also three times in the *Aeneid* as the patron of
women's work of spinning and weaving. Aeneas' prize to
Sergestus after the boat-race is 'a slave-woman, not un-
skilled in the tasks of Minerva';[2] Camilla when she first
appears is described as 'a warrior maid, her hands all
unaccustomed to the distaff or baskets of Minerva'[3]—a
good phrase, by the way, for 'a work-basket'; and the
hour of midnight is described as the time 'when first a
woman, whose task it is to support life by the distaff and
thin-spun Minerva,[4] rouses the ashes and the slumbering
flames' for her work; here we again have the use of the
deity for the concrete thing with which she is associated.
Finally, there is the description of the spider as 'hated of
Minerva';[5] Servius adduces legend for this, but it is
probable that behind it lies the idea of a rival in the craft.

[1] A. viii. 699 contra Neptunum et Venerem contraque Minervam
        tela tenent.
[2] A. v. 284 olli serva datur operum haud ignara Minervae.
[3] A. vii. 805 bellatrix, non illa colo calathisve Minervae
        femineas adsueta manus.
[4] A. viii. 408   cum femina primum,
        cui tolerare colo vitam tenuique Minerva
        impositum, cinerem et sopitos suscitat ignis.
[5] G. iv. 246   invisa Minervae
        laxos in foribus suspendit aranea cassis.

Pallas, then, had taken over Minerva and absorbed her in almost all her associations, but once again the old Italian conception survives, uncontaminated by the intrusion of Pallas. It is a good example of Virgil's knowledge and scrupulousness.

4. *Diana (Artemis)-Hecate*. Among the deities with both Greek and Roman names may be included Diana, for although Artemis, with whom she was directly identified, is not mentioned by Virgil, her chthonic counterpart, Hecate, occurs not infrequently. Virgil reflects, too, the complicated history of Diana with her Italian and Greek associations in Roman religion and mythology. As a Latin goddess of the woods and groves, she was worshipped particularly in her grove at Aricia. She seems at one time to have been the central deity of the Latin league, and it was probably in order to establish herself in the headship of the league that Rome founded a cult of Diana on the Aventine. Her character as a deity of the woods led to her identification with the Greek huntress-goddess Artemis, daughter of Zeus and Latona and sister of Phoebus Apollo. From Artemis Diana took over new associations. She became a moon-goddess, sister of Phoebus, the sun, and assimilated various legends belonging to Artemis. She also acquired the chthonic associations which had accrued to Artemis from her merging with the underworld deity, Hecate. Virgil scrupulously refrains from attributing these chthonic associations to Diana herself; he frequently refers to Hecate, and as a kind of 'half-way house' he uses the cult-title *Trivia*, derived from the worship of the chthonic Artemis at the cross-ways (τριοδῖτις), alike for the chthonic Hecate and for the Italian Diana; it is in fact the most frequent of his names for Diana and acts as a link between the upper- and lower-world associations. There are thus in Virgil four names for the goddess—

Diana, Latonia, Trivia, Hecate—all suggesting different associations.

In the first place Diana appears in her true Italian character as the deity of groves and in particular of the grove of Aricia,[1] where she has her 'wealthy altar easily appeased',[2] and near to which is the 'lake of Trivia'[3] (Lake Nemi), which was popularly known as 'Diana's mirror'. Her legendary associations in the grove are indicated by its description as 'the wood of Egeria'[4] and more specifically by the strange Graeco-Roman story of Hippolytus,[5] whose son appears in the ranks of the Italian army.[6] Hippolytus, it was said, after he had been thrown from his chariot and killed, was restored to life by Aesculapius and 'the love of Diana',[7] but Iuppiter (Zeus) in indignation slew the physician with a thunderbolt; Diana (Artemis), however, hid Hippolytus in the grove of Aricia under the care of the nymph Egeria. There he was known by the new name of Virbius, which was interpreted by the commentators as signifying *vir bis*, the 'twice-born'. And this is the reason, adds Virgil,[8] why horses are excluded from the grove, because they were the cause of Hippolytus' death. If an attempt is to be made to unravel this tangled skein, it would seem that on the Italian side there were two minor spirits or attendants associated with Diana in the grove of Aricia, Egeria and Virbius,[9] and that there was an

[1] A. iii. 681 silva alta Iovis lucusve Dianae.

[2] A. vii. 764 pinguis ubi et placabilis ara Dianae.

[3] A. vii. 516 audiit et Triviae longe lacus; Servius notes 'hic est, qui Dianae speculum dicitur'.   [4] A. vii. 763 Egeriae lucis.   [5] A. vii. 761–82.

[6] A. vii. 761 ibat et Hippolyti proles pulcherrima bello,
        Virbius, insignem quem mater Aricia misit.

[7] A. vii. 769 Paeoniis revocatum herbis et amore Dianae.

[8] A. vii. 778 unde etiam templo Triviae lucisque sacratis
        cornipedes arcentur equi, quod litore currum
        et iuvenem monstris pavidi effudere marinis.

[9] Servius (*ad* A. vii. 761) seems to suspect something of the sort: revera ... Virbius est numen coniunctum Dianae, ut Matri deum Attis.

ancient taboo forbidding horses to enter the grove. On the Greek side there was the legend that Hippolytus, who was of course a devotee of Artemis, had been restored after death. After the identification of Diana and Artemis and the accretion of myths to Italian cults, the Italian goddess and her protégé Virbius seemed to provide a ready explanation of the survival of Hippolytus, and his story a cause for the taboo on horses. It is an interesting and almost unique instance of the happy conflation of Greek and Italian customs and ideas. We may notice in passing that the name Trivia is used in the story as a mere synonym for Artemis-Diana.

The other legend in the *Aeneid* which closely concerns Diana is that of Camilla,[1] the story of whose infancy and her subsequent prowess and death in battle against the Aeneadae occupies the greater part of the second half of book xi. The name appears to be nothing but the feminine of *camillus*, the ordinary word for an attendant at a sacrifice; if we can believe Virgil's statement[2] that there was an older form *Casmilla*, it might, like *Casmenae* (*Camenae*) and *Carmentis* be derived from the root of *carmen* and suggest a prophetic nymph. We may probably see again in Camilla a woodland nymph associated with Diana in the grove of Aricia, nor is there any reason here for suspecting the intrusion of the legend of Artemis. The story of the fleet-footed warrior nymph may have been an old Italian legend, which either became attached popularly to the Aeneas story, or was consciously adopted by Virgil for

[1] A. vii. 803–17, xi. 498 ff., 648 to end.
[2] A. xi. 542   matrisque vocavit
              nomine Casmillae mutata parte Camillam.
Servius (D), commenting on the line, states on the authority of Statius Tullianus that *casmillus* is Greek and was used by Callimachus. Müller refers this to a Cabeiric god known as Casmilus (Cadmus). This is conjecture. For *camilla* as the feminine of *camillus* Servius refers to Pacuvius, caelitum camilla exspectata advenis, used of Medea.

his own purposes.[1] Here again it may be noticed that the name Trivia is twice used as nothing but a straightforward synonym of Diana.[2]

To balance these traces of Italian tradition there are certain places where Diana is undoubtedly the Greek Artemis. Aeneas, greeted on his way to Carthage by his mother in disguise, inquires if she is 'Phoebus' sister or one of the race of nymphs';[3] a more explicit reference occurs in a simile later in the same book: 'even as on the banks of Eurotas or in the glades of Cynthus Diana trains her bands, and in her wake gather from all sides a thousand mountain nymphs; she bears her quiver on her shoulder and, as she strides, o'er-tops all the goddesses.'[4] From the Artemis legend, too, comes the story of the devastation of Calydon by the wild boar,[5] owing to the failure of King Oeneus to sacrifice to the goddess—a story quoted by Iuno as a justification for the persecution of the Trojans. Under the name Phoebe, Diana twice appears as a moon-goddess,[6] and is alluded to in this character in a passage[7] which contains an interesting combination of Diana's functions, when Nisus, 'looking up to the moon' prays to 'the daughter of Lato, glory of the stars and

[1] Conington on *Aen*. vii. 803 states dogmatically that Camilla is an invention of the poet's, but it seems improbable that there should not be some tradition behind a person who plays so important a part in the story.

[2] A. xi. 566 donum Triviae (Metabus' spear); ibid. 836 Triviae custos (Opis).

[3] A. i. 329 an Phoebi soror an nympharum sanguinis una?

[4] A. i. 498 qualis in Eurotae ripis aut per iuga Cynthi
   exercet Diana choros, quam mille secutae
   hinc atque hinc glomerantur Oreades; illa pharetram
   fert umero gradiensque deas supereminet omnis.

[5] A. vii. 305   concessit in iras
   ipse deum antiquam genitor Calydona Dianae.

[6] G. i. 431   vento semper rubet aurea Phoebe.
A. x. 215   almaque curru
   noctivago Phoebe medium pulsabat Olympum.

[7] A. ix. 405 astrorum decus et nemorum Latonia custos.

guardian of groves'. This description of Diana (Artemis) as the 'daughter of Lato' is twice used in the story of Camilla. Under this name Diana addresses the nymph Opis,[1] and Metabus dedicates his daughter to the goddess as 'dweller in the forests, virgin daughter of Lato'.[2] It is noticeable that the title derived from Greek mythology is thus used in a story connected with the Italian Diana.

Still more interesting is the association of Trivia with Apollo at Cumae. Aeneas seeks 'the heights over which lofty Apollo presides'[3] and the cave of the Sibyl, but it is 'the grove of Trivia' which he enters. Deiphobe, later on, is described as 'the priestess of Phoebus and Trivia',[4] just as is Haemonides in book x,[5] and Aeneas vows that, if he is granted a home in Latium, he will 'build a temple of solid marble to Phoebus and Trivia, and appoint festal days in the name of Phoebus'.[6] Now Trivia is here primarily the Olympian Artemis, Phoebus' sister. This is made clear by the passage last quoted, which is, as Servius saw,[7] an anticipation of the building of the Palatine temple to Apollo, in which a statue of Artemis stood by the god's side, and the institution of the *ludi Apollinares* by Augustus. But in view of the subsequent action of the sixth book, there can be little doubt that in all this description of Cumae

---

[1] A. xi. 534   has tristis Latonia voces
           ore dabat.
[2] A. xi. 557   alma, tibi hanc, nemorum cultrix, Latonia virgo,
           ipse pater famulam voveo.
[3] A. vi. 9   at pius Aeneas arces quibus altus Apollo
           praesidet horrendaeque procul secreta Sibyllae,
           antrum immane, petit.
Ibid. 13   iam subeunt Triviae lucos atque aurea tecta.
[4] A. vi. 35   Phoebi Triviaeque sacerdos.
[5] A. x. 537   nec procul Haemonides, Phoebi Triviaeque sacerdos.
[6] A. vi. 69   tum Phoebo et Triviae solido de marmore templum
           instituam festosque dies de nomine Phoebi.
[7] Servius *ad Aen.* vi. 69 ut solet, miscet historiam; nam hoc templum in Palatio ab Augusto factum est.

Trivia is meant to suggest also the lower world Hecate, who figures largely in the adventures of Aeneas among the shades. It is perhaps intentional that Virgil in this context never uses the name Diana, but always Trivia, which more easily suggests chthonic associations.

Hecate herself is prominent in the sixth book as one of the principal deities of the lower world. It was she who, as we are twice told, had set the Sibyl 'to rule over the Avernian groves';[1] 'and when Aeneas makes his sacrifice of black heifers to the deities of the underworld he 'calls aloud on Hecate mighty in heaven and in Erebus';[2] here we have a link between the chthonic Hecate and the Olympian Artemis in her lunar character. So, again, when Dido's priestess makes her appeal to the chthonic deities she calls on 'the triple Hecate, the three-faced virgin Diana';[3] this is definitely Greek, for Artemis is similarly called Τρισσοκέφαλος in Greek,[4] either as the Olympian Artemis, the moon, and the chthonic Hecate, or perhaps rather because she looks down all the roads at the τρίοδος, and it is interesting to see that here, with this inclusive reference, Virgil does employ the essentially Latin title Diana. In the same spirit later on Dido appeals to 'Hecate summoned with shrieks at night at the crossways throughout the cities'.[5]

This Diana-Artemis-Trivia-Hecate is perhaps the most complete Graeco-Roman conflation which we find in Virgil, yet even here he seems to be conscious of the diverse elements and to be careful of the contexts in which he employs the various titles.

[1] A. vi. 117   potes namque omnia, nec te
              nequiquam lucis Hecate praefecit Avernis.
  A. vi. 564 sed me cum lucis Hecate praefecit Avernis.
[2] A. vi. 247 voce vocans Hecaten caeloque Ereboque potentem.
[3] A. iv. 510 ter centum tonat ore deos, Erebumque Chaosque
          tergeminamque Hecaten, tria virginis ora Dianae.
[4] Orph. *Argon.* 974.
[5] A. iv. 609 nocturnisque Hecate triviis ululata per urbes.

VII

THE GRAECO-ROMAN GODS

III. GODS WITH GREEK NAMES

THERE are certain deities, who though fully recognized by the Latin poets and even sometimes admitted to the Roman State-cult, yet for various reasons never acquired Roman names. Some of these, such as Aeolus and Iris, had merely an epic value and were never the objects of cult; they are part of the poetic tradition. Others, such as Apollo and Cybele, were worshipped at Rome, but having no obvious equivalents among the Roman deities retained their Greek names.

1. *Phoebus Apollo.* By far the most important of these Greek deities, both in the State-cult and in the poems of Virgil, is Apollo; his treatment by Virgil also forms the most interesting study. He was the first of the Greek gods to be received at Rome and was introduced early in the fifth century B.C. from the Greek colony of Cumae, bringing with him, either then or shortly afterwards, the oracles of the Sibyl, destined to play a large part in the history of Roman religion. He came first to Rome as a god of healing and medicine, but from early times his prophetic and oracular side was prominent. Oracles were unknown to the genuine Italian cult, though it recognized prophetic persons such as Faunus; and Rome but rarely had recourse to any oracles but those of the Sibyl; nevertheless she became acquainted with the prophetic seats of Apollo at Delphi, Delos, Claros, and elsewhere. Apollo's character as a sun-god was also well known to the poets, though it was not admitted in cult. Similarly, it was literature rather than cult which acquainted Rome with Apollo's function as patron of poetry, music and the arts, and the Augustan

poets frequently appeal to him in this capacity. But an even stronger link of connexion in Virgil's own day was forged when Augustus selected Apollo as his own special patron and seems to have permitted himself to be regarded as Apollo's son or even as an incarnation of the god. These last two aspects of Apollo were consecrated by the erection of the great temple on the Palatine, at once library and Augustus' offering to his divine patron.

Apollo, although he does not play a personal part in the *Aeneid* as the three great gods do, is yet mentioned in Virgil more frequently than any other deity with the possible exception of Iuppiter. Once, in a solemn passage,[1] he is given both his names, Phoebus Apollo; ordinarily he is either Apollo or Phoebus and there seems to be no distinction between the two names; they are interchangeable and are frequently varied within the limits of the same incident. His cult-titles, derived chiefly, as will be seen, from the seats of his oracles, are often applied to him, but seldom stand alone.

Virgil refers to Apollo in all the capacities mentioned, but far and away the most frequent reference is to his prophecies and oracles. They are indeed an essential part of the divine framework of the *Aeneid*, yet Phoebus' intervention is never, except in one incident,[2] so personal as that of the three great gods, and in an important and significant passage we are expressly told that he is but the mouthpiece of the will of higher powers. The Harpy Celaeno claims to derive her inspiration from Phoebus,[3] but states that Apollo in his turn derives his knowledge from Iuppiter.

---

[1] A. iii. 251.   [2] A. ix. 638 ff.

[3] A. iii. 250 accipite ergo animis atque haec mea figite dicta,
              quae Phoebo Pater omnipotens, mihi Phoebus Apollo
              praedixit.

For Apollo's position as the interpreter of Zeus, Conington compares Aesch. *Eum.* 19 Διὸς προφήτης δ' ἐστὶ Λοξίας πατρός.

This is good doctrine, and it explains why, in spite of his frequent mentions, Apollo yet occupies a comparatively subordinate position.

As the oracular god Apollo appears in a popular aspect as the solver of riddles in the *Eclogues*,[1] but throughout the *Aeneid* and specially in the earlier books he holds a far more dignified position as the inspirer of oracles. In Sinon's story in the second book[2] the Greeks send to consult him as to the propitiation required to secure a prosperous return home, and Calchas interprets the god's sinister reply. The third book, which might almost be called 'The Book of the Prophets', is full of Apollo. Aeneas consults him in his Temple at Delos and receives the characteristically ambiguous oracle 'seek your ancient mother',[3] which sends the Trojans in mistake to Crete. When the mistake is discovered Anchises suggests a return to the oracle at Delos,[4] but the Penates, appearing in a vision to Aeneas, explain that it was not Crete but Italy that 'Delian Apollo' bade them seek.[5] Driven to the islands called the Strophades, the Trojans encounter the Harpies,[6] and Celaeno, inspired by Apollo, again prophesies the voyage to Italy and the 'eating of the tables'. Then comes the meeting with Andromache and Helenus and his more explicit prophecies,[7] and it may be noted that Helenus, prophet as he is, takes Aeneas to the temple of Apollo that he may receive fuller inspiration,[8] and even then asserts that he can

---

[1] E. iii. 104 dic quibus in terris—et eris mihi magnus Apollo—
      tris pateat Caeli spatium non amplius ulnas.

[2] A. ii. 114 suspensi Eurypylum scitatum oracula Phoebi
      mittimus.

[3] A. iii. 73–120.   [4] A. iii. 143–89.

[5] A. iii. 161   non haec tibi litora suasit
      Delius aut Cretae iussit considere Apollo.

[6] A. iii. 210–67.   [7] A. iii. 294–505.

[8] A. iii. 371   meque ad tua limina, Phoebe,
      ipse manu multo suspensum numine ducit.

only tell him 'a few things out of many, for the fates prevent Helenus from knowing more and Iuno, Saturn's daughter, forbids him to speak'.[1] Once again, Apollo's prophet, if not Apollo himself, is subordinate to a higher will. In the fourth book Aeneas tells Dido that 'the Lycian Apollo' has bidden him to seek Italy and make it his home,[2] and later on that Apollo's prophecy has been fortified by the direct command of Iuppiter, delivered by Mercurius.[3] In the sixth book Aeneas, meeting Palinurus in the lower world, complains that Apollo had falsely prophesied that his helmsman should reach Italy alive, but learns that he did in fact do so.[4] Later in the poem Evander tells Aeneas that he was driven from Arcadia to Italy by 'fortune the all-powerful and fate irresistible' and by 'the warnings of the nymph Carmentis and the god Apollo who urged me';[5] it may be noticed here that Apollo appears as the mouth of destiny rather than of Iuppiter, and the interchangeability of the two ideas is significant. By far the most explicit account of Apollo's oracular powers occurs, of course, in the earlier part of the sixth book; it is, indeed, one of the most detailed records of oracular possession in antiquity. Aeneas, landing at Cumae, 'approaches the heights, over which Apollo presides and the vast cavern, the deep and

[1] A. iii. 377   pauca tibi e multis . . .
            expediam dictis; prohibent nam cetera Parcae
            scire Helenum farique vetat Saturnia Iuno.

[2] A. iv. 345   sed nunc Italiam magnam Gryneus Apollo,
            Italiam Lyciae iussere capessere sortes.

[3] A. iv. 376   nunc augur Apollo,
            nunc Lyciae sortes, nunc et Iove missus ab ipso
            interpres divum fert horrida iussa per auras.

[4] A. vi. 337–83.

[5] A. viii. 333 me pulsum patria pelagique extrema sequentem
            fortuna omnipotens et ineluctabile fatum
            his posuere locis, matrisque egere tremenda
            Carmentis nymphae monita et deus auctor Apollo.

hidden abode of the dread Sibyl'.[1] There he finds Deiphobe, the Sibyl, 'the priestess of Phoebus and Trivia'[2] (see
p. 161). She leads them into the cave and at once begins
to be seized with prophetic frenzy, 'her face, her colour was
changed, her hair dishevelled; her breast heaves and her
heart swells wildly beneath the madness; larger she seems
in stature and her voice more than mortal, since she is
inspired by the nearer influence of the god'.[3] She bids
Aeneas pray and sacrifice before the oracle can be given.
Then, 'not yet able to endure Phoebus, she rages wildly
in the cave, if but she might shake off the great god from
her heart; yet all the more he wearies her raving mouth,
subduing her fierce heart, and quieting her, bends her
to his will'.[4] At last comes the prophecy: 'the Trojans
shall reach the kingdom of Lavinium, but there shall
be wars, and strife over Aeneas' marriage; but he must
meet his fortune bravely and he shall receive help
from a Greek city.'[5] The earlier oracles have all been
working up to this great scene, which shows the mystery
and might of oracular possession and the greatness of
the prophetic Apollo; the god at every stage performs
his part and the prophetess is a mere instrument in his
hands.

[1] A. vi. 9 at pius Aeneas arces, quibus altus Apollo
praesidet horrendaeque procul secreta Sibyllae,
antrum immane, petit.

[2] A. vi. 35 Phoebi Triviaeque sacerdos:

[3] A. vi. 47   non vultus, non color unus,
non comptae mansere comae; sed pectus anhelum,
et rabie fera corda tument, maiorque videri
nec mortale sonans, adflata est numine quando
iam propiore dei.

[4] A. vi. 77 at Phoebi nondum patiens immanis in antro
bacchatur vates, magnum si pectore possit
excussisse deum; tanto magis ille fatigat
os rabidum, fera corda domans, fingitque premendo.

[5] A. vi. 81–97.

From the various seats of his oracles Apollo derives the many cult-titles given him by Virgil. He is lord of Delos,[1] of Cynthus,[2] and of Thymbra,[3] and in Asia Minor of Claros[4] and the Grynean grove[5] and of Patara, whence he derives the title 'Lycian';[6] his shrine at Actium is also mentioned.[7] All these seats of Apollo's oracular power are known to Virgil, but he reserves his fullest description for the site best known to and most closely connected with Rome, at Cumae.

In close association with his prophetic character it is Apollo who instructs the augurs and gives them power. Helenus is the 'interpreter of the gods, who knows the inspiration of Phoebus, the tripods, the laurels of Claros, the stars, the voices of birds and the omens of the flying wing',[8] the Sibyl is, of course, his prophet, and to Iapyx he 'gave augury and the lyre and his swift arms'.[9] He is himself once *augur*,[10] and more than once in a prophetic capacity *auctor*,[11] a word which cannot but suggest *augur* and *augurium*.

In a more general sense Virgil speaks of the worship of Apollo. Anchises in Delos sacrifices to him with Neptune,[12]

---

[1] Delius A. iii. 162, A. vi. 12.   [2] Cynthius E. vi. 3, G. iii. 36.
[3] Thymbraeus G. iv. 323, A. iii. 85.
[4] Clarii lauros A. iii. 360.
[5] Gryneus A. iv. 345; Gryneum nemus E. vi. 72.
[6] Lyciae sortes A. iv. 346, 377; cf. A. xii. 516.
[7] A. iii. 274; cf. A. viii. 704 Actius . . . Apollo.
[8] A. iii. 359 Troiugena, interpres divum, qui numina Phoebi,
        qui tripodas, Clarii lauros, qui sidera sentis
        et volucrum linguas et praepetis omina pennae.
[9] A. xii. 393   laetus Apollo
        augurium citharamque dabat celerisque sagittas.
[10] A. iv. 376 augur Apollo.
[11] A. viii. 336.
A. xii. 405 nulla viam fortuna regit, nihil auctor Apollo
        subvenit.
[12] A. iii. 118   meritos aris mactavit honores,
        taurum Neptuno, taurum tibi, pulcher Apollo.

and Dido to 'Ceres the lawgiver and Phoebus and father Lyaeus'.[1] Prayer is made to him not only in connexion with the great occasions of prophecy, but, for instance, by Arruns before his attack on Camilla.[2] Several times we hear of priests of Apollo, apart from his prophets. Thus Panthus in Troy was 'priest of the citadel and of Phoebus',[3] that is, of a temple of Apollo on the citadel (for Apollo was 'founder of Troy',[4] since he built its walls for Laomedon), though in his need his 'great piety and the fillet of Apollo saved him not'.[5] Anius on Delos was 'king of men and priest of Phoebus, his temples bound with ribbons and the sacred laurel',[6] and Haemonides, like the Sibyl herself, was 'priest of Phoebus and Trivia'.[7] And in connexion with his worship the laurel was Apollo's favourite tree.[8]

Once only does Phoebus himself appear as a sun-deity and that in a conventional description of sunset, when 'rosy Phoebus dips his weary steeds in the Hiberian sea',[9] but the sun itself is twice described as 'Phoebus' torch'.[10] It may be that Virgil shrank from this un-Roman attribution of deity to the sun even as a poetic convention.

Apollo appears as a god of medicine in the last book of

[1] A. iv. 57   mactant lectas de more bidentis
        legiferae Cereri Phoeboque patrique Lyaeo.
[2] A. xi. 785.
[3] A. ii. 319 Panthus Othryades, arcis Phoebique sacerdos.
[4] G. iii. 36 Troiae Cynthius auctor.
[5] A. ii. 429   nec te tua plurima, Panthu,
        labentem pietas nec Apollinis infula texit.
[6] A. iii. 80 rex Anius, rex idem hominum Phoebique sacerdos,
        vittis et sacra redimitus tempora lauro.
[7] A. x. 537 Haemonides, Phoebi Triviaeque sacerdos; cf. A. vi. 35.
[8] e.g. E. vii. 62, 64, A. iii. 360, vii. 62.
[9] A. xi. 913 ni roseus fessos iam gurgite Phoebus Hibero
        tingat equos.
[10] Phoebea lampas A. iii. 637, iv. 6.

the *Aeneid*,[1] where he is said to have taught 'the power of herbs and the practice of healing' to Iapyx, his favourite, who nevertheless was unable to heal Aeneas' wound 'with his doctor-hand and Phoebus' powerful herbs', until Venus brought the plant of dictamnum. The same aspect of the god is to be recognized in the account of Lichas, 'cut from his mother's womb after she had died and sacred, Phoebus, to thee; what availed it that as a child he was suffered to escape the perils of the steel?'[2] So, too, Asclepius, who raised Hippolytus from the dead, 'the discoverer of such a healing art', is described, as in the Greek legend, as 'the son of Phoebus'.[3]

The connexion of Apollo with shipping is suggested when his temple on a dangerous promontory at Actium is described as 'Apollo dreaded by sailors',[4] and more explicitly when 'the gilded Apollo' is the headpiece of Abas' ship.[5]

As patron of music and poetry Apollo, as is natural, plays a large part in the *Eclogues*, and the references there are very miscellaneous. Mythologically he is the father of the singer Linus,[6] and Silenus sings the song 'which Eurotas heard as Phoebus was practising'.[7] More frequently he

[1] A. xii. 391 ff.; esp. 393:
   ipse suas artis, sua munera, laetus Apollo
   augurium citharamque dabat celerisque sagittas.
   ille ut depositi proferret fata parentis,
   scire potestates herbarum usumque medendi
   maluit.
402 multa manu medica Phoebique potentibus herbis
   nequiquam trepidat.
[2] A. x. 315 inde Lichan ferit exsectum iam matre perempta
   et tibi, Phoebe, sacrum; casus evadere ferri
   quo licuit parvo?
[3] A. vii. 772 repertorem medicinae talis et artis | ... Phoebigenam.
[4] A. iii. 275 et formidatus nautis aperitur Apollo.
[5] A. x. 170 una torvus Abas: huic totum insignibus armis
   agmen et aurato fulgebat Apolline puppis.
[6] E. iv. 56 quamvis ... adsit | ... Lino formosus Apollo.
[7] E. vi. 82 omnia quae Phoebo quondam meditante beatus
   audiit Eurotas.

is the inspirer and rival of the singing shepherds: Codrus can 'sing a song second to Phoebus',[1] and the ambitious shepherd 'strives to surpass Phoebus in his singing',[2] but 'Phoebus loves' the shepherd poet.[3] After the death of Daphnis, Apollo and Pales might well leave the fields,[4] and the shepherd must build two altars for Phoebus and two for Daphnis.[5] Here, if Daphnis is Julius Caesar, we are approaching contemporary events and persons, and twice this connexion becomes explicit. In a passage, which to modern ears sounds rather oddly, Virgil in dedicating the sixth *Eclogue* to Varus says: 'nor is any page more acceptable to Phoebus than that which has the name of Varus written at its head.'[6] Earlier in the same poem Virgil puts Apollo in direct connexion with himself;[7] it was Cynthius, who, when the poet was wishful to sing of kings and battles, 'twitched his ear' and warned him that a shepherd should sing 'a slenderer song'. In a higher strain than anything in the *Eclogues*, Virgil tells us in the *Aeneid* of the special place reserved in Elysium for those 'who had spoken words worthy of Phoebus'.[8]

The sixth *Eclogue* brings Apollo into touch with Virgil and his contemporary poets, nor does he in the *Aeneid* shrink from the recognition of Apollo as the special patron of Augustus. This is, as it were, foreshadowed in the one

---

[1] E. vii. 22 proxima Phoebi | versibus ille facit.
[2] E. v. 9 quid, si idem certet Phoebum superare canendo?
[3] E. iii. 62 et me Phoebus amat.
[4] E. v. 34   postquam te fata tulerunt,
    ipsa Pales agros atque ipse reliquit Apollo.
[5] E. v. 65   en quattuor aras;
    ecce duas tibi, Daphni, duas altaria Phoebo.
[6] E. vi. 11   nec Phoebo gratior ulla est
    quam sibi quae Vari praescripsit pagina nomen.
[7] E. vi. 3 cum canerem reges et proelia, Cynthius aurem
    vellit et admonuit: 'pastorem, Tityre, pinguis
    pascere oportet ovis, deductum dicere carmen.'
[8] A. vi. 662 quique pii vates et Phoebo digna locuti.

passage[1] where Apollo makes an appearance in the poem as the protector of the young Iulus, the ancestor of the Julian house; he congratulates him on his first victory in battle and, assuming the form of Butes, warns him against further fighting.

So in the celebrations at the tomb of Anchises Ascanius leads the *Ludus Troiae*, a foreshadowing of Augustus' Actian games in honour of Apollo.[2] In more direct reference still, the birth of the child in the fourth *Eclogue* heralds the reign of Apollo,[3] and on the shield of Aeneas Apollo of Actium is represented as turning his bow against Cleopatra and the Egyptians;[4] while on the day of triumph Augustus surveys the procession 'seated on the snow-white threshold of bright Phoebus',[5] of the Palatine temple of Apollo, that is, whose dedication is anticipated by Aeneas' vow before his descent to the lower world.[6]

Apollo is a fascinating figure in Virgil. He is essentially a Greek god, and the conception of his character and functions is built up on Greek ideas and precedents, but Virgil lays his emphasis on the points of connexion with Rome, in the Sibylline oracles, in the patronage of the Augustan poets, and in his direct relation with Augustus himself.

2. *The Muses.* Closely allied to Apollo in his capacity of god of poetry are the Muses. Their treatment by Virgil is purely conventional. The Muse is invoked by the poet at the outset of the *Aeneid*[7] in a passage reminiscent of the

[1] A. ix. 638–63.
[2] A. v. 545–603; see esp. 596–603.
[3] E. iv. 10 casta fave, Lucina; tuus iam regnat Apollo.
[4] A. viii. 704 Actius haec cernens arcum intendebat Apollo desuper.
[5] A. viii. 720 ipse sedens niveo candentis limine Phoebi.
[6] A. vi. 69 tum Phoebo et Triviae solido de marmore templum instituam festosque dies de nomine Phoebi.
[7] A. i. 8 Musa, mihi causas memora.

Iliad and *Odyssey*, the 'goddesses' are twice summoned to 'open Helicon',[1] and declare first the kings and people ranged against Aeneas in war, and later the hosts that came by ship from Etruria to his aid. Calliope, the epic Muse, is called upon with her sisters to inspire the poet with the story of Turnus' ἀριστεία,[2] and with less appropriateness Erato, strictly the lyric Muse, to tell of the state of Latium on Aeneas' arrival.[3] In one place the Camenae, the accepted Latin equivalent of the Muses, are mentioned in a similar context.[4] A more definite invocation is that to 'the Muses of Sicily' in the fourth *Eclogue*,[5] to the inspiration, that is, of Theocritus, who is Virgil's accepted model. Twice only have the Muses any kind of personality, once when Calliope is mentioned as the mother of Orpheus,[6] and once in a characteristically modern context,[7] when Silenus tells in his song 'how one of the sisters guided Gallus, wandering at the streams of Parnassus, to the Aonian mountains'.

The Muse, like other deities, had suffered an eclipse of her personality and in several places in the *Eclogues* appears in a 'faded' sense as the equivalent of 'poetry' or 'song'. Tityrus 'meditates the woodland muse on slender pipe';[8] 'Pollio', says Damoetas, 'loves our muse, though she is rustic';[9] and Virgil tells Varus that he will 'meditate

[1] A. vii. 641, x. 163 pandite nunc Helicona, deae.
[2] A. ix. 525 vos, o Calliope, precor, aspirate canenti.
[3] A. vii. 37 nunc age, qui reges, Erato, quae tempora, rerum
        quis Latio antiquo fuerit status, . . . expediam.
[4] E. iii. 59 amant alterna Camenae.
[5] E. iv. 1 Sicelides Musae, paulo maiora canamus.
[6] E. iv. 56   mater quamvis . . . adsit
        Orphei Calliopea.
[7] E. vi. 64 tum canit errantem Permessi ad flumina Gallum
        Aonas in montis ut duxerit una sororum,
        utque viro Phoebi chorus adsurrexerit omnis.
[8] E. i. 2 silvestrem tenui musam meditaris avena.
[9] E. iii. 84 Pollio amat nostram, quamvis est rustica, musam.

the muse of the fields on slender reed';[1] all three expressions are very similar, but the variation of the adjective shows the range of the themes of bucolic poetry.

3. *Cybele*. At this point it will perhaps be well to consider Virgil's treatment of Cybele, the great mother-goddess of Phrygia, who, though not strictly a Greek goddess, was yet introduced to Rome under the direction of the Sibylline books in 202 B.C. The cult never became in any real sense Roman; citizens were forbidden to take part in it or hold priesthoods, but the processions of her orgiastic worshippers, the Phrygii and the mutilated galli, singing and dancing orgiastically and 'cutting themselves with knives and lancets after their manner' must have been familiar in the streets, and the great festival of the Megalensia was held in her honour. Cybele's procession made a profound impression on the Roman poets; it is described at length by Lucretius (ii. 600 ff.) and referred to several times by Virgil. The future empire of Rome, with her long line of citizens and their descendants (*felix prole virum*), is compared by Anchises to 'the Berecyntian mother riding in her car with turreted crown through the cities of Phrygia, rejoicing in her progeny of gods, embracing her hundred grandchildren, all dwellers in heaven, all having their abode in the heights above'.[2] So Aeneas, addressing her after his ships returned to their form as nymphs, cries to the 'Gracious mother of the gods on Ida, who lovest Dindyma and the tower-capped cities and the twin lions yoked to the car',[3] and Turnus in a moment of scorn cries

---

[1] E. vi. 8 agrestem tenui meditabor harundine Musam.
[2] A. vi. 784   qualis Berecyntia mater
         invehitur curru Phrygias turrita per urbes
         laeta deum partu, centum complexa nepotes,
         omnis caelicolas, omnis supera alta tenentis.
[3] A. x. 252 alma parens Idaea deum, cui Dindyma cordi
         turrigeraeque urbes biiugique ad frena leones.

to the Trojans:'Phrygian maids, not Phrygian men, go your way over lofty Dindyma, where the two-holed pipe plays its song to those who know it; the timbrels and the Berecyntian flute of the mother of Ida are summoning you.'[1] So, after the transformation of the ships, there appears a vision in the sky of the 'Idaean bands'.[2] In a playful passage of the *Georgics*, where Virgil is giving directions for causing bees to swarm, he tells his farmer, in a phrase closely imitated from Lucretius, to 'rouse the tinkling sounds and shake the cymbals of the Mother all around'.[3]

But in spite of all these signs of familiarity with the cult Virgil tends always to think of Cybele as the Phrygian deity with her home on Ida and Dindyma. This is seen in the epithets and synonyms which he employs; there is the old form of her name 'Cybebe',[4] she is 'the Phrygian mother',[5] she is Idaea[6] and Berecyntia,[7] and in accordance with the original Asiatic idea, she is, as is seen in Anchises' simile, the mother of all the gods, an idea repeated often elsewhere.[8]

[1] A. ix. 617 o vere Phrygiae, neque enim Phryges, ite per alta Dindyma, ubi adsuetis biforem dat tibia cantum. tympana vos buxusque vocat Berecyntia Matris Idaeae.

[2] A. ix. 110   ingens visus ab Aurora caelum transcurrere nimbus Idaeique chori.

[3] G. iv. 64 tinnitusque cie et Matris quate cymbala circum; cf. Lucr. ii. 618 tympana tenta tonant palmis et cymbala circum | concava.

[4] A. x. 220   nymphae, quas alma Cybebe numen habere maris nymphasque e navibus esse iusserat.

[5] A. vii. 139 Idaeumque Iovem Phrygiamque ex ordine matrem invocat.
Note here the combination with the Iuppiter of Mt. Ida in Crete; the two Idas led to identification not only in poetry but in ritual.

[6] A. x. 252, ix. 620 (see above, n. 1).

[7] A. vi. 784 (see p. 174, n. 2), ix. 619 (see above, n. 1). A. ix. 82 ipsa deum fertur genetrix Berecyntia magnum vocibus his adfata Iovem.

[8] G. iv. 64, A. ii. 788, vii. 139, ix. 82, x. 252.

Nor is Virgil content to leave Cybele as a vague Phrygian Mother-goddess, but in a manner peculiar to himself
makes her a special deity of Troy, worshipped there before
its fall, and still appealed to by Aeneas and his wandering
companions. Anchises tells how even before the coming of
Teucer there had reached Troy from Crete 'the Mother
who dwells in Cybelus, and the brass of the Corybantes and
the grove of Ida, the loyal silence at the rites and the lions
yoked to the goddess' car'.[1] So Aeneas' follower Chloreus
had once been 'sacred to Cybelus and her priest' in Troy,[2]
and when the lost Creusa appears to Aeneas she tells him
that she will not accompany him or see the promised land:
'the great Mother of the gods keeps me behind on these
shores.'[3] Later on Aeneas, in his solemn appeal to many
deities on landing in Italy, couples the 'Phrygian Mother'
with the Iuppiter of the Cretan Ida,[4] and again invokes the
Idaean Mother in the stress of battle: 'my leader in the
fight, do thou duly bring the fulfilment of augury, and
come, goddess, to the Phrygians with favouring foot.'[5]
This is a very remarkable invocation and suggests a relation between the Trojans and Cybele comparable to the
connexion with Venus. The same idea is prominent on
the one occasion in the story of the *Aeneid* when Cybele
plays an active part.[6] The ships of Aeneas are threatened
with fire and Cybele appeals to Iuppiter to save the pines

---

[1] A. iii. 111 hinc mater cultrix Cybeli Corybantiaque aera
      Idaeumque nemus, hinc fida silentia sacris,
      et iuncti currum dominae subiere leones.
Note that here the worship of the Mother is even thought to be derived from
Crete. Cybelus is a mountain in Phrygia.
  [2] A. xi. 768 sacer Cybelo Chloreus olimque sacerdos.
  [3] A. ii. 788 sed me magna deum genetrix his detinet oris.
  [4] A. vii. 139, see p. 175, n. 5.
  [5] A. x. 252 alma parens Idaea deum . . .
         tu mihi nunc pugnae princeps, tu rite propinques
         augurium Phrygibusque adsis pede, diva, secundo.
  [6] A. ix. 82 ff.

grown on her beloved Ida from destruction. Iuppiter grants her prayer and permits them to be turned into sea-nymphs, and later on Aeneas recognizes them as they play around his own ship.[1]

In his treatment of Cybele then Virgil is not only true to her real character as the Phrygian Mother-goddess, but uses that character to create a new supporter for Aeneas and his Trojans. It is a natural development, but without precedent in previous legend.

Certain other minor Greek gods and supernatural beings occur in the *Aeneid*, not as objects of worship or in any way connected with religious thought or feeling, but as part of the traditional Homeric machinery of epic.

4. *Aeolus* in the first book at the request of Iuno raises a storm to destroy Aeneas and his followers, but the winds are rebuked by Neptunus, and Aeolus is told to remain in the cave, his proper domain;[2] the whole incident is based directly on the story in the tenth *Odyssey*.

5. *Iris* appears, as in Homer, as the messenger of the gods and shares this function with Mercurius-Hermes, but on every occasion but one she is the messenger of Iuno, as he is of Iuppiter. She is sent by Iuno to cut the lock from the hair of Dido and thus release her from her sufferings in death;[3] to inspire the Trojan matrons to set fire to the fleet in Sicily during the progress of the funeral games;[4] to urge Turnus to attack while Aeneas is absent with Evander.[5] In one of the later celestial debates Iuno seems almost to claim Iris as her own: 'where now is Iuno or Iris dispatched from the clouds?'[6] The only exception to this appropriation occurs when, in one of the earlier battles, Iris is dispatched by Iuppiter[7]—but she is sent to Iuno to tell her

---

[1] A. x. 219 ff. [2] A. i. 50 ff., 124 ff. [3] A. iv. 693 ff. [4] A. v. 604 ff.
[5] A. ix. 1 ff. [6] A. x. 73 ubi hic Iuno demissave nubibus Iris?
[7] A. ix. 803   aëriam caelo nam Iuppiter Irim
        demisit germanae haud mollia iussa ferentem.

to moderate her assistance to Turnus and withdraw him from the attack on the Trojan camp. It is as though the husband sent a message to his wife by her maid and does not preclude the conclusion that Iris was to Virgil Iuno's particular satellite.

6. *Proteus* has his place in the story of Aristaeus in the fourth book of the *Georgics*,[1] just as he has in Odysseus' adventures in the *Odyssey*.

7. *Supernatural Monsters.* Several of the supernatural monsters of Greek legend find their place in Virgil. Most important of these are the Erinys and the Eumenides with their Latin counterparts, the Furiae and the Dirae. Virgil seems to make little distinction between these beings; Erinys is in effect the singular of Eumenides, and Furiae and Dirae seem to be used indifferently as the Latin equivalents, the latter being no less concrete and personal than the former. But once again his use of these personages is interesting. Twice they appear in their proper place in Greek legends, when Dido's madness in her love for Aeneas is compared to the plight of Pentheus when he sees the 'hosts of the Eumenides', or of Orestes, when he flees from his mother 'armed with torches and black serpents, and the avenging Dirae sit upon the threshold'.[2] To complete the comparison, as it were, Dido in her misery calls on 'the avenging Dirae' with Hecate and the 'gods of dying Elissa'.[3] The Eumenides also have their place in the lower world. On the threshold of Orcus Aeneas sees 'the iron chambers of the Eumenides and mad Discord';[4] the Sibyl

---

[1] G. iv. 387 ff.; cf. *Od.* iv. 384 ff.
[2] A. iv. 469 Eumenidum veluti demens videt agmina Pentheus . . .
   aut Agamemnonius scaenis agitatus Orestes
   armatam facibus matrem et serpentibus atris
   cum fugit ultricesque sedent in limine Dirae.
[3] A. iv. 609 nocturnisque Hecate triviis ululata per urbes
   et Dirae ultrices et di morientis Elissae.
[4] A. vi. 280 ferreique Eumenidum thalami et Discordia demens.

rebukes Palinurus for desiring, while yet unburied, 'to look on the waters of Styx and the stern river of the Eumenides';[1] as the Lapithae reproduce their fatal banquet in the world beneath, 'the greatest of the Furies has her seat at their side and prevents them from touching the tables with their hands, and rises brandishing her torch and thunders with her voice'.[2] So, too, in the *Georgics* in the front of his new temple Virgil will picture 'wretched Envy fearing the Furies and the stern river [the same words as in *Aen.* vi] of Cocytus'.[3] Among these monstrous beings of the lower world *Tisiphone* is specified by name; as 'the avenger girt with her whip, she assaults and chastises the guilty and holding her grim snakes towards them in her left hand she summons the wild bands of her sisters'.[4] She sits, too, before the iron tower 'girt with her blood-stained cloak and sleepless night and day she guards the entrance'.[5] During the plague described in the third book of the *Georgics*, 'summoned to the light from Stygian darkness pale Tisiphone drives before her the Diseases and Fear',[6] and in the battle in the tenth book of the *Aeneid* she 'raves amid the thousands of the combatants'.[7] These hellish

[1] A. vi. 374 tu Stygias inhumatus aquas amnemque severum
           Eumenidum aspicies.
[2] A. vi. 605   Furiarum maxima iuxta
           accubat et manibus prohibet contingere mensas,
           exsurgitque facem attollens atque intonat ore.
[3] G. iii. 37 Invidia infelix furias amnemque severum
           Cocyti metuet.
[4] A. vi. 570 continuo sontis ultrix accincta flagello
           Tisiphone quatit insultans, torvosque sinistra
           intentans anguis vocat agmina saeva sororum.
Cf. *Culex* 218 obvia Tisiphone, serpentibus undique compta,
           et flammas et saeva quatit mihi verbera.
[5] A. vi. 554   stat ferrea turris ad auras,
           Tisiphoneque sedens palla succincta cruenta
           vestibulum exsomnis servat noctesque diesque.
[6] G. iii. 551 saevit et in lucem Stygiis emissa tenebris
           pallida Tisiphone Morbos agit ante Metumque.
[7] A. x. 761 pallida Tisiphone media inter milia saevit.

monsters are all purely Greek in origin, but it is noticeable how frequently they are combined with personified abstractions, which perhaps gave them more familiarity to Latin ears. The evil spirit Allecto, whom Iuno rouses to spur Amata to rouse the Latin matrons against Aeneas, is described as Erinys and must therefore be regarded as one of the Eumenides of the lower world.[1] These chthonic creatures may be roused to earth to take their part in battle: Aeneas in the falling Troy is 'carried on into the flames and the warfare, whither the grim Erinys calls and the turmoil and the battle-cry rising to the heavens',[2] and on the shield of Aeneas at the battle of Actium 'amid the strife rages Mavors fashioned by the chisel, and the grim Dirae in the sky'.[3] In the opening of the final scene of the *Aeneid* Iuppiter summons one of the Dirae to go to earth and in the form of a bird to strike terror into Turnus and to warn Iuturna that her help to her brother is no longer of any avail.[4] A still more concrete manifestation of an Erinys is that in the form of Celaeno, the Harpy, who describes herself in the words used later of the figure in the lower world as 'the greatest of the Furies'.[5] The *Harpies*, then, who play so prominent a part in the disconcerting of Aeneas and his companions on the Strophades islands,[6] might be regarded as identified with the Eumenides, but most probably, except for this one phrase, Virgil thought of them as independent and rather more concrete beings: they appear again in the description of the lower world in

[1] A. vii. 447 tot Erinys sibilat hydris; ibid. 570, quis condita Erinys, | invisum numen, terras caelumque levabat.

[2] A. ii. 337 in flammas et in arma feror, quo tristis Erinys,
        quo fremitus vocat et sublatus ad aethera clamor.

[3] A. viii. 700   saevit medio in certamine Mavors
        caelatus ferro, tristesque ex aethere Dirae.

[4] A. xii. 845 ff.

[5] A. iii. 252 Furiarum ego maxima.

[6] A. iii. 210 ff.

connexion with the Gorgones.[1] Once more then in his treatment of these malign beings connected with the underworld Virgil is at once strict in his conception of them in Greek legend, elastic in the expansion of ideas which he allows himself, and careful to attach them to conceptions which would be more familiar to Romans.

[1] A. vi. 289 Gorgones Harpyiaeque.

VIII

ORIENTAL GODS—COSMOLOGICAL GODS— WORSHIP OF THE EMPEROR

(a) Oriental gods

IT is characteristic of Virgil's outlook that with the exception of Cybele the oriental deities, whose worship was so prevalent in Rome at the end of the Republic, find no place in the *Aeneid*. The Egyptian deities, Isis and Serapis, who play so prominent a part in Propertius and had clearly an important position in the lives of Roman women at the time, are nowhere to be found. Their only representative is 'the barking Anubis', who with 'the monstrous shapes of all manner of gods' leads the degenerate fleet of Antony and Cleopatra at the battle of Actium against the great deities of Rome.[1] The reason of course is that one of the main purposes of Augustus' religious reforms was to exile these ascetic and orgiastic Oriental cults and re-establish the full worship of the Graeco-Roman deities, and in this aim Virgil seconded him with the zeal and consistency of complete abstention.

(b) Cosmological deities

A word may be said about the cosmological deities, which occasionally find their place in Virgil. The worship of sun and moon was not natural or original in Italy, though it seems to have established itself comparatively early in Rome. *Sol* in Virgil is for the most part a mythological personification of the sun who 'drives his chariot across the heavens'. Thus, in the *Georgics*, Virgil speaks of

---

[1] A. viii. 698 omnigenumque deum monstra et latrator Anubis
contra Neptunum et Venerem contraque Minervam
tela tenent.

the time of year when 'the swift Sol has not yet touched winter with his horses',[1] or the summer season 'when the golden Sol has routed winter and driven it beneath the earth and opened up the sky with the light of summer'.[2] In the *Aeneid* he appears rather in descriptions of place, 'where Sol in his course to and fro looks upon either ocean',[3] 'the mighty realms on which Sol used once to look as he came from furthest Olympus',[4] 'whoever is cut off by the zone of relentless Sol which stretches midmost of the four'.[5] He attains a little more personality in the phrase about Carthage, 'nor does Sol yoke his horses so aloof from the Tyrian city',[6] and has a full Greek mythological importance when Circe is described as 'the daughter of Sol'[7] (Helios). Twice he is addressed as a deity to whom prayer may be made, once by Dido in her distress,[8] once by Aeneas in taking the oath before the single combat in a passage more cosmological than mythological, 'Be Sol now my witness and this Terra as I call.'[9] Virgil then in his use of Sol and his apparent unwillingness to admit him as a full deity is true to Roman tradition.

Luna appears more rarely in this kind of personification. Once she has the full personality of Selene in Greek

[1] G. ii. 321   cum rapidus Sol
       nondum hiemem contingit equis.

[2] G. iv. 51   ubi pulsam hiemem Sol aureus egit
       sub terras caelumque aestiva luce reclusit.

[3] A. vii. 100   qua Sol utrumque recurrens
       aspicit Oceanum.

[4] A. vii. 217   regnis, quae maxima quondam
       extremo veniens Sol aspiciebat Olympo.

[5] A. vii. 226   si quem extenta plagarum
       quattuor in medio dirimit plaga Solis iniqui.

[6] A. i. 568 nec tam aversus equos Tyria Sol iungit ab urbe.

[7] A. vii. 11 Solis filia.

[8] A. iv. 607 Sol, qui terrarum flammis opera omnia lustras.

[9] A. xii. 176 esto nunc Sol testis et haec mihi Terra vocanti.

mythology, 'Pan, the god of Arcadia captured and deceived thee, Luna, calling thee into the deep woods; nor didst thou reject his call.'[1] She appears with the same sort of vague personification as Sol in the *Georgics*: 'Luna herself has ordained days in varying order to be lucky for work',[2] 'Luna who rises beholden to her brother's rays';[3] and, again, in the *Aeneid*, 'the fair Luna bars not their course'.[4] Once only she has the full dignity of a goddess, when Nisus makes his prayer 'looking up to Luna on high',[5] but it is clear from his words, 'Thou goddess, do thou come and aid our toil, glory of the stars and daughter of Lato, guardian of the woods', that Luna here is a mere synonym for Artemis-Diana. Luna then, consistently with Roman thought and usage, is still less of a deity in Virgil than Sol.

Stranger, because less naturally Roman, is the occasional personification and deification of *Terra*, the earth. Tellus was of course prominent among the old deities, but not Terra. Mythologically in Virgil she appears as the equivalent of the Greek Ge, the mother of the giants who assailed Olympus: 'Terra with awful birth created Coeus and Iapetus and cruel Typhoeus and the brothers who conspired to break open the sky.'[6] So in the lower world Aeneas sees 'the ancient brood of Terra, the Titan youths, hurled down by the thunderbolt and

---

[1] G. iii. 392 Pan, deus Arcadiae, captam te, Luna, fefellit
　　　　　in nemora alta vocans; nec tu aspernata vocantem.
[2] G. i. 276 ipsa dies alios alio dedit ordine Luna
　　　　　felicis operum.
[3] G. i. 396 nec fratris radiis obnoxia surgere Luna.
[4] A. vii. 9 nec candida cursus | Luna negat.
[5] A. ix. 403 suspiciens altam Lunam sic voce precatur:
　　　　　'tu, dea, tu praesens nostro succurre labori,
　　　　　astrorum decus et nemorum Latonia custos.'
[6] G. i. 278　　　　　　　　　　　tum partu Terra nefando
　　　　Coeumque Iapetumque creat saevumque Typhoea
　　　　et coniuratos caelum rescindere fratres.

wallowing in the lowest depth',[1] and later on there was 'Tityos, fosterling of Terra the all-mother, stretching over nine acres of land'.[2] Earlier in the book she appears with a fuller deification, but still as the Greek Ge, when Aeneas sacrifices a black lamb to 'the Mother of the Eumenides (Night) and her great sister (Terra)'.[3] In a more cosmological sense Aeneas, as has been seen, invokes to his oath Sol and Terra,[4] and Latinus in his reply swears by earth, sea, and stars;[5] in the latter instance we need hardly suppose them personified, if it were not for the parallel invocation of Aeneas. A more unexpected combination occurs in Turnus' frightened appeal to Faunus and Terra to check the spear of Aeneas, 'if I have ever worshipped you duly'.[6] Perhaps Terra is here really the Italian Tellus. We must reckon, too, among the cosmological deities the 'sea and stars' of Latinus' oath; this may be due to philosophical ideas, though it is more likely that the inclusion of the stars comes from astrology.

There are two more deities to be added, which are of a less concrete character, Nox and Aurora. *Nox* is recognized in a fully Greek mythological setting, as 'the Mother of the Eumenides';[7] the latter idea is repeated with a Roman twist in the description of 'the twin pests, the Dirae by name, whom with Tartarean Megaera timeless

---

[1] A. vi. 580 hic genus antiquum Terrae, Titania pubes,
    fulmine deiecti fundo volvuntur in imo.
[2] A. vi. 595 nec non et Tityon, Terrae omniparentis alumnum
    cernere erat, per tota novem cui iugera corpus
    porrigitur.
[3] A. vi. 249   ipse atri velleris agnam
    Aeneas matri Eumenidum magnaeque sorori
    ense ferit.
[4] A. xii. 176; see p. 183, n. 9.
[5] A. xii. 197 haec eadem, Aenea, terram, mare, sidera, iuro.
[6] A. xii. 777 'Faune, precor, miserere', inquit, 'tuque optima ferrum
    Terra tene, colui vestros si semper honores.'
[7] A. vi. 249. See above, n. 3.

B b

Nox bore at one and the same birth'.[1] Myth is almost passing into allegory here, and Nox has the epithet *intempesta*, so often applied to night as a common noun. As a personification of cosmological night Nox is conceived as performing a journey across the sky, just as the sun does by day: she 'rushes up from the Ocean',[2] 'riding on her car dark Nox holds the sky',[3] 'damp Nox drives her course in mid heaven',[4] 'and now damp Nox had touched the mid turning-point of heaven';[5] all these expressions carry but a faint sense of personality and are little more than picturesque descriptions. Once only does Nox appear to be the object of worship, when on Latian soil Aeneas prays to 'the Genius of the spot, and Tellus, oldest of the gods, and the Nymphs and streams he knows not yet and then to Nox and the rising constellations of Nox'.[6]

Aurora's treatment is much the same, except that the cosmological personification is far more frequent and there is no trace of actual worship. In her Greek mythological character (Eos) she is the mother of Memnon,[7] and the wife of Tithonus in the frequently repeated phrase, 'Aurora rises leaving the saffron couch of Tithonus',[8] where the mythology is but a conventional ornament of

[1] A. xii. 845 dicuntur geminae pestes cognomine Dirae,
        quas et Tartaream Nox intempesta Megaeram
        uno eodemque tulit partu.
Cf. A. xii. 860 talis se sata Nocte tulit terrasque petivit.
[2] A. ii. 250 ruit Oceano Nox.
[3] A. v. 721 et Nox atra polum bigis subvecta tenebat.
[4] A. v. 738 torquet medios Nox umida cursus.
[5] A. v. 835 iamque fere mediam caeli Nox umida metam
        contigerat.
[6] A. vii. 136   Geniumque loci primamque deorum
        Tellurem Nymphasque et adhuc ignota precatur
        flumina, tum Noctem Noctisque orientia signa | . . . invocat.
[7] A. i. 751 nunc quibus Aurorae venisset filius armis.
[8] G. i. 446   ubi pallida surget
        Tithoni croceum linquens Aurora cubile.
Cf. A. iv. 585, ix. 460.

the cosmological idea. As the personified dawn Aurora is introduced in a large variety of more or less conventional phrases. Once she simply 'comes',[1] elsewhere she 'shows her rising',[2] 'brings back day',[3] 'sprinkles the earth with new light',[4] 'moves away the dark shadows from the sky',[5] 'shows her gracious light to wretched mortals',[6] 'touches a man with her light'.[7] With a slightly less vague personification 'she routs the stars and blushes',[8] 'rises and leaves Ocean',[9] or in the most definitely conceived personal pictures 'shines saffron-coloured in her rosy car',[10] or 'glows as she drives on her purple wheels'.[11] In all this there is no suggestion of worship and Aurora's personification is of the thinnest; in most of these places she might almost as well be written with a small 'a'.

These cosmological deities, then, with the possible exceptions of Sol and Nox, have very little religious significance and are either mythological inheritances from the Greek or faint personifications of natural phenomena.

(c) *Worship of the Emperor*

The problem of Virgil's attitude to emperor-worship in the persons of Iulius Caesar and Augustus is complex and difficult, but exceedingly interesting as a study of opinion at the time; it has been admirably dealt with recently by

[1] A. x. 241 Aurora . . . veniente.
[2] G. iv. 544 post ubi nona suos Aurora ostenderit ortus; cf. ibid. 552.
[3] G. i. 249 aut redit a nobis Aurora diemque reducit.
[4] A. iv. 584, ix. 459 et iam prima novo spargebat lumine terras . . . Aurora
[5] A. iii. 589, iv. 7 umentemque Aurora polo dimoverat umbram.
[6] A. xi. 182 Aurora interea miseris mortalibus almam
extulerat lucem.
[7] A. iv. 568 si te his attigerit terris Aurora morantem.
[8] A. iii. 521 iamque rubescebat stellis Aurora fugatis.
[9] A. iv. 129, xi. 1 Oceanum interea surgens Aurora reliquit.
[10] A. vii. 26 Aurora in roseis fulgebat lutea bigis.
[11] A. xii. 76   cum primum crastina caelo
puniceis invecta rotis Aurora rubebit.

Professor Ross Taylor in *The Divinity of the Roman Emperor*. A careful distinction must be drawn between the poet's conception of the divinity of Iulius and that of Augustus, and again between his views at different times.

There can be little doubt that Iulius Caesar welcomed the attribute of divine honours to himself in his lifetime, and it is certain that popular sentiment ascribed divinity to him immediately after his death. Except in the *Eclogues*, Virgil refers to Iulius comparatively rarely, but his tone is unmistakable. In the ninth *Eclogue* he mentions the famous comet, which appeared shortly after his death and was popularly taken as a sign of his translation to heaven: 'Daphnis, why regard the ancient risings of the stars? lo the star of Caesar, Venus' son, has come forth, that star at which the crops might rejoice in their fruit, and the grape don its colour on the sunny hills.'[1] It is interesting to note that the beginning of the era of Caesarian prosperity is here regarded as a time of agricultural fertility. In the *Georgics* comes another reference to Caesar's death in the eclipse of the sun which followed in November 45 and is regarded by Virgil as a prelude to the further civil wars which were to follow: 'the sun too pitied Rome when Caesar died, and hid his shining face in dim rusty red, and that impious generation feared eternal night.'[2] Here there is no overt suggestion of Caesar's divinity, but that is explicit in the fifth *Eclogue*,[3] if, as there can hardly be any doubt, Daphnis is there to be regarded as an allegory of Iulius. The song of Mopsus tells of Daphnis' death at

[1] E. ix. 46 Daphni, quid antiquos signorum suspicis ortus?
 ecce Dionaei processit Caesaris astrum,
 astrum quo segetes gauderent frugibus et quo
 duceret apricis in collibus uva colorem.
[2] G. i. 466 ille etiam exstincto miseratus Caesare Romam,
 cum caput obscura nitidum ferrugine texit,
 impiaque aeternam timuerunt saecula noctem.
[3] E. v. 20–80.

which all nature and the wild beasts wept; for it was Daphnis who 'taught men to yoke Armenian lions to the car, to lead the dancing bands of Bacchus and with gentle leaves to twine the pliant spears'[1]—a strange eulogy which Servius refers to a reintroduction by Iulius Caesar of the cult of Bacchus; since his death Pales and Apollo—the Italian and Greek shepherd gods—have left the fields;[2] but the shepherds make a tomb for Daphnis and place on it the legend: 'I was Daphnis in the woods, famous from earth to stars, guardian of the lovely flock, lovelier myself.'[3]

Then Menalcas offers to 'raise thy Daphnis to the stars; we will bear Daphnis to the stars: Daphnis loved us too'.[4] He then describes Daphnis' arrival on the threshold of Olympus and the immediate joy that seized the world now at peace, 'good Daphnis loves peace',[5] the very rocks and thickets cry aloud, 'a god, a god was he'.[6] Altars shall be raised to Daphnis and Phoebus and annual rites performed: 'as to Bacchus and Ceres, so to thee the country-folk shall make their prayer year by year; thou too shalt bind the suppliant to his vow.'[7] Here we have the quite definite

---

[1] E. v. 29 Daphnis et Armenias curru subiungere tigris
instituit, Daphnis thiasos inducere Bacchi
et foliis lentas intexere mollibus hastas.
Cf. Serv. ad loc. hoc aperte ad Caesarem pertinet; quem constat primum sacra Liberi patris transtulisse Romam.

[2] E. v. 34   postquam te fata tulerunt,
ipsa Pales agros atque ipse reliquit Apollo.

[3] E. v. 43 Daphnis ego in silvis, hinc usque ad sidera notus,
formosi pecoris custos, formosior ipse.

[4] E. v. 51   Daphnimque tuum tollemus ad astra;
Daphnin ad astra feremus; amavit nos quoque Daphnis.

[5] E. v. 61 amat bonus otia Daphnis.

[6] E. v. 63   ipsae iam carmina rupes,
ipsa sonant arbusta: 'deus, deus ille, Menalca.'
sis bonus o felixque tuis! en quattuor aras;
ecce duas tibi, Daphni, duas altaria Phoebo.
Cf. Lucr. v. 8 deus ille fuit, deus, inclute Memmi.

[7] E. v. 79 ut Baccho Cererique, tibi sic vota quotannis
agricolae facient: damnabis tu quoque votis.

ideas of an ascent into heaven and reception into Olympus, the institution of an annual worship, and the association of Caesar's divinity with peace: it is interesting to notice that the words *deus, deus ille*, are the words in which Lucretius addressed his master Epicurus, and to remember that at this time Virgil was living at Siro's Epicurean school at Naples.

By the time of the *Aeneid* Iulius' worship was fully established and he is referred to by his due divine title, Divus.[1] There is a strange passage in the first book in Iuppiter's prophecy to Venus which has been claimed with equal confidence as referring to Iulius and to Augustus: 'Of the noble stock a Trojan Caesar shall be born, who will extend his rule to the Ocean and his fame to the stars, Iulius, a name transmitted from great Iulus. Him in time to come thou shalt receive in heaven, laden with the spoils of the East; he too shall be called upon in prayer.'[2] The reference in this passage is much disputed, but in spite of the expression *spoliis Orientis onustum*, which does seem more applicable to Augustus, I believe that Servius is right in attributing the passage to Iulius for the following reasons: (1) Iulius at the date of the *Aeneid* would naturally mean the elder Caesar; it is rarely used of Octavian and would be no longer at this time; (2) 'extending his sway to Ocean' is just the phrase used by Cicero of Caesar after his conquests in Gaul (Cic. *de Prov. Cons.* xii. 29 quid Oceano longius inveniri potest? cf. xiv. 34); (3) *vocabitur hic quoque votis* is strongly reminiscent of *damnabis tu quoque votis* used of Iulius in *Eclogue* v. 80; (4) *spoliis Orientis onustum* is not

---

[1] A. vi. 792 Augustus Caesar, Divi genus.
[2] A. i. 286 nascetur pulchra Troianus origine Caesar,
    imperium Oceano, famam qui terminet astris,
    Iulius, a magno demissum nomen Iulo.
    hunc tu olim caelo spoliis Orientis onustum
    accipies secura; vocabitur hic quoque votis.
    aspera tum positis mitescent saecula bellis.
Serv. ad loc. hic est qui dictus est Gaius Iulius Caesar.

inappropriate to Iulius, when one remembers that Egypt was reckoned as part of the Orient; (5) the verses which follow and especially the reference to the closing of the 'gates of war' seem to refer to Augustus, but in 291 *tum* should be stressed—'after Iulius' reception into heaven will come the reign of peace and justice', i.e. the reign of Augustus. Thus interpreted the passage makes a close and natural parallel to *Eclogue* v and puts just the view found there of Caesar's deification. Virgil, then, in regard to Iulius, follows closely the run of popular thought. In the *Eclogues* his emphasis is on the recent comet and the thought of the moment of apotheosis; by the time of the *Aeneid* the divinity of Divus Iulius is established and it has ushered in Augustus' reign of peace.

The attitude of Virgil to the divinity of Augustus is much more complex and varying and far more interesting as representing the trend of thought and the workings of Augustus' mind. He was far less willing than Iulius had been to receive divine honours in his lifetime, and, at any rate after his power was fully established, seems to have thought of himself as a mortal who after death might win to divinity. In the *Eclogues* we seem to find the first outburst after Philippi at Augustus' success and the natural impulse to regard him as a divine being. In the first poem there is Virgil's gratitude for the restoration of his father's farm: 'it is a god', cries Tityrus, 'who has brought us this peace, for he will ever be a god in my eyes, his altar a tender lamb from my flocks shall stain with his blood again and again';[1] 'I could not', he adds later, 'elsewhere have found divine beings (*divos*) so present to aid.'[2] The

---

[1] E. i. 6 O Meliboee, deus nobis haec otia fecit;
namque erit ille mihi semper deus, illius aram
saepe tener nostris ab ovilibus imbuet agnus.
[2] E. i. 41 nec tam praesentis alibi cognoscere divos.

expression here is far from formal and, as a recent writer has well put it, it is an 'indication of the ready way in which an Italian or a Roman could turn to the forms of personal cult as the natural means of making his gratitude known'.[1] In the famous fourth *Eclogue*, whoever may be the child whose birth is sung, and I am myself reluctant to imagine it to be any other than the expected heir of Octavian,[2] the poem is a magnificent expression of the hopes of a new golden age which it was thought must now succeed the long civil strife, but does not necessarily imply any apotheosis.

By the time of the *Georgics* Virgil had become a member of Maecenas' circle and practically a court poet, and his utterances are more cautious; he seems to accept Octavian's view that his divinity is to come after death, and yet, like Horace, to make a protest against it. In the opening to the first book he invokes the rustic deities of Greece and Rome to aid him in his task, and finally adds to them Caesar, 'though it is not certain what councils of the gods will have him for their own',[3] whether he will be a god of earth and rule cities and favour the crops and control the weather, or of the sea, or become (like his father) a new constellation in the sky—the only certainty is that he will not be a god of the underworld—and then comes the interesting conclusion, 'grant a prosperous course and favour my daring task, and pitying the country-folk who know not the right way, advance with me, and *here and now* become used to be called upon in prayer'.[4] The idea of the

[1] L. Ross Taylor, op. cit., p. 111.
[2] W. W. Tarn (*Class. Quart.* 1932, p. 154) has, however, advanced cogent reasons for believing that the reference is to a child of Antony and Octavia.
[3] G. i. 24–42 and esp. 24
　　　　　tuque adeo, quem mox quae sint habitura deorum
　　　　　concilia incertum est.
[4] G. i. 40 da facilem cursum, atque audacibus adnue coeptis,
　　　　　ignarosque viae mecum miseratus agrestis
　　　　　ingredere, et votis iam nunc adsuesce vocari.

future divinity is elaborated in every way and yet it ends with the appeal to Augustus to be even now a *praesens divus* and to accept worship and prayer, even as his father had; *votis vocari* must once again be intended to suggest *damnabis tu quoque votis*. The official view of the future deification is echoed at the end of the first book: 'long has the palace of heaven, Caesar, grudged thee to us and complained that thou carest for the triumphs of men.'[1] The opening of the third book is vaguer;[2] it suggests for Augustus the character and privileges of the gods but without specifying whether it will be in this life or hereafter. Virgil by his songs will build a great marble temple, 'in the midst of it will be Caesar, who will dwell in the temple';[3] Virgil will drive the cars of triumph to him: 'even now it is my joy to lead the solemn pomp to the shrines and to see the steers slain'[4] and the games celebrated, and on the doors of the temple will be depicted Octavian's victories. There is the same protesting *iam nunc*, yet the cautious use of the future. A more explicit exposition of the official view is seen in the conclusion of the whole *Georgics*: Virgil has been telling of the culture of fields and flocks and trees 'while mighty Caesar is thundering in battle by the deep Euphrates, and in triumph is giving laws to willing nations, and *setting foot on the path to Olympus*'.[5] It is the first step, not the completed road, to divinity.

In the *Aeneid* Octavian has become 'Augustus Caesar, son of Divus', and this full official title designates clearly

[1] G. i. 503 iam pridem nobis caeli te regia, Caesar,
        invidet atque hominum queritur curare triumphos.
[2] G. iii. 13–44.
[3] G. iii. 16 in medio mihi Caesar erit templumque tenebit.
[4] G. iii. 22   iam nunc sollemnis ducere pompas
        ad delubra iuvat caesosque videre iuvencos.
[5] G. iv. 560   Caesar dum magnus ad altum
        fulminat Euphraten bello victorque volentis
        per populos dat iura viamque adfectat Olympo.

the emperor's own view of his character. He is the son of
one who has attained to a special kind of godhead, Divus
not *deus*; he himself is a man as yet, but with a special
kind of sanctity expressed in the old ritual title. Yet even
here there are two ideas which appear in association with
Augustus, one that he has brought back the golden age of
peace, the other that after death a place is awaiting him
in heaven among the gods. Both these ideas find their
expression in the great vision of Rome's heroes at the close
of the sixth book. 'Turn hither', Anchises says to his son,
'thine eyes, gaze on this stock of thy Romans. Here is
Caesar and all the offspring of Iulus, *which is one day to come
to the great vault of heaven.* This is the man, yea this, whom
thou hast often heard promised to thee, Augustus Caesar,
the son of Divus, *who shall found again the golden age* in the
fields once the realm of Latin Saturn.'[1] In the two pictures
of Augustus on the shield of Aeneas he is still more
definitely the mortal monarch, and even the hint of
divinity is wanting. The first is the vision of the battle
of Actium: 'on the one side is Caesar Augustus leading
the Italians to battle, with the fathers and the people, the
Penates and the great gods, standing on the lofty poop.'[2]
He is not divine himself, but the ancient gods of Rome are
on his side and with him. The second picture is of Augustus'
triumph,[3] 'Caesar riding into the walls of Rome in triple

---

[1] A. vi. 788   huc geminas nunc flecte acies, hanc aspice gentem
              Romanosque tuos. hic Caesar et omnis Iuli
              progenies, magnum caeli ventura sub axem.
              hic vir, hic est, tibi quem promitti saepius audis,
              Augustus Caesar, Divi genus, aurea condet
              saecula qui rursus Latio regnata per arva
              Saturno quondam.
[2] A. viii. 678   hinc Augustus agens Italos in proelia Caesar
                cum patribus populoque, penatibus et magnis dis,
                stans celsa in puppi.
[3] A. viii. 714–28.

triumph, was dedicating his deathless vow to the gods of Italy, three hundred lofty shrines throughout the whole city'[1] . . . 'before the altars the slaughtered steers were strewn upon the ground. He himself, sitting on the snow-white threshold of glorious Phoebus, reviews the gifts of the nations and fits them to the lofty doorposts.'[2] He is again mortal, but we are reminded of his great religious work in the renewal of the temples and in the building of the great temple of Apollo on the Palatine. It is as if the emperor's restraining hand was on the poet and he could not say all he would. But as though by way of compensation, he says it of the characters of his epic, who are at once the ancestors and the prototypes of Augustus. Apollo himself addresses the young Iulus: 'Good luck to thee in thy new honour, boy: this is the path to the stars, son of the gods and father of gods to be.'[3] This is explicit enough, and the poet's feeling becomes plainer still in the last book, when Iuppiter urges Iuno to cease her obstructive tactics and let Aeneas enter on his due success, 'Thou knowest thyself and dost confess that thou dost know that Aeneas, god of our soil (*indigetem*) is due to heaven and is being raised by destiny to the stars.'[4] Aeneas, if not an allegory, is the prototype of Augustus, and it is impossible to doubt that Virgil intended the inference.

We are left then with the impression of Virgil at first

[1] A. viii. 714 at Caesar, triplici invectus Romana triumpho
   moenia, dis Italis votum immortale sacrabat,
   maxima ter centum totam delubra per urbem . . .
[2] A. viii. 719 ante aras terram caesi stravere iuvenci.
   ipse sedens niveo candentis limine Phoebi,
   dona recognoscit populorum aptatque superbis
   postibus.
[3] A. ix. 641 macte nova virtute, puer, sic itur ad astra,
   dis genite et geniture deos.
[4] A. xii. 794 indigetem Aenean scis ipsa et scire fateris
   deberi caelo fatisque ad sidera tolli.

saluting the saviour of his country with enthusiastic accla-
mation as a divine being like his father, and then gradually
tempered to the moderation of Augustus himself, but
always with an eye to the supernatural results of his rule
on earth and the glorification that is to come after his
death. The fact is that the court poets, and Horace perhaps more than Virgil, outran the official pace; they not
only supported Augustus in his reforms, in many ways
they led the way. And if one asks how far this feeling of his
divinity was genuine, it is hard to doubt that it was. It
is difficult for us to put ourselves back into the mind of the
age, to realize how little a polytheism would resent the
addition of a new divinity and how strong was the influence of the oriental idea of divine kingship, which had
come to Rome through Alexandria. It was indeed hard
at that time to conceive of a Soter or a Euergetes who was
not also in his nature divine and it was clearly all that
Augustus could do to keep the people of Rome from
regarding him as a god in his lifetime. Virgil's sympathy
was with the popular view, but as he fell more and more
under the influence of the court, he learned to keep his
own inclinations in check.

(d) Combinations of deities

Not a little light is thrown on the state of religious habits
and feelings in Virgil's age by a consideration of the combinations of deities, which he invokes or makes his characters invoke in prayer or vow. Sometimes, though rarely,
these are the traditional combinations of the old religion,
more often Roman and Greek gods are placed side by
side, and, especially in the longest and most solemn
invocations, we find gods, Greek and Roman, old spirits
of the country-side, cosmological deities, and sometimes
Caesar, run together in an incongruous but yet strangely

impressive congeries. At times we can see the reason for his combinations, at others they remain mysterious, but it is unlikely that his choice is ever really haphazard. It will be worth while to pursue this idea in several fields.

The old household gods are found in just the combination in which an Italian of the earliest days might have worshipped them. Aeneas in the early morning in Sicily 'rouses the sleeping flames and in supplication worships the Lar of Pergamus and the shrine of hoary Vesta with sacred meal and a full censer'.[1] The only extraneous touch is the epithet of the Lar *Pergameum*, which arises from the story; the Lar and Vesta were worshipped together from of old. The combination is even more complete in Ascanius' oath to Nisus: 'by the great Penates and the Lar of Assaracus and the shrine of hoary Vesta I swear.'[2] The list is made more comprehensive by the inclusion of the Penates and the Trojan touch is given here by the mention of the Lar of Assaracus.

The gods of agriculture and the country-side naturally appear in *Eclogues* and *Georgics*, and there it is significant that in two prominent places Caesar-worship affects the combination. In the passage already noticed in the fifth *Eclogue*[3] comes the prophecy that in future the country-folk will pay their annual vows to Daphnis-Iulius as well as to Bacchus, lord of the vine, and Ceres, deity of the corn. More impressive and more indicative of the peculiar syncretism of the age is the great invocation to the deities of the country-side at the opening of the *Georgics*.[4] There are

[1] A. v. 743 haec memorans cinerem et sopitos suscitat ignis,
  Pergameumque Larem et canae penetralia Vestae
  farre pio et plena supplex veneratur acerra.
[2] A. ix. 258   per magnos, Nise, Penatis
  Assaracique larem et canae penetralia Vestae
  obtestor.
[3] E. v. 79 ut Baccho Cererique, tibi sic vota quotannis
  agricolae facient.   [4] G. i. 5-42.

the old Italian country gods, Liber and Ceres, who have charge of the corn-crop, Silvanus and the Fauni, the Italian deities of wood and field, but the Fauni are combined with the Greek Dryades and reduplicated in the Greek Pan; there are the Graeco-Roman deities, Neptunus representing Poseidon Hippios and Minerva standing for Pallas, the protectress of the vine, and the two Greek heroes, Aristaeus the bee-keeper and Triptolemus the inventor of the plough. And most characteristically the invocation opens with the appeal to the cosmological deities, the stars, who 'lead on the gliding year in the sky', and ends with Caesar, who may be about to become a deity of the country-side and must in any case 'even now grow accustomed to be called upon in prayer'. As though with a certain sense of incongruity these two form, as it were, the frame to a picture, which is orthodox and traditional.

At the conclusion of the first book comes an invocation to the gods of the State: 'Ye gods of our country, old gods of the land (*indigetes*) and Romulus and Mother Vesta, who dost preserve Tuscan Tiber and the Roman Palatia.'[1] The question has often been raised why Virgil here specifies Romulus and Vesta, but the following line supplies the clue; it is again a covert hint at the divinity of Octavian. Romulus, deified as Quirinus, was a prototype of the deified Augustus (it is notable that the only other occurrence of the word *indiges* in the poem is in reference to Aeneas in a passage where the suggestion of Augustus is unmistakable), and as for Vesta, Octavian had a special liking for her, and later on (12 B.C.), breaking away from tradition, was to establish a special cult for her in his own

---

[1] G. i. 498 di patrii, Indigetes, et Romule Vestaque mater,
      quae Tuscum Tiberim et Romana Palatia servas.
Cf. A. xii. 794 indigetem Aenean.

palace on the Palatine; it looks almost as if Virgil already knew that he had this in mind.

Another group which we meet in definite contexts is that of the sea-gods. Cloanthus, longing to win the boat-race, cries to the 'gods, who have the sway over the sea, on whose waters I speed',[1] and his prayer was heard by 'all the band of the Nereids and of Phorcus and the maid Panopea, and father Portunus himself with his great hand pushed the vessel as it went'[2]—a strange combination of the nymphs of Greek mythology and the old Roman deity, clearly thought of here by Virgil as the 'god of harbours' (*portus*). So, again, when the Trojans are about to set sail for Crete Anchises 'sacrificed the due meal of honour on the altars, a bull to thee, Neptunus, a bull to thee, beauteous Apollo, a black sheep to Hiems, and a white sheep to the favouring Zephyrs'.[3] Neptune's place as Poseidon is obvious, Apollo was the protector of Troy and had just given the oracle which Anchises believed he was obeying in making for Crete, and to these are added the half-personified meteorological beings, Storms and Winds. Here is a sophisticated combination.

So, again, in Dido's appeals to the deities of the lower world, the choice is obvious but the combination curious.[4] The priestess 'thunders aloud to the three hundred gods (a strange expression, not yet fully explained), to Erebus and Chaos, to triple Hecate, the three aspects of the virgin

[1] A. v. 235 di, quibus imperium est pelagi, quorum aequora curro.

[2] A. v. 239   audiit omnis
        Nereidum Phorcique chorus Panopeaque virgo,
        et pater ipse manu magna Portunus euntem
        impulit.

[3] A. iii. 118 sic fatus meritos aris mactavit honores,
        taurum Neptuno, taurum tibi, pulcher Apollo,
        nigram Hiemi pecudem, Zephyris felicibus albam.

[4] A. iv. 509   crinis effusa sacerdos
        ter centum tonat ore deos, Erebumque Chaosque,
        tergeminamque Hecaten, tria virginis ora Dianae.

Diana'. Here is Artemis in her character of the chthonic Hecate, yet with remembrance of her connexion with the upper world and, as the moon, with the sky, Erebus the personified lower world of mythology, and Chaos, its cosmological counterpart. And so later on[1] Dido makes her own more complex appeal to Sol, who illuminates the world, to Iuno, who knows the cares of love and marriage, to the mighty Hecate, the avenging Dirae, and 'the gods of the dying Elissa', who probably represent the Roman idea of the 'Iuno' of women corresponding to the Genius of men, tinged perhaps with the notion of the Greek δαίμων, one of whose functions, as Norden has shown,[2] was to lead the dying to the lower world. It is a strange complex of ideas derived from many sources.

On certain other special occasions it is possible to trace the motive of the combination of deities. Dido and her sister Anna on the morning after Aeneas' arrival at Carthage 'duly sacrifice chosen sheep to Ceres the law-giver, to Phoebus and father Lyaeus, and above all to Iuno, who cares for the bonds of wedlock'.[3] Iuno's place is obvious, Phoebus may be there to represent the Trojans, and Ceres in her character of Demeter Θεσμοφόρος to secure the establishment of the new colony. But there may be other grounds: Henry has noticed that Ceres, Apollo, and Bacchus are mentioned in the *Pervigilium Veneris* (43) as deities of marriage. And Virgil himself has illustrated the passage, for on the previous night Dido had made prayer

---

[1] A. iv. 607 Sol, qui terrarum flammis opera omnia lustras,
tuque harum interpres curarum et conscia Iuno,
nocturnisque Hecate triviis ululata per urbes,
et Dirae ultrices et di morientis Elissae,
accipite haec.

[2] E. Norden, *Vergilius, Aeneis Buch VI*, p. 33.

[3] A. iv. 57   mactant lectas de more bidentis
legiferae Cereri Phoeboque patrique Lyaeo,
Iunoni ante omnis, cui vincla iugalia curae.

to Iuppiter, the protector of strangers,[1] and asked for the
presence of 'Bacchus giver of joy and kindly Iuno'.[2] Ceres
and Lyaeus then may be here as deities of hospitality and
feasting. But probably several motives may have worked
in Virgil's mind towards his choice.

Other special instances are less complicated than this.
On first landing in Thrace Aeneas worships 'the rustic
Nymphs',[3] the spirits that is of the country-side, and Mars,
'who presides over the fields of the Getae', the local protecting deity. When they first land in Italy the Trojans
pray to the 'holy power of Pallas, of the rattling arms, who
first received them in their happiness',[4] for their first sight
was one of her temples, and 'by the ordinance of Helenus
to Iuno of Argos', for she was their bitter foe and no chance
of propitiating her must be lost. An interesting combination, to which reference has been already made,[5] is seen in
the protectors of Augustus' fleet at Actium as represented
on Aeneas' shield—Neptune, because it was a sea battle,
Venus as the protectress of the Julian house, and Minerva,
either in her capacity as Pallas, deity of fighting, or as representing the Capitoline triad (see p. 156).

There are some passages in the *Aeneid* where, as in the
exordium of the *Georgics*, Virgil has wished to give a very
special religious feeling to his story, and here his collocations
of deities are particularly interesting. Such a one occurs
in the seventh book when the fulfilment of the prophecy

---

[1] A. i. 731 Iuppiter, hospitibus nam te dare iura loquuntur.
[2] A. i. 734 adsit laetitiae Bacchus dator et bona Iuno.
[3] A. iii. 34   Nymphas venerabar agrestis,
      Gradivumque patrem, Geticis qui praesidet arvis.
[4] A. iii. 543   tum numina sancta precamur
      Palladis armisonae, quae prima accepit ovantis . . .
      praeceptisque Heleni, dederat quae maxima, rite
      Iunoni Argivae iussos adolemus honores.
[5] A. viii. 699 contra Neptunum et Venerem contraque Minervam
      tela tenent.

of the 'consumed tables' leads Aeneas to the realization that this is the land of their destiny.[1] His invocation is wide in its scope and full of significance: he prays first to the 'Genius of the spot and Earth oldest of the gods'—that is, to the new land which he has reached; then to the spirits of its natural features, to the Nymphs and the streams which as yet he knows not; then, for the sun has now set, to Night and the rising constellations; then to the gods of his own country, Iuppiter of Ida and the Phrygian mother; and finally, becoming yet more personal, to 'his two parents in heaven and in Erebus', Venus and Anchises —a strange collocation and one of the few undoubted instances in Virgil of prayer to a dead hero and therefore definitely Greek in idea. Here it is easy to account for each item in the list, but the combination of them all produces a strange sense of inconsequence. Perhaps the most interesting and significant passages of all are met with in the taking of the oaths before the single combat by Aeneas and Latinus. Aeneas[2] calls on Sun and this Earth, 'for whose sake I have been able to endure such heavy toils'—the main conception is cosmological but Terra is localized as the land of Latium; then come the great Roman gods, Iuppiter, 'the omnipotent father', and his wife Saturn's daughter ('be now more gracious, even now goddess, I pray') and Mars the lord of war; then he turns

[1] A. vii. 136   Geniumque loci primamque deorum
Tellurem Nymphasque et adhuc ignota precatur
flumina, tum Noctem Noctisque orientia signa
Idaeumque Iovem Phrygiamque ex ordine Matrem
invocat, et duplicis caeloque Ereboque parentis.

[2] A. xii. 176   esto nunc Sol testis et haec mihi Terra vocanti,
quam propter tantos potui perferre labores,
et pater omnipotens et tu Saturnia coniunx,
iam melior, iam, diva, precor; tuque inclute Mavors,
cuncta tuo qui bella, pater, sub numine torques;
fontisque fluviosque voco, quaeque aetheris alti
religio et quae caeruleo sunt numina ponto.

to the local *numina*, 'ye streams and rivers and the divine beings in the sky above and the spirits in the blue deep': three distinct strata of thought combined in the one appeal. Latinus replies in the same strain, but with an even wider embrace:[1] he swears by earth, sea, and stars, not necessarily, as has been seen, regarded here as deities, by 'the two children of Latona', Phoebus and Artemis, perhaps, as the parallel of Aeneas' prayer suggests, here sun and moon, 'by Ianus the twin-faced' (the Latin deity), 'the might of the gods below the earth and the precincts of cruel Dis'—the appeal to the underworld gods gives additional force and terror to the oath—and finally returning to Iuppiter he prays, 'may the Father hear this, who sanctifies treaties by his thunderbolt'. Both these lists would have been impossible at any earlier stage of Latin thought, for they imply gods Roman, Greek, and cosmological, but they are typical of the syncretistic religion of the early empire and are significant documents for the permutations and combinations of religious thought which were then prevalent.

[1] A. xii. 197 haec eadem, Aenea, terram, mare, sidera, iuro,
Latonaeque genus duplex Ianumque bifrontem,
vimque deum infernam et duri sacraria Ditis;
audiat haec genitor qui foedera fulmine sancit.

IX

FATE AND THE GODS

No account of the religious ideas in Virgil would be complete without a consideration of his conception of Fate and the relation of Fate to the gods; it is indeed in some senses the widest and deepest of his religious ideas. This is a well-worn theme; 'much', says Warde Fowler,[1] 'has been written about the part of the Fates in the *Aeneid* and their relation to Jupiter', and not a little of the best was written by himself. But there is perhaps still room for a rather minuter study of the subject than has hitherto been made.

The idea of Fate is all-pervading in Virgil, and especially of course in the *Aeneid*. In it the words *fatum* and *fata* occur some 120 times, besides several instances of the derivative adjective *fatalis*. To these must be added *Parcae*, the personification of the Fates, together with many instances in which in one sense *fortuna*, in another *numen* and *iussa deum* are in various contexts tantamount in Virgil's mind to *fatum*. If all these be put together, and it is also borne in mind that there are large tracts of the poem in which the idea is necessarily absent, some idea can be formed of the astonishing penetration of the whole work by this one dominating conception.

But, as soon as one is on the look-out for the word *fatum* and pays attention to its meaning in the context, it becomes obvious that Virgil uses it in a very considerable range of different senses. If an attempt is made to classify these, certain main categories soon emerge, overlapping no doubt and running into one another in borderline

[1] *R.E.*, p. 425, n. 12.

examples, but on the whole distinct. From such a classifi-
cation it is possible to make a general analysis of the idea
and to draw certain conclusions as to the main lines of
Virgil's thought.

One must ask as preliminary, what was Virgil's inheritance? There can be no question that the word *fatum* is
connected with the verb *fari*, 'to speak', and that it is in
fact its passive participle, meaning 'the spoken word'.
What idea did that convey to a Roman? To Virgil himself
it seems to have implied primarily the notion of the 'spoken
word' of divine beings and in particular of Iuppiter, which
was the expression of his will and so of the destiny of mankind. So, as will be seen (pp. 224–232), Virgil speaks often
of the *fata deum*, *fata dei* or *fata Iovis*, and *fata* are also assigned
to Iuno. Some authorities[1] believe this to have been the
original meaning in Latin, but early instances are lacking
and it is not easy, if this is so, to derive other usages from it.
It is more probable that the original Latin sense is rather
that of the 'spoken word' of the prophet or seer, in which
he declares future events, regarded not as the will of divine
beings, but rather as part of a fixed order. The idea is
possibly more akin to magic than religion; the prophet
knows of himself and his word contains its own validity,
just as in origin the bird of omen was thought of as bringing
the weather, not as declaring the intentions of a divine
power. This older meaning, too, is well known to Virgil
and may be recognized in many passages of the *Aeneid*; the
characteristic verb with *fata* is here *canere*. Thus Helenus
tells Aeneas of the cavern at Cumae, where the Sibyl 'sings
her prophecies'.[2] When Aeneas approaches her, she cries
to him that it is 'time to demand the prophecies',[3] and

[1] e.g. Peter, in Roscher's *Lexicon*, s.v.; but see Otto, in P.W., s.v.
[2] A. iii. 443 insanam vatem aspicies, quae rupe sub ima
      fata canit.
[3] A. vi. 45 poscere fata | tempus.

shortly afterwards he promises her that he will make a shrine in which to place her 'secret prophecies',[1] and will consecrate decemvirs to watch over them. So, too, Cassandra 'opens her mouth to utter prophecies of the future',[2] just as in similar phrase Proteus 'opens his mouth for prophecy'[3] to Aristaeus in the *Georgics*, and Aeneas tells how his father Anchises in his prophecy of his son's future 'left me such secrets of the fates'.[4] The last passage is important because it is the expression 'the secrets of the fates', which is found also in a very interesting but ambiguous passage at the outset of the poem,[5] when Iuppiter is solacing Venus and assuring her of Aeneas' ultimate success after many hardships; in an etymological sentence, more in the manner of Ovid, Iuppiter says, 'I will speak out, since this anxiety is harassing you, and unrolling them far ahead will stir up the secrets of the fates.' It is clear that *fabor* and *fata* are meant to suggest the etymology of the word, but are the *fata* here the 'spoken word' or will of Iuppiter himself, which he now intends to declare, or is Iuppiter here rather in the position of a prophet to the other gods, declaring, like an earthly prophet, the destiny laid up for Aeneas? Probably the latter, but this does not preclude the thought that that destiny itself is divinely willed.

From this primary sense of 'the seer's prophecy', *fatum* passed by a natural development to mean the 'destiny' which the seer prophesied; the belief that the future could be foretold implied that the future was ordained. This

---

[1] A. vi. 72 hic ego namque tuas sortis arcanaque fata
      dicta meae genti ponam lectosque sacrabo,
      alma, viros.

[2] A. ii. 246 fatis aperit Cassandra futuris | ora.

[3] G. iv. 452 fatis ora resolvit.

[4] A. vii. 122   genitor mihi talia namque
      (nunc repeto) Anchises fatorum arcana reliquit.

[5] A. i. 261   fabor enim, quando haec te cura remordet,
      longius et volvens fatorum arcana movebo.

'destiny' would most frequently be the destiny of an individual or family or nation, as in Naevius' famous gibe *fato Metelli Romae consules fiunt*, but as ideas grew and perspective widened it came to designate the more general conception of a destiny which rules the world. And so in a more philosophical context, such as Cicero's treatise *De Fato*,[1] it acquires, under the strong influence of Greek thought, the more exact significance of 'determinism'. Similarly, in religious contexts it has the sense already noticed of the 'decree' of the god or the gods, which is binding on men, and so can be naturally applied to the responses of oracles.

The natural sense then of the word *fatum* in Latin is the destiny, which is the content of the spoken word, primarily of the seer, and later and more commonly, of a deity. When the Roman poets fell under the sway of Greek literature, they found there several conceptions which corresponded to their own notions of *fatum*, but gave them a richer and wider content. There was first the idea, common in the poets from Homer onwards, of μοῖρα, the root-notion of which seems to be the 'portion', 'lot', or 'destiny' of the individual. Secondly, there was the conception of εἰμαρμένη or τὸ πεπρωμένον, the 'destiny' which guides the whole world, connected by the scientific writers with the idea of 'natural law' (ἀνάγκη) and so becoming the principle of determinism; 'I would rather', says Epicurus in a famous passage,[2] 'follow the myth about the gods than be a slave to the determinism (εἰμαρμένη) of the physicists'. Finally, there was from the first the religious idea that 'fate' was a lot apportioned by the gods and in particular by Zeus; this view was 'philosophized' by the Stoics and

[1] Cicero's definition of *fatum*, quoted by Servius *ad Aen.* iii. 376 is: fatum est conexio rerum per aeternitatem se invicem tenens, quae suo ordine et lege sic variatur ut ipsa varietas habeat aeternitatem.

[2] *Ep. ad Men.*: D.L. x. 134.

taken up into their theory that the destiny of the world was the will, the 'providence' (πρόνοια), of the great world-spirit. The germs of all these Greek conceptions were present in the Latin associations of *fatum*, but they defined and distinguished them and to some extent crystallized them.

Virgil was influenced by each and all of these ideas, but the secret of his apparent inconsistency in his use of the word *fatum* and the ideas connected with it is to be found in the influence of the Greek rather than the Latin conceptions; at any rate his usages fall most easily into the Greek categories. *Fatum* appears as the 'lot' of the individual or of the race and as the ultimate destiny of the world; but the most deep-seated of his beliefs about fate lies in the Stoic conception of 'providence'; that is, it might be said, the keynote of the whole poem. An attempt must be made to examine these three senses in some detail.

I. *The 'Lot' of the Individual*

Of *fatum* or *fata* used in the simple and unmistakable sense of the 'lot' or 'destiny' of the individual person there are many examples in the *Aeneid*. A large number naturally concern the destiny of Aeneas. Thus Aeneas assures the Sibyl that 'the kingdom I seek is due to my destiny',[1] Anchises, later in the sixth book, promises him, 'I will tell you your destiny',[2] and in the eighth book Aeneas, gazing on the pictures wrought on the shield which Vulcan had made for him, 'wonders at the fame and destinies of his descendants'.[3] So Ilioneus, the envoy of the Trojans, takes an oath to Latinus by 'the destiny of Aeneas and his strong right arm'.[4] Outside the lot of Aeneas we have other

---

[1] A. vi. 66 non indebita posco | regna meis fatis.
[2] A. vi. 759 te tua fata docebo.
[3] A. viii. 730 miratur . . . famamque et fata nepotum.
[4] A. vii. 234 fata per Aeneae iuro dextramque potentem.

examples. Deiphobus in the lower world tells Aeneas 'it was my own destiny and the fatal crime of Helen which plunged me in these miseries;'[1] Iuppiter prevents Pallas and Lausus meeting in combat, for 'soon their destinies await them beneath a greater foe',[2] and later consoles Hercules for the death of his favourite Pallas by reminding him that Turnus too is 'being summoned by his destiny'.[3] In the instances quoted the genitive or possessive pronoun makes the conception of individual destiny certain; there are many others where the same idea is clear, though less explicit. Sinon, the traitor, in words closely recalling Aeneas' thought of his descendants, tells the Trojans that, if the wooden horse is taken into the city, Asia would come to attack Greece and 'that is the destiny that awaits our descendants';[4] it is their μοῖρα. Similarly, Aeneas assures the disguised Venus in the first book that in undertaking his voyage he was 'following the allotted destiny',[5] Aeneas and his wife and son implore Anchises 'to be willing to yield to the destiny pressing upon him',[6] Deiphobus, as Aeneas parts from him, prays that he may 'enjoy a better destiny than his own',[7] and the dying Orodes reminds Mezentius that 'the like destiny awaits thee too'.[8] A remarkable example of this idea occurs in the passage where Anchises speaks of the souls on the banks of Lethe's

[1] A. vi. 511 sed me fata mea et scelus exitiale Lacaenae
his mersere malis.
[2] A. x. 438 mox illos sua fata manent maiore sub hoste.
[3] A. x. 471 etiam sua Turnum | fata vocant.
[4] A. ii. 194 nostros ea fata manere nepotes.
[5] A. i. 382 data fata secutus.
[6] A. ii. 653 fatoque urgenti incumbere vellet.
[7] A. vi. 546 melioribus utere fatis.
[8] A. x. 740 te quoque fata | prospectant paria.

Similar examples will be found in iv. 13 and xii. 795, and there are many which are on the borderline of this sense and that of the universal fate (εἱμαρμένη).

water 'to whom a second life is due by destiny';[1] even the unborn souls have their μοῖρα. In all these instances the notion of the individual 'lot' is clear.

Occasionally this use of *fatum* declines into what might be called a 'faded' sense and means little more than 'adventures', as when the ghost of Hector tells Aeneas to take the Penates as 'the companions of his destiny'.[2] Far more often it is in effect a synonym for death. Dido tells her sister that Aeneas alone has touched her heart 'since the fate of my poor Sychaeus',[3] Anna rebukes her on the funeral pyre, 'thou shouldest have summoned me to the same fate',[4] Euryalus reminds Nisus that together they 'follow high-souled Aeneas and their destined end',[5] Latinus rends his robe, 'stunned by his wife's fate',[6] and Iapyx learns medicine 'in order that he might postpone the death [or 'prolong the life'] of his sick father'.[7] To this meaning belongs the use of the adjective *fatalis* in the sense of 'deadly', 'fatal'.[8]

The notion of the special destiny (μοῖρα) is applied not only to individual persons, but also to countries and races. Most frequently it is the destiny of Troy which Virgil thus contemplates. Thus it was 'the destiny of Troy' which led to the bringing of the wooden horse within the walls,[9] and twice in the poem, once in life and once as a ghostly visitant, Anchises addresses Aeneas as 'my son, harassed by the destiny of Ilium'.[10] So, too, Iuppiter, near the outset

[1] A. vi. 713   animae, quibus altera fato
                     corpora debentur.
[2] A. ii. 294 hos cape fatorum comites.
[3] A. iv. 20 miseri post fata Sychaei.
[4] A. iv. 678 eadem me ad fata vocasses.
[5] A. ix. 204 magnanimum Aenean et fata extrema secutus.
[6] A. xii. 610 coniugis attonitus fatis.
[7] A. xii. 395 ut depositi proferret fata parentis.
[8] e.g. A. xii. 232 fatales manus; xii. 919 telum fatale.
[9] A. ii. 34 sive dolo seu iam Troiae sic fata ferebant.
[10] A. iii. 182, v. 725 Iliacis exercite fatis.

of the story, assures Venus that 'the destiny of thy people remains unshaken'.[1] It is noticeable that in the first two of these instances the destiny of Troy is regarded as an evil fate, from which Aeneas has to escape; in Iuppiter's promise to Venus alone is there the glimpse of the brilliant future which was to convert the evil destiny of Troy into the glorious destiny of Rome. Besides the 'lot' of Troy we find this sense of the destiny of a race when Diomede tells Aeneas' envoys that if Troy had borne two more such heroes as Aeneas, the Trojans would have attacked the cities of Argos and 'Greece would have mourned the reversal of her destiny'.[2]

The last instance introduces a very interesting feature in the lot of the individual. Μοῖρα in the Greek conception is limited and may be overruled by the wider and more universal εἱμαρμένη. That Virgil inherited this conception is proved by two limitations to the individual *fatum* which appear from time to time in the *Aeneid*.

In the first place the destiny of man or nation may be avoided or postponed. Thus Evander lamenting over Pallas says, 'by living I have conquered my fate, a father surviving my son',[3] Iuppiter tells Iuno that if she craves delay for Turnus, she may 'wrest him from the destiny which is now coming on him',[4] and in the most striking instance of all, Anchises addresses the unborn soul of

---

[1] A. i. 257   manent immota tuorum
                fata tibi.
[2] A. xi. 287 versis lugeret Graecia fatis.
[3] A. xi. 160 contra ego vivendo vici mea fata, superstes
                restarem ut genitor.
The complement of this notion is seen in *Culex* 227, where the gnat, which died before its time to save the shepherd, says,
                'instantia vici
                alterius, sine respectu mea fata reliquens',
i.e. it abandoned the fate allotted to it in order to ward off the fate threatening the shepherd.
[4] A. x. 624 instantibus eripe fatis.

Augustus' son-in-law, 'Ah! wretched boy, thou, if thou couldst but burst through thy harsh fate, thou shalt be Marcellus.'[1]

Particularly interesting in this context are certain passages in which human action or effort are set parallel to or even in opposition to fate as a determinant of the course of human life. 'He would have lived to whom God or his right hand had given life';[2] his survival in the combat might have been due either to the will of heaven or to his own valour, thwarting his destiny; 'this place alone is open to thy deserts and thy fortune';[3] chance and his own valour both have the opportunity of enabling Aeneas to retrieve his position with Evander, just as on the other side Dido's death was not due either to fate, which might have given her a longer span of life, or to any great crime she had committed.[4] The same combination is seen in Ilioneus' oath by Aeneas' 'fate and his strong right arm',[5] in Ascanius' reference to his 'fortune and his confidence',[6] and in Anchises' reflection on the 'character and deeds' of his descendants as well as their 'destinies and fortunes'.[7] It is not fanciful in all these passages to see a protest in favour of the free will of the individual, which by exceptional actions may thwart or modify the μοῖρα appointed for him by fate.

The limitation of the individual destiny is brought out almost more strikingly in passages where individual *fata* are spoken of in contrast or even in conflict. Thus at the outset of the poem Venus tells Iuppiter that she used to console herself for the fall of Troy by the thought of the coming of the Roman race, 'thus weighing fate against

[1] A. vi. 882 heu, miserande puer, si qua fata aspera rumpas,
    tu Marcellus eris.
[2] A. xi. 118.   [3] A. xi. 179.
[4] A. iv. 696.   [5] A. vii. 234.
[6] A. ix. 260.   [7] A. vi. 683.

fate',[1] the present destiny of Aeneas, that is, against the fate of Troy. So too, if the meaning be pressed, Aeneas' saying to Helenus that 'we are summoned from one fate to another'[2] may mean a transference from the ill fortune of the Trojans to the great destiny of Rome. A more notable instance of conflict occurs in Iuno's outburst against the Trojans: 'Ah! hateful stock and the fate of the Phrygians set against our fate.'[3] If the destinies of nations can thus strive against one another, one at least must give way and yield to the destiny of the world, which is above them. In a sense the whole *Aeneid* might be said to be the story of the conflict of μοῖραι and its ultimate decision by a higher fate.

To sum up; *fatum* in its μοῖρα sense is used by Virgil first of the lot of the individual, then of the destiny of a country or a people. These lesser 'fates' of individuals or races may come into conflict with one another and may in some cases be postponed or even avoided altogether, sometimes even by the free action of the person concerned. They are at all times subordinate to the world-destiny which affects all men and races alike.

The relation of *fortuna* to *fatum* in Virgil's usage will have to be considered at length,[4] but here it may be noticed that *fortuna* is used as the equivalent of *fatum* both in reference to the individual and to the nation. Thus, to take a passage in which the words are combined, Aeneas, saying farewell to Helenus and Andromache, exclaims: 'Live in happiness, ye whose fortune is now accomplished; we are summoned

---

[1] A. i. 238 hoc equidem occasum Troiae tristisque ruinas
      solabar fatis contraria fata rependens.

[2] A. iii. 494 nos alia ex aliis in fata vocamur.

[3] A. vii. 293 heu stirpem invisam et fatis contraria nostris
      fata Phrygum!
The significance of the expression *nostris . . . fatis* must be considered in estimating the relation of the gods to fate; see p. 221.

[4] See appendix to this chapter, pp. 234–240.

from one fate to another';[1] it is not possible here to distinguish between the 'fortune' of Helenus and the 'fate' of Aeneas. Or, again, to compare parallel expressions, 'is it some fortune that harries you?'[2] is not different from the twice-repeated 'harassed by the destiny of Troy'. It is equally clear in application to nations. *Fortuna* is used of the destiny of Troy when in the cave of the Sibyl Aeneas prays to Phoebus 'thus far may the fortune of Troy have pursued us',[3] and of the destiny of the Latin race when the orator Drances tells Latinus that all his subjects know 'what the fortune of the people is bringing to pass'.[4] The inclusion of such instances of the use of *fortuna* widens the range of Virgil's thought of the destiny of the individual, but does not in any way alter its significance.

II. *The 'Destiny' of the World*

Though the conception of the destiny or 'lot' of the individual is thus very prominent in the *Aeneid*, yet the prevailing idea is wider, that of a general fate or destiny, which rules the world and overrides the 'lot' of a man or a race in a higher 'fate'. It is not easy to say how far these two ideas were distinct in Virgil's conception, and they no doubt merge into one another; for the 'lot' of the individual must in the ultimate analysis be a part of the universal 'destiny'. There are, therefore, certain borderline cases in which it would not be easy to say which of the two ideas was uppermost in the poet's mind. At the very outset of the *Aeneid* the poet tells us that Aeneas came to Italy

---

[1] A. iii. 493 vivite felices, quibus est fortuna peracta
       iam sua; nos alia ex aliis in fata vocamur.
[2] A. vi. 533 an quae te fortuna fatigat? Cf. A. iii. 182, v. 725; see p. 210, n. 10.
[3] A. vi. 62 hac Troiana tenus fuerit fortuna secuta.
[4] A. xi. 344   cuncti se scire fatentur
       quid fortuna ferat populi.

'exiled by fate':[1] is 'fate' his individual lot or a wider conception? Seeing that here the keynote of the poem is struck, probably the latter; it was the destiny of the world which brought Aeneas to the Latin shores. Later on in the first book Venus sends Mercurius to earth, lest Dido, 'ignorant of fate',[2] should keep the Trojans from her borders; here again it is surely the great destiny which the Trojans were fulfilling, not Dido's own calamitous future, which was in Venus' mind. A peculiarly interesting passage[3]—not a borderline instance, but one where the two ideas are combined—occurs in the twelfth book, when Iuturna is appealing to Iuno for further help for Turnus; Iuno replies, 'where fortune seemed to grant it and the goddesses of Fate (Parcae) allowed events to go fairly for Latium, I protected Turnus and your walls; now I see that the youth is meeting his foe with unequal destiny, and the day of the Fates and the force of his foe draw near him'. Here it is the working of the ultimate fate, personified in the three sisters, which causes Turnus to meet Aeneas with an unequal lot: εἱμαρμένη gives the colour to μοῖρα. This ultimate destiny overrules the wishes and intentions of men: 'alas,' cries Latinus, 'we are broken by fate and borne on by the storm.'[4] Similarly, it may nullify the will of a god; Iuno, it is said at the beginning of the poem, was destining Carthage to be the seat of a world-empire, 'if by any means

---

[1] A. i. 2 Italiam fato profugus Lavinaque venit
     litora.
[2] A. i. 299   ne fati nescia Dido
       finibus arceret.
Servius here has an interesting note: *ne fati nescia Dido*: non sui, nam si sciret exitum suum, multo magis vetaret, sed *fati* dixit voluntatis Iovis.
[3] A. xii. 147 qua visa est Fortuna pati Parcaeque sinebant
          cedere res Latio, Turnum et tua moenia texi;
          nunc iuvenem imparibus video concurrere fatis,
          Parcarumque dies et vis inimica propinquat.
[4] A. vii. 594 frangimur heu fatis, inquit, ferimurque procella.

the fates permitted it';[1] but later on, when she sees she cannot keep the Trojans from the shore, she cries indignantly, 'Forsooth I am forbidden by fate';[2] even a powerful goddess cannot make headway against the universal destiny. An interesting note of Servius on a 'borderline' passage in the first book shows how the Roman mind conceived this relation between the god's will and destiny. 'The Trojans', Virgil says, 'were wandering for many years from sea to sea, driven by fate.'[3] Servius raises the question, 'if they were harried by the hatred of Iuno, how could he say *acti fatis?*' He has two instructive answers. It may be that 'fate' here means the will of Iuno, as in Book viii he speaks of 'the fates of cruel Iuno', but he seems rather to incline to the other explanation, 'it is because even Iuno's hatred is itself ordained of fate'; 'for', he adds, and it is significant for the conception of the whole poem, 'Virgil is at pains to ascribe nothing to the merit of the Trojans, but all to fate'. Gods and men must ultimately bow to the world-destiny, of which Aeneas and his followers are the instruments.

In the passages just noticed the wider fate has been seen in its relation to the individual destiny, but in very many places in Virgil 'fate' is a general conception of a destiny which rules the world and shapes its events. Men are aware of it and make their plans subject to its permission. 'If fate had permitted him', says Aeneas to Dido, 'to live his life at his own choice',[4] he would have stayed and

---

[1] A. i. 17   hoc regnum dea gentibus esse,
      si qua fata sinant, iam tum tenditque fovetque.

[2] A. i. 39 quippe vetor fatis.

[3] A. i. 31   multosque per annos
      errabant acti fatis maria omnia circum.
Servius, ad loc.: si odio Iunonis fatigabantur, quomodo dicit *acti fatis?* sed hoc ipsum Iunonis odium fatale est.

[4] A. iv. 340 me si fata meis paterentur ducere vitam
      auspiciis.

founded a new Troy at Carthage; Aeneas is told by the
Sibyl that he will have no difficulty in plucking the golden
bough, 'if the fates summon thee'.[1] The son of Aunus was
foremost of the Ligurians, 'so long as the fates suffered him
to cheat';[2] Ilioneus, in the presence of Dido, says that he and
his companions have no fear 'if the fates preserve Aeneas'.[3]
Even the gods know their subjection to this great destiny;
Iuno in her last prayer to Iuppiter that the defeated Latins
may not have to change their name to Trojans, enforces it
with the statement that 'this prayer is checked by no law
of fate'.[4] It is indeed often ignorance of fate that may
cause men to get into trouble. Aeneas, 'forgetful of the
fate'[5] he knew, is tempted to settle in Sicily, and the mind
of man in general, 'because it knows not fate',[6] is unduly
puffed up by prosperity. Yet when the future seems difficult and obscure to gods and men 'the fates will find a
way',[7] though it often seems cruel[8] or malignant[9] to men
and even to break them by its opposition.[10] In one interesting passage fate acts in accord with the powers of nature,
almost in the manner of the scientific ἀνάγκη: 'what winds,
what fates,' Andromache asks Aeneas, 'have granted thee
thy course?'[11] At other times it is in harmony with man's

[1] A. vi. 147 si te fata vocant.
[2] A. xi. 701 haud Ligurum extremus, dum fallere fata sinebant.
[3] A. i. 546 quem si fata virum servant.
[4] A. xii. 819 illud te nulla fati quod lege tenetur,
      pro Latio obtestor.
[5] A. v. 701 nunc huc ingentis, nunc illuc pectore curas
      mutabat versans, Siculisne resideret arvis
      oblitus fatorum, Italasne capesseret oras.
[6] A. x. 501 nescia mens hominum fati sortisque futurae
      et servare modum rebus sublata secundis.
[7] A. iii. 395, x. 113 fata viam invenient.
[8] G. iv. 495 crudelia retro | fata vocant.
[9] A. iii. 17 fatis ingressus iniquis.
[10] A. vii. 594; see p. 215, n. 4.
[11] A. iii. 337 sed tibi qui cursum venti, quae fata dedere?

own will; Aeneas tells Pallas that he is willingly driven by the fates,[1] and Evander assures him that the alliance which he proffers is demanded by the fates.[2]

A clearer notion of the action of the Virgilian fate may be obtained from a survey of the fields in which it acts. Once only is it applied to an inanimate object: 'Camerina, never permitted by the fates to be moved.'[3] Occasionally it has a very wide sphere of influence, as for instance when it is applied to the age-long conflict of Europe and Asia exemplified in the Trojan war,[4] or in Apollo's prophecy of all the future wars 'destined to come by fate',[5] which will yet be quelled by the Romans, the race of Assaracus, an idea echoed in the 'rough fate of war',[6] which Aeneas knows to be summoning him from the dead Pallas to 'other tears'. But more usually it is the action of fate on individuals and peoples which comes uppermost in Virgil's mind, a wider setting, as it were, of the individual μοῖρα. Thus Dido, when she realizes Aeneas' treachery, 'prays for death, staggered by fate';[7] Lavinia is irrevocably destined by fate as Aeneas' wife;[8] Arruns, when he makes his attack on Camilla, is already 'due to fate';[9] and in the realm of prophecy Anchises foretells that 'the fates will but reveal' the young Marcellus 'to the world, nor suffer him longer

[1] A. viii. 131 sed mea me virtus et sancta oracula divum . . . fatis egere volentem.

[2] A. viii. 477 fatis huc te poscentibus adfers.

[3] A. iii. 700   fatis numquam concessa moveri
                    apparet Camerina.

[4] A. vii. 223   quibus actus uterque
                    Europae atque Asiae fatis concurrerit orbis.

[5] A. ix. 642   iure omnia bella
                    gente sub Assaraci fato ventura resident.

[6] A. xi. 96 nos alias hinc ad lacrimas eadem horrida belli
                    fata vocant.

[7] A. iv. 450 tum vero infelix fatis exterrita Dido
                    mortem orat.

[8] A. vii. 314 immota manet fatis Lavinia coniunx.

[9] A. xi. 759 fatis debitus Arruns.

life'.[1] So of groups of people the leaders of the Danai after ten years' siege of Troy are 'broken by war and baffled by fate',[2] and Aeneas and his Trojans, though destined for ultimate victory, are yet in their course constantly harried by fate. Aeneas himself is 'exiled by fate',[3] he approaches the land of the Trojan Lycurgus 'with fate against him',[4] and in the lower world addresses what fate ordains to be his last words to Dido;[5] he and his men are 'driven by fate from sea to sea'.[6] But by far the most frequent occurrence of the idea is in reference to the fatal settlement in Italy of Aeneas and the Trojan fugitives—that is the purpose to which fate is directing the whole course of events in the story. At the outset Aeneas consoles his companions and reminds them of their destiny: 'through many chances and many hazards we are making for Latium, where the fates reveal our quiet home; there it is ordained that the realm of Troy shall rise again',[7] and Iuno in her last struggle against the hated band, yet grants that 'he has sought Italy with the fates to back him'.[8] In the period of his entanglement with Dido Aeneas forgets 'the cities granted him by fate',[9] but when he awakes again to his task he realizes that by his dallying he is defrauding Ascanius his son of 'his kingdom in Hesperia and the fields destined for him'.[10] By

[1] A. vi. 869 ostendent terris hunc tantum fata neque ultra esse sinent.
[2] A. ii. 13   fracti bello fatisque repulsi ductores Danaum.
[3] A. i. 2 fato profugus.
[4] A. iii. 17 fatis ingressus iniquis.
[5] A. vi. 466 extremum fato quod te adloquor hoc est.
[6] A. i. 32 errabant acti fatis maria omnia circum.
[7] A. i. 204 per varios casus, per tot discrimina rerum tendimus in Latium, sedes ubi fata quietas ostendunt; illic fas regna resurgere Troiae.
[8] A. x. 67 Italiam petiit fatis auctoribus: esto.
[9] A. iv. 225 fatisque datas non respicit urbes.
[10] A. iv. 355 quem regno Hesperiae fraudo et fatalibus arvis.

the time of their arrival in Italy their course is clear; Aeneas at once greets the land as 'due to me by fate',[1] and not long after Venulus is sent to inform Diomedes of Aeneas' claim that he is 'summoned by fate as king'.[2] Fate has many ramifications and affects many individuals, but has one great end in view which is never lost sight of.

Synonymous with 'fate' in this wider sense are the Parcae, the personified Fates, 'harmonious', as they are described in the fourth *Eclogue*, 'in the unchanging will of fate'.[3] Thus 'the Parcae ordain'[4] is one of the regular formulae of destiny, and 'the day of the Parcae' determines,[5] as has been seen, the individual's death. They have been met already in several other quotations; their presence does not alter the meaning, but gives colour and vividness to the conception of fate. A far more frequent synonym for 'fate' is *fortuna*, whose case will be considered separately.[6]

III. *Fate and the Gods*

Hitherto Fate has been seen shaping the 'lots' of men and nations and in a wider sense guiding the destiny of the world, which overrules the purposes and even the 'fates' of men. But as one reads the *Aeneid* fate seems not to be the only disposer of events; the gods, too, have their wills to which men must conform. In particular the will of the three great gods stands out above all others, Venus and Iuno striving for and against the Trojans, Iuppiter acting, as it were, as umpire between them and ordaining the final upshot of their quarrel. What is the relation of the will of the gods to the impersonal destiny? This was of course one

[1] A. vii. 120 salve fatis mihi debita tellus.
[2] A. viii. 12 fatis regem se dicere posci.
[3] E. iv. 47 concordes stabili fatorum numine Parcae.
[4] A. i. 22 sic volvere Parcas.
[5] A. xii. 149; see p. 215, n. 3.
[6] See appendix, pp. 234–240.

of the fundamental problems of ancient religion, to which thinkers and poets from the time of Aeschylus onwards had addressed themselves. Virgil's answer, based on the theory of the Stoic philosophy, is that they are identical. This conclusion has not universally been accepted and needs demonstration.

If we go back first to the μοῖρα sense of *fatum*, an important question is raised by the reference of Iuno to 'the fate of the Phrygians set against our fate'.[1] What does Iuno mean by 'set against our fate'? Does she mean the fate of her favourites, the Greeks, or her destiny as a person, or, as Servius' note *voluntatibus* suggests, 'set against my will'? The first is an unnatural interpretation, nor is it possible to suppose that either Virgil or any Greek before him thought that a god had a 'destiny' like a mortal's, even though, as has been seen, fate may overrule a god's intentions. One is forced back on the conclusion that the sense is 'my will as a goddess', and this conclusion is borne out by other passages where Virgil speaks of the *fatum* of the deity meaning his 'will', a sense which really approaches the old Latin meaning of the god's 'spoken word'. Thus Hercules is said to have been compelled to endure his labours under Eurystheus 'by the fate of cruel Iuno',[2] clearly meaning her 'will' or 'decree'. So, too, Turnus complains that 'enough has been granted to the fates and to Venus',[3] almost, if not quite, a hendiadys for 'the will of Venus'. This interpretation of *fatum* is strongly supported by passages in which we find combined with it the unmistakable word *numen*, which can only mean the 'will' of the god. Thus Evander in his prayer for Pallas cries to the gods, 'if your will, if the fates preserve Pallas for me, then

[1] A. vii. 293; see p. 213, n. 3.
[2] A. viii. 292 fatis Iunonis iniquae.
[3] A. ix. 135 sat fatis Venerique datum.

I pray for life'.[1] Here, even if we do not connect *fata* as well as *numina* with *vestra*, as is grammatically possible, it is clear that the 'fates' are the will of the gods concerned. So again the infuriated Latins 'demand war against the omens, against the fates of the gods, whose will is adverse to them';[2] it is impossible here to distinguish the 'fates' of the gods from their 'will'. Once more Latinus is warned by the anger of the gods that 'Aeneas is borne on by destiny, by divine will clear to see';[3] the two are again identified. It is significant too that Iuno in the passage first quoted, picks up the idea of 'our fates' immediately afterwards by *numina*: 'my will forsooth at last is worn out and perishes';[4] 'my will' can hardly be distinguished from 'my fates'.

It thus appears that the *fata* or 'will' of a deity for any individual or nation may correspond closely to the μοῖρα; like the μοῖρα it is partial in its outlook and may be thwarted by the will of another god or a higher power than that of either. In this context we may raise the question of the true significance of the two goddesses, Venus and Iuno, who under Iuppiter play the most prominent part in the development of the story of the *Aeneid*. How did Virgil conceive and interpret their action in relation to the idea of fate, and what is their place in the religious economy of the poem? It is clear that they are not 'divine persons' in the sense of the Homeric gods; they have not in the poem any personal history or interests apart from the fate of the

[1] A. viii. 574   si numina vestra
    incolumem Pallanta mihi, si fata reservant . . .
    vitam oro.
[2] A. vii. 583 illicet infandum cuncti contra omina bellum,
    contra fata deum perverso numine poscunt.
Perverso numine has also been taken to mean 'under an evil inspiration', which is surely less natural.
[3] A. xi. 232 fatalem Aenean manifesto numine ferri
    admonet ira deum.
[4] A. vii. 297 at, credo, mea numina tandem
    fessa iacent.

mortal heroes and heroines with whom they are concerned; they do not, like the Homeric gods, intervene
arbitrarily, as the whim seizes them, to interpose their will.
Both have a perfectly consistent purpose, which they pursue unswervingly throughout, and indeed they exist only
for the carrying out of that purpose. Their speeches in the
councils of the gods are a rhetorical statement of the case
for and against Aeneas and his men, and their actions are
a translation of those arguments and pleadings into deeds.
Nor again is it enough to describe them as part of the
'divine machinery' of the poem, or as a convention which
Virgil embodied as a convention and nothing more. They
have a far greater reality and force than that. A key to
what Virgil intended by these two goddesses seems to lie
in the conception of the μοῖρα of men and races. Venus
clearly stands in close relation to the μοῖρα of Aeneas and
his men, the μοῖρα which is to bring them through all
difficulties to success and lead on to the foundation of the
Roman empire. But she is more than an embodiment or
personification or symbol of that μοῖρα; she is, as it were,
the divine element in it, that which makes it not merely
the working of a blind fate, but the expression of a divine
will. The *fatum Veneris* is the indication that the *fatum
Aeneae* is born of the will of heaven. The position of Iuno
is a little more complicated: in the second book of the
Aeneid she represents the μοῖρα of the Greeks, here trium-
phant over the destiny of Troy. In the fourth, though less
clearly, she represents the μοῖρα of Carthage, which will
measure itself in the struggle with Rome under that
avenger whom Dido prophesies. In the later books of the
Aeneid she represents the μοῖρα of the Latin peoples in their
stand against the invaders. In all these different parts of
the poem Iuno is the divine element in the fate of other
races which are 'contrary to the fates of the Phrygians'.

But she is more than this; she is, as it were, Aeneas' evil genius, the fate which drives him into misfortune, *Teucris addita Iuno*.[1] It would perhaps be truest to say that Venus represents that which, in the divine will, made for the success or happiness of the Aeneadae, Iuno that which made for their misery and thwartings; they are the good and evil sides of the divine will expressed in their μοῖρα.

This idea may perhaps seem fanciful, but it is greatly strengthened by the consideration of the much more frequent and definite evidence that Virgil regarded the ultimate fate, εἰμαρμένη, as itself the will of the gods or of God. For it is spoken of in three different ways, all of which lead to the same conclusion, first as the collective will of the gods, secondly and less frequently, as the will of 'god', and thirdly and quite definitely as the will of Iuppiter. All these usages require careful examination.

The most frequent and obvious indication that fate is the will of the gods is given in the constantly recurring phrase the 'fate' or 'fates of the gods'. Laocoon, in the second book of the *Aeneid*, would have urged the Trojans to pierce the wooden horse, 'if the fates of the gods and his own mind had not thwarted him',[2] and later on Sinon, the traitor, opened the horse 'protected by the cruel fates of the gods'.[3] The dead Palinurus, attempting to cross the Styx unburied, is warned by the Sibyl 'not to hope that the fates of the gods can be changed by prayer'.[4] Ilioneus, the ambassador, tells Latinus that 'the fates of the gods have driven us to seek out your land',[5] the Latins seek to make

[1] A. vi. 90.
[2] A. ii. 54 et, si fata deum, si mens non laeva fuisset,
      impulerat ferro Argolicas foedare latebras.
[3] A. ii. 257 fatisque deum defensus iniquis | . . . laxat claustra Sinon.
[4] A. vi. 376 desine fata deum flecti sperare precando.
[5] A. vii. 239 sed nos fata deum vestras exquirere terras
      imperiis egere suis.

war 'against the fates of the gods',[1] Aeneas, in his story to Dido, 'was recounting the fates of the gods',[2] and Latinus 'by the fate of the gods'[3] had lost his only son as a child. What exactly in all these passages is the meaning of the 'fate' or 'fates of the gods'? No doubt in expression it goes back to the original sense of the word, 'the thing said'; Servius in a note puts this from the grammatical point of view: '*fata* is a participle, that is, what the gods say.'[4] *Fata deum* is thus 'the decrees of the gods', and this is borne out by the occurrence in parallel passages of *iussa deum*, 'the commands of the gods'. Thus Anchises, interpreting an oracle of Phoebus, calls to his companions, 'Come then, and let us follow where the commands of the gods lead us',[5] a phrase closely resembling many in which we have seen *fata* used alone; Aeneas at Carthage, after receiving Mercurius' message, though sad at heart, 'yet carries out the gods' command and goes back to the fleet';[6] after the alliance with Tarchon 'the Lydian people boards the fleet by the command of the gods'.[7] No doubt in these passages there is reference to a more explicit expression of the gods' will in message or oracle, as there is in Turnus' boast, 'I am not affrighted by any fateful answers of the gods which these Phrygians may flaunt',[8] but the phraseology is just that which is used of the unrevealed 'fates of the gods'. The 'fates' then are in the primary sense the 'spoken words' of the gods. But there is a deeper idea as well, for it is

---

[1] A. vii. 583; see p. 222, n. 2.
[2] A. iii. 717 fata renarrabat divum.
[3] A. vii. 50 filius huic fato divum prolesque virilis
             nulla fuit.
[4] *ad* A. ii. 54.
[5] A. iii. 114 ergo agite et divum ducunt qua iussa sequamur.
[6] A. iv. 396 iussa tamen divum exsequitur classemque revisit.
[7] A. x. 155 classem conscendit iussis gens Lydia divum.
[8] A. ix. 133   nil me fatalia terrent,
             si qua Phryges prae se iactant, responsa deorum.

impossible to contemplate the many phrases in which the absolute 'fate' or 'the fate of the gods' seem to be used indifferently without inferring that to Virgil his words meant in effect 'fate, which is the will of the gods'. This is shown in passages where the two ideas are combined. In the opening of the third book Aeneas tells Dido that 'after it had seemed good to the gods above to overthrow the empire of Asia and the race of Priam . . . we were driven by the auguries of the gods . . . unknowing whither the fates are carrying us';[1] we cannot there separate 'what seemed good to the gods', 'the auguries of the gods', and 'the fates'; if they are not absolutely identical, they are at least working in perfect harmony. Take again a passage[2] in the account of the fight in Troy, where immediately after the famous phrase used of the death of Rhipeus, 'it seemed good otherwise to the gods', Aeneas says of his own actions in the battle 'if it had been fated that I should fall, I swear that I deserved it by my deeds'; 'fate' and 'the will of the gods' are together directing the course of events, they are in effect identical. Fate, we may infer, is to Virgil the will of the gods, and the will of the gods finds its expression in the fate which decides a man's actions and sufferings and guides the whole course of events.

The same conclusion is to be drawn from certain passages where the singular *deus* is combined with *fatum* or *fortuna* or both. It might be expected that in such cases *deus* would refer to a particular god and sometimes this is the case. 'I was placed in this spot', says Evander to Aeneas, 'by fortune the all-powerful and fate irresistible; the fearsome warnings of my mother, the nymph Car-

---

[1] A. iii. 1 postquam res Asiae Priamique evertere gentem | immeritam visum superis . . . (5) auguriis agimur divum . . . (7) incerti quo fata ferant.

[2] A. ii. 428 dis aliter visum . . . (432) testor . . . (433) si fata fuissent | ut caderem, meruisse manu.

mentis, drove me on and Apollo the god as my guide.'[1]
Here no doubt the 'spoken word' is that of Apollo, but he,
like the prophetess-nymph Carmentis, is not enunciating
merely his own will, but the will of a higher and more
universal fate. In other cases, where the same combination
of fate, fortune, and god is found, the meaning of *deus* is
much more general. 'Already', says Turnus to Iuturna,
'the fates have the upper hand; away with delay; let us
follow whither god and cruel fortune summon us.'[2] Here
'god' has no definite reference, and fate, fortune, and god
are in effect the same. So again in Aeneas' reply to the
Latin envoys: 'What cruel fortune, Latins, has involved
you in this great war? ... I had not come, but that the fates
had given me this place for my abode ... he would have
lived, to whom god or his own right hand had given life.'[3]
Once again the general idea is that of a divinely willed
destiny. Two more instances may be mentioned, where
fata and *deus* are combined: Aeneas in the fourth book is
unmoved by the appeal of Anna: 'the fates forbid it, and
god stops the unhearing ears of the hero';[4] and later in the
same book Dido, as she looks her last on Aeneas' couch and
garments, cries, 'Relics sweet to me, while god and fate
permitted, receive my soul and free me from my cares';[5]
here the connexion is still closer. In other places *fatum* is
linked not with *deus*, but with *numen* or *numina*, clearly a

[1] A. viii. 333 me pulsum patria pelagique extrema sequentem
        fortuna omnipotens et ineluctabile fatum
        his posuere locis, matrisque egere tremenda
        Carmentis nymphae monita et deus auctor Apollo.

[2] A. xii. 676 iam iam fata, soror, superant; absiste morari;
        quo deus et quo dura vocat fortuna sequamur.

[3] A. xi. 108 quaenam vos tanto fortuna indigna, Latini, | implicuit bello
... | (112) nec veni, nisi fata locum sedemque dedissent | ... (118) vixet cui
vitam deus aut sua dextra dedisset.

[4] A. iv. 440 fata obstant placidasque viri deus obstruit auris.

[5] A. iv. 651 dulces exuviae, dum fata deusque sinebat,
        accipite hanc animam meque his exsolvite curis.

synonym for *deus* in the broad sense of the divine will. 'Do thou go forward,' says Evander to Aeneas, 'to whose youth and birth the fates are kindly, thou whom the divine will demands';[1] later on in prayer to the gods above (*superi*) Evander cries, 'if your divine wills, if the fates are keeping Pallas safe for me',[2] and when he passes to the alternative, he uses the third synonym, 'but if, fortune, thou dost threaten me with some unutterable mischance'; the combination is exactly that which has been noticed with *deus*. With the same meaning the poet expresses Latinus' thought that 'Aeneas is borne on by the clear will of heaven, guided by fate'.[3]

If any doubt is felt whether Virgil in the passages quoted in the last paragraph uses *deus* in the general philosophic sense of ὁ θεός, and if it be held that *deus* according to normal Latin usage must refer to some particular god, then the solution must be that that god is Iuppiter. For the most striking of all the indications that his *fatum* is, often at least, the divine will is its identification with Iuppiter or with his will. Virgil seems to expound the doctrine in that early passage of the first book,[4] which has been quoted to illustrate the use of *fatum* as 'the word of the god'. Consider it again for its content: 'the fate of thy loved ones', Iuppiter says to Venus, 'abides unchanged for thee . . . my purpose changes not. Aeneas (for I will speak out and far ahead will I reveal the secrets of the fates) shall wage a

---

[1] A. viii. 511   tu, cuius et annis
　　　　et generi fata indulgent, quem numina poscunt.
[2] A. viii. 574   si numina vestra
　　　　incolumem Pallanta mihi, si fata reservant . . .
(578) sin aliquem infandum casum, fortuna, minaris.
[3] A. xi. 232 fatalem Aenean manifesto numine ferri.
[4] A. i. 257 manent immota tuorum | fata tibi . . .
(260)   neque me sententia vertit.
　　　hic tibi (fabor enim, quando haec te cura remordet,
　　　longius, et volvens fatorum arcana movebo)
　　　bellum ingens geret Italia.

great war in Italy.' The special μοῖρα of Aeneas and his men is in accord with the ultimate εἱμαρμένη and that is the purpose of Iuppiter. Just, then, as Virgil speaks of the *fata deum*, so too he speaks of the *fata Iovis*[1], which required that Aeneas shall come to Carthage, and the fates and fortune are elsewhere combined with Iuppiter just as they are with 'the gods'. In a famous passage,[2] just before the final contest of Aeneas and Turnus, which is modelled very closely on Homer, Iuppiter places the fates of the two heroes in the balance: Iuppiter is above the separate μοῖραι and has to judge between them. But much more usually Iuppiter is set in direct relation with the supreme fate, εἱμαρμένη. Thus Venus complains that Iuno is still restless though 'broken by the command of Iuppiter and by the fates',[3] Iuppiter himself tells Venus that 'neither the almighty father nor the fates forebade Troy to stand' for ten years more.[4] In both these passages it is hard to distinguish between the two ideas and in the latter Iuppiter's epithet *omnipotens* seems deliberately to place him on a level with fate, as having supreme and universal control. Once again, later in the poem, Venus asks why, if Aeneas and his men have carried out the oracular commands of gods above and gods below, 'why has any one now the power to change thy bidding or ordain new fates?',[5] just as earlier in the story, confused by the events in Carthage, she had complained, 'Uncertain is my guidance by the fates, if Iuppiter should wish that there should be one city for the

---

[1] A. iv. 614 sic fata Iovis poscunt.
[2] A. xii. 725 Iuppiter ipse duas aequato examine lances
    sustinet et fata imponit diversa duorum,
    quem damnet labor et quo vergat pondere letum.
[3] A. v. 784 nec Iovis imperio fatisque infracta quiescit.
[4] A. viii. 398 nec Pater omnipotens Troiam nec fata vetabant
    stare decemque alios Priamum superesse per annos.
[5] A. x. 34   cur nunc tua quisquam
    vertere iussa potest aut cur nova condere fata?

Tyrians and the exiles from Troy.'¹ But the most significant utterance of all comes in the final pronouncement of
Iuppiter in the heavenly council in the tenth book: 'to
every man his own undertaking shall bring his labours
and his fortune. King Iuppiter is the same for all; the
fates will find a way.'² Iuppiter is impartial; his will is
fate and it will decide the portion allotted to every man.

Lest it be thought that the identity of fate with the will
of Iuppiter has been too lightly assumed, the passages cited
above must be submitted to a closer investigation. There
are three possible solutions: that the will of Iuppiter is
subordinate to the universal destiny, that it is independent
but parallel in its action, and that it is identical. The first
conception is probably that of early Greek thought, as seen
in Homer, which was challenged by Aeschylus, who sought
to show that the workings of fate were not blind but just,
and were indeed the expression of the will of Zeus. But
there is at least no direct indication of such a view in
Virgil. The *fata* are the *fata Iovis*,³ again and again the
command or bidding of Iuppiter is put together with the
fates as the supreme controlling forces with no suggestion
that one is subordinate to the other.⁴ In two only of the
passages is the idea of subordination possible. When
Iuppiter holds up the scales and places in them the 'fates'
of Aeneas and Turnus, it might be argued that he is not
responsible for the result, that he is trying an experiment
to see 'whom his toil condemns and with which weight
death sinks the scale'.⁵ Even if this were so, it would be

¹ A. iv. 110 sed fatis incerta feror, si Iuppiter unam
        esse velit Tyriis urbem Troiaque profectis.
² A. x. 111   sua cuique exorsa laborem
        fortunamque ferent. rex Iuppiter omnibus idem;
        fata viam invenient.
³ A. iv. 614; see p. 229, n. 1.
⁴ A. v. 784, p. 229, n. 3; A. viii. 398, p. 229, n. 4; A. x. 34, p. 229, n. 5;
A. iv. 110, n. 1, above.   ⁵ A. xii. 725, p. 229, n. 2.

possible to defend a divergence from Virgil's normal view on the ground of the Homeric parallel, but this is unnecessary. Here are two conflicting μοῖραι and the ultimate victory of one or other will be determined by the universal destiny; Iuppiter holds the scales, because it is he who decides the course of that supreme destiny. Again the great saying of Iuppiter at the heavenly council might be interpreted to mean 'Iuppiter shows no favour to one man more than another; it is left to the fates to discover the course of events'.[1] But if Iuppiter is powerless to influence fate, what would be the good of his favouring any man? It is surely implied that his power is not less than that of fate.

These passages then do not make for subordination; are the two controlling forces parallel, in the sense in which some modern thinkers have supposed the action of the brain and the movements of thought to be two concomitant series, set to run, as it were, at the same pace? Of such a view there is no hint in Virgil or indeed in any Greek or Latin author and it would surely have appeared to them absurd. If Iuppiter's will were 'set to run' parallel to the decrees of fate, then it would in fact be determined and subordinate to them.

There is left the solution, set out in the previous discussion, that the will of Iuppiter is in fact identical with the fates. It is to my mind the natural interpretation of the passages which have been considered and it is strongly borne out by the evidence of the two preceding sections. The *fata deum*, *deus*, and the will of Iuppiter appear again and again in Virgil in contexts exactly similar to those in which the controlling force is *fatum* or *fortuna*; they are all identical: Iuppiter is himself the *deus* and, as *rex divum*, the representative of the gods' collective will. And if so, then

[1] A. x. 111, p. 230, n. 2.

Virgil's ultimate conception must be something closely akin to that of the Stoic πρόνοια, the will of the world-god, which manifests itself in the universal destiny. It has been seen how this conception shows itself in the persons of Venus and Iuno, representing the divine element in the μοῖραι of Aeneas' men and their successive opponents. So the will of Iuppiter deifies, as it were, the ultimate εἱμαρμένη; it too, the destiny of the world, is not mechanical or arbitrary— it is the expression of the will of a world-god. Iuppiter knows fate and can speak it, because it is his will.

IV. *Conclusion*

What then is the upshot of this examination of the use by Virgil of the word *fatum* and its kindred ideas? In the first place it shows that here as elsewhere Virgil is using his inheritance of conceptions both Roman and Greek. On the Roman side he is conscious of the root-meaning of *fatum* as 'the thing spoken', the word of the prophet or the oracle, which is in fact the word of the god. He attributes to it also, especially in the plural, the derivative sense of 'fate', the destiny governing the lives of men and the course of events. And on the Greek side he uses ideas which are in part coincident with Roman conceptions but have a definiteness and precision of which the Italian mind was not capable. There is μοῖρα, the lot of the individual man or of the race, which may conflict with the lot of another man or race, and may be modified or even escaped or over-ruled by a higher fate. And there is εἱμαρμένη, the ultimate destiny, which is inexorable and is the controlling power which moulds and governs the course of events as a whole. But behind and in all these there is a religious idea, akin to the Stoic conception of πρόνοια, the divine providence, which ordains the destiny of the world. This is the supremely important point in Virgil's conception of fate.

It is not a mechanical force, arising from the laws of nature, like the Greek ἀνάγκη, or an unmeaning caprice, as we find fate sometimes represented in the Greek poets, but a deliberate purpose of the divine beings who are above the world and in the world. The 'divine machinery' of the *Aeneid*, even though in its setting it is often conventional and has little significance beyond tradition, is yet the ultimate religious idea lying behind the whole poem. The μοῖραι of Troy and Greece, of Aeneas and Dido, of the Aeneadae and the Italians, are given their divine sanction by their representation in the persons of Venus and Iuno, and above them dictating the final fate is the collective will of the gods, or of Iuppiter, who is god. The struggle on earth has its counterpart in heaven, for it is the outcome of the divine will. This is perhaps too definite a theology and it is not to be supposed that the poet was at all times conscious of the reconciliation of the many diverse elements he uses, derived from different sources; he is here as always an eclectic. But he is feeling towards a monotheism in which Iuppiter is supreme and, like the Stoic world-god, expresses his will in the decrees of fate. It is perhaps in this conception that we meet Virgil's highest and deepest religious conviction.

And if it be asked what is the content of this divine purpose, to what practical end is it guiding events, there can be no doubt as to the answer. It is the fulfilment of Aeneas' destiny, his arrival in Italy, the establishment of his power, and beyond that the foundation of Rome and the expansion of Rome's empire over the world; the great passages at the end of Book vi, where by common consent Virgil most clearly expresses his own religious thoughts, leave that indubitable. This may well seem a narrowing conception, but it must not be judged by modern ideas. To the Roman of Augustus' time there was no other real power, no other civilizing influence in the world but Rome, and the greatest blessing which could befall other peoples was that they should be brought within the sphere of Rome's influence. Philosophy, especially Stoicism, which by the time of the *Aeneid* was more than any other philosophical theory Virgil's creed, was developing a monotheistic conception of a universal god, which was destined to supersede narrower national ideas. But the process was as yet incomplete, and Iuppiter, though omnipotent, was still in conception a tribal god. The fate of mankind, then, was the destiny of Rome, but this destiny was the will and purpose of the divine power, which was the object of man's worship and the supreme controlling force of the world.

Appendix to Chapter IX

THE MEANING OF 'FORTUNA' IN VIRGIL

IT has been noticed in the previous chapter[1] that *fortuna* is used by Virgil as an equivalent of *fatum* both in the sense of the individual 'lot' and of the universal 'destiny'. In each place a larger number of instances might have been quoted to strengthen the general argument, but it seemed better to reserve for independent treatment the whole question of the meaning of *fortuna* in Virgil.

The normal meaning of the word in Latin is undoubtedly 'luck' or 'chance', its equivalents being in Latin *casus* and in Greek τύχη. In more philosophical and reflective passages this implies that which, though it occurs in the ordinary course of events and by the action of the laws of nature, is yet 'unpredictable' by men, such, for instance, as the fall of a meteoric stone. But popular ideas attributed to 'fortune' an arbitrary independence of its own; it is that which is due to some freak or, as Lucretius might have said, to some 'swerve' in the order of nature which produced an exceptional or abnormal result. And it is in this sense that the word is ordinarily used.

[1] pp. 213, 220.

But behind this popular idea of 'chance' lies another which is possibly more fundamental.[1] If, as is highly probable, *fors* and *fortuna* are derived from the root of *fero* in its sense of 'childbirth', then *fortuna* is not 'chance' but 'destiny', the fate, the μοῖρα in fact, which attaches to the new-born child. It was undoubtedly in this sense that the goddess Fortuna was worshipped at Praeneste, where 'fortunes' were 'told' by means of the sacred lots (*sortes*). In this sense, too, Horace,[2] celebrates the goddess of Antium, whose companion is 'Necessity'.

Virgil has both these uses in mind, and it is possible to arrange the instances of their occurrence in a kind of ascending scale from the meaning of 'chance' to the full sense of 'fate'. It is, however, probably true to say that even where the 'chance' sense is most prominent, that of 'fate' is lurking beneath the surface, and where *fortuna* seems most equivalent to *fatum*, there yet remains a touch of 'chance' in its significance.

(i) '*Fortuna*' as '*luck*'. In several passages *fortuna* seems to mean 'good luck'. Thus the Latin envoys to Diomedes argue that it is not obvious what Aeneas has in mind, nor 'what issue to the fight he craves, if fortune follow him'.[3] When Iasides is applying medicaments to the wounded Aeneas, 'no fortune rules his way, Apollo comes not to his aid with prompting';[4] Iuno, angered as ever at Venus' sneers, cries, 'I myself will be queen, if there is yet any fortune in my toils.'[5] Sometimes *fortuna* in this sense fades almost into the sense of 'opportunity'. Arruns, wishing to attack Camilla, tries 'what will be the easiest fortune',[6] and Aeneas in his last attack on Turnus 'chooses fortune with his eyes'[7]—looks, that is, for his opportunity. Conversely there are places where *fortuna* seems definitely to have the sense of 'bad

---

[1] See Warde Fowler, *Roman Ideas of Deity*, pp. 61 ff.
[2] Hor. *Od.* i. xxxv.
[3] A. viii. 15 quid struat his coeptis, quem, si fortuna sequatur, eventum pugnae cupiat.
[4] A. xii. 405 nulla viam fortuna regit, nihil auctor Apollo subvenit.
[5] A. vii. 559   ego, si qua super fortuna laborum est, ipsa regam.
[6] A. xi. 761 quae sit fortuna facillima temptat.
[7] A. xii. 920 sortitus fortunam oculis.

luck'. The story of the suicide of Amata is introduced with the phrase 'this (ill) fortune too beset the weary Latins';[1] Aeneas receives the envoys from Latinus, asking for a burial truce, with the question 'what cruel fortune has involved you in this great war?'[2] and in a remarkable passage, where he replies to Aeneas' envoys, Diomedes exclaims, 'O peoples blessed by (good) *fortune*, realms of Saturn, Ausonians of ancient stock, what (ill) *fortune* disturbs your peace and urges you to provoke blind wars?';[3] here good fortune and bad fortune are contrasted.

(ii) *'Fortuna' in an intermediate sense.* In a second group of passages the idea of 'chance' seems to be merging into that of 'fate', so that it would be hard to say which notion is uppermost. Conspicuous here are the many places in which fortune is said to show or to refuse a way, whether to some minor accomplishment or to the main goal of Aeneas' adventures. Thus in the passage already noticed[4] fortune 'does not guide the way' for the healing of Aeneas, Drances promises Aeneas to unite him to Latinus 'if fortune will grant the way',[5] and when Aeneas, on leaving Carthage, meets the storm, he tells his followers that they cannot struggle against it: 'since fortune has the upper hand, let us follow, and turn our course, whither she calls.'[6] Coroebus in the flight from Troy proposes to put on Greek armour for disguise: 'where first fortune reveals the path of safety, let us follow.'[7] In a wider sense Venus, pleading to Iuppiter for the young Ascanius, is ready to forfeit Aeneas: 'let Aeneas be tossed in unknown waters and follow wherever fortune

[1] A. xii. 593 accidit haec fessis etiam fortuna Latinis.
[2] A. xi. 108 quaenam vos tanto fortuna indigna, Latini,
    implicuit bello?
[3] A. xi. 252 o fortunatae gentes, Saturnia regna,
    antiqui Ausonii, quae vos fortuna quietos
    sollicitat suadetque ignota lacessere bella?
[4] A. xii. 405; see p. 235, n. 4.
[5] A. xi. 128 et te, si qua viam dederit fortuna, Latino
    iungemus regi.
[6] A. v. 22   superat quoniam fortuna, sequamur,
    quoque vocat vertamus iter.
[7] A. ii. 387   qua prima, inquit, fortuna salutis
    monstrat iter, quaque ostendit se dextra, sequamur.

shall grant him a path.'[1] So Dido, already on the pyre, exclaims, 'My life is over, I have accomplished the course which
fortune had given me.'[2] Closely parallel to these passages is
Turnus' exclamation, 'what fortune now promises me safety?'[3]
So, too, in the debate in the palace he argues 'if we are so
deserted, if when our line has once been broken we have utterly
perished and fortune grants us not to retrace our steps, let us
pray for peace'.[4] In the same vein Virgil speaks of Pallas and
Lausus, 'alike lovely in form, but fortune had denied them return
to their land'.[5] In all these passages, where fortune is said to
open or block the way, what may have seemed to the actors
'luck' seems to be thought of by the poet as destiny or fate.
There are other places, too, where 'fortune' seems to hover
between the meanings of 'chance' and 'destiny'. Nisus after the
foot-race claims that he had deserved the first prize, 'had
not hostile fortune beset me, as she did Salius',[6] Euryalus,
setting out on his dangerous expedition, prays that 'fortune
may fall favourable, not adverse'.[7] Nautes, consoling Aeneas
after a storm, cries, 'Goddess-born, let us follow where the
fates drag us to and fro; whatever may come, every fortune
can be overcome by patience';[8] here is an instructive combination of *fata* and *fortuna* in almost identically the same
meaning. Again, when Iuno sent Iris to announce favourable winds, 'fortune changed and renewed its promises',[9] as
also in the famous *audentis fortuna iuvat*, there is the note of

[1] A. x. 48 Aeneas sane ignotis iactetur in undis
    et quacumque viam dederit fortuna sequatur.
[2] A. iv. 653 vixi et quem dederat cursum fortuna peregi.
[3] A. xii. 637 quae iam spondet fortuna salutem?
[4] A. xi. 412 si tam deserti sumus et semel agmine verso
    funditus occidimus neque habet fortuna regressum,
    oremus pacem.
[5] A. x. 435 egregii forma, sed quis fortuna negarat
    in patriam reditus.
[6] A. v. 356 ni me, quae Salium, fortuna inimica tulisset.
[7] A. ix. 282   tantum fortuna secunda,
    haud adversa cadat.
[8] A. v. 709 nate dea, quo fata trahunt retrahuntque sequamur;
    quidquid erit, superanda omnis fortuna ferendo est.
[9] A. v. 604 hinc primum fortuna fidem mutata novavit.

destiny.[1] In all the passages 'fortune' is very little removed from 'fate'.

(iii) In the third group may be placed passages in which *fortuna* seems indistinguishable from *fatum* in one of the three senses (μοῖρα, εἱμαρμένη, πρόνοια) which have been already discerned in it.

(a) It is perhaps natural, if it be true that a touch of the popular sense of 'luck' always clings to *fortuna*, that in the majority of these instances it has the sense of the 'lot' of the individual. Examples of this have already been given,[2] but others may here be added. Now and then the identity of meaning in *fortuna* and *fatum* is made clear by their combination. Thus Anchises, when found by Aeneas in the lower world, is meditating on his future descendants: 'he chanced to be counting all the tale of his progeny and his beloved descendants, the destinies and fortunes of the men, their characters and deeds.'[3] It is possible here to make a distinction between the words, the fixed destinies of the men and the chances which would befall them, *fortuna* being used in its looser sense, but that would be pressing the phrase rather hard. In other instances the identity of meaning is guaranteed by the similarity of phraseology. 'Go to meet him more boldly along the path which your fortune will allow'[4] is not different in thought from Iuno's cry, 'forsooth I am forbidden by the fates.'[5] When Aeneas says of Pallas, 'fortune grudged thee to me',[6] he is using the same language as Aeneas when he addresses Latium as 'land due to me by fate'. When Dido prays for a short respite 'till my fortune teach me to grieve in submission',[7] she might as well have spoken of her 'fate' as of her 'fortune'. Finally, 'fortune' takes the place of 'fate' in

[1] A. x. 284.
[2] See p. 213.
[3] A. vi. 681   omnemque suorum
    forte recensebat numerum carosque nepotes,
    fataque fortunasque virum moresque manusque.
[4] A. vi. 95   contra audentior ito
    qua tua te fortuna sinet.
[5] A. i. 39 quippe vetor fatis.
[6] A. xi. 43 te . . . invidit fortuna mihi. Cf. A. vii. 120 fatis mihi debita tellus.
[7] A. iv. 434 dum mea me victam doceat fortuna dolere.

several of the passages quoted in which human endeavour is set
against destiny.[1]

(*b*) Several of the examples cited above might almost equally
well be assigned to the εἱμαρμένη sense, and there are some in
which *fortuna* seems clearly to be so used. In one again we have
the two words in combination without any perceptible difference of meaning: 'I have been placed in this spot', says Evander,
'by all-powerful fortune and fate irresistible';[2] the one phrase is
but the amplification of the other. Servius in an interesting note
on this passage says that Virgil is using the language of the Stoics,
who assigned birth and death to fate, and all intermediate events
to fortune. Virgil may have had this in mind in other places,
but not here, for there is no question of either birth or death and
the two ideas seem identical. 'Unhappy people, for what doom
does fortune reserve you?'[3] gives us an example in which *fortuna*
certainly refers to death, and it cannot be separated in thought
from many similar expressions where the poet uses *fatum*. In
Evander's prayer there is the interesting phrase, 'if thou, fortune,
dost threaten us with some awful chance',[4] where fortune, as the
supreme destiny, seems to have control of the inferior chance.
Again, 'if fortune shall forbid this'[5] is not different from 'I am
forbidden by the fates', and 'if fortune has made Sinon wretched'[6]
is very like 'if the fates preserve him'.

(*c*) Finally, passages have been noticed (pp. 226–228)[7] already
in which *fortuna*, like *fatum*, is combined with *deus* or *numen* and
so indicates the divine character of the destiny which guides individuals or rules the world. To these may be added two other places
in which there is the still more remarkable combination of *deus*
with *casus*, a word more definitely indicating 'chance' than *fortuna* itself and even subordinated to it, as has been seen above.[8]

[1] See p. 212.
[2] A. viii. 333 me . . . | fortuna omnipotens et ineluctabile fatum
        his posuere locis.
[3] A. v. 624 o gens | infelix, cui te exitio fortuna reservat?
[4] A. viii. 578 sin aliquem infandum casum, fortuna, minaris.
[5] A. ix. 214 si qua id fortuna vetabit; cf. i. 39.
[6] A. ii. 79 miserum fortuna Sinonem | finxit; cf. i. 546.
[7] e.g. A. viii. 333 ff., xii. 676, xi. 108; see p. 227.
[8] A. viii. 578; see n. 4, above.

Nisus says to Euryalus, before they start out on their fatal expedition, 'if any chance or god should bring us to misfortune, I should wish thee to survive';[1] and again, when Aeneas is wounded by the arrow from an unseen hand, 'it was uncertain', says the poet, 'who brought this high praise to the Rutulians, whether chance or a god'.[2]

It seems then that *fortuna* had for Virgil a wide range of meaning. It was not infrequently used in the popular sense of 'luck', especially with the notion of 'good luck' or 'bad luck'. In other passages it appears to be verging towards the meaning of destiny, though still retaining the notion of 'chance'. In yet a third group it is the equivalent of *fatum*, with which it is often combined, in references alike to the destiny of individuals, to the world destiny, and to the divine providence. Its usage in this last sense confirms, but in no way modifies, the view of Virgil's use of *fatum*, which has been taken in the preceding chapter.

---

[1] A. ix. 211 si quis in adversum rapiat casusve deusve,
   te superesse velim.

[2] A. xii. 320 incertum . . . | quis tantam Rutulis laudem, casusne deusne
   attulerit.

A close parallel to this passage occurs in *Culex* 193:
   qui casus sociarit opem numenne deorum,
   prodere sit dubium.

The *Culex* (347) also provides an instance of the combination of the will of the gods with the influence of the stars: seu caelesti fato seu sideris ortu. This idea is otherwise unknown in Virgil.

X

THE DEAD AND THE UNDERWORLD

THE study of Virgil's statements with regard to the dead, both as to their fate and as to the attitude of men towards them, is one of supreme interest, for here we seem to come nearest to his own conception of religion in relation to the individual, just as in the idea of fate we approach most closely to his religious conception of the world. It is, however, a difficult and complicated sphere of investigation and it is necessary, as in other fields, to start by obtaining briefly a notion of his inheritance from Italian and Graeco-Roman sources.

The earliest Italian practice, as we may see from the great cemeteries of Bologna, and the burial-ground beneath the Forum at Rome, was to place the dead of the community, whether buried or cremated—the more usual practice—in a common cemetery, herded and huddled together without distinction of individuality. There was some notion of survival or continued activity beneath the ground, but it was a collective activity; the dead were known by the common title of Manes, 'the kindly ones'—doubtless a euphemistic appellation for those whose action was to some extent a ground of fear—and it was thought that they had an influence on the growth of the crops and possibly in a wider manner on the fate of the living. Side by side with this goes a feeling that the dead could return to the house in which they had lived and pester the inhabitants. Against this danger precautions were taken at the time of burial in the removal of the corpse feet foremost from the house and in elaborate purification. This feeling is shown prominently in the primitive festival of the Lemuria, when the Lemures or Larvae (the spirits of the

dead regarded as hostile) were exorcized by the paterfamilias with magic charms and driven from their old
home with the formula 'Manes exite paterni'.[1] Later the
practice of individual burial arose and family tombs or
special tombs for single persons became the habit at any
rate in the more aristocratic and noble houses. It is to this
period of the individual tomb that the later and more
obviously civilized festival of the Parentalia seems to
belong, at which the family visited the tombs of its dead
(the *di parentes*), laid wreaths and offerings of food and
drink upon them, and returned home to celebrate a kind
of family love-feast, the Caristia or Cara Cognatio, in
which the dead were thought to have their part.

The Greeks from early times, at least for important
persons, used the individual tomb; even in the shaft-graves
at Mycenae the bodies are separately interred and both
tholos-tombs and chamber-tombs were the burial-places
of single persons or of a family. This practice engenders
the idea that the dead still resides in his tomb and offerings
of food and drink to sustain him are consequently made,
and even poured down a hole or channel (βόθρος) in the
mound in order to reach the dead beneath. Connected
with this tendance at the tomb is the hero-cult, which is so
characteristic of Greek religion, in which the great dead
are worshipped with prayer and offering. Thus the earliest
Greek conception of the fate of the dead would seem to be
that the spirit, like the body, was present in the tomb, but
already by the time of Homer we find an alternative idea,
connected possibly with the practice of cremation, which
destroys the body and liberates the spirit. The soul of the
dead man is now supposed to leave the body and pass away
into a distant land, not in Homer's account beneath the
world, but in the far west, where the dead live a faint feeble

---

[1] Ov. *Fast.* v. 443.

existence, like that of life, but in every way less real and effective (ἀμενηνὰ κάρηνα). In a later stage, just becoming visible in the second part of the Nekyia of *Odyssey* xi, there is introduced the idea of the rewards and punishments of the dead, on which is built, as Norden has shown in the introduction to his edition of *Aeneid* vi, a gradually developing popular 'theology' of the world of the dead, with its regions and divisions, and the differentiation of fate apportioned to various classes of persons, the dead infants, the murdered, the prophets, the heroes, and so on. Later on in historical times two new influences came to bear on popular belief. On the one hand were the mystery religions, and in particular Orphism, which promised to the initiate a future life of happiness, on the other the theories of philosophers. Here the doctrine of the Pythagoreans, which was early connected with Orphism, taught a belief in metempsychosis, and influenced the speculations of Plato, while the later teaching of the Stoics, rooted in the belief in the individual soul as a 'fiery particle' of the divine *anima mundi*, also laid stress on a life after death.

All these conceptions seem to have been familiar to Virgil and, though in his more detailed and reflective account of the lower world in the sixth book of the *Aeneid* it is Greek 'theology' and philosophy by which he is most attracted, the older ideas of the dead in the tomb and even the Roman conception of the undistinguished *manes* find their place in his poems. The *Aeneid* at least shows the eclectic conservation of all that in thought or tradition made the strongest appeal to Virgil, both as a poet and as a man for whom religion contained the ultimate explanation of the world. We may consider first what he says of the fate of the dead and then pass to the attitude of men towards them.

A. *The Fate of the Dead*

1. *The Importance of Burial.*

It was a common belief of the Greeks, shared probably by the early Italians, that it was of supreme importance to the dead to be duly buried; otherwise, as Virgil makes clear in several passages,[1] they could not enter the lower world and find their due resting-place. This idea is specially brought out in the sixth book of the *Aeneid* in connexion with two of Aeneas' companions, lost during the voyage.

Misenus, the trumpeter, in a moment of exaltation had challenged the gods to a musical contest, and was pulled into the sea and drowned by the indignant Triton.[2] The Sibyl had warned Aeneas that he would not be able to enter the lower world until he had buried the body of a lost companion, and the corpse of Misenus was shortly afterwards found on the shore. Aeneas gives it due burial; the details of the funeral are very interesting and must be considered when the cult of the dead is under discussion.[3]

The idea of the miserable fate of the unburied dead is emphasized more strongly in the story of Palinurus, the helmsman of Aeneas, who, as he was steering his ship by night, was overcome by sleep and fell into the water still clasping the rudder.[4] Seated on it he was driven by the winds for three days and nights and washed up on the Italian shore, where, however, he was slain by the inhabitants and his corpse left to be washed by the waves. As Aeneas approaches the rivers of the lower world he recognizes Palinurus, who in answer to his question tells

[1] e.g., A. vi. 326   hi, quos vehit unda, sepulti.
                nec ripas datur horrendas et rauca fluenta
                transportare prius quam sedibus ossa quierunt.
[2] A. vi. 171 ff.   [3] See p. 287.
[4] A. v. 854–71, vi. 347–62.

his story.[1] Then he turns to Aeneas with a piteous appeal: 'By the sweet light and breezes of the sky, by thy father, I pray thee and the hope of Iulus, rising to manhood, save me, unconquered hero, from my ills; either return to the harbour of Velia and cast earth upon me, or else, if there be any means, if thy goddess mother shows thee the way . . . give thy hand to thy wretched friend and carry me with thee through the waters, that I may at least rest in the peaceful abodes in death.'[2] The idea that an unburied person should cross the Styx horrifies the Sibyl; it is an attempt to change the 'fates of the gods by prayer',[3] but she consoles him by the prophecy that the Italians of Velia, spurred by 'portents from heaven', presumably a plague, 'will make atonement to thy bones and erect a mound and pay due honours at the mound, and the spot shall for ever bear the name of Palinurus'.[4] The hero is comforted and 'joys in the thought of a land named after him'.[5] The poignancy of the position of the unburied is finely brought out, all the more by the scene of Aeneas' encounter with his helmsman on the banks of the Styx. The same conception which has been noticed in these two passages is expressed again later when Aeneas on the morning after the first great battle exhorts his companions to commit the

[1] A. vi. 337 ff.
[2] A. vi. 363 quod te per caeli iucundum lumen et auras,
      per genitorem oro, per spes surgentis Iuli,
      eripe me his, invicte, malis: aut tu mihi terram
      inice, namque potes, portusque require Velinos,
      aut tu, si qua via est, si quam tibi diva creatrix
      ostendit . . .
      da dextram misero et tecum me tolle per undas,
      sedibus ut saltem placidis in morte quiescam.
[3] A. vi. 376 desine fata deum flecti sperare precando.
[4] A. vi. 378 nam tua finitimi, longe lateque per urbes
      prodigiis acti caelestibus, ossa piabunt,
      et statuent tumulum et tumulo sollemnia mittent,
      aeternumque locus Palinuri nomen habebit.
[5] A. vi. 383 gaudet cognomine terra.

unburied bodies of their companions to earth, 'for this is the sole honour in Acheron below'.[1]

A much stranger conception of the liberation of the spirit in order that it may enter the lower world is mentioned in connexion with the death of Dido.[2] Iuno in pity at Dido's long death agony sends Iris 'to release her struggling soul and loose her compacted limbs. For since she was dying neither by destiny nor by a death she had provoked, but miserably before her time and fired by a sudden madness, Proserpina had not yet taken the yellow lock from her hair or condemned her head to Stygian Orcus.'[3] Iris then cuts the lock as an offering to Dis and Dido's spirit departs. We meet with the idea of the cutting of the lock of hair from the dead in Euripides' *Alcestis*,[4] and Turnebus was probably right in explaining it on the analogy of a sacrifice, where hairs are cut from the victim's head and given as a first-offering to the gods of the lower world. We know, too, from Virgil himself, that those who died prematurely were regarded as a special class (see p. 270), but the combination of these two ideas in the notion that Proserpina could not herself perform the function in the case of the prematurely dead is, as far as we can tell, Virgil's own supposition, based obviously on Greek precedent.

The sacredness of the tomb owing to the indwelling of

---

[1] A. xi. 22   interea socios inhumataque corpora terrae
              mandemus, qui solus honos Acheronte sub imo est.

[2] A. iv. 693–705.

[3] A. iv. 694   Irim demisit Olympo
              quae luctantem animam nexosque resolveret artus.
              nam quia nec fato merita nec morte peribat,
              scd misera ante diem subitoque accensa furore,
              nondum illi flavum Proserpina vertice crinem
              abstulerat Stygioque caput damnaverat Orco.

[4] Eur. *Alc.* 74 στείχω δ' ἐπ' αὐτὴν ὡς κατάρξωμαι ξίφει·
              ἱερὸς γὰρ οὗτος τῶν κατὰ χθονὸς θεῶν,
              ὅτου τόδ' ἔγχος κρατὸς ἁγνίσῃ τρίχα.

the dead spirit in it is well illustrated in the story of Aeneas' encounter with the murdered Polydorus in the third book.[1] Landing on the coast of Thrace and wishing to sacrifice to the gods, Aeneas proceeds to pluck up some cornel bushes growing on a neighbouring mound. But he finds the roots dripping with blood; three times to his horror this experience is repeated, and then he hears groans and a voice from the mound telling him that below lies the buried Polydorus, Priam's son, robbed and slain by the traitor Polymestor. Aeneas gives Polydorus a renewed funeral, after which the spirit lies in peace.[2] The details of the ritual must again be considered later, but here it may be noted that the passage forms an interesting contrast to those considered above, in that while there the spirit is eager to enter the realm of the dead, here it is to be laid to rest in the tomb. Virgil is eclectic in his ideas and uses one or another, as it suits his purpose.

2. *Spirits of the Dead.*

From time to time in Virgil we hear of visions of the spirits of the dead. They are described as *umbrae* or *simulacra*, and the conception of the dead spirits seems to belong partly to folk-lore, but from the literary point of view it follows the Homeric tradition of the ἀμενηνὰ κάρηνα. Thus when Orpheus raised his song in the lower world 'the thin shades moved and the images of them that had lost the light of day, as many as are the thousands of birds that hide among the leaves, when evening or a wintry storm drives them from the hills, mothers and men and the bodies of great-souled heroes quit of life, boys and unmarried maidens and youths laid upon the pyre before

[1] A. iii. 22 ff.
[2] A. iii. 62 ergo instauramus Polydoro funus. In spite of some commentators (e.g. Conington, ad loc.) I believe that *instauramus* here means 'renew' in reference to the previous hasty interment after Polydorus' murder.

their parents' eyes'.[1] Three of these lines are repeated in
the sixth book of the *Aeneid* to describe the crowd of souls
whom Aeneas sees waiting to be ferried across by Charon.
So, too, when Iuno is fashioning the wraith of Aeneas to
deceive Turnus and lead him away from the battle 'she
gives him empty words, and a voice without a mind, and
feigns his walk as he moves, even as legend has it that the
figures of the dead flit around, or like the dreams which
deceive the senses in sleep'.[2] The comparison of the dead
spirits to the visions of sleep is interesting and recalls the
Epicurean doctrine that both were due to *simulacra* ranging
at large: Virgil is imitating Lucretius closely here.[3]

These are pictures of the dead in the world below. In the
second book are two instances of the appearance of particular dead persons to the living, both of which are of
great interest. Hector appears to Aeneas, not as a vague
'shade' or 'image', but as he was at the moment of death,
'dragged at the chariot-wheel, as once before, and black
with gory dust, the thongs piercing through his swelling
feet';[4] he urges Aeneas to fly and to take with him the
Penates of Troy, and has the strength 'to bear from the
inmost shrines the fillets and mighty Vesta and her eternal
flame'. This is a substantial vision, but the ghost of Creusa

---

[1] G. iv. 471–7: note especially 472 umbrae ibant tenues simulacraque
luce carentum, the Homeric words σκιά and εἴδωλον with a reminiscence of
the Lucretian simulacra modis pallentia miris (i. 123); cf. A. vi. 306–8.

[2] A. x. 639   dat inania verba,
        dat sine mente sonum gressusque effingit euntis,
        morte obita qualis fama est volitare figuras
        aut quae sopitos deludunt somnia sensus.

[3] Cf. Lucr. i. 132–5; iv. 749–83.

[4] A. ii. 270–97; see especially 272–3:
        raptatus bigis ut quondam, aterque cruento
        pulvere perque pedes traiectus lora tumentis,
and 296–7:
        sic ait et manibus vittas Vestamque potentem
        aeternumque adytis effert penetralibus ignem.

is nearer to the Homeric conception: 'there appeared before my eyes the image and shade of Creusa herself, a vision greater in stature than her whom I knew'.[1] This is the shade-vision, but it has acquired a new dignity. Creusa too warns Aeneas to fly and prophesies his long journey and his arrival in Italy and at the Tiber; she herself must not share his wanderings, but is detained in Troy by the great Mother of the gods. And then comes the significant conclusion, 'she departed into the thin air. Thrice I strove to fling my arms about her neck, thrice the vision grasped in vain escaped my hands, like the light winds or a fleeting dream.' The spirit of the dead may for recognition by the living assume the appearance and trappings of life, but in reality it is the thin unsubstantial shade. Once more we may notice the comparison to the dream-figure.

3. *The Lower World.*

If the appearances of the dead and the general descriptions of their condition suggest the feeble shade existence of the first part of Homer's Nekyia, the later idea of rewards and punishments, which is briefly suggested in the *Odyssey*, is the basis of the great description of the lower world in the sixth book of the *Aeneid*. It is amplified by the legend of the judgement of Minos and Rhadamanthus, and by a wealth of infernal 'topography', which no doubt had its roots in popular belief and was elaborated in the

---

[1] A. ii. 771–95; see especially 772–3:

> infelix simulacrum atque ipsius umbra Creusae
> visa mihi ante oculos et nota maior imago,

and 791–4:

> tenuisque recessit in auras.
> ter conatus ibi collo dare bracchia circum;
> ter frustra comprensa manus effugit imago,
> par levibus ventis volucrique simillima somno.

Almost the same language is used in G. iv. 499–502 of the shade of Eurydice fleeing from Orpheus.

traditional 'theology'. Many attempts have been made to analyse Virgil's picture and to give it a logical consistency which is hardly to be sought for in the vision of a poet. Here all that can be attempted is to sketch an outline of Virgil's conceptions and to notice some salient features in it.

(*a*) *Gods of the Underworld.* Virgil knows of certain definite deities and other lesser figures who hold sway or dwell in the underworld. Greek influence is at work in them all, even if they are not all certainly of Greek origin. The male deity of the underworld is once given his Greek name Pluton,[1] elsewhere he is known as Dis, or less frequently as Orcus. Dis was almost certainly an importation from Greece; the name Dis (*sc.* Dives) looks like a translation of Pluton, and there is no mention of him at Rome until the foundation of the cult of Dis and Proserpina by order of the Sibylline books in the stress of the first Punic war in 249 B.C. The Romans had apparently a notion of shadowy underworld gods (*di inferi*), such as Acca Larentia and Tarpeia, dwelling among the Manes, but the idea of a king of the lower world was due to Greece. In Virgil Dis is for the most part a pallid figure, a mere synonym, almost geographical, for the lower world. Thus we find the 'gateway of Dis' and 'the doorway of Dis'; so also 'the palace of Dis' and with perhaps a more personal touch 'the chamber of Dis'.[2] Once the lower world is thought of as a town rather than a house and we hear of the 'walls of Dis',[3] and in the valley of Ampsanctus of 'the breathing-holes of Dis'.[4] When Latinus in taking his oath swears by 'the might of the infernal gods and the sacred precincts of cruel

---

[1] A. vii. 327 odit et ipse pater Pluton.
[2] G. iv. 467, A. viii. 667 ostia Ditis, A. vi. 127 ianua Ditis; cf. A. vi. 106 inferni ianua regis, A. v. 731, vi. 269 domos Ditis, A. vi. 397 thalamo Ditis.
[3] A. vi. 541 Ditis moenia.
[4] A. vii. 568 spiracula Ditis.

Dis',[1] there is certainly an advance towards a personal conception, and this becomes more explicit when Dido's lock is described as 'sacred to Dis'.[2] The most completely personal reference to Dis is in the story of Orpheus in the fourth book of the *Georgics*, where after his loss the bard 'mourns for Eurydice snatched from him and the fruitless gift of Dis';[3] here he is the king of the lower world, who had allowed Orpheus to lead Eurydice away. Dis appears again as the 'Stygian king',[4] to whom Aeneas builds altars and sacrifices victims before his journey to the lower world, and similarly Iuppiter makes oath by 'the streams of his Stygian brother';[5] Pluto in Greek mythology was Zeus' brother, to whom was assigned the kingship of the lower world, as that of the sea was given to Poseidon. Once, too, he appears as 'the Stygian Iuppiter'[6] (Ζεὺς χθόνιος) to whom Dido announces her intention of completing a sacrifice already begun.

Parallel to Dis, and apparently used as a mere synonym, is Orcus. There is some doubt whether Orcus was a figure in Italian folk-lore, like Tarpeia and Acca Larentia, connected with the lower world, or whether his name is merely a transliteration of the Greek Ὄρκος, which is sometimes found in connexion with Pluton.[7] In any case after the

---

[1] A. xii. 199 vimque deum infernam et duri sacraria Ditis.
[2] A. iv. 703   hunc ego Diti
       sacrum iussa fero.
[3] G. iv. 519   raptam Eurydicen atque inrita Ditis
       dona querens.
[4] A. vi. 252 tum Stygio regi nocturnas incohat aras.
[5] A. x. 113 Stygii per flumina fratris . . . adnuit.
[6] A. iv. 638 sacra Iovi Stygio.
[7] The former, which is the more generally held view, was adopted by Wissowa in the first edition of *R.K.* (p. 192), but in the second (p. 310) he inclines to the latter, chiefly on the ground that G. i. 277 (quoted in n. 6, p. 252, below) is a literal translation of Hesiod, *Op.* 803 ἐν πέμπτῃ γάρ φασιν Ἐρίνυας ἀμφιπολεύειν | Ὅρκον γεινόμενον, τὸν Ἔρις τέκε πῆμ' ἐπιόρκοις. But does this prove more than that Virgil recognized the Ὅρκος of Hesiod as

Graeco-Roman period he became little more than an equivalent of Hades. In Virgil, like Dis, he mostly appears in quite colourless contexts with no indication of a clear personality. Thus Charon is the 'ferryman of Orcus',[1] and Cerberus his 'janitor',[2] and in front of the vestibule of the lower world is the 'corridor of Orcus'.[3] A twice-used synonym for slaying a foe in battle is to 'send him down to Orcus',[4] and similarly Proserpina 'had not yet condemned the head of Dido to Orcus',[5] till Iris came to cut the fatal lock. Once the god seems more personal: Virgil warns the farmer that the fifth of the month is unlucky, for on it 'pale Orcus and the Eumenides were born';[6] this comes straight from Hesiod and is purely Greek.

The goddesses of the lower world in Virgil are Proserpina and Hecate, but their connexion with one another is not so close as that of Dis and Orcus. Proserpina is of course a transliteration of Persephone, who in Greek legend was the daughter of Zeus and Demeter, carried off by Pluto to the lower world, as she was gathering flowers in the fields of Henna, and there established as his queen, returning for one-third of the year to her mother in the world above, To this legend Virgil refers once,[7] when in the opening of the *Georgics* he expresses the hope that the young Caesar will not wish to rule in the world below, though it has its attractions, for 'Proserpina recalled cares

equivalent to Orcus, whom he knew? Orcus seems to me too well established in Italian thought to have so flimsy a Greek origin.

[1] G. iv. 502 portitor Orci.   [2] A. viii. 296 ianitor Orci.

[3] A. vi. 273 vestibulum ante ipsum primis in faucibus Orci.
Norden is probably right in interpreting *fauces* in an architectural sense here.

[4] A. ii. 398 multos Danaum demittimus Orco; A. ix. 527 quem quisque virum demiserit Orco.

[5] A. iv. 698 nondum illi flavum Proserpina vertice crinem
          abstulerat Stygioque caput damnaverat Orco.

[6] G. i. 277   quintam fuge: pallidus Orcus
          Eumenidesque satae.

[7] G. i. 39 nec repetita sequi curet Proserpina matrem.

not to follow her mother'. ⌐Elsewhere she is definitely the wife of Dis and queen of the lower regions, but it is noticeable that she has a far more definite personality than Dis himself. 'In chastity she sits guarding the threshold of her uncle [Dis as Iuppiter's brother]',[1] to her in his initial sacrifice Aeneas offers a barren cow,[2] to her he must bear the golden bough as the price of his admission to the lower world.[3] It is again Proserpina who should have shorn the lock from Dido's head for her acceptance in the world below,[4] and finally—the most completely personal reference of all—it is Proserpina who makes with Orpheus the condition of Eurydice's return, that he must not look back.[5] This more distinct personality of Proserpina is in accordance with Roman usage: she always remained a figure of legend and mythology and never faded, like Dis and Orcus, into a symbol of the lower world.

The other female deity of the lower world, namely Hecate, is, as has been seen (p. 162), closely associated with Diana as the Latin counterpart of the Greek Artemis. She appears usually in the *Aeneid*[6] as a lower-world deity to whom prayer and sacrifice are made, and once in a more personal aspect as giving to the Sibyl the charge of the Avernian groves. What was the respective authority of Hecate and Proserpina in the underworld is a question which Virgil himself would probably have found it hard to answer. Dis and Orcus may fairly be identified, but the two goddesses remain distant.

Besides the definite deities there appear also in Virgil

[1] A. vi. 402 casta licet patrui servet Proserpina limen.
[2] A. vi. 251 sterilemque tibi, Proserpina, vaccam.
[3] A. vi. 142 hoc sibi pulchra suum ferri Proserpina munus
　　　　　instituit.
[4] A. iv. 698 nondum illi flavum Proserpina vertice crinem | abstulerat.
[5] G. iv. 486 redditaque Eurydice superas veniebat ad auras
　　　　　pone sequens (namque hanc dederat Proserpina legem).
[6] A. iv. 511, 609, vi. 118, 247, 564; passages quoted in notes, p. 162.

the well-known figures of legend and folk-lore associated with the lower world. The three of definitely human shape are Charon, Minos, and Rhadamanthus. Charon, the ferryman of buried souls across the infernal rivers, is described by the poet in picturesque language: 'he guards the waters and the streams in fearful filth; a long white beard hangs unkempt from his chin, his eyes are alive with flame, a frowzy garment hangs knotted from his shoulders. He pushes off the raft with his pole and minds the sails, and carries the bodies over in his rust-black boat, an old man by now, but the old age of a god is fresh and green.'[1] One may note that he is definitely described as a god. On the shore is seen the vast throng of the dead waiting for their transport, but the unburied may not enter the boat until they have waited for a hundred years.[2] Palinurus' attempt to persuade Aeneas to take him across in the boat with him is most sternly suppressed by the Sibyl.

Minos and Rhadamanthus are not gods, but great heroes ; Minos, the king of Cnossos, and Rhadamanthus, his brother, who were exalted to be the judges of souls in the lower world and to assign to them their destiny and the region in which they are to dwell. Aeneas has separate visions of them; 'Minos, as prevailing judge shakes the urn; he summons a jury of the silent ones and inquires into men's lives and the charges brought against them.'[3] The

[1] A. vi. 298   portitor has horrendus aquas et flumina servat
              terribili squalore Charon, cui plurima mento
              canities inculta iacet, stant lumina flamma,
              sordidus ex umeris nodo dependet amictus.
              ipse ratem conto subigit velisque ministrat,
              et ferruginea subvectat corpora cumba,
              iam senior, sed cruda deo viridisque senectus.
[2] A. vi. 329   centum errant annos volitantque haec litora circum;
              tum demum admissi stagna exoptata revisunt.
[3] A. vi. 432   quaesitor Minos urnam movet; ille silentum
              consiliumque vocat vitasque et crimina discit.
Concilium has better manuscript authority than *consilium* and would mean

language here is that of the Roman law-court, and the idea of Minos as presiding over a jury, whose votes he takes in the urn, is otherwise unknown. Nor can we be sure to whom his judgement extends; probably only to the class of souls mentioned just before, those who in life were unjustly condemned. 'Cnossian Rhadamanthus' appears later in the story and seems to have a more autocratic position: 'Here he has his cruel realm, and hears and punishes crimes, and compels each man to confess the atonements for sin, which rejoicing in vain wickedness, he has incurred and put off to the late hour of death'.[1] The meaning of the last very difficult phrase has been discussed above (p. 86), but it may be noticed that Rhadamanthus sits without a jury and apparently has a wider jurisdiction over all the souls of the guilty. It is, however, doubtful whether Virgil intended any such distinction between the authority of the two brothers. The third judge of the dead in legend, Aeacus, is not mentioned by Virgil.

The supernatural monsters of the lower world, the Eumenides and Erinyes, with their Latin counterparts, the Furiae and Dirae, have already been noticed (p. 178), and among them Tisiphone and Allecto have an individual personality. To them should be added the dog Cerberus[2] and the monstrous Hydra,[3] but neither of these can be said to have any religious significance; they are only the bogies of folk-lore.

'he summons the throng of the dead before him'. But this will not obviate the difficulty of Minos sitting with a jury, which is implied in *quaesitor*, the technical term for the judge presiding in a jury-court, in *urnam movet*, and also in 431 nec vero hae sine sorte datae, sine iudice, sedes, where *sors* must refer to the *sortitio iudicum*. On this ground I prefer *consilium* which completes instead of confusing the picture.

[1] A. vi. 566 Gnosius haec Rhadamanthus habet durissima regna,
         castigatque auditque dolos subigitque fateri
         quae quis apud superos furto laetatus inani,
         distulit in seram commissa piacula mortem.
[2] G. iv. 483, A. vi. 400, 417.   [3] A. vi. 287, 576, vii. 658, viii. 300.

The deities of the underworld, who have been hitherto mentioned, Dis, Orcus, Proserpina, and Hecate, are *di inferi*, gods in the same sense as the *di superi*, but holding sway in the lower world; as has been seen, they are all either Greek in origin or Grecized in conception. Orcus alone may be native Italian. But side by side with them and often interconnected is the essentially Italian conception of the Manes. Its development is not easy to trace; the Manes are primarily, as has been noticed (p. 241), the undiscriminated mass of the spirits of the dead; they were thought of as hostile and given the euphemistic title of 'the kindly ones'. And though this hostile association died away, there survived a sense of the supernatural power of the dead and they were collectively worshipped as the Di Manes, an expression which it is noticeable that Virgil never uses. As far back as the Twelve Tables we find the injunction, 'Let the rights of the Di Manes be sacred',[1] and there is extant an early Republican inscription to them.[2] This was a general worship of the spirits of the dead, but it gradually became more individualized. With the practice of the family tomb the Di Manes were identified with the Di Parentes, the sanctified dead of the family. A further stage of development is seen when the individual tomb leads to the thought of the dead spirit of a particular person. Now there was no singular of *manes* and so the plural word is used somewhat illogically of the single spirit. The first extant usage in this sense occurs in a speech of Cicero's,[3] but from the early empire the common form of epitaph on a tomb is 'Dis Manibus of so-and-so'.[4] In

[1] Deorum Manium iura sancta sunto, Cic. *Leg.* ii. 9. 22.
[2] *C.I.L.* i. 1410.
[3] Cic. *in Pis.* 7. 16 a me quidem etiam poenas expetistis quibus coniuratorum manes mortuorum expiaretis, and even here the reference is plural.
[4] This explanation, which is in general supported by W. F. Otto, *Die*

other epitaphs 'Dis Manibus' is followed by the dative of the person commemorated. This represents a consecration to the Di Manes in general and a dedication to the person. Where the genitive is used it may be supposed that 'Manibus' represents the spirit of the individual and that 'Dis' is prefixed by false analogy. The usage need not be taken to imply worship of the dead individual. A second and quite different development of Di Manes took place, when after the introduction of the Greek ideas of gods of the underworld, it becomes interchangeable with the title Di Inferi and is applied to the personal rulers of the lower world.

Now this development has left its traces in Virgil's treatment of the Manes at varying stages and with very varying emphasis. The oldest use of Manes for the undistinguished mass of the dead spirits survives, if anywhere, only in the striking passage where Virgil is describing the revelation of Cacus' cave when Hercules threw down the great stone at its entrance; 'just as if the earth opened deep by some force were to unlock the abodes below and reveal the pale realms, and from above a vast chasm were seen and the Manes were to tremble at the light let in upon them'.[1] Here the Manes seem to be just the collected spirits of the dead, though it is possible that even here the word may rather be used in a derivative sense, of which Virgil is fond, of the 'realm of the dead' with a local meaning, corresponding to that which he sometimes gives to Dis and Orcus; in this sense it is accompanied by the adjective *imi* or *profundi*. Thus Evander prays to be allowed to bring the news of Turnus' death to his son Pallas 'in the lowest

---

Manen, pp. 53–63, is at least more probable than the theory noticed by Servius in a long note on *Aen.* iii. 63 that every man had two Manes or Genii attached to him which accompanied him in death.

[1] A. viii. 243–6; see especially 246 trepident immisso lumine Manes.

Manes',[1] Dido prophesies that the news of Aeneas' punishment will reach her 'in the lowest Manes',[2] and the divine Iuturna prays that 'the earth might yawn for her and send her, goddess as she is, to the lowest Manes'.[3] Similarly, in his description of the *mundus* Virgil says that the lower pole 'is looked on beneath our feet by dark Styx and the deep Manes'.[4] In all these instances *Tartara* might be substituted for *manes* without any change of meaning, and the geographical sense seems to be derived from the conception of the lower world as the home of the collected spirits of the dead. To these examples may be added a natural extension when in describing a storm at sea Aeneas says: 'we are borne up to heaven on the billowing surge, and again as the wave withdraws we sink to the lowest Manes.'[5]

But, if he is sparing in his use of the word in its old Roman collective sense, Virgil has many examples of the later developments. In two passages *manes* is clearly used of the family dead, the Di Parentes. Aeneas speaks in magnanimity to Lausus, whom he has just killed: 'keep thy arms, in which thou didst rejoice, I give thee back to the Manes and ashes of thy parents, if thou hast any care for that',[6] and Camilla, addressing Ornytus, whom she has slain, cries: ' 'twill be no light fame that thou wilt bear to the Manes of thy fathers, that thou didst fall by the weapon

---

[1] A. xi. 180   non vitae gaudia quaero,
    nec fas, sed nato manis perferre sub imos.
[2] A. iv. 387 audiam et haec manis veniet mihi fama sub imos.
[3] A. xii. 883   o quae satis ima dehiscat
    terra mihi, manisque deam demittat ad imos?
[4] G. i. 242 hic vertex nobis semper sublimis; at illum
    sub pedibus Styx atra videt manesque profundi.
[5] A. iii. 564 tollimur in caelum curvato gurgite, et idem
    subducta ad manis imos desedimus unda.
[6] A. x. 827 arma, quibus laetatus, habe tua; teque parentum
    manibus et cineri, si qua est ea cura, remitto.

of Camilla.'[1] Elsewhere the reference is unmistakably to the individual spirit. Mago pleads for his life with Aeneas 'by the Manes of thy father and the hopes of the young Iulus', and Aeneas rejecting his offered bribes replies, 'this is the purpose of the Manes of my father Anchises, this of Iulus';[2] the two lines are absolutely parallel and the meaning in the first is simply 'thy father's buried spirit'. So again Anna, urging Dido to marry again after Sychaeus' death, asks, 'dost thou believe that his ashes or buried Manes care for thy widowhood?',[3] and later in the book Dido, protesting that she had not harmed Aeneas, says, 'I never violated the ashes or the Manes of thy father Anchises.'[4] In the last instance *manes* comes near to meaning the dead body, and we may notice in both these passages once again the combination of *manes* with *cinis*, the spirit and the cremated body. In one famous passage 'ashes' is used by itself as a synonym for 'manes':[5] 'it will be a joy to have sated my mind with the fire of vengeance and to have appeased the ashes of my kin.' Orpheus again is said by his lyre to have 'availed to summon the Manes of his wife',[6] once more a rather concrete instance, something like 'ghost' in sense. ⌊Aeneas, too, tells Deiphobus that he made a tomb for him on the Rhoetean shore and 'thrice summoned thy Manes aloud',[7] the last cry to the dead at the funeral. In two important passages, which must be

---

[1] A. xi. 688   nomen tamen haud leve patrum
          manibus hoc referes, telo cecidisse Camillae.

[2] A. x. 524 per patrios manis et spes surgentis Iuli, and 534 hoc patris Anchisae manes, hoc sentit Iulus.

[3] A. iv. 34 id cinerem aut manis credis curare sepultos?

[4] A. iv. 427 nec patris Anchisae cineres manisve revelli.

[5] A. ii. 586   animumque explesse iuvabit
        ultricis flammae et cineres satiasse meorum.

[6] A. vi. 119 potuit manis accersere coniugis Orpheus.

[7] A. vi. 505 tunc egomet tumulum Rhoeteo litore inanem
       constitui et magna manis ter voce vocavi.

discussed more fully when the cult of the dead is considered (p. 297), *manes* may be used for the spirit of the individual dead. In the account of the renewed funeral of Polydorus it is said that 'altars stand there to the Manes',[1] and Andromache, during her ceremony in honour of Hector in Thrace, 'was calling on the Manes'[2] at the empty tomb. In the latter case it is very difficult to resist the conclusion that it was Hector's spirit and not the collective dead whom she was summoning. Finally, we must assign to this usage of *manes*, as applied to the single individual, the famous phrase in the sixth book, 'we each of us suffer our own shades'.[3] There can be no doubt of Virgil's usage of *manes* as applied to the individual and it is perhaps significant of the custom and thought of the Augustan age that this use prevails over any other.

There remain some instances of the second development of *manes* which has been noticed, its use for the 'powers of the lower world'. This was more usually denoted in Latin by Di Manes, but Virgil does not use that title. It is true, as has been seen, that even old Latin sentiment attributed a certain collective divinity to the dead, but this had no doubt been crystallized in the Augustan age by the Graecized conception of the deities of the lower world and in some at least of the Virgilian instances *manes* appears to be the direct equivalent of *di inferi*. Iuno in her supreme effort to move the Latins to hostility to Aeneas cries in famous words, 'if I cannot bend the gods on high, I will

---

[1] A. iii. 63 stant manibus arae.

[2] A. iii. 303   manisque vocabat
        Hectoreum ad tumulum.

[3] A. vi. 743 quisque suos patimur manis; see further discussion on p. 277. W. F. Otto, *Die Manen*, p. 58, notices that this use of the plural *manes* for the spirit of the single person influenced other words as well, so that Virgil can represent Aeneas as saying (A. v. 81) in reference to the spirit of Anchises, animaeque umbraeque paternae.

stir up Acheron';[1] the opposition there with the *di superi* makes it clear that the vague term 'Acheron' signifies the *di inferi*, and her action in stirring up the Fury Allecto confirms this. Further, when Venus later on complains to Iuppiter of Iuno's action, she has the corresponding contrast between *superi* and *manes*: 'now she even stirs up the Manes, this realm of the world remained before untouched.'[2] Here the Manes are the lower-world deities and as if to emphasize it Venus has already in the same speech declared that the Trojans in seeking Italy were following the oracles given by 'the gods above and the Manes', *di superi et inferi.*[3] The same use of *manes* becomes clear in the story of Orpheus in the fourth book of the *Georgics*. In the hope of recovering Eurydice 'he entered the jaws of Taenarum, the high gates of Dis and the grove dark with black fear, and approached the Manes and the dread king';[4] here the combination with 'the king' makes the idea of the infernal deities manifest. So later in the story when he has lost Eurydice again, the poet exclaims: 'by what lamentation could he move the Manes, what divine powers by his words?';[5] here in just the same way the combination with *numina* makes the sense clear. So at the fatal moment when he looked round his fault 'was pardonable, if the Manes know how to pardon'.[6] To this same use must be ascribed the vaguer phrase in the description of the ivory gate, by which 'the Manes send false dreams to

[1] A. vii. 312 flectere si nequeo superos, Acheronta movebo.
[2] A. x. 39 nunc etiam Manis (haec intemptata manebat
        sors rerum) movet.
[3] A. x. 33   sin tot responsa secuti
        quae superi Manesque dabant.
[4] G. iv. 467 Taenareas etiam fauces, alta ostia Ditis
        et caligantem nigra formidine lucum
        ingressus, manisque adiit regemque tremendum.
[5] G. iv. 505 quo fletu manis, quae numina voce moveret?
[6] G. iv. 489 ignoscenda quidem, scirent si ignoscere Manes.

the upper air';[1] the idea of the gate of dreams is Greek, and the Manes here are the Graecized gods of the lower world.

Thus in his use of *manes* Virgil touches all those known to the Roman or Graeco-Roman religion. There is the oldest meaning of the indiscriminate mass of the dead with its local extension, and the two later developments, the spirit of the individual, in connexion with which he is influenced by Greek hero-worship, and the lower-world deities, where his practice is coloured by the far more clear and precise Greek conceptions of the rulers of the dead. He does not attempt to find consistency between these ideas, but after his manner as a poet uses any one of them to suit his mood and context and yet does not leave his readers with any sense of uncertainty or contradiction. Once again his usage is, as in many other fields, an epitome of Roman thought.

(*b*) *The Lower World—Destinies of the Souls.* By far the most explicit exposition in Virgil of the fate of the souls of the dead is of course contained in the picture of the lower world, which occupies the greater part of the sixth book of the *Aeneid*. Much has been written about its sources, its topography, its inconsistencies, and its difficulties; I propose here merely to review its main features and to detect, if possible, something of the various strains which Virgil has woven together, if not into a consistent and logical account, yet into a great poetic and artistic vision, which seems at the same time to contain his deepest thoughts on the life of the individual as seen by religion.[2]

[1] A. vi. 896 sed falsa ad caelum mittunt insomnia Manes. To these instances in the authenticated poems may be added *Culex* 214:

at mea Manes
viscera Lethaeus cogunt transnare per undas,

where *Manes* clearly stands for the powers of the lower world.

[2] For recent work on this subject see A. Dieterich, *Nekyia* (esp. pp. 150–9), E. Norden, *Aeneis Buch VI*, Einleitung, and in English a sane and sound statement of results in the Introduction to H. E. Butler's edition of *Aeneid VI*.

We must begin by considering in rather more detail the accounts and beliefs with which Virgil's description shows kinship. In the first place the view that the dead spirit remains in or near the tomb, which, as has been seen, Virgil not infrequently adopts, is here entirely thrown away. The whole picture is based on the conception of the passing of the spirit to a world of the dead, and its literary foundation is Homer's Nekyia in *Odyssey* xi. Yet, though Virgil has followed Homer in certain episodes, there are wide differences. Homer's world of the dead is in the far north-west, but still apparently on earth, Virgil's is below the earth and is entered by the cave near Lake Avernus. Homer is concerned only with the great personages of legend, Virgil tells also of the fate of the ordinary man. The great bulk of the Homeric description is of a vague shadowy existence of weak, almost witless forms; Virgil tells of the 'shades' with a full personality and a recollection of their lives on earth. Most noticeable of all differences, Homer, though in a probably later addition he speaks of the punishment of sinners, knows nothing of the idea of purification, still less of the idea of the re-birth of the souls in other human bodies, which supplies Virgil with the magnificent pageant of Roman heroes at the end of the book.

For the origin of such ideas we must clearly look elsewhere. There can be little doubt that the theme of the lower world was a favourite in popular Greek folk-lore, and its ideas were probably embodied in popular 'theologies', such as those of which Norden has suspected the existence. These would have supplied the idea of the punishment of the wicked for their sins on earth and the rewards of the good, and doubtless have contained many details of lower-world topography. Perhaps the paintings in the Etruscan tombs with their pictures of the banqueting and revelling of the good and the torture of the evil by Charun and his attendant demons may give us some idea of the general belief.[1] But these notions of folk-lore became focused and crystallized and greatly developed in the philosophy of the Pythagoreans and the Orphic mysteries. These two coalesced in southern Italy and were expressed, as Dieterich has shown,[2] in poetic narratives of 'Descents' (καταβάσεις) into the lower world. √The new features which they added to popular belief were firstly the conception of punishment as a purification of the spirit, which was probably the contribution of Orphism, and secondly the idea of metempsychosis, the return of the spirit after a period spent in the lower world, to another life of probation on earth. The resultant picture was of a tri-partite division of the lower world,' in which the incorrigible sinners remained for ever in Hell, the great saints went straight to the 'Islands of the Blest', and those who had lead 'intermediate' lives,[3] after being punished and purified in Acheron, were admitted to the realm of the blessed, whether with or without a further life on earth.

It is this conception of the future world which we meet in Greek authors of the classical period, and especially in the works of Pindar and Plato.[4] A well-known fragment of Pindar[5] gives a glorious description of the Elysian fields, and a still better-known passage in the *Olympians*[6] tells us that even the good cannot dwell there for ever, but must come back to spend two more lives on earth—the second apparently in the body of a hero or a saint—and then 'those who have thrice had strength to keep their souls pure from all deeds of wrong, pass by the highway of Zeus into the tower of Kronos, where the ocean-breezes blow

[1] See F. Poulsen, *Etruscan Tomb Paintings*.
[2] *Nekyia*.   [3] Plat. *Phaedo*, 113 d οἳ ἂν δόξωσι μέσως βεβιωκέναι.
[4] The relevant passages are collected and quoted by Butler, op. cit., Introd., pp. 23–30.   [5] Fr. 129.   [6] *Ol.* ii. 58 ff.

around the Islands of the Blest'. In Plato[1] the myths of the *Phaedo, Phaedrus, Gorgias,* and *Republic* are obviously based on the same Pythagoreo-Orphic conceptions. Differing in certain details they all have the idea of judgement, of Acheron, and the 'islands of the blest', of the periods of purification, and the return of the souls to the new life on earth. The *Phaedo* emphasizes the tripartite division of the lower world, the *Phaedrus* the idea of metempsychosis and the periods, and the *Gorgias* the judgement, while the myth of the *Republic* has a marvellous summing up of all these elements. The reading of these great descriptions leaves no doubt of the general kinship to them of *Aeneid* vi, and two special points may be noticed, which are prominent in Virgil. The *Phaedo*[2] states that the holy—and the holy to Plato are the philosophers—are released from any sojourn in the world below and go straight to a καθαρὰ οἴκησις upon earth, while the *Phaedrus*[3] similarly reduces the period of purgation for the philosophers from 10,000 to 3,000 years; and both in *Gorgias*[4] and *Republic*[5] there is special mention of the fate of the ἰδιῶται, the common men, as well as of that of the great heroes and sinners.

Last, but not least, of the influences upon Virgil in this matter was the Stoic doctrine of the *anima mundi,* the world-spirit, which is God, which runs through every part of the universe, and of which every living thing has a 'particle' or a 'spark', for the world-spirit itself is 'a breath like fire'.[6] This becomes clogged and corrupted during man's life on earth, but by purification may be refined again. This doctrine does not of course affect the greater part of Virgil's description, but becomes prominent in the speech of Anchises.

How far all these Greek antecedents were known to Virgil it is impossible to say. Homer was of course known

---

[1] *Phaedo,* 113 ff., *Phaedrus,* 248 ff., *Gorgias,* 523 ff., *Republic,* 615 ff.   [2] 114 d.
[3] 249 a.   [4] 525 e.   [5] 615 d.   [6] Aët. i. 6. 1 πνεῦμα νοερὸν καὶ πυρῶδες.

to him and there is no reason why he should not have been familiar with the odes of Pindar, nor, since we know his great interest in the study of philosophy, with the dialogues of Plato. The traditional 'theology' may have been known to him from many sources and among them he may well, as Dieterich believes, have had access to some Orphic κατάβασις. With the general doctrine of Stoicism he was certainly well acquainted.

The sixth book of the *Aeneid* thus looks back to Greek sources in the main, to a tradition, partly popular, partly poetical, partly philosophical. In Latin the only extant description of a future life, which is certainly antecedent to Virgil, is the vision in the sixth book of Cicero's *De Republica*, which is usually known as the *Somnium Scipionis*. This resembles Virgil's picture in its strongly patriotic tone and its insistence on the rewards for the great heroes and those who have saved their country, but its foundation is more definitely Stoic than Virgil's and the future world is placed in the heavens among the 'nine' stars. It bears, as will be seen, a closer analogy to the Stoic passage in the *Georgics* than to *Aeneid* vi.

Besides the *Somnium Scipionis* there is another extant description of the lower world in the poem known as the *Culex*, which is usually supposed to be an early work of Virgil's own. If so, this part of it may be regarded as a kind of 'dress rehearsal' for the account in the sixth book of the *Aeneid*; in any case it may be taken as a more or less contemporary work and therefore as expounding the current ideas of the time. Both its resemblances to and its differences from *Aeneid* vi are instructive. The lower world is conceived as a city surrounded by walls.[1] At the

---

[1] *Culex* 216   vidi et flagrantia taedis
limina; conlucent infernis moenia templis.

threshold are Tisiphone and Cerberus.[1] It is divided into its regions, but here apparently there are only two. In the region of the punishments are the great sinners,[2] a longer catalogue described with more conventional mythology than in the *Aeneid*. There are the giants who rose against Olympus, Tityos, Tantalus, Sisyphus, the Danaids, Medea, Procne and Philomela, Eteocles and Polynices. To correspond to these in Elysium comes a procession, unknown to the *Aeneid*, of the heroines of Greek legend,[3] who are now the handmaids of Persephone, Alcestis, Penelope, and Eurydice, whose story is narrated at full length. Then follow the heroes of the Trojan war,[4] Peleus and Ajax, Achilles with Hector, scowling at one another still, and Odysseus and Agamemnon with the Greeks who were wrecked on their return from Troy. Next to them are all the great heroes of Roman history and legend,[5] the Fabii and Decii, Horatius, Metellus and Curtius, Mucius and Curius, Flaminius, and the Scipios. A little later there is reference to the judgement of Minos.[6] This description, as will be seen, anticipates much of the material of *Aeneid* vi, Tartarus and Elysium, the great sinners and heroes of Greece, and the addition of the historical heroes of Rome. But it is a much cruder work and is lacking in two of the great features of the sixth book. On the one hand it is without the element of philosophical reflexion, which gives its supreme interest to the speech of Anchises, and, what is perhaps more noteworthy there is no reference to the fate of the common people. It would thus seem that it is more definitely due to poetic tradition, founded on the eleventh book of the *Odyssey*, and lacks both philosophy

---

[1] *Culex* 218 obvia Tisiphone, serpentibus undique compta,
        et flammas et saeva quatit mihi verbera. pone
        Cerberus et diris latrantia rictibus ora.

[2] *Culex* 233–57.   [3] *Culex* 260–95.   [4] *Culex* 296–357.
[5] *Culex* 358–71.   [6] *Culex* 374–5.

and that element of folk-lore which was an essential feature of the underworld 'theology'. Still, whether Virgil's work or not, it bears a notable analogy to the far finer treatment in *Aeneid* vi.

With this background in mind we may follow the journey of Aeneas and the Sibyl through the lower world. The first point that strikes the reader is the firm division of the different portions of the country—if one may so call it—and the definite separation of the inhabitants to be found there. This is, we may be sure, in the main part of the tradition and, thanks to the researches of Norden, it is often possible to trace it and to add some explanation to Virgil's account.

The first place reached is described as being 'right before the entrance and in the very corridor of Orcus'.[1] Here are the personified spirits, Grief, Care, Disease, &c., ending with 'War and the iron dwellings of the Eumenides and mad Discord'. Such personification goes back to Homer and Hesiod, and may possibly have been suggested by Lucretius,[2] though, as Butler thinks, it is more probable that the ideas come from some Greek Nekyia. The Eumenides take their place among these abstractions as their counterparts, the Dirae, do at the battle of Actium.[3] In the middle is the great elm tree, which is the abode of the dreams[4]—an idea to which no exact parallel can be found—and close by are the forms of the monsters of mythology, Centaurs, Scylla, Chimaera, Gorgons, and Harpies. One may notice how skilfully Virgil separated these from the personifications; they belong of course to a much more primitive stage of thought. All this is reached before the crossing of the lower-world rivers, and so is the

[1] A. vi. 273–81: note 273 vestibulum ante ipsum primis in faucibus Orci.
[2] Lucr. iii. 65.   [3] A. viii. 701 tristesque ex aethere Dirae.
[4] A. vi. 282–94.

next scene which is laid on the bank of the Acheron.[1] Charon is there with his ferry-boat and towards him is rushing the whole crowd of the recently dead. 'They stood there praying to be the first to make the crossing and held out their hands in longing for the further bank.' This is a picturesque setting of the old mythological idea. Charon transports now one group and now another, but some he utterly refuses. In reply to Aeneas' question the Sibyl tells him that these are the unburied dead, who have to wait a hundred years before they can be taken across: here again we clearly meet popular tradition and the definiteness of the assigned period is characteristic. This leads to the meeting with the unburied Palinurus and the Sibyl's prophecy of his coming burial (see p. 245). Not less typical of folk-lore is Charon's stern refusal to carry the living Aeneas across, until he is constrained by the sight of the golden bough. The legend of the bough itself has no parallel in Greek and Latin literature, but must represent the content of some popular idea. Indeed Norden has shown that the mistletoe (*viscus*) with which Virgil compares the golden bough, as a winter plant and an evergreen, was a symbol at once of death and of life and was considered an apotropaic against underworld demons. He has conjectured with some plausibility that it was used in the rites of Persephone and so was introduced by Virgil as the suitable gift to her and the key for admission to the lower world.

Thanks to his possession of the bough Aeneas is ferried across the river.[2] He is now on the outskirts of Tartarus,

---

[1] A. vi. 295–416; see especially 313:

> stabant orantes primi transmittere cursum
> tendebantque manus ripae ulterioris amore;
> 327 nec ripas datur horrendas et rauca fluenta
> transportare prius quam sedibus ossa quierunt;
> 391 corpora viva nefas Stygia vectare carina.

[2] A. vi. 417–547; Cerberus 417–25; Limbo 426–9; falsely condemned 430–3; suicides 434–7; victims of love 440–76; killed in war 477–547.

but not yet within the realm of the lower-world deities. Here is Cerberus, the guardian, in his cave, who has to be put to sleep with the honey-cake. In this 'suburban' region there are two divisions, inhabited by various classes of souls, who are not permitted to enter the infernal city. The first is Limbo, the abode of the souls of those who have died in infancy. Next is a region given up to those who have died a violent death, and various classes of these are specified, those falsely condemned, the suicides, the victims of love, among whom Aeneas meets Dido, and lastly and nearest the citadel, those killed in war, among whom Aeneas converses with Deiphobus. Norden has shown that all these classes are recorded in the 'traditional theology' and further that the popular belief was that such victims of violent death could not enter the realm of Tartarus until they had completed what would have been the full span of their natural life. An interesting point arises with regard to the first class of those unjustly condemned on earth. Minos is said to sit in judgement over them and, as has been seen (p. 255), his procedure is described in the terms of the Roman law-court; but it is not clear what he is doing. He does not appear to be reversing the judgement given in the upper world, but 'hearing of their life and the charges' and then assigning to them the quarter in which they should dwell. One may presume that, if he thought they were guilty of crime, they would have, when their time came, to go to Tartarus; if he found them innocent, after they had completed their span of years, they might in due course reach the Elysian fields. It should perhaps be further noted that Dido appears, not among the suicides but among the victims of love, with Phaedra and Procris—perhaps a sympathetic touch.

Aeneas and his guide have now reached the parting of

the ways;[1] the right road leads beneath the walls of Dis to Elysium, the abode of the righteous souls, the left to Tartarus, where the sinners are punished. Anchises, who is the object of Aeneas' search, will clearly be in Elysium, but Virgil, the poet, must not lose the chance of the description of Tartarus as well. His device is ingenious, yet not forced. Aeneas looks round and sees the great walls surrounded by the stream Phlegethon; there is the gate of adamant, and the iron tower guarded by Tisiphone, and the cries of the tortured victims and the clanking of their chains may be heard. Aeneas exclaims in horror and the Sibyl explains that no holy (*castus*) person such as he, may enter the threshold, but that Hecate once took her over it all, and she can tell him what is within. It is here that Rhadamanthus holds his court, and he appears to have a wider jurisdiction than Minos, for he judges all the souls of sinners and on their confessions assigns to them their punishment, which is executed by Tisiphone and her Fury sisters. A momentary opening of the gates shows the vision of Megaera and the Hydra and Tartarus stretching beyond. Then the Sibyl tells him of those who are being punished within— there are the great Homeric sinners, Tityos and Ixion and the other criminals of Greek legend, the Titans and Aloidae who assailed heaven, Salmoneus, who made himself equal to Zeus, the Lapithae, and Pirithous. And from them she turns to the sinners among ordinary men, those who had been impious to their relations, the fraudulent, the avaricious, the adulterers, the rebels, and their punishments are briefly hinted at. There again are the traitors, the bribed politicians, and the incestuous. The list is arbitrary, oddly composed and curiously interrupted by

[1] The double road, A. vi. 540–3; the walls of Dis 548–58; Rhadamanthus' judgement 566–9; Tisiphone 571–8; the sinners of legend 576–607; the ordinary sinners 608–27. For the conception of the lower world as a walled city cf. *Culex* 217 conlucent infernis moenia templis.

the description of the punishments, but it is interesting to note that here, just as afterwards in Elysium, we have at once the distinction and also the combination of the persons of legend and the persons of everyday life. We may note, too, that in this 'traditional' narrative there is no hint of an escape from Hell or a limitation to the punishments, as there is in the philosophical doctrine later expounded by Anchises.

As they pass the walls of the palace, Aeneas fixes the golden bough to the portal, as Proserpina's gift,[1] and then they pursue their way to Elysium and the 'blessed abodes'. A brief but beautiful description tells us of the fields and groves of the blessed, which know an 'ampler air' and 'sun and stars of their own', beneath which the happy souls engage in their sports and dances and songs. Then we find again the same division of the inhabitants, the mythical figures first and then the ordinary mortals. Among the former are Musaeus and Orpheus with the crowd hanging expectant on his song. They are there of course as the great prophets of old, but, though he never explicitly says so, Virgil is no doubt thinking of the Orphic mysteries, which offered man the key to the happiness of Elysium. To these he adds with that patriotic and historic twist, which becomes so clear in the last part of the book, the great Trojan ancestors, Ilus, Assaracus, and Dardanus. And then follow the lesser men, once again arranged in groups, those who died for their country, the priests and prophets, the inventors of arts, and the benefactors. As in the description of Tartarus, there is no particularization here for the obvious reason that Virgil's thoughts are on historic times in Greece and Rome, long after the day of

---

[1] Persephone's gift vi. 628–36; Elysium 637–44, note specially 640–1:
    largior hic campos aether et lumine vestit
    purpureo, solemque suum, sua sidera norunt.

Aeneas. He is anticipating here just as much as in the avowed prophecy of Anchises of the future heroes of Rome.

Under the guidance of Musaeus Aeneas finds his father in a green valley.[1] With another of Virgil's anticipating touches Anchises is brooding over the long line of his descendants, whose future souls he sees before him. This is the first hint of the metempsychosis idea, which is to play so large a part in Anchises' account of the state of the dead. Anchises greets his long-expected son and Aeneas rushes forward to embrace him but—and here we turn suddenly back to the primitive conception of the shadowy dead—the unsubstantial 'image' escapes him, just as did the wraith of Creusa;[2] the actual wording is the same. It is almost as if Virgil, conscious that he was now about to embark on more philosophic ideas, yet wished to link them on with the old popular tradition.

Anchises leads his son on to what is in effect a third division of the lower world,[3] the banks of Lethe on which are gathered 'like a swarm of bees' the souls destined to return for another life to the upper world. Let us first look at the outline of the narrative and then return for comment. Aeneas questions Anchises and asks who these people are and receives the famous philosophical account of the life in the underworld, which must later be examined carefully. And then in the spirit of prophecy Anchises adapts his explanation to the thought of his descendants, which was in his mind when Aeneas arrived and unrolls the great pageant of the heroes of Rome, from the Alban kings and the first kings of Rome, through the heroes of the Republic, to Julius, Augustus, and the young Marcellus.

[1] Mythical figures A. vi. 645–55, 667–8; ordinary mortals 660–5; search for Anchises 666–78; the meeting of Aeneas and Anchises 679–702.

[2] A. ii. 791–4.

[3] The banks of Lethe and the souls A. vi. 703–9; Anchises' explanation 710–51; the heroes of Rome 752–892; Aeneas' return 893–901.

Historical order is not fully observed, but links are found where they come easiest. Augustus comes in as the direct descendant of Romulus and the young Marcellus—in a passage perhaps added later—as the offspring of the great Marcellus of Sicily. And so when Aeneas has been conducted over all he is dismissed again to the upper world, through the mysterious ivory gate, by which the false dreams come to men.

In all this great passage of culmination there are many interesting points of detail, but three marked characteristics stand out. In the first place there is a conspicuous change of atmosphere and idea. Hitherto the pictures of the lower world have been based on popular belief and literary legend and the fate of the souls is regarded as fixed and permanent. There is no hint that the prisoners in Tartarus will ever cease to be punished, no suggestion that the dwellers in Elysium are anything but permanent inhabitants, no expectation that any of them will ever come back to earth in another life. But now we are plunged— abruptly, but so delicately that the transition is hardly perceptible—into the more philosophical notion of metempsychosis. Here on the banks of Lethe are gathered the souls, which, having already spent one life in the world above, are now waiting their turn to enter another human body, and indeed their destiny is already shaped and it is already ordained who they shall be in this second existence. The ideas are as yet still concrete and popular, in so far as the mysteries which taught these doctrines were popular, and they lead up, as it were, to the more strictly philosophic account in the speech of Anchises.

Secondly, Virgil uses the *motif* of metempsychosis for patriotic purposes. All these souls, waiting for their new life, are the royal descendants of Aeneas or the great heroes of historical Rome, just as in the first vision of the Elysian

fields the Trojan ancestors had their place. It might perhaps be thought, from a modern point of view, that there
was a certain bathos in this and that the idea is narrowed.
But it must be remembered that to Virgil the thought of
Rome was always closely bound up with his religion and
especially with its deepest ideas. As has been seen (p. 233),
his highest conception of fate, in which it is at once world-
wide and closely linked with the will of Iuppiter and the
gods, manifests itself in the destiny of Rome. It may be a
defect in Virgil, the sign of the want of a sufficiently broad
outlook, but both here and there the manifestation of a religious idea in the history of Rome is immensely characteristic.

Lastly, we advance from a vague metempsychosis to the
far more precise idea of the meaning and purpose of life
and the sojourn in the lower world, which is set out in the
famous words of Anchises.[1] The mysteries and several
strains of philosophy are here mingled and the result is a
picture which, eclectic as is its material, is Virgil's own
vision. The passage must be examined in detail. The
basis of the theory enunciated by Anchises is that of the
Stoic *anima mundi*, the world-spirit, present in every part of
the universe.[2] This is clearly set out in the opening section
of the speech, and may be compared with the famous
passage in the *Georgics* about the instinct of the bees.[3] 'By
these tokens and following these indications some have
said that the bees have a part of the divine mind and a
draught from the heavenly source; for god, they say, goes
through all lands and the tracts of the sea and the depths of

---

[1] Anchises' speech 724–51.
[2] The world-spirit A. vi. 724–9. Dieterich, op. cit., p. 153, compares
Orphic cosmogonical passages in Ap. Rhod. i. 496 ff. and Eur. *Melanippe*, fr.
484, but both of these are more nearly akin to the traditional cosmogony of
the pre-Socratics (e.g. the idea of the separation of the elements) and lack
the Stoic idea of the nourishing spirit, which is the keynote of Virgil's
description.   [3] G. iv. 219–27.

heaven. Hence come flocks and herds, men and all the race of wild beasts; each at his birth draws the thin breath of life.' The last three lines may be held over for the moment.

Then follows the result of this in human life: 'all have the "fiery vigour" (notice *igneus*) and the heavenly source in their seeds, but their sinful bodies impede them and earthly limbs and members due to death weaken them.'[1] The contact with the body tends to blur the pure ethereal fire. To this combination of soul and body are due 'their fears and desires, their joys and griefs, and shut in the darkness of their blind prison they cannot see the light'. Here we have the first touch of Pythagoreanism, mingled with pure Stoicism, the famous doctrine of the body as the soul's prison-house (σῶμα σῆμα), which plays so large a part in Plato's *Phaedo*. But though the element is alien, it is not in any way inconsistent with Stoicism.

Then comes the consequence of this continuation in the after-life.[2] 'When at the last day life departs, yet not all evil nor all bodily pests leave the wretched souls, but it must needs be that much long hardening in them festers in wondrous wise. And so they are plied with punishment and pay the penalty for their former evils. Some are stretched out to the empty winds, others have the engendered sin washed from them beneath the vast sea or burned away by fire; we each suffer our own life as shades.' Stoicism conceived the progress of the soul as a gradual rising to the upper ether from which it started, through the grades below and imagined something like a purgation

---

[1] The earthly life A. vi. 728–34.

[2] The purification of the souls A. vi. 735–43. For purification by 'hanging up', cf. Plat. *Gorg.* 525 c ἀνηρτημένους ἐκεῖ ἐν ᾍδου ἐν τῷ Δεσμωτηρίῳ, and the account in Diog. Laert. viii. 21 of Pythagoras' κατάβασις: φησὶ Δὲ Ἱερώνυμος κατελθόντα αὐτὸν εἰς ᾍδου τὴν μὲν Ἡσιόδου ψυχὴν ἰΔεῖν πρὸς κιόνι χαλκῷ Δεδεμένην καὶ τρίζουσαν, τὴν Δὲ Ὁμήρου κρεμαμένην ἀπὸ Δένδρου καὶ ὄφεις περὶ αὐτὴν ἀνθ' ὧν εἶπον περὶ θεῶν. For purification by water cf. the Orphic κατάβασις, fr. 154 ἐν τῷ Ἀχέροντι καθαίρονται (Dieterich, op. cit., p. 154).

taking place in the grosser atmosphere near the earth (ἀήρ), from which the soul reached the sphere of the stars and so the upper heaven. If we turn back now to the *Georgics* passage,[1] this doctrine is clearly and correctly enunciated: 'to this [the god which is in all things] all are restored and brought back after dissolution, nor is there any place for death, but living they fly to join the stars, and then reach to the lofty sky.' Why did Virgil desert this orthodox explanation here? For two reasons. Firstly, following popular beliefs he had placed the abode of the departed below the earth and it was impossible to reconcile with this the idea of the souls rising to the stars and the high heaven, and secondly, that this vision of the souls was to lead up to the very concrete picture of the Roman heroes; he must, therefore, work away from the strictly philosophical and almost physical notion of the soul, which was his inheritance from the Stoics, towards a more personal conception which would serve his purpose later on. This we can see him doing with consummate skill. He turns from the Stoic idea to that of the mysteries and indeed to that of popular belief; the purgation from evil elements becomes the punishment for sin. But the change is not yet complete and we have the curious idea—not of course inconsistent with Roman notions of *lustratio*—of the purification of the souls by wind or water or fire—an idea for which we know no literary precedent, but which once again may have come to Virgil from some of the traditional 'theologies'. And then we come back again to the very personal conception and to Roman phraseology in the famous words *quisque suos patimur manes*, which must be briefly discussed. The view which seems recently to have won most favour, and is supported by Norden (p. 33), is that the *manes* here are the Greek δαίμων, which is often in Graeco-Roman

[1] G. iv. 225-7.

writers equated with the *genius*. Reference is made to Plato's *Phaedo* (107d, 113d) where it is said that the Δαίμων assigned to him in life leads every man at his death to 'a place where the soul suffers many things' and this is borne out by a passage in Plutarch (*de Gen. Socr.* 22, 592 b–c). The idea is further complicated by a note in Servius on this passage in Virgil, in which he explains that at birth every man has two *genii*, one which exhorts him to good, the other to evil; the *manes* are thus the two *genii*. This looks like a later explanation, after the genius—Δαίμων assimilation had been established, in order to explain the use of the plural *manes*. It is not of course impossible that there may have been some Greek conception in Virgil's mind, but I find it hard to believe in view of the conclusions in previous examinations (p. 256) that Virgil's use of *manes* is strictly in accordance with Roman ideas, he should have used it differently here. And it is far more natural that this line should be explained in accordance with Virgil's normal use of the word. It has been seen that *manes*, which originally denoted the collective and undistinguished mass of the dead, came to be employed to denote the dead spirit of the individual and that Virgil has very many instances of this usage. So I believe it is here; 'we each of us suffer his own dead spirit', meaning 'we each of us suffer our existence as spirits',[1] much as a Pythagorean, holding the doctrine of the body as a prison might say of living men, *quisque suum patimur corpus*, 'we all suffer our life in the body'. This is in effect the view of Warde Fowler (*R.E.*, p. 386), who would translate 'each individual of us must endure his own individual ghosthood'. We may perhaps further note that Virgil, as if conscious

[1] This view is supported by Servius' first note on the passage: supplicia quae sunt apud manes, ut si quis dicat 'iudicium patimur' et significat ea quae in iudicio continentur. So Dieterich, p. 155, who compares Statius, *Theb.* viii. 84: at tibi quos, inquit, manis, qui limite praeceps | non licito per inane ruis?

of the difficulty of the use of the plural of the individual spirit, has preferred to write *patimur* rather than *patitur*.

Virgil has thus returned to the concrete and Roman conception which he needed for the great pageant he was about to describe. This is maintained in the opening sentence of the last section of the speech, which deals with the purgation in Elysium.[1] This sentence, too, has been the subject of much discussion and contention, but I have little doubt that the right view is that which regards *et pauci laeta arva tenemus* as a parenthesis. There are in Elysium two classes of souls, those who have undergone the first purgation and now are allowed a sojourn in Elysium, that by its influence they may be further purged before they return to earth for another life, and the few who are permitted to stay permanently in the blessed fields.[2] These would be those who have accomplished the whole round of their lives in the world above and their purgation below—Pindar's souls who have reached the tower of Kronos—and the few exceptional souls of the great heroes and saints who need no further earthly life, those in fact who were described in the earlier picture of Elysium. And if we ask why Virgil refers to them thus parenthetically here, I think the answer is a dramatic necessity, that it would be manifestly inappropriate that Anchises himself should be one of the souls waiting for a further probationary life. So far we are again in a concrete world with a legendary picture before us; and then quite suddenly comes a plunge right back into the soul-idea and the Stoic view of *divinae particula animae* with which the

[1] The purgation in Elysium 743–51; cf. Plat. *Rep.* 615, Phaedr. 249.
[2] For the period of a thousand years (A. vi. 748) as the time of purgation before the return to a second life see Plat. *Rep.* 615 a. In *Phaedr.* 248 e the period of the κύκλος is put at 10,000 years, but it is reduced to 3,000 for the philosophers. In *Phaedo* 114 b the holy, like the *pauci* here, go up at once to the καθαρὰ οἴκησις.

whole speech started; 'Long ages will take away the fester-
ing sore and leave untainted the ethereal sense and the
flame of pure air'[1]—the soul will be cleansed of the im-
purities which have gathered round it in the earthly life
and will be once more the spark of πνεῦμα πυρωᾶές, which
was implanted in the body at first. It is an audacious
welding of philosophy and mythology which at once
emphasizes and yet by its art conceals the mingling of
inconsistent ideas which is really latent throughout, but
which it is important to disentangle in analysis.

Here, if anywhere, we have Virgil's own belief as to the
fate of the individual soul and the cycle of its existence. It
is not a consistent philosophy, it is not a clear-cut mythological picture, but is not this blending of abstract thought
and concrete picture characteristic at all times of the religious mind? It is trying to conceive things which are
beyond the ken of its own experience, and is forced back
into a kind of visualization in the lines and colours which
it knows. The medieval conception of Hell and Purgatory
and Heaven inherited much both from the pagan 'theology',
which lay behind Virgil's account and from the philosophy
which he has assimilated to it, and when Dante chose
Virgil as his guide in the lower world it was not merely
a matter of literary 'imitation', it was the admission that
his own highest thoughts of the life after death must of
necessity be cast in the same mould.

This protracted examination of Virgil's statements or
implications as to the nature of the soul and its fate after
death has revealed him once more as the poet and the
eclectic. He chooses for the purpose of his poetry at one
time one conception and at another another; and with that

---

[1] A. vi. 745 donec longa dies perfecto temporis orbe
              concretam exemit labem, purumque relinquit
              aetherium sensum atque aurai simplicis ignem.

antiquarian spirit, which was so deeply engrained in him, he seems to have wished to embody them all. There is the idea of the spirit enclosed in the tomb, and the ghost-notion closely allied with it; there is the conception of the spirit-world elaborated with the contributions of traditional 'theology', of mythology, and of philosophy. Nor is there any attempt to reconcile inconsistencies or to preserve one underlying conception throughout. It is welded together by his imagination, and the greatness of that imagination is tested by the absence of any sense of inconsistency on the part of the reader. This is all characteristic of the Virgil we have recognized throughout the inquiry, indeed it is the most consummate instance of his art. And yet here, almost alone, we feel justified in claiming that we have some glimpse of Virgil's own beliefs. There is a depth and a sense of conviction in his picture of the lower world in the sixth *Aeneid* which makes it stand by itself and the summing up of it all in the speech of Anchises leaves one with an irresistible sense that there, if ever, we have the thoughts of Virgil himself. In one other sphere, and one only, is there anything like the same assurance, and that is in the conception of Iuppiter and of his relation to fate.

B. *Cult of the Dead*

One of the most vexing and vexed problems in the study of Roman religion is the question whether the Romans worshipped the dead, and whether ancestor-worship played any part in their religious life. The solution of this problem turns no doubt largely on inquiries which do not come into question here, such as the significance of the Lar and the intention of the festival of the Compitalia, and no answer derived from Virgil's poems could be decisive on the general problem. But an effort can be made to clear up the ideas expressed by Virgil, to trace the origin of his conceptions and so perhaps to gain some notion as to the prevalent beliefs of his contemporaries.

It must be remembered in the first place that the two elements, both in Greek and in Roman cult-worship, were offerings on the one hand and prayer on the other; these two elements may be taken as the test of worship. Offerings are not in themselves evidence of the worship of a being conceived of as divine. At the Parentalia, for instance, the festival of the dead in February, Ovid tells us that 'the Manes seek but little gifts; affection takes the place of a rich gift',[1] and he enumerates wreaths and offerings of corn and salt and bread dipped in wine and violets as constituting the normal gifts. Such offerings may in origin have been intended to sustain the strength of the dead, and Ovid clearly regards them rather as marks of honour than as offerings to deities. This conception is borne out by the culmination of the festival in the Caristia, a love-feast of the family at which the dead were thought to be present. *Parentatio*, the offering to the dead, is not in the full sense *sacrificium*. But where blood-offerings, sacrificed on an altar, are found together with prayer to the object of the cult, there can hardly be any doubt that there is worship of a divine being in the full sense.

If we turn to the inheritance from Greece, it is clear that in classical times, at least, there was no general worship of the dead and no ancestor-cult; the dead were even less regarded in normal religious thought than they were at Rome. Only at the Anthesteria do they emerge into cult in the notion of the temporary return of the spirits of the dead to the upper world, and at the end of the festival they are dismissed with the formula θύραζε κῆρες, οὐκέτ' Ἀνθεστήρια, which is singularly reminiscent of the *Manes exite paterni*

---

[1] Ov. *Fast.* ii. 535 parva petunt Manes: pietas pro divite grata est munere.

of the Roman Lemuria (see p. 242). But here there is no trace of worship. On the other hand there are three elements in Greek practice which seem to have had considerable weight with Virgil. In the first place the Greeks worshipped the lower world gods, such as Zeus Meilichios, Pluto himself, and in connexion with the mysteries, Persephone or Kore. Secondly, inherited from a dim past was the worship of local heroes, which was still vital in classical times and often supplied themes for the Greek tragedians. Such a hero-cult would naturally have special attractions for the author of a great heroic poem. Lastly, Rome was by Virgil's day in touch with the Hellenistic ideas of the deification of the dead. These were undoubtedly one of the main inspirations of the Caesar-cult, and that they had penetrated into the private life of Roman intellectual circles is clear from Cicero's half-serious proposal to erect a temple to his daughter Tullia. There can be little doubt that the prevalence of such notions made Virgil's treatment of the dead heroes seem less strange to his readers than they would have appeared a century earlier.

In the light of such antecedents Virgil's attitude may be examined. That Virgil recognized the worship of the *di inferi*, the named gods of the underworld, there is no doubt, even though the instances are not very many. The most important passage in this connexion is certainly that at the end of the fourth book of the *Aeneid*,[1] where Dido, in reality preparing her own funeral pyre, professes to be renewing a sacrifice to Iuppiter Stygius.[2] The details are interesting and important: Dido bids her nurse summon her sister Anna: 'bid her sprinkle her body with river-water, and bring with her sheep and the offerings of atonement

---

[1] A. iv. 632 ff.
[2] A. iv. 638 sacra Iovi Stygio, quae rite incepta paravi,
        perficere est animus finemque imponere curis.

ordained. Thus let her come and do thou thyself wreath thy temples with the holy fillet.'[1] Though the cult of Iuppiter Stygius itself may be derived from a Greek origin, Virgil is using the language of Roman ritual. There is the lustration of purification by water before the sacrifice, the offering is described as *piacula*, and the sheep are doubtless the black sheep which are prescribed as the right offering in a *piaculum* to the lower world gods in the sixth book.[2] Such a sacrifice might often have been made to the powers of the underworld in Rome, and there is a close parallel in Lucretius' description of the readiness of those who profess philosophic views to take to the old ways of religion, when they are in trouble: 'they make offering to the dead and slaughter black sheep and send their gifts to the divine Manes',[3] though Lucretius goes farther than Virgil in the identification of the underworld gods with the spirits of the dead. A similar offering occurs in the sixth book, when Aeneas 'prepares the altar of night worship for the Stygian king, and places on the flames the flesh of whole oxen';[4] at the same time he slays a barren cow to Proserpina.[5] There is no record of a sacrifice to Hecate, but she is once invoked for aid by Dido,[6] and again by Aeneas at his sacrifice before entering the lower world.[7] It is to be noted that in both these passages Hecate is combined with the Greek Erebos

[1] A. iv. 635 dic corpus properet fluviali spargere lympha,
et pecudes secum et monstrata piacula ducat.
sic veniat, tuque ipsa pia tege tempora vitta.
[2] A. vi. 153 duc nigras pecudes: ea prima piacula sunto.
[3] Lucr. iii. 51   parentant
et nigras mactant pecudes et manibu' divis
inferias mittunt.
[4] A. vi. 252 tum Stygio regi nocturnas incohat aras
et solida imponit taurorum viscera flammis.
[5] A. vi. 251 sterilemque tibi, Proserpina, vaccam.
[6] A. iv. 510 ter centum tonat ore deos, Erebumque Chaosque,
tergeminamque Hecaten, tria virginis ora Dianae.
[7] A. vi. 247 voce vocans Hecaten caeloque Ereboque potentem.

and in one also with Chaos, and that Hecate is definitely thought of as the lower-world counterpart of the Greek Artemis. There is thus sufficient evidence of the worship of the *di inferi* with Greek associations, but with appropriate Roman ritual.

But the worship of lower-world deities does not affect the question of the cult of the spirits of the dead themselves. Nor can any evidence be derived from Virgil's use of the word *manes* for the collective dead. There is no instance of their worship, though Turnus in the agony of approaching death might appear to make prayer to them: 'do you, Manes, be gracious to me, since the will of the gods above is turned from me.'[1] This might be interpreted as prayer to the collective dead, but the contrast with the *di superi* makes it far more probable that *manes* is used here as the equivalent of *di inferi*, which, as it has been seen (p. 260), is not infrequently the case in Virgil.

The crucial instances for the cult of the dead occur in Virgil in connexion with funerals and rites at tombs, and these contain, as will be seen, a perplexing mixture of the Roman funeral rites and the ritual of *parentatio* with Greek hero-worship, which often makes interpretation very difficult. We may deal with some minor instances first and take to begin with an extreme Greek case. In the battle in the tenth book Aeneas takes prisoner several youths 'in order to sacrifice them as offerings to the shades and drench the flames of the pyre with the blood of captives';[2] in the next book he sends them for this purpose with the body of Pallas.[3] The idea here is wholly un-Roman, for

[1] A. xii. 646   vos o mihi, Manes,
         este boni, quoniam superis aversa voluntas.
[2] A. x. 519 viventis rapit, inferias quos immolet umbris
         captivoque rogi perfundat sanguine flammas.
[3] A. xi. 81 vinxerat et post terga manus, quos mitteret umbris
         inferias, caeso sparsurus sanguine flammas.

human sacrifice is unknown at any rate in the developed Roman religion,[1] and the passage is a deliberate reminiscence of the sacrifice of captives at the pyre of Patroclus.[2]

At the other end of the scale we may place an instance where the funeral ritual is almost, if not quite, wholly Roman, the description of the general burial of the Trojan dead in *Aeneid* xi.[3] Aeneas and Tarchon, the Etruscan chief, 'built pyres on the winding shore';[4] all bring the bodies of their dead and the pyre is lighted. 'Clad in their shining arms thrice they ran round the kindled piles, thrice they circled the mournful funeral flame on horseback and wailed aloud.'[5] Then they throw on the blazing heap the spoils of the enemy and the armour of the dead. So far it is a typical Roman military funeral, and we may note as specially Roman the distinction, noted by Servius, between the *pyra* (185), the pyre before it is lighted, the *rogus* (189), the burning pyre, and the *bustum* mentioned later (201), the burnt-out heap; similarly the use of the ritual word *lustro* (190) to describe the procession round the pyre. And then there follows a description of the sacrifice: 'many bodies of oxen are slain around, and they kill and cast into the flames bristly sows and sheep ravaged from all the countryside.'[6] Here we have a blood-offering such

---

[1] It is fair to note that Servius on *Aen.* x. 519 says that such human sacrifice at a tomb was once the custom at Rome, but that in a more humane age the gladiatorial show in honour of the dead was substituted. Without accepting this particular theory, I am inclined to believe that in primitive Italy human sacrifice was not unknown.

[2] *Il.* xxiii. 175.

[3] A. xi. 183–202.

[4] A. xi. 184 iam pater Aeneas, iam curvo in litore Tarchon
        constituere pyras.

[5] A. xi. 188 ter circum accensos cincti fulgentibus armis
        decurrere rogos, ter maestum funeris ignem
        lustravere in equis ululatusque ore dedere.

[6] A. xi. 197 multa boum circa mactantur corpora Morti,
        saetigerosque sues raptasque ex omnibus agris
        in flammam iugulant pecudes.

as is made to a deity and it has the three elements of the *suovetaurilia*, the most complete sacrifice known to Roman ritual. To whom is it made? Is it to the *di inferi* or to the *manes* in general or to the spirits of the individual dead? As if conscious of the difficulty Virgil equivocates and says that the offering was made to 'Death', a personification, which never in Rome attained to the rank of a deity. Virgil seems almost to be shelving the problem which we are attempting to solve, and we must pass to certain fuller descriptions of ritual, which may bring us nearer to an answer. We have one complete account of a funeral and three of commemorative rites at tombs, all of which must be carefully examined.

The funeral is that of Misenus the trumpeter, whose due burial was, as has been seen (p. 244), a condition of Aeneas' admission to the lower world.[1] The Trojans, at Aeneas' bidding, repair to the woods to cut down logs to make a great pyre, on which to cremate the corpse,[2] a pyre, which Virgil in an odd phrase, which must be fully discussed later, describes, if the text be right, as 'the altar of the tomb'. The preparations being thus complete, the Trojans start to pay the last rites to 'the ashes that know no thanks'.[3] They build the pyre, weaving into it the funeral cypress and adorning it with 'shining armour'; they wash the corpse in warm water from caldrons and anoint it, lamenting the while.[4] The corpse is then lifted on to the bier and

[1] A. vi. 175-235.

[2] A. vi. 176 tum iussa Sibyllae, | haud mora, festinant flentes aramque sepulcri | (*MRb²cπ* and the MSS. of Servius, sepulcro *cett.*) congerere arboribus caeloque educere certant.

[3] A. vi. 213 cineri ingrato suprema ferebant. *Cinis* is used proleptically of what the corpse was to become, but implies, as it often does in its combination with *manes* or *umbra* in Virgil, the spirit of the dead. *Ingratus* is used of the general inability of the dead to express the gratitude, which their spirits might feel, another queer phrase, for which there is a close parallel in *Copa* 35 quid cineri ingrato servas bene olentia serta?; cf. also A. x. 827 teque parentum | manibus et cineri, si qua est ea cura, remitto.   [4] A. vi. 214 ff.

covered with bright garments, and the bier carried and placed on the pyre. Next they set light to the pyre with torches held beneath it, while they turn away their faces 'after the manner of their fathers',[1] probably, as Norden explains, so as not to risk seeing the ghost, as it escapes from the body. On the pyre are burnt offerings of incense, the 'sacred feast' (*dapes*)[2] and bowls of oil.[3] When the flames have died down, the relics are washed in wine, and the bones collected and placed in a brazen urn.[4] Finally, Aeneas purifies his companions from the taint of association with the dead by a lustration of 'pure water' scattered over them 'with a branch of fruitful olive',[5] and speaks the words of farewell to the spirit of Misenus. Then he heaps a great barrow over the ashes and places on it the hero's tools, his oar, and his trumpet, 'beneath a lofty mountain, which even now is called Misenus from him and keeps its name for ever through the ages'.[6]

The description of the burial is full and elaborate and shows Virgil's characteristic fondness for details of ritual. Some of it is undoubtedly Greek and is modelled on famous descriptions in Homer, such as that of the burial of Patroclus,[7] but distinctively Italian features may also be noted,

---

[1] A. vi. 223   subiectam more parentum
                   aversi tenuere facem.

[2] A. vi. 224   congesta cremantur
                   turea dona, dapes, fuso crateres olivo.

[3] Servius notes that whereas to the gods the oil was poured out in libation, in offerings to the dead it was thrown on to the pyre in the jars.   [4] A. vi. 226–8.

[5] A. vi. 229 idem ter socios pura circumtulit unda
                   spargens rore levi et ramo felicis olivae,
                   lustravitque viros dixitque novissima verba.
cf. Servius, *ad loc.* circumtulit, purgavit, antiquum verbum est.

[6] A. vi. 232 at pius Aeneas ingenti mole sepulcrum
                   imponit suaque arma viro remumque tubamque.
arma here must be taken in the general sense of 'implements of his trade, *remumque tubamque* being in apposition; it cannot be his armour, for that had already been burned on the pyre.

[7] Norden notices details of correspondence.

such as the lustration of the living at the end and the speaking of 'the last words'. Is there evidence of any worship of the dead Misenus as a divine being? Applying the tests suggested above, there is in the first place clearly no trace of prayer to the dead. The question turns on the offerings and the 'altar' and the problem is rather complex. The offerings of incense and olive oil are gifts to the dead, such as might be made at any *parentatio*;[1] what are the *dapes*? Again, they may well be such simple offerings as cakes and honey, given to honour the dead. But some critics have interpreted the word in its more formal ritual sense as a 'sacred banquet' and connected it with the Sibyl's instructions to 'bring black sheep';[2] we shall then have an offering that suggested sacrifice to lower world deities. But the Sibyl expressly says that the black sheep are to be *piacula*; this is a word which can hardly be applied to the offering on the tomb and it is more likely that it was to be a preliminary expiation to the lower world powers for the pollution caused by the unburied corpse. And even if the Sibyl's words do refer to the *dapes* on the pyre, they need not be an offering to Misenus, but to the under-world powers in general. The question of the 'altar' is complicated by the uncertainty of the text. If the dative, *aramque sepulcro*, be read, the 'altar for the tomb' is probably an altar erected in front of the tomb, as it is described in the passages which have next to be considered. If we adopt the genitive *sepulcri*, which has the authority of good manuscripts and Servius' note, it seems to imply that the tomb is itself an altar. Here Servius comes to our aid and explains that the original meaning of *ara* is 'a place where a fire is made'[3] which afterwards by association acquired a

[1] A. vi. 224; see p. 288, n. 2.
[2] A. vi. 153 duc nigras pecudes; ea prima piacula sunto.
[3] Servius ad *Aen*. vi. 177: pyram dixit, quae in modum arae construi lignis

religious sense: *ara sepulcri* in that case need not mean more than 'the pyre'. But this explanation sounds a little far-fetched and it may well be that Virgil did intend to describe the pyre itself as an 'altar' in the full sense. The significance of this must be reserved until after an examination of the other passages; it may be said here that the description of the funeral of Misenus does not necessarily imply worship of his spirit, but might easily be interpreted so as to indicate it.

We must pass now to the three main passages describing tomb-ritual. The first of these is, as it were, a half-way house between burial and anniversary celebrations like that of the *parentatio*, and describes the ceremonies at the tomb of the re-buried Polydorus. 'And so we renew the funeral for Polydorus, and a vast pile of earth is heaped on the mound; there stood *the altars for the Manes*, gloomy with black fillets and dark cypress, and all around the Ilian women with their hair loosened according to the rite. We bring bowls foaming with warm milk, and *platters of sacred blood*, and we lay the spirit in the tomb and call on the dead aloud for the last time.'[1] The ritual is that of a funeral and closely resembles the rites at the burial of Misenus. There are the simple bowls of milk and the last call to the dead with the explanation here that the purpose is to 'lay the spirit in the tomb'. An added and fully Italian detail is that of the loosening of the hair of the women, the avoidance, that is, of a knot which might

solebat . . . aram, quae ante sepulcrum fieri consuevit, intellegere non possumus. Cf. Norden on the passage.

[1] A. iii. 62–8 ergo instauramus Polydoro funus, et ingens
    aggeritur tumulo tellus; stant manibus arae
    caeruleis maestae vittis atraque cupresso,
    et circum Iliades crinem de more solutae;
    inferimus tepido spumantia cymbia lacte
    sanguinis et sacri pateras, animamque sepulcro
    condimus et magna supremum voce ciemus.

impede the working of sacred influences. Once again there is no trace of prayer, but there is a blood-offering and there are altars described here as 'altars to the Manes'.

The second passage describes the worship paid by Andromache at a cenotaph to Hector which she had erected in Epirus: 'I started from the harbour', says Aeneas, 'leaving my fleet and the shore, just when outside the city in a grove by the waters of a feigned Simois Andromache was offering to the ashes the annual feast and the gifts of mourning, and was summoning the Manes to the tomb of Hector, an empty tomb which she had consecrated with green turfs and by it *two altars*, a source of tears.'[1] Here the occasion is clearly an annual offering at the tomb of the dead, which is exactly the form of the private *parentatio*. The 'gifts' (*dapes* once again) may well be the simple meal offered to sustain the dead—there is no suggestion of blood-offering here—and the summoning of the *manes* is probably not a repetition of the last cry to the dead, but the calling up of the spirit to take the offering prepared for him. So far all might be Roman ritual, but then again come the altars, and this time Virgil specially states that there were two of them. The same problem is raised again.

The fullest description of ritual at a tomb is of course that of the rites at Anchises' grave in the fifth book.[2] Here again there is much to remind one of the simple Roman *parentatio*. The ceremony takes place on the anniversary of the burial of Anchises: 'the cycle of a year is completed, its months passed, since we buried in the earth the remains and bones

---

[1] A. iii. 300 progredior portu classis et litora linquens,
sollemnis cum forte dapes et tristia dona
ante urbem in luco falsi Simoentis ad undam
libabat cineri Andromache manisque vocabat
Hectoreum ad tumulum, viridi quem caespite inanem
et geminas, causam lacrimis, sacraverat aras.

[2] A. v. 42–103, 759–78.

of my divine father and consecrated the altars of mourning.'[1] Later Aeneas says that wherever he might be, 'he would celebrate the annual vow and the solemn rites in due order and would heap the altars with their due gifts',[2] and prays 'may he be willing that I should celebrate these rites for him year by year, when I have founded my city in the temple dedicated to him'.[3] The offerings, too, as described in one passage,[4] are such as could be given in simple commemoration at the tomb of a dead relative, wine, milk, and flowers, though the intrusion of blood among them here as, at the tomb of Polydorus, strikes a different note, which is emphasized in later descriptions. The spirit of the dead again is summoned, as at the tomb of Hector, to drink the offering, and we have the interesting suggestion that the *manes* are let out from Acheron to come and receive their gifts.[5] Aeneas' greeting to the shade of Anchises is once more in the spirit of the Roman greeting to the dead at the tomb: 'Hail, revered parent, once again: hail, ye ashes of him I rescued in vain, soul and shade of my father.'[6] It is greeting and no word of prayer as to a divine person. And then there follows an incident

[1] A. v. 46 annuus exactis completur mensibus orbis,
ex quo reliquias divinique ossa parentis
condidimus terra maestasque sacravimus aras.

[2] A. v. 53 annua vota tamen sollemnisque ordine pompas
exsequerer strueremque suis altaria donis.

[3] A. v. 59   haec me sacra quotannis
urbe velit posita templis sibi ferre dicatis.

[4] A. v. 77 hic duo rite mero libans carchesia Baccho
fundit humi, duo lacte novo, duo sanguine sacro,
purpureosque iacit flores.
  Note that the offerings here are double.

[5] A. v. 98 vinaque fundebat pateris animamque vocabat
Anchisae magni manisque Acheronte remissos.

[6] A. v. 80 salve, sancte parens, iterum salvete, recepti
nequiquam cineres animaeque umbraeque paternae.

(I take *recepti* as a genitive and *recepti nequiquam* to refer to Aeneas' rescue of Anchises from Troy—but it is a strange expression.)

very characteristic of Roman ideas. A snake appears and winds its way among the offerings and tastes them and then disappears again into the tomb.[1] Aeneas doubts whether it is 'the genius of the place or the attendant spirit of his father';[2] he would perhaps have been nearest the truth if he had combined the ideas and taken it to be the 'genius of his father'. The genius of the paterfamilias was at all times at Rome typified by the household snake, and the *manes* of the dead are often in reflective times, though not in the earliest period, identified with the genius of the living. The snake was indeed the spirit of Anchises which came to receive the offerings.

Yet in spite of these clear traces of the survival of Roman ideas in this anniversary ceremony at the tomb of Anchises, it is more deeply tinged with the Greek conception of the hero-cult than any of the tomb-rites, which have hitherto been considered. Aeneas addresses his father as *sancte parens*,[3] and the epithet is repeated at the end of the games celebrated to 'his holy father'. The epithet can, as has been seen (p. 77), be applied to living persons in the sense of 'chaste', 'pure', but here it has more naturally the meaning of 'divine' as applied to a person of more than mortal holiness, and this is brought out by the use of the adjective *divinus*,[4] which is unmistakable. Anchises is not quite thought of as deified, but as having attained in death to the sanctity of a hero. This idea is brought out by the twice-repeated description of the altars at the tomb as *altaria*,[5] a word used, according to Servius,[6] only of altars to the *di*

[1] A. v. 84–93.
[2] A. v. 95 incertus geniumne loci famulumne parentis
        esse putet.
[3] A. v. 80; see p. 292, n. 6; A. v. 603 hac celebrata tenus sancto certamina patri.
[4] A. v. 47 divinique ossa parentis.
[5] A. v. 54 strueremque suis altaria donis, 93 depasta altaria liquit.
[6] Serv. *ad* E. v. 66 novimus enim aras et dis esse superis et inferis conse-

superi, and not in the more general sense of *arae*. In two passages, too, the offerings are such as could not be made to a dead human being at the grave, but imply a more august divinity. Aeneas tells his followers at the outset that their Sicilian host, Acestes, has promised two oxen for each ship and bids them bring their Penates and those of Acestes to the festival[1]—another mark of its solemnity. And so, when the sacrifice is made, the offering is two sheep, two pigs, and two black heifers,[2] the *suovetaurilia* with its adaptation in colour to a lower-world divinity, and Aeneas' sacrifice is deliberately described as 'the honour paid to his father'.[3] Still more significant is Aeneas' vow that when he has founded his city he will celebrate the annual rites in a 'dedicated temple',[4] and even before he leaves Sicily, he not only founds the great temple to Venus of Eryx, but 'assigns to the tomb of Anchises a priest and a sacred grove'.[5] These are undoubtedly the mark of a hero-cult, and indeed they are so near to the cult of one of the *di superi*, as Servius observes, that one wonders whether Aeneas' establishment of the worship of his father is not intended to suggest Augustus' cult of the Divus Iulius. Lastly, we may notice that the funeral games, which occupy the greater part of the fifth book, though they had

cratas; altaria vero esse superorum tantum deorum, and on A. v. 54 ponit autem altaria quae superorum deorum sunt, et hoc ideo quia Anchises iam deus est. The last explanation goes too far; Reisch (P.W., s.v. *ara*) is inclined to regard *altaria* as a mere poetic synonym for *arae*.

[1] A. v. 61   bina boum vobis Troia generatus Acestes
        dat numero capita in navis; adhibete Penatis
        et patrios epulis et quos colit hospes Acestes.

[2] A. v. 96   caedit binas de more bidentis
        totque sues, totidem nigrantis terga iuvencos.

    Note that both in this and in the previous instance the offerings are again double.

[3] A. v. 94 inceptos genitori instaurat honores.

[4] A. v. 59; see p. 292, n. 3.

[5] A. v. 760   tumuloque sacerdos
    ac lucus late sacer additur Anchiseo.

been adopted as a Roman custom, are undoubtedly of Greek origin, and Virgil's model is of course the games in *Iliad* xxiii to the dead Patroclus.

Thus in the cult of Anchises we seem to see a deliberate and skilful blending of Roman ideas and practices with the Greek hero-cult, which implied a far more definite conception of the divine character of the dead person. It is all done with caution and so that it seems to make a consistent whole and it may be noticed here, that though offerings are full and worthy of the highest deity, yet, except in the vague 'let us pray for winds',[1] which might be addressed to any of the heavenly or lower powers, there is no suggestion of prayer to the dead for blessings to the living. Once again there is the puzzle of the altars, intensified here by the use of the word *altaria*.

Besides these four important passages in the *Aeneid* there is one more Virgilian tomb-rite which stands by itself, but must be considered together with them, that for the deified Daphnis in the fifth *Eclogue*.[2] If the parallel of Iulius Caesar is hinted at in the cult of Anchises, it is explicit in the deification of Daphnis, and in spite of other suggestions, it is inconceivable that Virgil either had any other person in mind in his allegory or intended it to be purely pastoral and refer only to the mythical shepherd Daphnis. Here we are dealing not with a hero, but with one who has actually become an Olympian: 'he marvels at the threshold of Olympus, a strange sight to him';[3] his two *arae* are to be combined with two altars (*altaria*) to Phoebus;[4] his annual

---

[1] A. v. 59 poscamus ventos. The one passage in Virgil where there appears to be clear evidence of prayer to the dead occurs in Aeneas' invocation on the landing in Italy: at the end of the list of deities to whom he prays we find (A. vii. 140) 'his parents in heaven and in Erebus', i.e. Venus and Anchises.   [2] E. v. 56–80.

[3] E. v. 56 candidus insuetum miratur limen Olympi.

[4] E. v. 65   en quattuor aras:
        ecce duas tibi, Daphni, duas altaria Phoebo.

cult is to be associated with the farmer's sacrifice to the nymphs and with the Ambarvalia;[1] he is to be on a level with Bacchus and Ceres, for 'the country-folk will each year make their vows to thee and thou shalt bind them to their vows'.[2] This exaltation of Daphnis to the *di superi* goes beyond anything in the *Aeneid* and can only be explained by its political significance. The analogy here is not that of the old Greek hero-cults, but the Hellenistic deification of kings and great men. But the apparent naturalness of the idea in the *Eclogue* shows how easily Rome had adopted Greek notions of the paying of divine honours to the great dead and how little incongruous the deification of Iulius would have seemed at the time.

Daphnis is undoubtedly worshipped with divine honours in a ritual which any Roman would recognize as that due to a fully acknowledged deity. What of the heroes of the *Aeneid*, Misenus, Polydorus, Hector, and Anchises? It has been seen that the foundation of their cult rests on the normal ritual of the Roman burial of the dead or of the celebration at the tomb on the anniversary of his death or burial (*parentatio*). But beyond this it is obvious that there appears with increasing clearness as one passes from one description to the other, a further element of worship, which is closer in spirit to the Greek hero-worship than to Roman practice. The question one would like to solve is: can this be ascribed entirely to Greek influence, or is it Roman in the sense that it implies a Roman worship of the deified dead? And if so, is such worship ancient or was it a recent growth? We could make a considerable step towards a solution if we could solve the question of the altars, which appear in all three descriptions. To whom are they

[1] E. v. 74 haec tibi semper erunt, et cum sollemnia vota
    reddemus Nymphis, et cum lustrabimus agros.
[2] E. v. 79 ut Baccho Cererique, tibi sic vota quotannis
    agricolae facient: damnabis tu quoque votis.

erected and are they part of Roman ritual or are they Greek? I doubt whether as yet there is sufficient material to answer the questions finally, but certain points may be cleared up.

Firstly, it might be suggested that the altars are erected to the Manes in the collective sense as representing the *di inferi*, and indeed Servius does suggest on *Aen*. iii. 305 that the two altars are to Dis and Proserpina. This explanation might be applied, though without much conviction, to the altars which 'stand to the Manes'[1] at Polydorus' tomb, but in Andromache's ritual to Hector,[2] the twin altars are so closely connected with the tomb and with the *manes*, here undoubtedly referring to the 'spirit' of Hector, which Andromache summons, that one is forced to the conclusion that the altars were erected to the dead hero himself. This becomes still clearer in the ritual to Anchises, where *arae* and even *altaria* are quite clearly dedicated to him in person.[3] With this weight of evidence in other passages, it seems most natural to suppose that the *ara sepulcri*[4] at the burial of Misenus, whatever quite it was, is also to be regarded as an altar to the dead hero.

The altars, it must be concluded, are dedicated to the dead hero himself and *manes* in all these passages stands for the spirit of the individual dead man. Is this a custom of Roman ritual or is it the Greek hero-cult? Servius,[5] commenting on the Polydorus passage, makes an effort on strangely Hellenistic lines, to attach the practice to Roman ideas. He states that the Manes are the same as the Genii— a belief for which he finds support in Apuleius[6]—and adds

---

[1] A. iii. 63.   [2] A. iii. 305.
[3] A. v. 48, 54, 86, 93, 762.   [4] A. vi. 177.
[5] *ad Aen*. iii. 63 Manes eosdem esse quos vetustas Genios appellavit, duosque Manes corporibus ab ipsa statim conceptione assignatos fuisse, qui ne mortua quidem corpora deserant, consumptisque etiam corporibus sepulcra inhabitent.   [6] Ap. *de deo Socr*. xv. 152.

that 'every man had two Genii, which remained even in the dead body, and when the body was consumed, dwelt in the tomb'. In a later passage Servius elaborates this idea and says that 'at birth we all receive two Genii, one of which exhorts us to good deeds, the other degrades us to evil'.[1] If we could accept this idea, we should have at hand an explanation not only of the erection of an altar, but of the two altars. But there is no trace of any such idea in the genuine Roman religion, which knows but one Genius for every living man and never uses the word for the spirit of the dead.[2] If the supposition be right (see p. 293) that Virgil thought of the snake as the genius of the dead Anchises—and the language is ambiguous—it may be that by his day this distinction between the genius of the living and the ghost or spirit of the dead was breaking down, but the language of Servius would have been unintelligible to him and is due to the sophistication of a later age, assisted by Greek conceptions of the δαίμων.

Are we then to say that the practices of the erection of altars at the tomb of the dead is derived from the Greek hero-cult and would have seemed totally foreign to Virgil's readers? The two questions must be distinguished. It is most probable that Virgil's model in these rituals was that of the Greek hero-cult, in which altars were erected at the tomb and offerings made as to divine beings. It must never be forgotten that Virgil is not telling of the funerals or cult of ordinary men, but of epic heroes, and derives, as has been seen, not a little of his ritual from Greek precedents and especially from Homer. But that is not to say that the idea of such worship of the dead would necessarily be strange to his contemporaries. For it has been seen that

---

[1] *ad Aen.* vi. 743 cum nascimur, duos Genios sortimur, unus est qui hortatur ad bona, alter qui depravat ad mala.

[2] This point is clearly brought out by W. F. Otto, *Die Manen*, pp. 59 ff.

Roman thought even before his day was moving in this direction under Hellenistic influence. It is significant that about this date was introduced the custom of inscribing the individual tomb to the 'Di Manes of so-and-so'.[1] That *manes* was intelligible as the equivalent of the spirit of the individual dead has become abundantly clear in the consideration of Virgil's use of the word, and the recurrent tomb inscription 'Dis Manibus' with the genitive, though it does not necessarily imply worship of the individual (see p. 256), suggests that the individual spirit was associated with the divinity inherent in the collective Di Manes of the lower world. It is clear further that in Imperial times the inscribed gravestone came to be regarded as an altar and was in fact frequently made in the shape of an altar. The conclusion is that Virgil's statements as to the erection of altars to the dead afford no kind of evidence for the existence of a worship of the dead in the genuine Roman religion, that his model was the Greek hero-cult and his descriptions based on poetical inheritance, but that the influx of Hellenistic ideas in his own time gave a naturalness to practices and thoughts which were gradually being embodied in the Graeco-Roman cult.[2]

A word must be said on the less important, but not uninteresting, point of the numbers of the altars in these passages. In the funeral rites to Polydorus, Virgil merely says, 'there stood altars to the dead';[3] in the account of the ritual at Anchises' tomb the plural is always used, some-

---

[1] The earliest instance occurs on a tomb of the end of the Republic. *C.I.L.* xi. 2464, Dessau 880.

[2] I am glad to be able to quote Professor H. J. Rose in support of the general view of the altars to the dead in Virgil, which has been taken here. He writes in a letter to me: 'The whole business has nothing to do with early Roman worship of the Di Manes, or the Di Parentum, but is Hellenistic, the sort of thing which a pious contemporary of Virgil might do—a less extravagant form of Cicero's proposed temple to Tullius.'

[3] A. iii. 63 stant manibus arae.

times *arae* and sometimes *altaria*, but there is no specifica-
tion as to number.[1] But Andromache had dedicated 'twin
altars' to Hector,[2] and in the fifth *Eclogue* there are four
altars, two for Phoebus and two for the deified Daphnis.[3]
It is not unnatural to suppose that the plural in the other
passages also stands for two. Further, in the description
of the rites at the tomb of Anchises in the fifth Book of the
Aeneid the offerings are in three different passages said to
be duplicated, 'two sheep, two oxen, two bowls of wine'[4]
and so on. What reason can there be for the double altar
and double offerings to dead heroes? Servius suggests
that it is because the lower world powers 'rejoice in an
even number, whereas the gods above like an uneven'.[5]
This is sufficiently refuted by Virgil in the *Eclogue* passage;
for there Phoebus, a full Olympian, has two altars, and
however Daphnis is to be regarded there, he is certainly
not a *deus inferus*. Warde Fowler[6] has discussed the
question and notes that both in the worship at the tomb
of Anchises and in certain state offerings the cult of the
dead is combined with a *votum*. Offerings are given to the
dead spirit and at the same time prayers are made to the
Di Manes for future benefits. The occasion is regarded as
specially solemn and the duplication of offerings therefore
means 'particular emphasis in sacrifice'. This is, I think,
the only suggestion which can safely be made in the
present state of our knowledge; the plurality of offerings
indicates an emphatic appeal and the plurality of altars
is a mark of special honour and respect. It is clear that
Daphnis, placed on a level with Phoebus, is to be regarded

---

[1] arae A. v. 48, 86, 762; altaria 54, 93.
[2] A. iii. 305 geminas . . . sacraverat aras.
[3] E. v. 65 en quattuor aras: ecce duas tibi, Daphni, duas altaria Phoebo.
[4] A. v. 61, 77, 96.
[5] *ad Aen.* iii. 305 quia inferi pari gaudent numero . . . superi vero impari.
[6] *Class. Rev.* xxxi, pp. 163 ff.

as an Olympian of high position, and we find in the *Aeneid* that Neptune is once to be worshipped with four altars.[1] We may suppose then that Andromache, wishing to give peculiar honours to Hector, erected two altars to his *manes*, and that a similar distinction was paid to Polydorus and Anchises.[2]

The general conclusion then as to Virgil's treatment of the cult of the dead seems to be that once again he has accomplished a fusion of Roman and Greek elements. His descriptions are founded on Roman customs of burial and the ritual of the *parentatio* at the tomb on the anniversary of the death. But there is no doubt that he also builds on the Greek practice of offering divine honours to the dead hero, and the altars and the blood-offerings are to be assigned to this source. In adjusting this conception to Roman ideas he has further made use of a habit based on Hellenistic notions which was becoming customary in his day. In all this there is no inconsistency. Virgil is again the poet, choosing the ideas which suit him at the moment, but never introducing conceptions which would seem offensive or unnatural to his contemporaries.

[1] A. v. 639 en quattuor arae | Neptuno. Warde Fowler in a note (*ibid.* p. 167) suggests that the four others here had been erected by the four competitors in the boat race, but I suspect a ritual reason.

[2] Professor Rose suggests to me that the practice 'may be connected with the old fashion of being complimentary by addressing a person twice as the beginning and the end', and quotes Theocr. xvii. 1 ἐκ Διὸς ἀρχώμεσθα καὶ ἐς Δία λήγετε, but I doubt if it is possible to be as precise as this.

XI

CONCLUSION

Some attempt must now be made to put together what has been learnt of Virgil's attitude to religious ideas and cults, and to see what inferences can be drawn as to the habits of thought of his contemporaries and, if possible, as to his own convictions.

It has been seen in the first place that he recognizes with a tender affection the early Italian tradition. The more vague the conception of deity and the nearer therefore to the primitive animism, the more sincere appears to be Virgil's recognition of its spiritual value. The spirits of the country-side, the Nymphs and Fauns in their undefined groups, are recalled by him in words of affectionate and almost impassioned reverence. In a lesser degree this is true of the divinities of the household, the Lar, Vesta, and the Penates, when he is thinking of them as the objects of the simple domestic cults. Something of the same feeling extends, too, to the functional deities of the agricultural seasons, the protectors of the farmers' crops and herds, to Ceres and to Pales, as to Liber-Bacchus and Pallas-Minerva, the protectors of the vine and the olive. So also in describing the old cult-forms, although, as in his description of the worship of Ceres in the first book of the *Georgics*,[1] he is sometimes guilty of conflation between one rite and another, yet he lingers over the details of ceremonial with a more than merely archaeological devotion. This is again specially true of the simple rites of the household worships and of the festivals of the country-side. And once more in his use of the great fundamental words of the old religion, *numen*, *sacer*, *pius*, and their cognates and

[1] G. i. 338 ff.

derivatives, though Virgil is ready to expand and develop them so as to meet modern conceptions, he is yet instinct with the sense of their traditional meaning, and they may fairly be said to strike the keynote of the poem. And if we ask why these old Italian traditions were dear to him, it is not, I think, fanciful to believe that in their vague suggestion of the presence of supernatural forces in the world and in man's life, they come nearer to his own religious thought than the more clear-cut figures and customs of anthropomorphism.

For, secondly, in his treatment of the deities of the State-cult and its ceremonies we miss the note of sympathetic devotion and to some extent the note of what we might call genuine religious feeling. But their place is taken by what to us, though probably not to Virgil himself, seems the secondary religious thought of the majesty and sanctity of Rome. When Evander in the eighth book of the *Aeneid* reveals to Aeneas the great sites of the future city of Rome, the *religio*, so vivid in the *Georgics*, is, except in certain great moments,[1] absent; the Ara Maxima, the Lupercal, the Scala Caci, are not memorable to him because they commemorate the sense of a supernatural presence, but because they will be landmarks in the *urbs Roma*. But the sanctity of the city stands out clearly in all the references to its cults. It seems to concentrate itself round three main figures: Ianus, who is the essentially Roman god, Saturnus, who is often coupled with him, possibly to link Rome with the wider religion of ancient Italy as a whole, and Hercules, who similarly may have his place there as the representative of the *di novensides*. And behind these three, though but rarely mentioned in a cult-connexion, stands

[1] e.g. in the momentary recurrence to the thought of the country-side deities, A. viii. 314 ff., and in the great description of the *religio* of the Capitol, A. viii. 349 ff.

the majestic figure of Iuppiter,[1] the ultimate embodiment of the majesty of the Roman State. Or, if we turn to worship, in the careful and elaborate descriptions of the making of treaties, the offering of spoils, the triumph, even of the opening of the gate of Ianus itself, though there is unmistakable dignity, there is not the feeling of a profoundly religious observance. The State-cults seem to provoke Virgil's antiquarian interest to the full, but only to rouse his sense of religion in so far as that is bound up with the position and history of Rome.

The consideration of the Graeco-Roman anthropomorphic deities is a more complex matter, for here there enters in a new strain of influence, which to some extent cuts across purely religious thought, that of the poetic mythological tradition. No doubt, as may be seen in the provinces of Gaul and Germany and elsewhere, it was both the popular and the official habit of the Romans to identify the deities whom they found among conquered peoples with their own gods. But Greek civilization, and in particular Greek poetry, caused the process in this instance to go much farther, so that the Greek legends of their gods were taken over by Latin poets and attached wholesale to the identified Roman deities. It has been seen that Virgil has no scruple in following out this literary tradition; the adopted Greek gods, like Apollo, come to him with all their wealth of associations and legends; those who in assimilation were known both by Greek and by Roman names, like Pallas-Minerva, had their Greek connexions attached to the Roman as well as their Greek names, and even those, like Mars, who were always true to their Roman name, yet acquired the characteristics of their

---

[1] It is perhaps noticeable that as the conclusion of Evander's expression of the *religio* of the Capitol and after the typically old-world phrase, *quis deus incertum est*, comes the statement that the Arcadians believe that it is Iuppiter whom they have seen (A. viii. 352).

Greek counterparts. Poetically, then, the fusion is complete, yet even here it has been noticed that Virgil still seems jealous of truly Italian tradition and refuses, for example, to attach to Pallas the essential functions of the Italian craft-goddess, Minerva;[1] the spirit which prompted his affection for the old deities of the country-side makes him scrupulous in his preservation of strictly Italian traits. He seems, moreover, less conscious of Greek mythology and associations in the *Aeneid* than in the earlier poems.

Here, too, as among the gods and ceremonies of the State-cult, the sanctity of Rome has its part as a moulding religious influence and it has further a marked contemporary bias. Not only do the deified Iulius and the deified, or soon to be deified, Augustus take their place among the State-gods, but the new Caesar-cult has also its effect on the treatment of Apollo, Augustus' patron, and, in a sense, his heavenly counterpart, and does not leave untouched even the conception of Iuppiter; for the reign of Augustus is alike the reflection and the culmination of the success of Aeneas, which is the primary outcome of Iuppiter's direction of events in the poem.

Again, it has been seen that the three great gods, Venus, Iuno, and Iuppiter, who almost alone have a personal part in the story of the *Aeneid*, are closely linked with the conception of fate—Venus and Iuno with the destinies of individuals and races, which may conflict and fail to work themselves out in full, and Iuppiter with the world-fate, which is above these lesser fates, and is through this identification the expression of the divine will for the whole world. And even here the bias of the Roman State-cult is felt, for the world-fate is in fact the destiny of the Roman Empire.

Finally, in an inquiry which stands necessarily by itself

[1] See pp. 155–7.

we have traced Virgil's conception of the fate of the dead. Here, in a fusion more subtle, more artistic, and more definitely his own, Virgil has blended many strains. He has linked the old Italian conception of the chthonic Manes, the undiscriminated dead, who have an influence on the products of the soil beneath which they lie, with the traditions of folk-lore and popular Greek 'theology' of an underworld in which the actions of this life receive their reward and punishment. And these notions in their turn are attached to the higher conceptions of the mystery religions and the speculations of philosophy, to the metempsychosis beliefs of the Pythagoreans and the Stoic idea of the divine fire in the soul, contaminated and de-graded by the sins of this life and gradually purified again hereafter. We are left with the conception of the refining of the soul in a process extending over epochs in this life and the life below, until it is worthy to take its place with the souls of the great heroes in Elysium; of purgatory, if we may translate into the terms of Dante and the Christian Church, complicated by the return to the upper world, ending in the enjoyment with the Saints of a life in Heaven. And among these souls the great ones are to be deemed worthy, like the Greek heroes, of a cult-worship.

Such in brief outline is the picture which we have been led to draw of 'Religion in Virgil'. Must it be left at that or is it possible to make any deductions as regards con-temporary thought in that complex Augustan age or as to Virgil's own beliefs?

In the first place it may safely be said that this strange medley of Greek and Roman ideas, of popular folk-lore and the abstract speculations of philosophers, would certainly not have appeared unnatural to an Augustan reader. We never hear of any outcry against Virgil's 'un-orthodoxy', and the same mingling of conceptions meets us in contemporary poets : in Horace with a more marked note of scepticism, in Ovid with the added savour of flippancy. For this ready acceptance many reasons might be adduced. It is notorious that a polytheism is always prepared to add new gods to its pantheon; Rome was in this respect no exception, and, as she developed intellectually, she was correspondingly ready to include new ideas in her theology. And if the result was confusion as well as fusion, let us remind ourselves that popular religious beliefs are always vague and floating, frequently confused, and not rarely inconsistent. The problem of the relation of fate to the will of the gods might here be taken as typical; there can be little doubt that the ordinary man in Virgil's day believed in both as governing his life and the events of the world, and made far less attempt to work out their relation than we have seen reason to attribute to Virgil himself. Similarly, for many generations now, through the existence of temples and cult-statues, he had become used to the anthropomorphic conception of his deities, the State-religion had accustomed him by official recognition to the fusion of Greek and Roman deities, and in all this he would find nothing strange.

But here a caution must be entered. If it is said that these strange minglings of Fauns and Nymphs with Eumenides and Hydras, of a Thracian Ares with the Mars of the Campus Martius, of hero-cult with the Roman *parentatio* at the tomb, would not seem 'unnatural' to a contemporary, we must undoubtedly add 'unnatural for a poet'. We know that, because again we find it in the other Augustan poets. But this does not mean that all this weight of Greek mythology, which was so precious a treasure-house to the poet, had any really religious meaning for the average Roman, or entered in any sense into his religious thought or practice. Much of it must be thought away, if we are to try to reach contemporary belief, and that which must thus be subtracted is precisely that which Virgil himself, by his treatment of it, shows to be merely part of the poetic tradition, the actions of Neptunus and Aeolus and Iris, the 'faded' uses of Ceres and Bacchus and Mars, and much else that is felt at once to have no true religious significance.

With this proviso an attempt can be made to distinguish features in Virgil which point to genuine belief or permanent practice among his contemporaries. Firstly, there can be no reasonable doubt that his striking care for the old Italian elements in religion, even in the Graeco-Roman fusion, is evidence of a real vitality of these ancient cults. However sophisticated the town population had become, the agricultural worship of the farms and the *pagi* persisted and was destined as 'paganism' to make the last stand against the incursion of Christianity. The farmer no doubt still felt himself beholden to Ceres for the success of his harvest and to Pales for the prosperity of his flocks and herds, and continued to perform the Parilia or the Ambarvalia with a sense of their religious importance. It is probable, too, that to the more simple-minded the presence of Fauns and Nymphs or of the woodland Silvanus was a reality, and would explain to him the feeling of *religio* with which he still approached a sacred spring or entered a grove hallowed by tradition. Similarly, and that even in the urban communities, the domestic worship of the household gods was still practised, and the offering made with an intention not purely conventional at the household meals. For all this we can appeal to evidence outside Virgil. The *sacraria* and *lararia* in the houses at Pompeii give us practical witness; the descriptions of the rustic cults in the poems of Tibullus have the true ring; and more clearly than elsewhere we find testimony to a continued reality in the *Fasti*. In all the strange setting of worthless legend and false etymology and personal flippancy which fills his books, Ovid's descriptions of ceremonials such as the Parilia or the Robigalia, which he himself witnessed, stand out with a note of sincerity, and the basic thoughts of animism burst through now and again, as in his insistence that Vesta is nothing but 'the living flame'. There was about the old animism a spiritual, or at any rate non-sensual, notion of the supernatural, which survived the disruptive forces which made havoc of the anthropo-morphic gods and their legends.

Or again, Virgil's care for the details of religious cult and ceremonial points at least to permanence, if not necessarily vitality, in the performance of the rites of the State-cult. We are apt to believe that all this, though still no doubt carried out at the end of the Republic and the beginning of the Empire, had degenerated into meaningless conven-tion, disregarded altogether by most men and only cared for by the officiating priests or by a conscientious member of the College of Pontifices or of Augurs. So no doubt it was in the normal performance of traditional ceremonials, but history startles us occasionally by a great outburst of feel-ing when anything went wrong with one of these stereo-typed acts of worship. The violation of the rites of the Bona Dea, Caesar's neglect of Bibulus' omens, Clodius' repeal of the Lex Aelia Fufia, these things could not have caused public scandal, if all sense of sanctity had passed away. It is no doubt true that Virgil's interest here is more antiquarian and less religious, but it may be taken as evidence that the conservation of the State-cults was still a matter of importance and that *religio* would have caused a Roman citizen a strong, if rather vague, uneasiness, if any of them should be dropped or misconducted.

Nor, if Virgil be thought of in the immediate setting of his own generation, must the importance of Augustus' religious revival or the first beginnings of Caesar-worship be ignored or minimized; indeed in both these respects it has been often said that the poets led the way rather than followed. If Augustus, as he boasted, had restored more than eighty decayed temples of the gods, so Virgil by his introduction of traditional deities and ancient rites in his poems was similarly attempting to revive religious interest. And just as Augustus was anxious to reinstate Italian agriculture, so Virgil attached a religious sanction to his effort by the sense of the godliness of the farmer's life, which pervades the *Georgics*. It might perhaps be doubted how far this represented general or popular feeling; we know that the effort of Augustus was comparatively a failure, in so far as it attempted to renew belief in the Graeco-Roman cults, but it must at the time have aroused interest, if nothing more, and this is reflected in the poems of Virgil. Far otherwise was it with the Imperial cult, which undoubtedly represents a strong popular movement. During the greater part of the Republic the majesty of the Roman State was summed up in the figure of Iuppiter Capitolinus. But in the last century this had begun to decay, and now, when new hopes of the future were strong and there was a new sense of the destiny of Rome, popular feeling tended to focus it round the house of the Caesars. If the meaning of Virgil's treatment of Caesar-worship has here been rightly analysed, we can recognize something of the history of popular enthusiasm and Augustus' own efforts at moderation. There can be no doubt as to the outburst of feeling at the death of Julius, and the fifth *Eclogue* rightly represents the popular sense of his divinity, which showed itself in the building of the temple of Divus Iulius. It may be that Virgil's apotheosis of Octavian in the *Eclogues* rather outstripped popular belief; if so, we can see how it was moderated and restrained in the later poems. Augustus becomes *Divi filius*, a mortal still, though looking for ultimate divinity, and his immediate worship is to some extent deflected into the exaltation of Apollo, his patron and divine counterpart. In all this Virgil is following Augustus' wishes and no doubt in some degree trying to lead popular opinion, but certainly also reflecting currents of thought and emotion of his time. And as for the neglected Iuppiter, if he may no longer be the tribal god, he is reinstated as the world god, the ruling power whose will is fate, expressed in effect in the supremacy of Rome. Here, too, Virgil must reflect, if not quite popular thought, at least the thought of the educated.

For it must not be forgotten that Virgil's first appeal, indeed his main appeal, was bound to be made not to the vulgar, but to the educated and the literary, and if his poems are a reflection of contemporary opinion, they should represent primarily educated opinion. And here again he may safely be taken as a guide. For at least two generations before him, philosophy had, among the educated, largely supplanted religion; in Cicero's dialogue *De Natura Deorum* the discussion lies between representatives of the main philosophical sects, Stoics, Epicureans, and Academics, and the problem as regards the traditional religion and its theology is not what is their value, but how they are to be fitted into a philosophical scheme of the world. On the surface of Virgil's poems it might be said that this problem is not explicit, but it is there in his great underlying thoughts which from time to time rise to the surface. In the sixth book of the *Aeneid* the fact of an afterlife is indeed assumed, but with consummate art Virgil, accepting the pictures derived from legend and popular 'theology', causes them all to culminate in the philosophical view of the purgation of the soul, which is the heart and kernel of the book. So, too, if the events of the *Aeneid* appear to be due to the action of bickering goddesses, yet behind them lies the philosophic conception of the divine πρόνοια, which is the governing force! Here of course Virgil does not represent all educated opinion, for the Epicureans, for instance, would deny all idea of a divine governance of the world, and there would undoubtedly be a wide scepticism as to any survival of the soul after death, but it may justly be inferred that Virgil was no Athanasius, and that there was in his day a large section among the educated who, if they had rejected traditional religion, yet, like the Stoics, held a philosophical view of the world which might be reconciled with religion, and was in itself essentially religious.

It is now perhaps easier to approach the second question, that of Virgil's own religious beliefs, though the caution given at the outset of this inquiry must here be repeated, that in so impersonal a poet it is difficult with any certainty to claim knowledge of his own convictions. It might perhaps be argued that in all the points just mentioned, if Virgil's treatment may be taken as evidence of the thoughts of his contemporaries, it may also be regarded as proof of his own beliefs. But such an inference would not be safe, for antiquarian interest, even affectionate recollection, and care cannot necessarily be interpreted as evidence of belief; Lucretius himself had a pathetic love of the ritual of the old religion. And it must not be forgotten that Virgil, though possessed with a deep religious sense, was a philosopher. Brought up in the school of Siro, his early inclinations were no doubt to Epicureanism, which would have made him reject all popular religion and accept only an attenuated conception of the possibility of communion with the persons of the gods by means of their *simulacra*. But there are signs even in the *Georgics* that Epicureanism was being supplanted in his mind by Stoicism, and by the time of the writing of the *Aeneid*, when, as we know, he intended to devote the remaining years of his life to the study of philosophy, it would seem that he had given himself wholly to those philosophies which supported the religious view of life, Stoicism, Platonism, and the Pythagoreanism of the Mysteries.

What then could be the attitude of a philosopher to the multiplicity of functional deities which formed the basis both of the old animism and of the Graeco-Roman anthropomorphism? For popular belief there seems never to be difficulty in conceiving this specialized action, as it were, of a divine power, or, rather, in thinking of the divine as many, not one. The whole history of primitive and early religions bears testimony to it, and saint-cults in their popular form are evidence of it to-day. But to the thinking man polytheism seems always to be a difficulty. Plato tacitly substitutes θεός for θεοί, and the Stoics and Neoplatonists were at pains to explain the gods of popular theology either as aspects of the one god or as subordinate δαίμονες, spirits working beneath his guidance. It is therefore hard to suppose that Virgil, for all his love of the household and country cults, had a real belief in their individual deities except as a popular expression of a divine presence and intention. If we are to look for his own religious beliefs, they must be found in a more philosophic region.

Hence it is not surprising to find that in Virgil's treatment the great majority of the gods are little more than puppets. They are for the most part a purely poetic convention and their value is ornament. This is clear in the many uses of the 'faded' god-name; it is but a picturesque periphrasis for the object symbolized, Mars for *bellum* and *pugna*, Ceres for *panis*, Bacchus for *vitis* or *vinum*, &c. But it is true also of many of the more personal appearances of the gods: the raising of a storm by Aeolus, its quieting by Neptunus, the dispatch of Mercurius or Iris by Iuppiter or Iuno have no religious implications at all; they have a purely aesthetic value, both for the framing of a concrete picture and for the literary associations which they awake as part of the great epic tradition. If we except the three great gods for the moment, the only divine figure which has substantiality and appears to wake a genuine religious emotion is that of Apollo, and even here symbolism plays a large part. For Apollo stands either for the inspiration of the poet, as in the *Eclogues*, or for the prophecy which lies in close connexion with the ultimate divine purpose, or for the conservation of the reign and the aims of Augustus.

With the three great gods there enters in, as has been seen, a new element. For Virgil uses them, in effect, to express his underlying philosophic view of the life of the individual and the race, and of the destiny of the world. In a sense the outward treatment of Venus, Iuno, and Iuppiter does not differ much from that of the other gods. Venus and Iuno at least have no personality and no aims of their own and their debates in heaven are little more than a setting out of the arguments for and against the success of the Trojan followers of Aeneas; they are, as has been seen, the workings of the opposed μοῖραι. Even Iuppiter in his summings up does not, considered as a person, do much more than hold perpetually the scales which come into the scene dramatically at the end of the poem. And this is why their words and actions have often been described as mere 'epic machinery'. Yet these three deities have a symbolic significance which stands above that of all other gods and goddesses. For they are the expression of the widest and greatest of all Virgil's philo-

sophic ideas, the conception that destiny, which moulds
the affairs of men, is no blind caprice, no material determinism, but a divine force which controls the world and
makes itself felt in the lives and actions of individuals.
And it is the man who can best hear the dictates of this
divine controlling element and make himself the instrument of its execution, who is in Virgil's view most truly
pius. In its most fundamental manifestation Aeneas' *pietas*
lies not in his family relations, not in his conventional
worship of individual gods, not even in his obedience to his
divine mother, but rather in his whole-hearted acceptance
of the position assigned to him as 'the man of destiny'.
Even if Virgil was not consciously following the Stoic
doctrine of πρόνοια, he had at least adopted for himself
as his most ultimate thought the poetic equivalent of this
philosophic theory. Here then we may safely claim to see
the mind of the poet-philosopher and to believe that we
are acquainted with his widest and most far-reaching
thoughts on the world and human life.[1]

And there is one other region in which, as has been
hinted, the tone of lofty conviction which it is impossible to
miss indicates to us another philosophic belief. That is of
course in relation to the problem of the fate of the dead.
Virgil's procedure is again the same. He takes the traditions of folk-lore and myth and using them as his framework, refines them to the measure of his own philosophic
vision. The crude separation of the souls in popular

[1] An attempt to see in Virgil's poems something like a systematic
theological system has been made by Heinze, *Virgils Epische Technik*, pp.
288–316. Accepting the identity of Iuppiter and Fate as representing the
Stoic conception of the πρόνοια of the world-god, he regards the lesser gods
either as aspects of the supreme god working in the different spheres of
nature, or as allegorical externalizations of internal psychological processes
(e.g. Allecto). But this is too clear-cut for a poet, and involves ideas taken
from the later thought of Neoplatonism and Stoicism as it developed during
the Empire.

thought into the good and evil, the Sheep and the Goats, suffering their rewards and punishments eternally in the underworld, glides imperceptibly into the idea of the purgation and purification of the soul, which with his true poet's eclecticism he derives from several philosophical sources. Yet here again we may notice his peculiar bias. There is no doubt of the survival of the soul, its purgation, and its return to earth in another body; but through the purgation and especially in the final drinking of the waters of Lethe, though it preserves its identity in its second life, it in effect loses its personality. Virgil has no such crude idea of metempsychosis as that of the famous legendary soul which passed through the bodies of Euphorbus, Homer, Pythagoras, and Ennius, conscious to some extent at each stage of those which preceded. The souls which are waiting on the bank to become the heroes of Rome will be those heroes and no one else. And so it is in reality not individuality of purgation and rebirth which Virgil has at heart, but once more rather the permanence of the Roman race. If the high conception of a world-fate is narrowed, as we think, to the destiny of the Roman people, so the great ideas of the fate of the soul end with the procession of the great figures of Rome. This is no declination to Virgil's mind, but only again the expression of his real belief that the world-destiny is the Roman Empire. But in this vision of the purification of the soul from its earthly sins and its remission to earth to lead a nobler life, it is hardly possible to exclude the conclusion that we have Virgil's own deep conviction as to the after-life.

And if in these two tenets, inspired by the philosophic reflection of a poet, we may safely recognize what Virgil would have admitted as 'articles of belief', there is a wider sense, not based upon any of the investigations conducted in this essay, in which Virgil has always and may justly be recognized as a religious poet. For running all through his poems, and more particularly through *Georgics* and *Aeneid*, there is the recognition of the spiritual value of things and events. This manifests itself in a profound sympathy with suffering and sorrow, as though it were something not merely incidental to the lot of man, but its deepest meaning. It is seen in the *Georgics* even in reference to the ox, bereft of his yoke-fellow by the plague. It is the source of his understanding of the position of the unfortunate and the wrong-headed, which makes the grief of the evil Mezentius for his son Lausus as pathetic and appealing as that of the noble Evander for his son Pallas. It is this which has always made modern readers feel that their sympathy lies rather with Dido and Turnus than with 'pius Aeneas'. Nor is it merely a 'religion of humanity', but a deep sense, such as Christianity later consecrated, that in suffering man reaches the depth of religious experience. The appeal of the stricken mother of Euryalus, 'slay me, if you have any *pietas*',[1] goes to the roots of religious sentiment; her suffering can only be ended by the supreme suffering, and it is the duty of those who love her and have the true religious sense to give her this final relief of sacrifice.

This religious feeling of the value of suffering might be illustrated again and again; it is the motive, for instance, of the tears called out from Aeneas by the pictures on the walls of Dido's palace: *sunt lacrimae rerum et mentem mortalia tangunt*.[2] And yet it would not be true to say that Virgil's was a religion of pessimism. For the ultimate keynote of the *Georgics* is that through labour the farmer wins to prosperity, and of the *Aeneid*, in tones far more pronounced, that through suffering Aeneas will win the glorious consummation of the Roman Empire. Virgil's is a religion

---

[1] A. ix. 493.   [2] A. i. 462.

which looks not to the past, but to the future. He had the profound conviction that he stood at the outset of a new golden age of happiness for the world, compared with which the past would be but a dim thing. In his joyful moments, as for instance in the fourth *Eclogue*, whatever may have been its immediately inspiring motive, this sense of a future triumph, willed by the divine destiny, rings out clear. And it is none the less clear, perhaps even more brilliant through contrast with suffering, in the *Aeneid*. From this point of view it might be said that the *Aeneid* is the epic commentary on the lyric of the fourth *Eclogue*. A religion which looks to ultimate triumph coming through sacrifice and suffering is a higher and stronger creed than any facile optimism, and it is such a religion which we meet in Virgil.

The Church of the Middle Ages greeted Virgil as the prophet of Christ, and Dante made him his guide through the world of departed souls. These recognitions of his religious worth were based no doubt on the apparently Messianic character of the fourth *Eclogue* and on the description of the after-world in the sixth book of the *Aeneid*. But the truth in fact lay deeper, for Virgil, the philosopher and the poet, as he looked on life and tried to interpret it, had probed something of the secret which lay at the heart of Christianity.

INDEX

Actium, seat of oracle 28, 168, 170.
  games at 47, 172.
  battle of 92, 113, 115, 116, 120, 156, 180, 182.
Aeolus 118, 177, 308, 314.
agri lustratio 47, 54.
agriculture, deities of 29, 30, 38–42.
Allecto 61, 67, 148, 180, 255, 260.
altars 10, 99, 102.
  altaria and *arae* 293, 295, 297, 300.
  double altars 291, 297, 300.
  in cult of dead 287, 289–300.
Ambarvalia 47, 54, 296, 308.
Anubis 120, 182.
anima mundi 243, 265, 275.
Animism 3, 29–42, 60, 61, 62, 302, 309, 313.
Anthropomorphism 62, 88, 103, 122, 123, 304, 307, 309, 313.
Apollo, *see* Phoebus.
Ara Maxima 52, 55–8, 64, 78, 98, 123, 124, 303.
Astrology, 11, 15, 64, 185.
augur and augury 11, 15, 20, 21, 23, 41, 98, 168.
augurium 19–21, 168.
Augustus, worship of 191–6, 198, 305, 310, 311.
  as Caesar 193, 194, 198.
  as Divi filius 193, 194, 311.
Aurora 186, 187.
auspice 11, 15, 16, 21, 22, 23.
auspicia 21, 22.

Bacchus, 4, 6, 67, 74, 78, 147–52, 189, 197, 200, 201, 296, 302, 308.
  as Dionysus of the Bacchanals 147–50.
  as Iacchus of mysteries 152.
  as protector of vine 150.
  cult-title Lyaeus 54, 108, 150, 169.
  identification with Liber 38, 107, 147.
  used in sense of 'vine' 151.
  used in sense of 'wine' 56, 108, 150, 151, 313.
Bellona 115, 116.
birds, omens from flight and song of 11, 14, 15, 23.

Cacus 56, 57, 122, 124, 125.
Camilla, 159, 169.
Capitoline triad 51, 129, 133, 153, 156.
Carmentis 26, 36, 37, 166, 227.
Celaeno 27, 28, 164, 165, 180.
Ceres 38, 39, 70, 73, 106–9, 152, 169, 189, 197, 198, 200, 201, 296, 302, 308.
  connexion with Liber 106, 147.
  connexion with Tellus 106.
  cult in Troy 107.
  festival of 54, 98, 106.
  identified with Demeter 38, 54, 106, 107.
  used in sense of 'bread' or 'corn' 56, 108, 109, 151, 313.
Charon, 254, 264, 269.
Cicero 86, 190, 256, 266.
Claros 28, 163, 168.
cosmological deities 11, 46, 182–7, 196.
country-side, deities of 34–8, 88, 196, 197, 302, 313.
Cumae 25, 26, 28, 163, 166, 168.
Cupid (Cupido, Amor) 64, 67, 129.
  used in the sense of 'love' 129.
Cybele 66, 73, 75, 142, 174–7.
  as Magna Mater of Phrygia 4, 175, 202.
  association with Troy 176.

daps 51–3.
  in cult of the dead 288, 289, 291.
Dead, the 241–301.
  cult of 281–301.
  Greek attitude to 242.
  importance of burial of 244–7.
  Italian attitude to 241.
  spirits of 247–9.
  Virgil's conception of fate of 244–80, 306, 315.
Delos 24, 25, 28, 45, 74, 84, 163, 165, 168.
Delphi 24, 25, 26, 163.
Demeter, *see* Ceres.
di agrestes 34, 146.
di indigetes 55, 95.
di inferi 250–3, 256, 257, 260, 261, 283, 285, 287, 297.

di magni 91, 92.
di novensides 55.
di parentes 242, 256, 258.
di superi 63, 66, 228, 256, 261, 293, 294, 296.
Diana 10, 15, 74, 134, 157–62, 184.
as Greek Artemis 160, 203.
as Latin goddess 157.
association with Aricia 158, 159.
cult-title Trivia 98, 157, 159, 160, 167, 169.
identification with Hecate (q.v.) 157, 253.
Dis 90, 126, 136, 203, 246, 250–1, 253, 256, 257, 261, 271, 297.

Egeria 158, 159.
Emperor, worship of 187–96, 197, 283, 305, 310.
of Augustus 191–6, 310, 311.
of Iulius Caesar 188–91, 310.
Ennius 77.
epulae 51–3.
Erinyes 178–81, 255.
Etruria and Etruscans 3, 12, 51, 88, 129, 152, 153.
Etruscan tombs 263.
Euhemerism 26, 36, 40, 41, 91, 104, 144.
Eumenides 178–81, 185, 252, 255, 268, 307.
extispice 12, 16, 24.

Fate 1, 204–40.
as determinism (ἀνάγκη) 207.
as εἱμαρμένη, general destiny 207, 214–20.
as μοῖρα, lot of individual 207, 208–14, of races 210–11.
as πρόνοια, providence 207, 228–32.
conception of in Virgil 204–34.
Greek ideas of 207, 208.
relation to the gods 204, 220–34, 307.
relation to Iuppiter 204, 228–32.
Roman ideas of 205–7.
fatum 24, 204–40 passim.
fata dei 205, 224, 226–8, 231.
fata deum 205, 224–6, 231.
fata Iovis 205, 224, 228–32.
meaning of word 205–7.

Faunus (Pan) 19, 22, 35, 41, 44, 73, 144–7, 163, 185.
as Italian king 36, 41, 144.
as prophet 24–7, 37.
identification with Pan 145–6.
Fauni 30, 34–7, 61, 144, 198, 302, 307, 308.
Feronia 123.
Fides 97.
Fortuna 141, 204, 213, 214, 220, 226, 231, 234–40.
meaning in Latin 234–5.
use in Virgil 235–40; as 'luck' 235–6; in intermediate sense 236–8; as fate 238–40.
fountains (streams), spirits of 34, 35, 61, 203.
Furies (Furiae, Dirae) 27, 178–81, 200, 255, 271.

Genius, of man 30, 33, 278.
identified with *manes* 278, 293, 297, 298.
of place 33, 34, 186, 202.

Hecate as form of Diana (q.v.) 10, 157, 199, 200, 253.
as lower world deity 132, 162, 178, 199, 200, 252, 253, 256, 284.
Hercules 123–6.
connexion with Cacus 124, 125.
identity with Greek Heracles 123.
worship of at Ara Maxima (q.v.) 52, 55–8, 64, 78, 79, 98, 303.
hero-worship (Greek) 242, 262, 283, 285, 293, 296, 297, 298, 299, 301.
Hiems 45, 98, 199.
Horace 4, 27, 87, 192, 196, 235, 307.
household, deities of 30–4, 88, 197, 302, 313.

Ianus 30, 40, 41, 70, 73, 75, 104, 112, 115, 203, 303, 304.
in State-cult 89–91.
incense, use in offerings 45, 56.
incubation 26, 27, 44.
Iris 6, 18, 93, 119, 177–8, 237, 246, 252, 308, 314.
Italian religion 29–59, 308.
deities of 29–42.
worship in 42–59.

LIST OF PASSAGES REFERRED TO

Note: When passages of several lines are quoted in full in the footnotes, the first line only is indexed.

PRINTED IN
GREAT BRITAIN
AT THE
UNIVERSITY PRESS
OXFORD
BY
JOHN JOHNSON
PRINTER
TO THE
UNIVERSITY